WEBMASTER

IN A NUTSHELL

WEBMASTER

IN A NUTSHELL

Third Edition

Stephen Spainhour and Robert Eckstein

O'REILLY®

Beijing • Cambridge • Farnham • Köln • Paris • Sebastopol • Taipei • Tokyo

Webmaster in a Nutshell, Third Edition
by Stephen Spainhour and Robert Eckstein

Published by O'Reilly & Associates, Inc., 1005 Gravenstein Highway North, Sebastopol, CA 95472.

O'Reilly & Associates books may be purchased for educational, business, or sales promotional use. Online editions are also available for most titles (*safari.oreilly.com*). For more information, contact our corporate/institutional sales department: 800-998-9938 or *corporate@oreilly.com*.

Editor:	Linda Mui
Production Editor:	Colleen Gorman
Cover Designer:	Edie Freedman
Interior Designer:	David Futato

Printing History:

October 1996:	First Edition.
June 1999:	Second Edition.
December 2002:	Third Edition.

ISBN: 0-596-00357-9
[M]

Table of Contents

Part IV. JavaScript

Part V. CGI and Perl

Part VI. PHP

Part VII. HTTP

Part VIII. Server Configuration

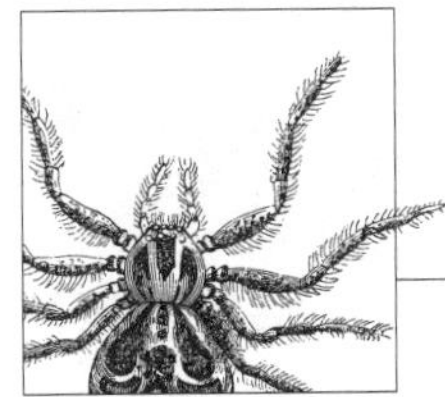

Preface

This book is for web developers, or anyone who works at the content end of the World Wide Web. Do you author or maintain web documents? Are you a programmer developing web-based client or server applications? Are you the administrator of a web site, responsible for maintaining and updating server software?

There are innumerable books and online resources for learning web-related skills. This book pares them down to a single desktop-sized volume for easy reference. You may be a whiz at JavaScript, but sometimes forget the details on an obscure function you seldom use. You may know HTML fairly well, but can never remember the correct syntax for creating tables. You might forget the directive for creating directory aliases on your server or how to enforce password protection on documents.

By no means is this book a replacement for more detailed books on the Web. But when those books have been digested and placed on your bookshelves with pride, this one will remain on your desktop.

Contents

In the years immediately after the first edition of this book was published in 1996, we watched the Web explode, with new technologies every month scrambling to make last month's technology obsolete. Then we watched the Web settle down, as standards caught up with features, and fiscal realities caught up with IPOs. The land grab was over as quickly as it began, and miraculously, the code you wrote last night still works after downloading the latest browser this morning. The Web has reached maturity.

As a result of the Web's maturation, this edition of *Webmaster in a Nutshell* is fairly stable. There haven't been new chapters introduced or old ones removed; what was relevant when we did the second edition in 1999 is still relevant today.

The technology has improved and the feature set has expanded, but the paradigms remain the same.

This book is separated into eight distinct subject areas.

Chapter 1, *The Web in a Nutshell*
: Introduces the book and the Web in general.

Part I: HTML

Chapter 2, *HTML Overview*
: Gives a brief background to HTML syntax and introduces the features of the latest specification, HTML 4.01.

Chapter 3, *HTML Reference*
: Lists the current set of HTML tags and their attributes.

Chapter 4, *Frames*
: Shows how to use HTML frames.

Chapter 5, *Tables*
: Shows how to use HTML tables.

Chapter 6, *Forms*
: Shows how to create HTML forms.

Chapter 7, *Character Entities*
: Lists the special characters recognized by HTML.

Chapter 8, *Color Names and Values*
: Lists the names accepted by HTML and CSS attributes for color values.

Part II: CSS

Chapter 9, *Cascading Style Sheets*
: Provides an overview and reference to the Cascading Style Sheets specification for HTML documents.

Part III: XML

Chapter 10, *XML*
: Provides an introduction and reference to XML.

Part IV: JavaScript

Chapter 11, *JavaScript*
: Provides a reference for the JavaScript language, Version 1.5.

Part V: CGI and Perl

Chapter 12, *CGI Overview*
: Gives a general overview to the Common Gateway Interface, or CGI.

Chapter 13, *Server Side Includes*
: Describes SSI, listing directives and environment variables and demonstrating their use.

Chapter 14, *The CGI.pm Module*
: Provides a reference to the Perl module CGI.pm, which simplifies CGI programming.

Chapter 15, *Web Server Programming with mod_perl*
: Provides a reference to mod_perl, an Apache module that can significantly enhance CGI performance.

Part VI: PHP

Chapter 16, *PHP*
: Lists the syntax and functions of PHP 4, a server-side, HTML-embedded scripting language.

Part VII: HTTP

Chapter 17, *HTTP*
: Provides an overview and reference to the Hypertext Transfer Protocol, Version 1.1.

Part VIII: Server Configuration

Chapter 18, *Apache Configuration*
: Lists the configuration directives used by the Apache 2.0 server.

Chapter 19, *Apache Modules*
: Lists the modules that you can use with Apache.

Chapter 20, *Web Performance*
: Gives specific suggestions for improving the performance of the Web.

Conventions Used in This Book

The following typographical conventions are used in this book:

`Constant width`
: Indicates headers, directives, attributes, code examples, and HTML tags.

`Constant width italic`
: Indicates variables in examples that should be replaced with user-supplied values.

Italic
: Indicates variables, filenames, directory names, URLs, and comments in examples.

Bold
: Indicates buttons and keys.

Comments and Questions

Please address comments and questions concerning this book to the publisher:

O'Reilly & Associates, Inc.
1005 Gravenstein Highway North
Sebastopol, CA 95472
(800) 998-9938 (in the United States or Canada)
(707) 829-0515 (international/local)
(707) 829-0104 (fax)

There is a web page for this book, which lists errata, examples, or any additional information. You can access this page at:

http://www.oreilly.com/catalog/webmaster3/

To comment or ask technical questions about this book, send email to:

bookquestions@oreilly.com

For more information about books, conferences, Resource Centers, and the O'Reilly Network, see the O'Reilly web site at:

http://www.oreilly.com

Acknowledgments

Some chapters in this book were researched from other books and some were contributed outright by other authors. We'd like to thank David Flanagan, Chuck Musciano, Bill Kennedy, Rasmus Lerdorf, and Clinton Wong for giving us permission to use their material as the basis for much of this one. We'd also like to thank Patrick Killelea for providing the chapter on server performance.

We'd especially like to thank Simon St. Laurent and Chuck Toporek for their effective, last-minute reviews of the book.

1
The Web in a Nutshell

The first edition of this book was published in 1996, when the Web was young and its possibilities were endless. As we write this third edition, the Web has since matured, and many of its possibilities have long been realized. Although the excitement of those early days has tempered and the technology has for the most part stabilized, it remains an integral part of our everyday lives. Venture capitalists might have moved on to newer ways to make a killing, but the Web's importance has not diminished, and its technology remains both vital and vibrant.

In this chapter, we give the world's quickest introduction to web technology. This book is by impatient writers for impatient readers, so don't expect much history or analysis here, just a basic tour of how everything fits together.

Clients and Servers

The tool most people use on the Web is a *browser*, such as Netscape Navigator, Internet Explorer, Opera, Mozilla, or Lynx. Web browsers work by connecting over the Internet to remote machines, requesting specific documents, and then formatting the documents they receive for viewing on the local machine.

The language, or *protocol*, used for web transactions is Hypertext Transfer Protocol, or HTTP. The remote machines containing the documents run HTTP *servers* that wait for requests from browsers and then return the specified document. The browsers themselves are technically HTTP *clients*.

Uniform Resource Locators (URLs)

One of the most important things to grasp when working on the Web is the format for URLs. A URL is basically an address on the Web, identifying each document uniquely (for example, *http://www.oreilly.com/products.html*). Since URLs are so fundamental to the Web, we discuss them here in a little detail. The simple syntax for a URL is:

```
http://host/path
```

host
The host to connect to: *www.oreilly.com* or *www.google.com*. (While many web servers run on hosts beginning with *www*, the *www* prefix is just a convention.)

path
The document requested on that server. This is not the same as the file-system path, as its root is defined by the server.

Most URLs follow this simple syntax. A more generalized syntax, however, is:

```
scheme://host/path/extra-path-info?query-info
```

scheme
The protocol that connects to the site. For web sites, the scheme is `http`; for FTP, the scheme is `ftp`.

extra-path-info and query-info
Optional information used by CGI programs. See Chapter 12.

HTML documents also often use a "shorthand" for linking to other documents on the same server, called a *relative URL*. An example of a relative URL is *images/webnut.gif*. The browser knows to translate this into complete URL syntax before sending the request. For example, if *http://www.oreilly.com/books/webnut.html* contains a reference to *images/webnut.gif*, the browser reconstructs the relative URL as a full (or *absolute*) URL, *http://www.oreilly.com/books/images/webnut.gif*, and requests that document independently (if needed). Often in this book, you'll see us refer to a URI, not a URL. A URI (Universal Resource Identifier) is a superset of URL, in anticipation of different resource naming conventions being developed for the Web. For the time being, however, the only URI syntax in practice is URL; so while purists might complain, you can safely assume that "URI" is synonymous with "URL" and not go wrong (yet).

Web Content: HTML, XML, CGI, JavaScript, and PHP

While web documents can conceivably be in any format, the universal standard is Hypertext Markup Language (HTML), a language for creating formatted text interspersed with images, sounds, animation, and hypertext links to other documents anywhere on the Web. Chapter 2–Chapter 8 cover the current version of HTML.

In 1996, a significant extension to HTML was developed: Cascading Style Sheets (CSS). Cascading Style Sheets allow web site developers to associate a number of style-related characteristics (such as font, color, spacing, etc.) with a particular HTML tag. This enables HTML authors to create a consistent look and feel in a set of documents. Chapter 9 provides an overview of and a reference to CSS.

While HTML remains the widespread choice for web site development, there is an heir apparent called XML (Extensible Markup Language). XML is a meta-language that allows you to define your own document tags. Chapter 10 covers XML.

XHTML

XHTML is a more rigorous version of HTML—essentially, an XML-compliant version of HTML. As such, its syntax and tags are (mostly) the same as HTML. See Chapter 2 for more information.

When static documents aren't sufficient for a web site's needs, you can use tools such as CGI, JavaScript, mod_perl, and PHP. CGI is a way for the web server to call external programs instead of simply returning a static document. *Chapters 12* through *15* are intended for CGI programmers and mod_perl programmers using the Perl programming language. JavaScript and PHP are both programming languages embedded directly into HTML documents, but that's where the similarities end: JavaScript is used primarily for client-side scripting, and PHP is used primarily for database access. See Chapter 11 and Chapter 16.

The HTTP Protocol

In between clients and servers is the network, which uses TCP (Transmission Control Protocol) and IP (Internet Protocol) to transmit data and find servers and clients. On top of TCP/IP, clients and servers use the HTTP protocol to communicate. Chapter 17 gives details on the HTTP protocol, which you must understand for writing CGI programs, server scripts, web administration, and just about any other part of working with a server.

What About Web Services?

"Web Services" is the name given to technologies such as SOAP and XML-RPC, which use existing Internet-related technologies (HTTP, XML, RPC) to exchange data between applications. Web services are so-called because they use the HTTP protocol, but as far as the Web is concerned, it's just another type of content. We don't cover web services in this book because they're more interesting to networked application developers than to web developers.

Web Servers

The runaway leader among Unix-based web servers is Apache. Chapter 18 deals with configuring Apache, while Chapter 19 discusses the various Apache modules. Regardless of the type of server you're running, there are various measures you can take to maximize its efficiency. Chapter 20 describes a number of these server optimization techniques for both the server side and the client side.

Who Are the Webmasters?

So if that's the Web in a nutshell, who are the webmasters? The title "webmaster," or "web developer", vaguely means a person who works on the content end of the web. When you examine what webmasters actually do, there are many different definitions. On a typical web site, the responsibilities can be broken into four general groups:

Content providers
: Work on the data itself—creating or editing HTML documents, incorporating images and forms, and maintaining the integrity of the links.

Designers
: Create the images and also define the "look" of the site.

Programmers
: Write CGI, Java, JavaScript, and other programs to incorporate to the web site.

Administrators
: Make sure that the server is running properly and efficiently at all times. They might also be responsible for establishing new content development areas, writing new scripts, and maintaining the security of sensitive documents and of the site in general.

On a large site, you might have a staff of 50 content providers, a group of five designers, 3 or 4 programmers, and 2 administrators. On a small site, one person might do it all herself.

Each of these people might justifiably call themselves "webmasters." And while a programmer may not be especially interested in HTML syntax or server configuration, and someone who works only in HTML markup may not need to know anything about HTTP, this book should be useful to all.

Recommended Books

This is a reference book for looking up things you already know. But what if you don't already know it? At the risk of blatant self-promotion, here are some books published by O'Reilly & Associates that we recommend heartily:

- Web content providers will find *HTML and XHTML: The Definitive Guide*, written by Chuck Musciano and Bill Kennedy, to be an essential reference. *Dynamic HTML: The Definitive Reference* by Danny Goodman contains just about everything you need to know to create dynamic web content.
- Designers who are getting started on the Web will find the basics of creating graphics and simple web pages in *Web Design in a Nutshell* and *Learning Web Design*, both by Jennifer Niederst. Designers who are interested in learning JavaScript should try *Designing with JavaScript* by Nick Heinle and Bill Peña.
- Programmers on web sites should flock to *CGI Programming with Perl* by Scott Guelich, Shishir Gundavaram, and Gunther Birznicks; *Perl in a Nutshell* by Ellen Siever, Stephen Spainhour, and Nathan Patwardhan; as well David Flanagan's *JavaScript: The Definitive Guide* and *Programming PHP* by Rasmus Lerdorf and Kevin Tatroe. For a Perl tutorial, we recommend *Learning Perl* by Randal Schwartz and Tom Phoenix, and *Perl for Web Site Management* by John Callendar; for more complete Perl documentation, we recommend the classic "Camel" book, *Programming Perl*, by Larry Wall, Tom Christiansen, and Jon Orwant. mod_perl programmers should also check out *Writing Apache Modules with Perl and C* by Lincoln Stein and Doug MacEachern.
- Anyone who works with HTTP directly, both programmers and administrators, will find *HTTP: The Definitive Guide* to be an absolutely indispensible.
- Web site administrators might also consider the following references for their shelves: *Apache: The Definitive Guide* by Ben Laurie and Peter Laurie, *Web Security and Commerce* by Simson Garfinkel (with Gene Spafford), and *Web Performance Tuning* by Patrick Killelea.

I

HTML

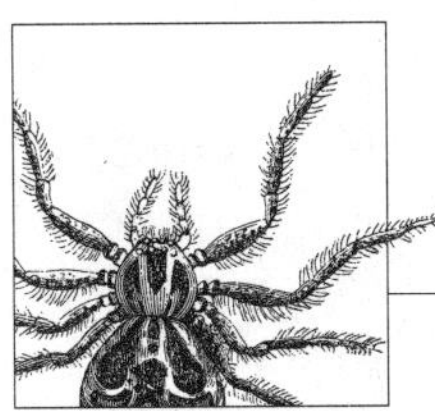

2
HTML Overview

Hypertext Markup Language (HTML) is the language that encodes World Wide Web documents. It is a document-markup and hyperlink-specification language that defines the syntax and placement of special, embedded directions that aren't displayed by a web browser but tell it how to display the contents of the document, including text, images, and other supported media. The language also tells you how to make a document interactive through special hypertext links, which connect your document with other documents on the network.

The syntax and semantics of HTML are defined in the HTML standard specification. The HTML specification and all other web-related standards issues are developed under the authority of the World Wide Web Consortium (W3C). Standards specifications and drafts of new proposals can be found at *http://www.w3.org*.

The latest HTML specification approved by the W3C is HTML 4.01. The latest generation of browsers have implemented the new standard almost fully. Although some support is still buggy, very few features of the specification remain unsupported. In the past, some browser makers implemented nonstandard extensions that could only be used on limited platforms. These extensions have been mostly done away with, although some platform-specific support still exists.

This section of the book summarizes the current state of HTML in seven chapters, as listed below. For more information on HTML, we recommend O'Reilly's *HTML and XMTML: The Definitive Guide,* by Chuck Musciano and Bill Kennedy.

- The current chapter introduces you to the background and general syntax of HTML. It also gives a brief introduction to XHTML, the XML-compliant version of HTML
- Chapter 3 describes the syntax of HTML tags and documents with descriptions of all the HTML tags in current use.
- For authors who want to use frames in HTML, Chapter 4 covers the frame tags in more detail and shows examples of using them.

- For authors using tables, Chapter 5 covers the table tags in more detail.
- Chapter 6 covers the form tags and shows examples of how to use them.
- Chapter 7 lists common character entities recognized in HTML documents.
- Chapter 8 contains listings of valid color values (for tags with attributes for specifying color).

HTML Document Structure

An HTML document consists of text, which comprises the content of the document, and tags, which define the structure and appearance of the document. The structure of an HTML document is simple, consisting of an outer `<html>` tag enclosing the document header and body:

```
<html>
<head>
<title>Barebones HTML Document</title>
</head>
<body>
<p>
This illustrates in a very <i>simple</i> way,
the basic structure of an HTML document.
</p>
</body>
</html>
```

Each document has a *head* and a *body*, delimited by the `<head>` and `<body>` tags. The head is where you give your HTML document a title and where you indicate other parameters the browser may use such as script and style sheets. The body is where you put the actual contents of the HTML document. This includes the text for display and document control markers (tags) that describe the text elements. Tags also reference media files like graphics and sound, and indicate the hot spots (*hyperlinks* or *anchors*) that link your document to other documents.

HTML Syntax

For the most part, HTML document elements are simple to understand and use. Every HTML element consists of a tag *name*, sometimes followed by an optional list of *attributes*, all placed between opening and closing brackets (< and >). The simplest elements are nothing more than the tag name enclosed in brackets, such as `<head>` and `<i>`. More complicated tags have attributes, which may have specific values defined by the author to modify the behavior of an element.

Attributes belong after the tag name, each separated by one or more tab, space, or return characters. The order of attributes in a single tag is not important. An attribute's value, if it has one, follows an equal sign after the attribute name. If an attribute's value is a single word or number, you may simply add it after the equal sign. All other values should be enclosed in single or double quotation marks, especially if they contain several words separated by spaces. The length of an attribute's value is limited to 1,024 characters. Here are some examples of tags with attributes:

```
<a href="http://www.ora.com/catalog.html" >
<h1 align="right">
<input name="filename" size="24" maxlength="80">
<link title="Table of Contents">
```

Tag and attribute names are not case-sensitive, but attribute values can be. For example, it is especially important to use the proper capitalization when referencing the URLs of other documents with the `href` attribute.

Most HTML elements consist of start and end tags that enclose a block of content. An end tag is the same as a start tag except it has a forward slash (/) before the tag name. End tags never contain attributes. For example, to italicize text, you enclose it within the <i> tags:

```
<i>This text in italics.</i>
```

You should take care when nesting elements in a document. You must end nested elements by starting with the most recent one and working your way back out. In this example, a phrase in bold (<b>) appears in the text of a link (<a href=...>) contained in a paragraph:

```
<p>
This is some text in the body, with a
<a href="another_doc.html">link, a portion of which
is <b>set in bold</b></a>
</p>
```

There are a handful of HTML elements that do not have end tags because they are standalone elements. For example, the image element (<img>) inserts a single graphic into a document and does not require an end tag. Other standalone elements include the line break (<br>), horizontal rule (<hr>), and others that provide information about a document that doesn't affect its displayed content such as <meta> and <base>.

XHTML

When the W3C defined the Extended Markup Language (XML), they also defined XHTML as a more rigorous, XML-compliant version of HTML. XHTML is designed to satisfy XML rules while still remaining legitimate HTML.

For example, although HTML specifies the <p> tag to start a paragraph, and the </p> tag to end it, you can easily omit the </p>, because HTML browsers will generally infer them. However, XHTML requires both <p> and </p> tags for all paragraphs, without exceptions.

The goal of the W3C is that eventually, HTML will migrate completely over to XHTML. However, that migration is likely to be slow. As long as people who write HTML documents manually can get away with omitting </p> tags and still have browsers parse them without complaint, they will continue to do so.

Most HTML authors today don't really need to worry about XHTML if all they're interested in is having their documents parsed by a web browser. But if you write tools that generate HTML, or if you expect that one day your document might be used in a venue other than the Web, you should take the time to learn XHTML.

The differences between XHTML and HTML are trivial compared to the benefits of writing XML-compliant documents.

For more information on XHTML, refere to *www.w3.org*, or to the book *HTML and XHTML: The Definitive Guide*.

Dynamic Content

One of the most important features provided by web page scripting is the ability to detect and react to events that occur while a document is loaded, rendered, and used. Web page authors can set up scripts that will be triggered by such events as a cursor passing over an image, clicking on a link, or even leaving a page. The scripting code that responds to these events may be placed within the `<script>` element or loaded from a separate file. A special set of common element attributes point to a script when their event is triggered. These attributes are called *event handlers*.

For example, you might want to invoke a JavaScript function when the user passes the mouse over a hyperlink in a document. You simply add a "mouse over" event handler for the `<a>` tag called `onMouseOver`

```
<a href=doc.html DEFANGED_OnMouseOver="document.status='Click me!'; return
true">
```

When the mouse passes over the example link, the browser executes the JavaScript statements. (Here, the JavaScript itself is embedded in the attribute, since it is so simple. Notice that the statements are enclosed in quotes and separated by a semicolon, and that single quotes surround the text-message portion of the first statement.)

While a complete explanation of this code is beyond our scope, the net result is that the browser places the message "Click me!" in the status bar of the browser window. Commonly, HTML authors use this simple JavaScript function to display a more descriptive explanation of a hyperlink, in place of the often cryptic URL the browser traditionally displays in the status window.

HTML supports a rich set of event handlers through related "on" event attributes. The value of any event handler attribute is either the name of a function defined elsewhere in the document, or a quoted string containing one or more script statements separated by semicolons. Extremely long statements can be broken across several lines, if needed.

At the lowest level, HTML event handlers are simply hooks defined by the browser manufacturer to access the Document Object Model of the browser. The DOM models the structure of the client as an interface for controlling it via scripting. For example, `document.title` is the interface for the title of a document, and `window.frame` is a single frame. Scripting can be used to alter these objects, whether it is to change their contents or how they are displayed.

An effort is underway at the W3C to implement a standard, platform-neutral DOM specification for web and XML applications. DOM Level 1 defined a core object model for HTML and XML documents. It provides for standard document navigation and manipulation. DOM Level 2 provides an event model and a model for style sheets and manipulating style information.

Currently, browsers support their own specific object models, which roughly comply with DOM Level 1. Currently, DOM Level 2 has been partially implemented in the latest generation of browsers.

Event Handler Attributes

Table 2-1 presents the current set of event handlers attributes. Some browsers support nonstandard event handlers; these are tagged with asterisks in the table.

Table 2-1. Event handlers

Event handler	HTML elements
onAbort	<img>*
onBlur	<a>
	<area>
	<body>*
	<button>
	<frameset>*
	<input>
	<label>
	<select>
	<textarea>
onChange	<input>
	<select>
	<textarea>
onClick	Most tags
onDblClick	Most tags
onError*	<img>
onFocus	<a>
	<area>
	<body>*
	<button>
	<frameset>*
	<input>
	<label>
	<select>
	<textarea>
onKeyDown	Most tags
onKeyPress	Most tags
onKeyUp	Most tags
onLoad	<body>
	<frameset>
	<img>*
onMouseDown	Most tags
onMouseMove	Most tags

Table 2-1. Event handlers (continued)

Event handler	HTML elements
onMouseOut	Most tags
onMouseOver	Most tags
onMouseUp	Most tags
onReset	<form>
onSelect	<input>
	<textarea>
onSubmit	<form>
onUnload	<body>
	<frameset>

Event handlers can be separated into user- and document-related events. The user-related ones are the mouse and keyboard events that occur when the user handles either device on the computer. Document-related events are special events and states that occur during the display and management of an HTML document and its elements by the browser.

User-related events are quite ubiquitous, appearing as standard attributes in nearly all the HTML elements. Clearly, some elements have no use for user-generated event handlers, e.g., <base> or <meta>. Similarly, many elements don't trigger document events.

Mouse-Related Events

The onClick, onDblClick, onMouseDown, and onMouseUp attributes refer to the mouse button. The onClick event happens when the user presses down and then quickly releases the mouse button, unless the user quickly clicks the mouse button a second time. In the latter case, the onDblClick event gets triggered in the browser.

If you need to detect both halves of a mouse click as separate events, use onMouseDown and onMouseUp. When the user presses the mouse button, the onMouseDown event occurs. The onMouseUp event happens when the user releases the mouse button.

The onMouseMove, onMouseOut, and onMouseOver events happen when the user drags the mouse pointer. The onMouseOver event occurs when the mouse first enters the display region occupied by the associated HTML element. After entry, onMouseMove events are generated as the mouse moves about within the element. Finally, when the mouse exits the element, onMouseOut occurs.

For some elements, the onFocus event corresponds to onMouseOver, and onBlur corresponds to onMouseOut.

Keyboard Events

Only three events are currently supported by the HTML 4.01 standard relating to user keyboard actions: onKeyDown, onKeyPress, and onKeyUp. The onKeyDown event occurs when the user depresses a key on the keyboard; onKeyUp happens when the key is released. The onKeyPress attribute is triggered when a key is pressed and released. Usually, you'll have handlers for either the up and down events or the composite keypress event, but not for both.

Document Events

Most of the document-related event handlers relate to the actions and states of HTML form controls. For instance, onReset and onSubmit happen when the user activates the respective reset or submit button. Similarly, onSelect and onChange occur as users interact with certain form elements. Please consult Chapter 6 for a detailed discussion of these HTML forms-related events.

There also are some document-related event handlers that occur when various document elements get handled by the browser. For instance, the onLoad event may happen when a frameset is complete or when the body of an HTML document gets loaded and displayed by the browser. Similarly, onUnload occurs when a document is removed from a frame or window.

JavaScript URLs

You can replace any conventional URL reference in a document with one or more JavaScript statements. The browser then executes the JavaScript code, rather than downloading another document, whenever the browser references the URL. The result of the last statement is taken to be the "document" referenced by the URL and is displayed by the browser accordingly. The result of the last statement is not the URL of a document; it is the actual content to be displayed by the browser.

To create a JavaScript URL, use javascript as the URL's protocol:

```
<a href="DEFANGED_javascript:generate_document()" >
```

In the example, the JavaScript function *generate_document()* gets executed whenever the hyperlink gets selected by the user. The value returned by the function, presumably a valid HTML document, is rendered and displayed by the browser.

It may be that the executed statement returns no value. In these cases, the current document is left unchanged. For example, this JavaScript URL:

```
<a href="DEFANGED_javascript:alert('Error!')" >
```

pops up an alert dialog box, and does nothing else. The document containing the hyperlink would still be visible after the dialog box gets displayed and is dismissed by the user.

See Chapter 11 for a complete reference on JavaScript.

3
HTML Reference

This section lists the tags and attributes in HTML 4.01.

Core Attributes

Prior to HTML Version 4, there were few attributes that could be used consistently for all HTML tags. HTML 4 changes this, defining a set of 16 core attributes that can be applied to almost all the tags in the language. For brevity, we list these core attributes in this section and spare you the redundancies in the table that follows:

`class=`*name*
: Specify a style class controlling the appearance of the tag's contents.

`dir=`*dir*
: Specify the rendering direction for text, either left to right (`ltr`) or right to left (`rtl`).

`id=`*name*
: Define a reference name for the tag that is unique in the document.

`lang=`*language*
: Specify the human language for the tag's contents with an ISO639 standard two-character name and optional dialect subcode.

`onclick=`*applet*
: Specify an applet to be executed when the user clicks the mouse on the tag's contents display area.

`ondblclick=`*applet*
: Specify an applet to be executed when the user double-clicks the mouse button on the tag's contents display area.

onkeydown=*applet*
: Specify an applet to be executed when the user presses down on a key while the tag's contents have input focus.

onkeypress=*applet*
: Specify an applet to be executed when the user presses and releases a key while the tag's contents have input focus.

onkeyup=*applet*
: Specify an applet to be executed when the user releases a pressed key while the tag's contents have input focus.

onmousedown=*applet*
: Specify an applet to be executed when the user presses down on the mouse button when pointing to the tag's contents display area.

onmousemove=*applet*
: Specify an applet to be executed when the user moves the mouse in the tag's contents display area.

onmouseout=*applet*
: Specify an applet to be executed when the user moves the mouse off the tag's contents display area.

onmouseover=*applet*
: Specify an applet to be executed when the user moves the mouse into the tag's contents display area.

onmouseup=*applet*
: Specify an applet to be executed when the user releases the mouse button when in the tag's contents display area.

style=*style*
: Specify an inline style for the tag.

title=*string*
: Specify a title for the tag.

A small handful of tags do not accept all of these attributes. They are:

<applet>	<embed>	<html>	<marquee>	<script>
<base>	<font>	<iframe>	<meta>	<server>
<basefont>	<frame>	<ilayer>	<multicol>	<spacer>
<bdo>	<frameset>	<isindex>	<nobr>	<style>
 	<head>	<keygen>	<noembed>	<title>
<comment>	<hr>	<layer>	<param>	<wbr>

In the reference section, we list all the attributes supported by these special tags, including the common ones. For all other tags, assume the common attributes in the preceding list apply.

HTML Tag and Attribute Descriptions

<a>

`<a> ... </a>`

Create a hyperlink (`href` attribute) or fragment identifier (`name` attribute) within a document.

Attributes

`accesskey=`*`char`*
: Define the hot-key character for this anchor.

`charset=`*`encoding`*
: Specify the character set used to encode the target.

`coords=`*`list`*
: Specify a list of shape-dependent coordinates.

`href=`*`url`*
: Specify the URL of a hyperlink target (required if not a name anchor).

`hreflang=`*`language`*
: Specify the language encoding for the target.

`name=`*`string`*
: Specify the name of a fragment identifier (required if not a hypertext reference anchor).

`rel=`*`relationship`*
: Indicate the relationship from this document to the target.

`rev=`*`relationship`*
: Indicate the reverse relationship of the target to this document.

`shape=`*`shape`*
: Define the region's shape to be `circ`, `circle`, `poly`, `polygon`, `rect`, or `rectangle`.

`tabindex=`*`value`*
: Define the position of this anchor in the document's tabbing order.

`target=`*`name`*
: Define the name of the frame or window to receive the referenced document.

`type=`*`type`*
: Specify the MIME type of the target.

Example

To create an anchor named `info` at some point in a document called *doc.html*, use the `<a>` tag with the `name` attribute:

```
<a name="info" >Information</a>
```

To provide a hyperlink to that point in *doc.html*, use the `<a>` tag with the `href` attribute appending the anchor name to the filename using a hash mark (#):

```
<a href="doc.html#info" >Link to information</a>
```

<abbr>

`<abbr> ... </abbr>`

The enclosed text is an abbreviation.

<acronym>

`<acronym> ... </acronym>`

The enclosed text is an acronym.

<address>

`<address> ... </address>`

The enclosed text is an address.

<applet>

`<applet> ... </applet>`

Define an executable applet within a text flow.

Attributes

align=*position*
: Align the <applet> region to either the top, middle, bottom (default), left, right, absmiddle, baseline, or absbottom of the text in the line.

alt=*string*
: Specify alternative text to replace the <applet> region within browsers that support the <applet> tag but cannot execute the application.

archive=*url*
: Specify a class archive to be downloaded to the browser and then searched for code class.

class=*name*
: Specify a style class controlling the appearance of the tag.

code=*class*
: Specify the class name of the code to be executed (required).

codebase=*url*
: URL from which the code is retrieved.

height=*n*
: Specify the height, in pixels, of the <applet> region.

hspace=*n*
: Specify additional space, in pixels, to the left and right of the <applet> region.

id=*name*
: Define a name for this applet that is unique to this document.

mayscript
: If present, allows the applet to access JavaScript within the page.

name=*string*
: Specify the name of this particular instance of the <applet>.

`object=`*`data`*
: Specify a representation of the object's execution state.

`style=`*`style`*
: Specify an inline style for this tag.

`title=`*`string`*
: Provide a title for the applet.

`vspace=`*`n`*
: Specify additional space, in pixels, above and below the `<applet>` region.

`width=`*`n`*
: Specify the width, in pixels, of the `<applet>` region.

<area>

`<area>`

Define a mouse-sensitive area in a client-side image map.

Attributes

`accesskey=`*`char`*
: Define the hot-key character for this area.

`alt=`*`string`*
: Provide alternative text to be displayed by nongraphical browsers.

`coords=`*`list`*
: Specify a comma-separated list of shape-dependent coordinates that define the edge of this area.

`href=`*`url`*
: Specify the URL of a hyperlink target associated with this area.

`nohref`
: Indicate that no document is associated with this area; clicking in the area has no effect.

`notab`
: This area should not be included in the tabbing order.

`onblur=`*`applet`*
: Specify an applet to be run when the mouse leaves the area.

`onfocus=`*`applet`*
: Specify an applet to be run when the mouse enters the area.

`shape=`*`shape`*
: Define the region's shape to be either `circ`, `circle`, `poly`, `polygon`, `rect`, or `rectangle`.

`tabindex=`*`value`*
: Define the position of this area in the document's tabbing order.

`taborder=`*`n`*
: Specify this area's position in the tabbing order.

`target=`*`name`*
: Specify the frame or window to receive the document linked by this area.

<b>

`<b> ... </b>`

Format the enclosed text using a `bold` typeface.

<base>

`<base>`

Specify the base URL for all relative URLs in this document.

Attributes

`href=`*`url`*
: Specify the base URL.

`target=`*`name`*
: Define the default target window of all `<a>` links in the document (mostly used for redirecting a link to other frames). There are four special values `_blank`, `_parent`, `_self`, and `_top`. These values are described in Chapter 4.

HTML Reference

<basefont>

`<basefont>`

Specify the font size for subsequent text.

Attributes

`color=`*`color`*
: Specify the base font's color.

`face=`*`name`*
: Specify the local font to be used for the base font.

`id=`*`name`*
: Define a name for this tag that is unique to this document.

`name=`*`name`*
: Specify the local font to be used for the base font.

`size=`*`value`*
: Set the basefont size from 1 to 7 (required; default is 3).

<bdo>

`<bdo> ... </bdo>`

Bidirectional override; changes the rendering direction of the enclosed text.

Attributes

`class=`*`name`*
: Specify a class style controlling the appearance of this tag.

`dir=`*`direction`*
: Specify the rendering direction for text, either left to right (`ltr`) or right to left (`rtl`).

`id=`*`name`*
: Define a name for this tag that is unique to this document.

`lang=`*`language`*
: Specify the language used for this tag's contents using a standard two-character ISO language name.

`style=`*`style`*
: Specify an inline style for this tag.

`title=`*`string`*
: Specify a title for this tag.

<bgsound>

`<bgsound>`

Define background audio for the document.

Attributes

`loop=`*`value`*
: Set the number of times to play the audio; *`value`* may be an integer or the value `infinite`.

`src=`*`url`*
: Provide the URL of the audio file to be played.

<big>

`<big> ... </big>`

Format the enclosed text using a bigger typeface.

<blink>

`<blink> ... </blink>`

Cause the enclosed text to blink.

<blockquote>

`<blockquote> ... </blockquote>`

The enclosed text is a block quotation.

Attributes

`cite=`*`url`*
: Specify the source URL of the quoted material.

<body>

`<body> ... </body>`

Delimit the beginning and end of the document body.

Attributes

`alink=`*`color`*
: Set the color of active hypertext links in the document.

`background=`*`url`*
: Specify the URL of an image to be tiled in the document background.

`bgcolor=`*`color`*
: Set the background color of the document.

`bgproperties=`*`value`*
: When set to `fixed`, prevent the background image from scrolling with the document content.

`leftmargin=`*`value`*
: Set the size, in pixels, of the document's left margin.

`link=`*`color`*
: Set the color of unvisited hypertext links in the document.

`onblur=`*`applet`*
: Specify an applet to be run when the mouse leaves the document window.

`onfocus=`*`applet`*
: Specify an applet to be run when the mouse enters the document window.

`onload=`*`applet`*
: Specify an applet to be run when the document is loaded.

`onunload=`*`applet`*
: Specify an applet to be run when the document is unloaded.

`text=`*`color`*
: Set the color of regular text in the document.

`topmargin=`*`value`*
: Set the size, in pixels, of the document's top margin.

`vlink=`*`color`*
: Set the color of visited links in the document.

`<br>`

Break the current text flow, resuming at the beginning of the next line.

Attributes

`class=`*`name`*
: Specify a style class controlling the appearance of this tag.

`clear=`*`margin`*
: Break the flow and move downward until the desired margin, either `left`, `right`, or `all`, is clear.

`id=`*`name`*
: Define a name for this tag that is unique to this document.

`style=`*`style`*
: Specify an inline style for this tag.

`title=`*`string`*
: Specify a title for this tag.

<button>

`<button>`

Create a push-button element within a `<form>`.

Attributes

`accesskey=`*char*
: Define the hot-key character for this button.

`disabled`
: Disable the button, preventing the user from clicking it.

`name=`*name*
: Specify the name of the parameter to be passed to the form-processing application if the input element is selected (required).

`onblur=`*applet*
: Specify an applet to be run when the mouse moves out of the button.

`onfocus=`*applet*
: Specify an applet to be run when the mouse moves into the button.

`type=`*type*
: Specify the button type, either `button`, `submit`, or `reset`.

`tabindex=`*n*
: Specify this element's position in the tabbing order.

`value=`*string*
: Specify the value of the parameter sent to the form-processing application if this form element is selected (required).

<caption>

```
<caption> ... </caption>
```

Define a caption for a table.

Attributes

`align=`*position*
: For Netscape, set the vertical position of the caption to either `top` or `bottom`. Default is top, centered. For Internet Explorer, set the horizontal alignment of the caption to either `left`, `center`, or `right`, or the vertical position to `top` or `bottom`. The default is top, centered. You cannot set both the horizontal and vertical position with this attribute alone.

`valign=`*position*
: Set the vertical position of the caption to either `top` or `bottom`. Default is top. Use this with a horizontal specification to `align` to set both vertical and horizontal caption positions.

See Chapter 5 for more information on using tables.

<center>

```
<center> ... </center>
```

Center the enclosed text.

<cite>

`<cite> ... </cite>`

The enclosed text is a citation.

<code>

`<code> ... </code>`

The enclosed text is a code sample.

<col>

`<col>`

Set properties for a column (or columns) within a `<colgroup>` of a table.

Attributes

`align=`*`value`*
: Specify alignment of text in the cells of a column. Value can be `center`, `left`, or `right`.

`char=`*`character`*
: Specify the alignment character for text in these cells.

`charoff=`*`value`*
: Set the offset within the cell at which the alignment character will be placed.

`span=`*`n`*
: Specify the number of columns to be affected by the `<col>` settings.

`valign=`*`position`*
: Set the vertical alignment of text within the column to either `top`, `middle`, or `bottom`.

`width=`*`n`*
: Set the width of the column, in pixels or as a percentage.

<colgroup>

`<colgroup>`

Set properties for designated column or columns within a table. Also indicates where vertical rules will be drawn when `rules=`*`groups`* is set in the `<table>` tag.

Attributes

`align=`*`value`*
: Specify alignment of text in the cells of columns in the `<colgroup>`. Values can be `center`, `left`, or `right`.

`char=`*`character`*
: Specify the alignment character for text in these cells.

`charoff=`*`value`*
: Set the offset within the cell at which the alignment character will be placed.

`span=`*n*
: Specify the number of columns in the `<colgroup>`.

`valign=`*position*
: Set the vertical alignment of text within the columns to either `top`, `middle`, or `bottom`.

`width=`*n*
: Set the width, in pixels or as a percentage, of each column in the group.

<comment>

`<comment> ... </comment>`

Place a comment in the document. Comments will be visible in all other browsers. Comments can be placed within `<!--` *comment text* `-->` for all browsers.

<dd>

`<dd> ... </dd>`

Define the definition portion of an element in a definition list.

<del>

`<del> ... </del>`

Delineate a deleted section of a document.

Attributes

`cite=`*url*
: Cite a document justifying the deletion.

`datetime=`*date*
: Specify the date and time of the deletion.

<dfn>

`<dfn> ... </dfn>`

Format the enclosed text as a definition.

<dir>

`<dir> ... </dir>`

Create a directory list containing `<li>` tags.

Attributes

`compact`
: Make the list more compact if possible.

`type=`*bullet*
: Set the bullet style for this list to either `circle`, `disc` (default), or `square`.

<div>

`<div> ... </div>`

Create a division within a document.

Attributes

`align=`*type*
: Align the text within the division to `left`, `center`, or `right`.

`nowrap`
: Suppress word wrapping within this division.

<dl>

`<dl> ... </dl>`

Create a definition list containing `<dt>` and `<dd>` tags.

Attributes

`compact`
: Make the list more compact if possible.

<dt>

`<dt> ... </dt>`

Define the definition term portion of an element in a definition list.

<em>

`<em> ... </em>`

Format the enclosed text with additional emphasis.

<embed>

`<embed> ... </embed>`

Embed an application into the document.

Attributes

`align=`*position*
: Align the applet area to either the `top` or `bottom` of the adjacent text, or to the `left` or `right` margin of the page, with subsequent text flowing around the applet.

`border=`*n*
: Specify the size, in pixels, of the border around the applet.

`height=`*n*
: Specify the height of the area the embedded object will occupy.

`hidden`
: If present, hide the applet on the page.

`hspace=`*n*
: Define, in pixels, additional space to be placed to the left and right of the applet.

`name=`*name*
: Provide a name for the applet.

`palette=`*value*
: In Netscape, a value of `foreground` causes the applet to use the foreground palette in Windows only; `background` uses the background palette. Internet Explorer provides the foreground and background colors for the applet, specified as two color values separated by a vertical bar (|).

`pluginspage=`*`url`*
: Provide the URL of the page containing instructions for installing the plug-in associated with the applet.

`src=`*`url`*
: Supplies the URL of the data to be fed to the applet.

`type=`*`type`*
: Specify the MIME type of the plug-in to be used.

`units=`*`type`*
: Set the units for the height and width attributes to either `pixels` (the default) or `en` (half the text point size).

`vspace=`*`n`*
: Define, in pixels, additional space to be placed above and below the applet.

`width=`*`n`*
: Specify the width, in pixels, of the applet.

<fieldset>

`<fieldset> ... </fieldset>`

Create a group of elements in a form.

<font>

`<font> ... </font>`

Set the size, color, or typeface of the enclosed text.

Attributes

`class=`*`name`*
: Specify a style class controlling the appearance of this tag.

`color=`*`color`*
: Set the color of the enclosed text.

`dir=`*`dir`*
: Specify the rendering direction for text, either left to right (`ltr`) or right to left (`rtl`).

`face=`*`list`*
: Set the typeface of the enclosed text to the first available font in the comma-separated list of font names.

`id=`*`name`*
: Define a name for this tag that is unique to this document.

`lang=`*`language`*
: Specify the language used for this tag's contents using a standard two-character ISO language name.

`size=`*`value`*
: Set the size to an absolute value (1 to 7), or relative to the `<basefont>` size using `+n` or `-n`.

`style=`*`style`*
: Specify an inline style for this tag.

`title=`*`string`*
: Specify a title for this tag.

<form>

`<form> ... </form>`

Delimit a form.

Attributes

`accept-charset=`*`list`*
: Specify a list of character sets accepted by the server processing this form.

`action=`*`url`*
: Specify the URL of the application that will process the form. The default is the current URL.

`enctype=`*`encoding`*
: Specify how the form element values will be encoded.

`method=`*`style`*
: Specify the parameter-passing style, either `get` or `post`. The default is `get`.

`name=`*`name`*
: Supply a name for this form for use by JavaScript.

`onreset=`*`applet`*
: Specify an applet to be run when the form is reset.

`onsubmit=`*`applet`*
: Specify an applet to be run when the form is submitted.

`target=`*`name`*
: Specify the name of a frame or a window to receive the results of the form after submission.

<frame>

`<frame> ... </frame>`

Define a frame within a frameset.

Attributes

`bordercolor=`*`color`*
: Set the color of the frame's border to *`color`*.

`class=`*`name`*
: Specify a style class controlling the appearance of this tag.

`frameborder=`*`value`*
: If *`value`* is `yes` (Netscape only) or `1` (Netscape and Internet Explorer), enable frame borders. If *`value`* is `no` (Netscape only) or `0` (Netscape and Internet Explorer), disable frame borders.

`id=`*`name`*
: Define a name for this tag that is unique in the document.

`longdesc=`*`url`*
: Provide the URL of a document describing the contents of this frame.

`marginheight=`*`n`*
: Place *n* pixels of space above and below the frame contents.

`marginwidth=n`
: Place *n* pixels of space to the left and right of the frame contents.

`name=string`
: Define the name of the frame.

`noresize`
: Disable user resizing of the frame.

`scrolling=type`
: Always add scrollbars (yes), never add scrollbars (`no`), or add scrollbars when needed (`auto`).

`src=url`
: Define the URL of the source document for this frame.

`style=style`
: Specify an inline style for this tag.

`title=string`
: Specify a title for this tag.

See Chapter 4 for more information on using frames.

<frameset>

`<frameset> ... </frameset>`

Define a collection of frames or other framesets.

Attributes

`border=n`
: Set size in pixels of frame borders within a frameset. Default border width is five pixels.

`bordercolor=color`
: Set the color for frame borders in a frameset.

`cols=list`
: Specify the number and width of frames within a frameset.

`frameborder=[yes|no]`
: Enable or disable the displaying of 3D borders or regular borders for frames. The default is yes (3D borders).

`frameborder=[1|0]`
: Enable or disable the displaying of 3D borders for frames within a frameset. The default is `1` (borders on).

`framespacing=n`
: Add additional space between adjacent frames in pixels.

`onblur=applet`
: Specify an applet to be run when the mouse leaves this frameset.

`onfocus=applet`
: Specify an applet to be run when the mouse enters this frameset.

`onload=applet`
: Specify an applet to be run when this frameset is loaded.

`onunload=`*`applet`*
    Specify an applet to be run when this frameset is unloaded.

`rows=`*`list`*
    Specify the number and height of frames within a frameset.

See Chapter 4 for more information on using frames.

<h*n*>

`<hn> ... </hn>`

The enclosed text is a level *n* header; for level *n* from 1 to 6.

Attributes

`align=`*`type`*
    Specify the heading alignment as either `left` (default), `center`, or `right`.

<head>

`<head> ... </head>`

Delimit the beginning and end of the document head.

Attributes

`dir=`*`dir`*
    Specify the rendering direction for text, either left to right (`ltr`) or right to left (`rtl`).

`lang=`*`language`*
    Specify the language used for this tag's contents using a standard two-character ISO language name.

`profile=`*`url`*
    Provide the URL of a profile for this document.

<hr>

`<hr>`

Break the current text flow and insert a horizontal rule.

Attributes

`align=`*`type`*
    Specify the rule alignment as either `left`, `center` (default), or `right`.

`class=`*`name`*
    Specify a style class controlling the appearance of the rule.

`color=`*`color`*
    Define the color of the rule.

`id=`*`name`*
    Define a name for this tag that is unique to this document.

`noshade`
    Do not use 3D shading to render the rule.

`onclick=`*`applet`*
: Specify an applet to be executed when the mouse button is clicked on this tag.

`ondblclick=`*`applet`*
: Specify an applet to be executed when the mouse button is double-clicked on this tag.

`onkeydown=`*`applet`*
: Specify an applet to be executed when a key is pressed down while this tag has input focus.

`onkeypress=`*`applet`*
: Specify an applet to be executed when a key is pressed and released while this tag has input focus.

`onkeyup=`*`applet`*
: Specify an applet to be executed when a key is released while this tag has input focus.

`onmousedown=`*`applet`*
: Specify an applet to be executed when a mouse button is pressed down on this tag.

`onmousemove=`*`applet`*
: Specify an applet to be executed when the mouse is moved over this tag.

`onmouseout=`*`applet`*
: Specify an applet to be executed when the mouse moves out of this tag's display area.

`onmouseover=`*`applet`*
: Specify an applet to be executed when the mouse moves into this tag's display area.

`onmouseup=`*`applet`*
: Specify an applet to be executed when a mouse button is released while over this tag.

`size=`*`pixels`*
: Set the thickness of the rule to an integer number of pixels.

`style=`*`style`*
: Specify an inline style for this tag.

`title=`*`string`*
: Specify a title for this tag.

`width=`*`value`*
: Set the width of the rule to either an integer number of pixels or a percentage of the page width.

<html>

```
<html> ... </html>
```

Delimit the beginning and end of the entire HTML document.

Attributes

`dir=`*`dir`*
Specify the rendering direction for text, either left to right (`ltr`) or right to left (`rtl`).

`lang=`*`language`*
Specify the language used for this tag's contents using a standard two-character ISO language name.

`version=`*`string`*
Indicate the HTML version used to create this document.

<i>

`<i> ... </i>`

Format the enclosed text in an *italic* typeface.

<iframe>

`<iframe> ... </iframe>`

Define an inline frame.

Attributes

`align=`*`type`*
Align the floating frame to either the `top`, `middle`, `bottom` (default), `left`, or `right` of the text in the line.

`class=`*`name`*
Specify a style class controlling the appearance of the frame contents.

`frameborder=[1|0]`
Enable or disable the display of borders for the frame. Default is `1`, which inserts the border. The value `0` turns the border off.

`height=`*`n`*
Specify the height of the frame in pixels or as a percentage of the window size.

`id=`*`name`*
Define a name for this tag that is unique to this document.

`longdesc=`*`url`*
Provide the URL of a document describing the contents of the frame.

`marginheight=`*`n`*
Place *n* pixels of space above and below the frame contents.

`marginwidth=`*`n`*
Place *n* pixels of space to the left and right of the frame contents.

`name=`*`string`*
Define the name of the frame.

`scrolling=`*`type`*
Always add scrollbars (yes), never add scrollbars (`no`), or add scrollbars when needed (`auto`).

`src=url`
: Define the URL of the source document for this frame.

`style=style`
: Specify an inline style for this tag.

`title=string`
: Specify a title for this tag.

`width=n`
: Specify the width of the frame in pixels.

See Chapter 4 for more information on using frames.

<ilayer>

`<ilayer> ... </ilayer>`

Define an inline layer.

Attributes

`above=name`
: Place this layer above the named layer.

`background=url`
: Specify a background image for the layer.

`below=name`
: Place this layer below the named layer.

`bgcolor=color`
: Specify the background color for the layer.

`class=name`
: Specify a style class controlling the appearance of this tag.

`left=n`
: Define, in pixels, the position of the layer's left edge from the containing line of text.

`name=name`
: Provide a name for the layer.

`src=url`
: Supply the content of the layer from another document.

`style=style`
: Specify an inline style for this tag.

`top=n`
: Define, in pixels, the position of the layer's top edge from the containing line of text.

`visibility=value`
: Determine whether to `show` the layer, `hide` the layer, or `inherit` the visibility attribute from a containing layer.

`width=n`
: Define the width, in pixels, of the layer.

`z-index=n`
: Specify the layer's position in the stacking order.

<img>

<img>

Insert an image into the current text flow.

Attributes

align=*type*
: Align the image to either the top, middle, bottom (default), left, or right of the text in the line. For Netscape Navigator, additionally align to the texttop, absmiddle, absbottom, or baseline of the text.

alt=*text*
: Provide descriptive text for nonimage-capable browsers, tool tips, telephone browsers, and search engines.

border=*n*
: Set the pixel thickness of the border around images contained within hyperlinks.

controls
: Add playback controls for embedded video clips.

dynsrc=*url*
: Specify the URL of a video clip to be displayed.

height=*n*
: Specify the height of the image in pixels.

hspace=*n*
: Specify the space, in pixels, to be added to the left and right of the image.

ismap
: Indicate that the image is mouse-selectable when used within an <a> tag.

longdesc=*url*
: Provide the URL of a document describing the image.

loop=*value*
: Set the number of times to play the video; *value* may be an integer or the value infinite.

lowsrc=*url*
: Specify a low-resolution image to be loaded by the browser first, followed by the image specified by the <src> attribute.

src=*url*
: Specify the source URL of the image to be displayed (required).

name=*name*
: Provide a name for the image for use by JavaScript.

onabort=*applet*
: Provide an applet to be run if the loading of the image is aborted.

onerror=*applet*
: Provide an applet to be run if the loading of the image is unsuccessful.

`onload=`*`applet`*
: Provide an applet to be run if the loading of the image is successful.

`start=`*`start`*
: Specify when to play the video clip, either `fileopen` or `mouseover`.

`usemap=`*`url`*
: Specify the map of coordinates and links that define the hypertext links within this image.

`vspace=`*`n`*
: Specify the vertical space, in pixels, added at the top and bottom of the image.

`width=`*`n`*
: Specify the width of the image in pixels.

<input type=button>

`<input type=button>`

Create a push-button element within a `<form>`.

Attributes

`accesskey=`*`char`*
: Define the hot-key character for this element.

`disabled`
: Disable this control, making it inactive.

`name=`*`name`*
: Specify the name of the parameter to be passed to the form-processing application if the input element is selected (required).

`notab`
: Specify that this element is not part of the tabbing order.

`onblur=`*`applet`*
: Specify an applet to be run when the mouse leaves this control.

`onfocus=`*`applet`*
: Specify an applet to be run when the mouse enters this control.

`tabindex=`*`n`*
: Specify this element's position in the tabbing order.

`taborder=`*`n`*
: Specify this element's position in the tabbing order.

`value=`*`string`*
: Specify the value of the parameter sent to the form-processing application if the input element is selected (required).

<input type=checkbox>

`<input type=checkbox>`

Create a checkbox input element within a `<form>`.

Attributes

`accesskey=`*`char`*
: Define the hot-key character for this element.

`checked`
: Mark the element as initially selected.

`disabled`
: Disable this control, making it inactive.

`name=`*`string`*
: Specify the name of the parameter to be passed to the form-processing application if the input element is selected (required).

`notab`
: Specify that this element is not part of the tabbing order.

`readonly`
: Prevent user modification of this element.

`tabindex=`*`n`*
: Specify this element's position in the tabbing order.

`taborder=`*`n`*
: Specify this element's position in the tabbing order.

`value=`*`string`*
: Specify the value of the parameter sent to the form-processing application if this form element is selected (required).

See Chapter 6 for more information on using forms.

<input type=file>

`<input type=file>`

Create a file-selection element within a `<form>`.

Attributes

`accept=`*`list`*
: Specify list of MIME types that can be accepted by this element.

`accesskey=`*`char`*
: Define the hot-key character for this element.

`disabled`
: Disable this control, making it inactive.

`maxlength=`*`n`*
: Specify the maximum number of characters to accept for this element.

`name=`*`string`*
: Specify the name of the parameter that is passed to the form-processing application for this input element (required).

`notab`
: Specify that this element is not part of the tabbing order.

`onblur=`*`applet`*
: Specify an applet to be run when the mouse leaves this control.

`onchange=`*`applet`*
: Specify an applet to be run when the user changes the value of this element.

`onfocus=`*`applet`*
: Specify an applet to be run when the mouse enters this control.

`readonly`
: Prevent user modification of this element.

`size=`*`n`*
: Specify the number of characters to display for this element.

`tabindex=`*`n`*
: Specify this element's position in the tabbing order.

`taborder=`*`n`*
: Specify this element's position in the tabbing order.

`value=`*`string`*
: Specify the value of the parameter sent to the form-processing application if this form element is selected (required).

See Chapter 6 for more information on using forms.

<input type=hidden>

`<input type=hidden>`

Create a hidden element within a `<form>`.

Attributes

`name=`*`string`*
: Specify the name of the parameter that is passed to the form-processing application for this input element (required).

`value=`*`string`*
: Specify the value of this element that is passed to the form-processing application.

See Chapter 6 for more information on using forms.

<input type=image>

`<input type=image>`

Create an image input element within a `<form>`.

Attributes

`accesskey=`*`char`*
: Define the hot-key character for this element.

`align=`*`type`*
: Align the image to either the `top`, `middle`, or `bottom` of the form element's text.

`alt=`*`string`*
: Provide a text description for the image.

`border=`*n*
: Set the pixel thickness of the border of the image.

`disabled`
: Disable this control, making it inactive.

`name=`*string*
: Specify the name of the parameter to be passed to the form-processing application for this input element (required).

`notab`
: Specify that this element is not part of the tabbing order.

`src=`*url*
: Specify the source URL of the image (required).

`tabindex=`*n*
: Specify this element's position in the tabbing order.

`taborder=`*n*
: Specify this element's position in the tabbing order.

`usemap=`*url*
: Specify the URL of a map to be used with this image.

See Chapter 6 for more information on using forms.

<input type=password>

`<input type=password>`

Create a content-protected text-input element within a `<form>`.

Attributes

`accesskey=`*char*
: Define the hot-key character for this element.

`disabled`
: Disable this control, making it inactive.

`maxlength=`*n*
: Specify the maximum number of characters to accept for this element.

`name=`*string*
: Specify the name of the parameter to be passed to the form-processing application for this input element (required).

`notab`
: Specify that this element is not part of the tabbing order.

`onblur=`*applet*
: Specify an applet to be run when the mouse leaves this control.

`onchange=`*applet*
: Specify an applet to be run when the user changes the value of this element.

`onfocus=`*applet*
: Specify an applet to be run when the mouse enters this control.

`onselect=`*applet*
: Specify an applet to be run when the user clicks this element.

`readonly`
: Prevent user modification of this element.

`size=`*n*
: Specify the number of characters to display for this element.

`tabindex=`*n*
: Specify this element's position in the tabbing order.

`taborder=`*n*
: Specify this element's position in the tabbing order.

`value=`*string*
: Specify the initial value for this element.

See Chapter 6 for more information on using forms.

<input type=radio>

`<input type=radio>`

Create a radio-button input element within a `<form>`.

Attributes

`accesskey=`*char*
: Define the hot-key character for this element.

`checked`
: Mark the element as initially selected.

`disabled`
: Disable this control, making it inactive.

`name=`*string*
: Specify the name of the parameter that is passed to the form-processing application if this input element is selected (required).

`notab`
: Specify that this element is not part of the tabbing order.

`readonly`
: Prevent user modification of this element.

`tabindex=`*n*
: Specify this element's position in the tabbing order.

`taborder=`*n*
: Specify this element's position in the tabbing order.

`value=`*string*
: Specify the value of the parameter that is passed to the form-processing application if this element is selected (required).

See Chapter 6 for more information on using forms.

<input type=reset>

`<input type=reset>`

Create a reset button within a `<form>`.

Attributes

`accesskey=`*`char`*
: Define the hot-key character for this element.

`disabled`
: Disable this control, making it inactive.

`notab`
: Specify that this element is not part of the tabbing order.

`readonly`
: Prevent user modification of this element.

`tabindex=`*`n`*
: Specify this element's position in the tabbing order.

`taborder=`*`n`*
: Specify this element's position in the tabbing order.

`value=`*`string`*
: Specify an alternate label for the reset button.

See Chapter 6 for more information on using forms.

<input type=submit>

`<input type=submit>`

Create a submit button within a `<form>`.

Attributes

`accesskey=`*`char`*
: Define the hot-key character for this element.

`disabled`
: Disable this control, making it inactive.

`name=`*`string`*
: Specify the name of the parameter that is passed to the form-processing application for this input element (required).

`notab`
: Specify that this element is not part of the tabbing order.

`tabindex=`*`n`*
: Specify this element's position in the tabbing order.

`taborder=`*`n`*
: Specify this element's position in the tabbing order.

`value=`*`string`*
: Specify an alternate label for the submit button, as well as the value passed to the form-processing application for this parameter if this button is clicked.

See Chapter 6 for more information on using forms.

<input type=text>

`<input type=text>`

Create a text input element within a `<form>`.

Attributes

`accesskey=`*`char`*
: Define the hot-key character for this element.

`disabled`
: Disable this control, making it inactive.

`maxlength=`*`n`*
: Specify the maximum number of characters to accept for this element.

`name=`*`string`*
: Specify the name of the parameter that is passed to the form-processing application for this input element (required).

`notab`
: Specify that this element is not part of the tabbing order.

`onblur=`*`applet`*
: Specify an applet to be run when the mouse leaves this element.

`onchange=`*`applet`*
: Specify an applet to be run when the user changes the value of this element.

`onfocus=`*`applet`*
: Specify an applet to be run when the mouse enters this element.

`onselect=`*`applet`*
: Specify an applet to be run when the user clicks this element.

`readonly`
: Prevent user modification of this element.

`size=`*`n`*
: Specify the number of characters to display for this element.

`tabindex=`*`n`*
: Specify this element's position in the tabbing order.

`taborder=`*`n`*
: Specify this element's position in the tabbing order.

`value=`*`string`*
: Specify the initial value for this element.

See Chapter 6 for more information on using forms.

<ins>

```
<ins> ... </ins>
```

Delineate an inserted section of a document.

Attributes

`cite=`*`url`*
: Specify the URL of the document justifying the insertion.

`datetime=`*`date`*
: Specify the date and time of the insertion.

<isindex>

`<isindex>`

Create a "searchable" HTML document.

Attributes

`action=`*`url`*
: Provide the URL of the program that will perform the searching action.

`class=`*`name`*
: Specify a class style controlling the appearance of this tag.

`dir=`*`direction`*
: Specify the rendering direction for text, either left to right (`ltr`) or right to left (`rtl`).

`id=`*`name`*
: Define a name for this tag that is unique to this document.

`lang=`*`language`*
: Specify the language used for this tag's contents using a standard two-character ISO language name.

`prompt=`*`string`*
: Provide an alternate prompt for the input field.

`style=`*`style`*
: Specify an inline style for this tag.

`title=`*`string`*
: Specify a title for this tag.

<kbd>

`<kbd> ... </kbd>`

The enclosed text is keyboard-like input.

<keygen>

`<keygen> ... </keygen>`

Generate key information in a form.

Attributes

`challenge=`*`string`*
: Provide a challenge string to be packaged with the key.

`name=`*`name`*
: Provide a name for the key.

<label>

`<label> ... </label>`

Define a label for a form control.

Attributes

`accesskey=`*`char`*
: Define the hot-key character for this label.

HTML Reference

`for=`*name*
: Specify the form element associated with this label.

`onblur=`*applet*
: Specify an applet to be run when the mouse leaves this label.

`onfocus=`*applet*
: Specify an applet to be run when the mouse enters this label.

<layer>

`<layer> ... </layer>`

Define a layer.

Attributes

`above=`*name*
: Place this layer above the named layer.

`background=`*url*
: Specify a background image for the layer.

`below=`*name*
: Place this layer below the named layer.

`bgcolor=`*color*
: Specify the background color for the layer.

`class=`*name*
: Specify a style class controlling the appearance of this tag.

`clip=`*edge*
: Define the layer's clipping region, in pixels. If `left` and `top` are 0, they may be omitted.

`left=`*n*
: Define, in pixels, the position of the layer's left edge from the containing line of text.

`name=`*name*
: Provide a name for the layer.

`src=`*url*
: Supply the content of the layer from another document.

`style=`*style*
: Specify an inline style for this tag.

`top=`*n*
: Define, in pixels, the position of the layer's top edge from the containing line of text.

`visibility=`*value*
: Determine whether to `show` the layer, `hide` the layer, or `inherit` the visibility attribute from a containing layer.

`width=`*n*
: Define the width, in pixels, of the layer.

`z-index=`*n*
: Specify the layer's position in the stacking order.

<legend>

`<legend> ... </legend>`

Define a legend for a form field set.

Attributes

`accesskey=`*`char`*
: Define the hot-key character for this legend.

`align=`*`position`*
: Align the legend to the `top`, `bottom`, `left`, or `right` of the field set.

<li>

`<li> ... </li>`

Delimit a list item in an ordered (`<ol>`) or unordered (`<ul>`) list.

Attributes

`type=`*`format`*
: Set the type of this list element to the desired format. For `<li>` within `<ol>`: `A` (capital letters), `a` (lowercase letters), `I` (capital Roman numerals), `i` (lowercase Roman numerals), or `1` (Arabic numerals; default). For `<li>` within `<ul>`: `circle`, `disc` (default), or `square`.

`value=`*`n`*
: Set the number for this list item to *n*.

<link>

`<link>`

Define a link in the document `<head>` between this document and another document. Currently this tag is implemented to provide links to style-sheet definition files and font definition files.

Attributes

`charset=`*`charset`*
: Specify the character set used to encode the target of this link.

`href=`*`url`*
: Specify the hypertext reference URL of the target document.

`hreflang=`*`lang`*
: Specify the language used for the target's contents using a standard two-character ISO language name.

`media=`*`list`*
: Specify a list of media types upon which this object can be rendered.

`rel=`*`relation`*
: Indicate the relationship from this document to the target. For Internet Explorer 3.0, `rel=`*`style`* indicates the existence of an external style sheet.

`rev=`*`relation`*
: Indicate the reverse relationship from the target to this document.

`type=text/css`
: Specify the MIME type for the linked document. Normally used in conjunction with links to style sheets, when the type is set to `text/css`.

<listing>

`<listing> ... </listing>`

Same as `<pre width=`*`n`*`>` ... `</pre>`; deprecated: don't use.

<map>

`<map> ... </map>`

Define a map containing hot spots in a client-side image map.

Attributes

`name=`*`string`*
: Define the name of this map (required).

<marquee>

`<marquee> ... </marquee>`

Create a scrolling-text marquee.

Attributes

`align=`*`position`*
: Align the marquee to the `top`, `middle`, or `bottom` of the surrounding text.

`behavior=`*`style`*
: Define marquee style to be `scroll`, `slide`, or `alternate`.

`bgcolor=`*`color`*
: Set the background color of the marquee.

`class=`*`name`*
: Specify a style class controlling the appearance of this tag.

`direction=`*`dir`*
: Define the direction, `left` or `right`, the text is to scroll.

`height=`*`value`*
: Define the height, in pixels, of the marquee area.

`hspace=`*`value`*
: Define the space, in pixels, to be inserted to the left and right of the marquee.

`loop=`*`value`*
: Set the number of times to animate the marquee; *`value`* is an integer or `infinite`.

`scrollamount=`*`value`*
: Set the number of pixels to move the text for scroll movements.

`scrolldelay=`*`value`*
: Specify the delay, in milliseconds, between successive movements of the marquee text.

`style=`*`style`*
Specify an inline style for this tag.

`vspace=`*`value`*
Define the space, in pixels, to be inserted above and below the marquee.

`width=`*`value`*
Define the width, in pixels, of the marquee area.

<menu>

`<menu> ... </menu>`

Define a menu list containing `<li>` tags.

Attributes

`compact`
Make the list more compact.

`type=`*`bullet`*
Set the bullet style for this list to either `circle`, `disc` (default), or `square`.

<meta>

`<meta>`

Provides additional information about a document.

Attributes

`charset=`*`name`*
Specify the character set to be used with this document.

`content=`*`string`*
Specify the value for the meta-information (required).For client pulls, `content="`*`n`*`;`*`url=url`*`"` tells the browser to load the specified *`url`* after *n* seconds. If no URL is specified, the source document will be reloaded. Must be used with `http-equiv="refresh"` within `<meta>`.

`dir=`*`direction`*
Specify the rendering direction for text, either left to right (`ltr`) or right to left (`rtl`).

`http-equiv=`*`string`*
Specify the HTTP equivalent name for the meta-information and cause the server to include the name and content in the HTTP header for this document when it is transmitted to the client. A value of `refresh` creates a "client-pull" within a document.

`lang=`*`language`*
Specify the language used for this tag's contents using a standard two-character ISO language name.

`name=`*`string`*
Specify the name of the meta-information.

`scheme=`*`scheme`*
Specify the profile scheme used to interpret this property.

<multicol>

```
<multicol> ... </multicol>
```

Format-enclosed HTML and text in multicolumn format. Text and elements will flow across specified number of columns to give them approximately equal length.

Attributes

`class=`*`name`*
: Specify a style class controlling the appearance of this tag.

`cols=`*`n`*
: Specify number of columns (required).

`gutter=`*`n`*
: Specify amount of space in pixels between columns. Default is 10 pixels.

`style=`*`style`*
: Specify an inline style for this tag.

`width=`*`n`*
: Specify width of columns in pixels.

<nobr>

```
<nobr> ... </nobr>
```

No breaks allowed in the enclosed text.

<noembed>

```
<noembed> ... </noembed>
```

Define content to be presented by browsers that do not support the `<embed>` tag.

<noframes>

```
<noframes> ... </noframes>
```

Define content to be presented by browsers that do not support frames.

See Chapter 4 for more information on using frames.

<noscript>

```
<noscript> ... </noscript>
```

Specify alternative content for browsers that do not support JavaScript. See Chapter 11 for more information on JavaScript.

<object>

```
<object> ... </object>
```

Insert an object into the document. This tag is used to specify applets, OLE controls, and other media objects.

Attributes

`align=`*`value`*
: Specify how the object is aligned with other elements in the document. Values include `baseline`, `center`, `left`, `middle`, `right`, `textbottom`, `textmiddle`, and `texttop`.

`archive=`*`list`*
: Specify a list of URLs of archives containing resources used by this object.

`border=`*`n`*
: Set the width of the object's border if it is a hyperlink.

`classid=`*`url`*
: Identify the class identifier of the object. The syntax of the URL depends on the object type.

`codebase=`*`url`*
: Identify the URL of the object's codebase. The syntax of the URL depends on the object.

`codetype=`*`codetype`*
: Specify the media type of the code.

`data=`*`url`*
: Specify the URL of the data used for the object. The syntax of the URL depends on the object.

`declare`
: Declare an object without instantiating it.

`height=`*`n`*
: Specify the height of the object in pixels.

`hspace=`*`n`*
: Specify the amount of space in pixels between the sides of the object and the surrounding elements.

`name=`*`url`*
: Specify the name of the object.

`notab`
: Do not make this object part of the tabbing order.

`shapes`
: Indicate shaped hyperlinks in object.

`standby=`*`message`*
: Specify message to display during object loading.

`tabindex=`*`n`*
: Specify this object's position in the tabbing order.

`type=`*`type`*
: Specify the media type for data.

`usemap=`*`url`*
: Specify image map to use with object.

`vspace=`*`n`*
: Specify the amount of space, in pixels, above and below object.

`width=`*`n`*
: Specify object width.

<ol>

`<ol> ... </ol>`

Define an ordered list containing numbered (ascending) `<li>` elements.

Attributes

`compact`
: Present the list in a more compact manner.

`start=`*n*
: Start numbering the list at *n*, instead of 1.

`type=`*format*
: Set the numbering format for this list to `A` (capital letters), `a` (lowercase letters), `I` (capital Roman numerals), `i` (lowercase Roman numerals), or `1` (Arabic numerals; default).

<optgroup>

`<optgroup> ... </optgroup>`

Define a group of options within a `<select>` element.

Attributes

`disabled`
: Disable this group, making it inactive.

`label=`*string*
: Provide a label for this group.

<option>

`<option> ... </option>`

Define an option within a `<select>` item in a `<form>`.

Attributes

`disabled`
: Disable this option, making it inactive.

`label=`*string*
: Provide a label for this option.

`selected`
: Make this item initially selected.

`value=`*string*
: Return the specified value to the form-processing application instead of the `<option>` contents.

See Chapter 4 for more information on using forms.

<p>

`<p> ... </p>`

Start and end a paragraph.

Attributes

`align=`*type*
: Align the text within the paragraph to `left`, `center`, or `right`.

<param>

`<param> ... </param>`

Supply a parameter to the <applet> or <object> surrounding this tag.

Attributes

id=*name*
: Define the unique identifier for this parameter.

name=*string*
: Define the name of the parameter.

type=*type*
: Specify the MIME type of the parameter.

value=*string*
: Define the value of the parameter.

valuetype=*type*
: Indicate the type of value. Can be one of three types: data indicates that the parameter's value is data (default); ref indicates that the parameter's value is a URL; object indicates that the value is a URL of another object in the document.

<plaintext>

`<plaintext>`

Render the remainder of the document as preformatted plain text.

<pre>

`<pre> ... </pre>`

Render the enclosed text in its original, preformatted style, honoring line breaks and spacing.

Attributes

width=*n*
: Size the text, if possible, so that *n* characters fit across the display window.

<q>

`<q> ... </q>`

Designate enclosed text as an inline quotation.

Attributes

cite=*url*
: Specify the URL of the source of the quoted material.

<s>

`<s> ... </s>`

The enclosed text is struck through with a horizontal line.

<samp>

`<samp> ... </samp>`

The enclosed text is a sample.

<script>

`<script> ... </script>`

Define a script within the document.

Attributes

`charset=`*`name`*
: Specify the character set used to encode the script.

`defer`
: Defer execution of this script.

`language=`*`lang`*
: Specify the language used to create the script.

`src=`*`url`*
: Specify the URL of an outside file containing the script to be loaded and run with the document.

`type=`*`type`*
: Specify the MIME type of the script.

See Chapter 10 for more information on JavaScript.

<select>

`<select> ... </select>`

Define a multiple-choice menu or scrolling list within a `<form>`, containing one or more `<option>` tags.

Attributes

`disabled`
: Disable this control, making it inactive.

`multiple`
: Allow user to select more than one `<option>` within the `<select>`.

`name=`*`string`*
: Define the name for the selected `<option>` values that, if selected, are passed to the form-processing application (required).

`onblur=`*`applet`*
: Specify an applet to be run when the mouse leaves this element.

`onchange=`*`applet`*
: Specify an applet to be run when the user changes the value of this element.

`onfocus=`*`applet`*
: Specify an applet to be run when the mouse enters this element.

`size=`*n*
: Display items using a pull-down menu for `size=1` (without `multiple` specified) and a scrolling list of *n* items otherwise.

`tabindex=`*n*
: Specify this element's position in the tabbing order.

See Chapter 6 for more information on using forms.

<server>

`<server> ... </server>`

Define a LiveWire script.

<small>

`<small> ... </small>`

Format the enclosed text using a smaller typeface.

<spacer>

`<spacer>`

Insert a whitespace element in a document.

Attributes

`type=`*type*
: Specify what type of spacer to use. `vertical` inserts space between two lines of text. `horizontal` inserts space between words or characters. `block` inserts a rectangular space such as an `<img>` object.

`size=`*n*
: Specify size in pixels for either width of `horizontal` spacer, or height of `vertical` spacer.

`width=`*n*
: Specify width in pixels of `block` spacer.

`height=`*n*
: Specify height in pixels of `block` spacer.

`align=`*value*
: Specify alignment of `block` spacer with surrounding text. Values are the same as for the `<img>` tag.

<span>

`<span> ... </span>`

Specify style-sheet formatting to text between tags.

Attributes

`style=`*elements*
: Specify cascading style-sheet elements for text in the span.

<strike>

`<strike> ... </strike>`

The enclosed text is struck through with a horizontal line.

<strong>

`<strong> ... </strong>`

Strongly emphasize the enclosed text.

<style>

`<style> ... </style>`

Define one or more document level styles.

Attributes

`dir=`*`dir`*
: Specify the rendering direction for the title text, either left to right (`ltr`) or right to left (`rtl`).

`lang=`*`language`*
: Specify the language used for this tag's title using a standard two-character ISO language name.

`media=`*`list`*
: Specify a list of media types upon which this object can be rendered.

`title=`*`string`*
: Specify a title for this tag.

`type=`*`type`*
: Define the format of the styles (i.e., `text/css`).

See Chapter 5 for more information on styles and style sheets.

<sub>

`<sub> ... </sub>`

Format the enclosed text as a subscript.

<sup>

`<sup> ... </sup>`

Format the enclosed text as a superscript.

<table>

`<table> ... </table>`

Define a table.

Attributes

`align=`*`position`*
: Align the table either `left` or `right` with the surrounding text flow.

`background=`*`url`*
: Specify an image to be tiled in the background of the table.

`bgcolor=`*`color`*
: Define the background color for the entire table.

`border=`*`n`*
: Create a border *n* pixels wide.

`bordercolor=`*`color`*
: Define the border color for the entire table.

`bordercolordark=`*`color`*
: Define the dark border-highlighting color for the entire table.

`bordercolorlight=`*`color`*
: Define the light border-highlighting color for the entire table.

`cellpadding=`*`n`*
: Place *n* pixels of padding around each cell's contents.

`cellspacing=`*`n`*
: Place *n* pixels of spacing between cells.

`cols=`*`n`*
: Specify the number of columns in this table.

`frame=[void|above|below|hsides|lhs|rhs|vsides|box|border]`
: Specify which sides of a table's outer border will be drawn. `void` removes outer borders; `box` and `border` displays all. `hsides` draws horizontal sides; `vsides` draws vertical sides. `lhs` draws left side; `rhs` right side.

`height=`*`n`*
: Define the height of the table in pixels.

`hspace=`*`n`*
: Specify the horizontal space, in pixels, added at the left and right of the table.

`nowrap`
: Suppress text wrapping in table cells.

`rules=[all|cols|groups|none|rows]`
: Turn off (`none`) or turn on rules between table cells by `cols`, `rows`, `groups`, or `all`.

`summary=`*`string`*
: Provide a description to summarize this table.

`vspace=`*`n`*
: Specify the vertical space, in pixels, added at the top and bottom of the table.

`width=`*`n`*
: Set the width of the table to *n* pixels or a percentage of the window width.

See Chapter 5 for more information on tables.

HTML Reference

<tbody>

`<tbody> ... </tbody>`

Create a row group within a table.

Attributes

`align=`*`position`*
: Align the table body cell contents to the `left`, `center`, or `right`.

`char=`*`char`*
: Specify the cell alignment character for the body group.

`charoff=value`
: Specify the offset of the alignment position within the cells.

`valign=position`
: Vertically align the body group cells' contents to the `top`, `center`, `bottom`, or `baseline` of a cell.

<td>

`<td> ... </td>`

Define a table data cell.

Attributes

`abbr=string`
: Specify an abbreviation for the cell's contents.

`align=type`
: Align the cell contents to the `left`, `center`, or `right`.

`axis=string`
: Provide a name for a related group of cells.

`background=url`
: Specify an image to be tiled in the background of the cell.

`bgcolor=color`
: Define the background color for the cell.

`bordercolor=color`
: Define the border color for the cell.

`bordercolordark=color`
: Define the dark border-highlighting color for the cell.

`bordercolorlight=color`
: Define the light border-highlighting color for the cell.

`char=char`
: Specify the cell alignment character.

`charoff=value`
: Specify the offset of the alignment position within the cell.

`colspan=n`
: Have this cell straddle *n* adjacent columns.

`headers=list`
: Provide a list of header cell names associated with this cell.

`height=n`
: Define the height, in pixels, for this cell.

`nowrap`
: Do not automatically wrap and fill text in this cell.

`rowspan=n`
: Have this cell straddle *n* adjacent rows.

`scope=scope`
: Define the scope of this header cell, either `row`, `col`, `rowgroup`, or `colgroup`.

`valign=type`
: Vertically align this cell's contents to the `top`, `middle`, `bottom`, or `baseline` of the cell.

`width=`*n*
: Set the width of this cell to *n* pixels or a percentage of the table width.

See Chapter 5 for more information on tables.

<textarea>

`<textarea> ... </textarea>`

Define a multiline text input area within a `<form>`; content of the `<textarea>` tag is the initial, default value.

Attributes

`accesskey=`*char*
: Define the hot-key character for this element.

`cols=`*n*
: Display *n* columns of text within the text area.

`disabled`
: Disable this control, making it inactive.

`name=`*string*
: Define the name for the text-area value that is passed to the form-processing application (required).

`onblur=`*applet*
: Specify an applet to be run when the mouse leaves this element.

`onchange=`*applet*
: Specify an applet to be run if a user changes the value of this element.

`onfocus=`*applet*
: Specify an applet to be run when the mouse enters this element.

`onselect=`*applet*
: Specify an applet to be run if the user clicks this element.

`readonly`
: Prevent user modification of this element.

`rows=`*n*
: Display *n* rows of text within the text area.

`tabindex=`*n*
: Specify this element's position in the tabbing order.

`wrap=`*style*
: Set word wrapping within the text area to `off`, `virtual` (display wrap, but do not transmit to server), or `physical` (display and transmit wrap).

See Chapter 6 for more information on forms.

<tfoot>

`<tfoot>`

Define a table footer.

Attributes

`align=`*position*
: Align the footer cell contents to the `left`, `center`, or `right`.

`char=`*char*
: Specify the cell alignment character.

`charoff=`*value*
: Specify the offset of the alignment position within the cell.

`valign=`*position*
: Vertically align the footer cells' contents to the `top`, `center`, `bottom`, or `baseline` of a cell.

<th>

`<th> ... </th>`

Define a table header cell.

Attributes

`abbr=`*string*
: Specify an abbreviation for the cell's contents.

`align=`*type*
: Align the cell contents to the `left`, `center`, or `right`.

`axis=`*string*
: Provide a name for a related group of cells.

`background=`*url*
: Specify an image to be tiled in the background of the cell.

`bgcolor=`*color*
: Define the background color for the cell.

`bordercolor=`*color*
: Define the border color for the cell.

`bordercolordark=`*color*
: Define the dark border-highlighting color for the cell.

`bordercolorlight=`*color*
: Define the light border-highlighting color for the cell.

`char=`*char*
: Specify the cell alignment character.

`charoff=`*value*
: Specify the offset of the alignment position within the cell.

`colspan=`*n*
: Have this cell straddle *n* adjacent columns.

`headers=`*list*
: Provide a list of header cell names associated with this cell.

`height=`*n*
: Define the height, in pixels, for this cell.

`nowrap`
: Do not automatically wrap and fill text in this cell.

`rowspan=`*n*
: Have this cell straddle *n* adjacent rows.

scope=*scope*
: Define the scope of this header cell: row, col, rowgroup, or colgroup.

valign=*type*
: Vertically align this cell's contents to the top, middle, bottom, or baseline of the cell.

width=*n*
: Set the width of this cell to *n* pixels or a percentage of the table width.

See Chapter 5 for more information on tables.

<thead>

<thead>

Define a table heading.

Attributes

align=*position*
: Align the header cells' contents to the left, center, or right.

char=*char*
: Specify the cell alignment character for heading cells.

charoff=*value*
: Specify the offset of the alignment position within the cell.

valign=*positiona*
: Vertically align the header cells' contents to the top, center, bottom, or baseline of a cell.

<title>

<title> ... </title>

Define the HTML document's title.

Attributes

dir=*dir*
: Specify the rendering direction for text, either left to right (ltr) or right to left (rtl).

lang=*language*
: Specify the language used for this tag's contents using a standard two-character ISO language name.

<tr>

<tr> ... </tr>

Define a row of cells within a table.

Attributes

align=*type*
: Align the cell contents in this row to the left, center, or right.

background=*url*
: Specify an image to be tiled in the background of the cell.

bgcolor=*color*
: Define the background color for this row.

`border=`*n*
: Create a border *n* pixels wide.

`bordercolor=`*color*
: Define the border color for this row.

`bordercolordark=`*color*
: Define the dark border-highlighting color for this row.

`bordercolorlight=`*color*
: Define the light border-highlighting color for this row.

`char=`*char*
: Specify the cell alignment character for this row.

`charoff=`*value*
: Specify the offset of the alignment position with cells of this row.

`nowrap`
: Disable word wrap for all cells in this row.

`valign=`*type*
: Vertically align the cell contents in this row to the `top`, `middle`, `bottom`, or `baseline` of the cell.

See Chapter 5 for more information on tables.

<tt>

`<tt> ... </tt>`

Format the enclosed text in typewriter-style (monospaced) font.

<ul>

`<ul> ... </ul>`

Define an unordered list of bulleted `<li>` elements.

Attributes

`compact`
: Display the list in a more compact manner.

`type=`*bullet*
: Set the bullet style for this list to either `circle`, `disc` (default), or `square`.

<var>

`<var> ... </var>`

The enclosed text is a variable's name.

<wbr>

`<wbr>`

Indicate a potential word-break point within a `<nobr>` section.

<xmp>

`<xmp> ... </xmp>`

Same as `<pre width=80>` ... `</pre>`; deprecated, do not use.

4 Frames

HTML frames allow you to divide the main browser window into smaller subwindows (frames), each of which simultaneously displays a separate document. Links in one frame can open in another frame by specifying its name as a target. All of the latest graphical browsers support frames.

Two tags are used to make frame documents: `<frameset>` and `<frame>`. The `<noframes>` element provides alternative content for nonframes browsers. This is a requirement for HTML 4.0 and later and should contain functional content, or a link to it, instead of telling someone to get a browser that supports frames.

A *frameset* is simply a collection of frames that occupy the browser's window. Column and row definition attributes for the `<frameset>` tag let you define the number and initial sizes for the columns and rows of frames. The `<frame>` tag defines what document—HTML or otherwise—initially goes into the frame, and is where you may give the frame a name to use for hypertext link targets.

Here is the HTML source for a simple frame document, which is displayed by the browser in Figure 4-1.

```
<html>
<head>
<title>Frames Layout</title>
</head>
<frameset rows="60%,*" cols="65%,20%,*">
  <frame src="frame1.html">
  <frame src="frame2.html">
  <frame src="frame3.html" name="fill_me">
  <frame scrolling=yes src="frame4.html">
  <frame src="frame5.html">
  <frame src="frame6.html">
  <noframes>
    You are using a browser that does not support frames.
    <a href="frame1.html">Take this link</a> to the first
    HTML document in the set.
```

```
  </noframes>
</frameset>
</html>
```

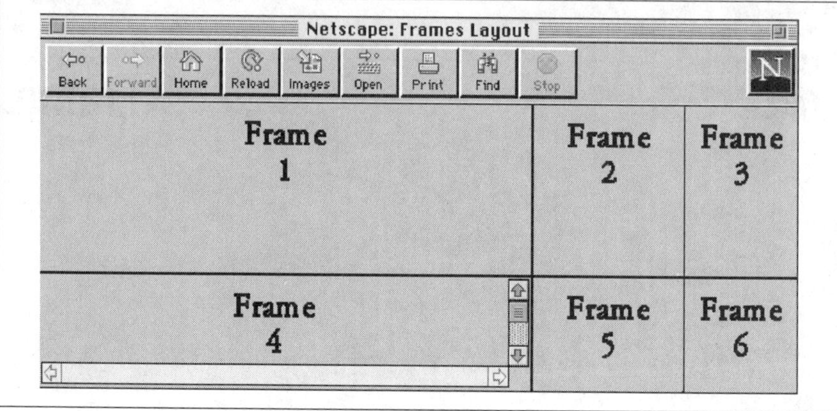

Figure 4-1. A simple six-panel frame layout in Netscape

The first thing to notice in the sample document is that Netscape fills the frames in the frameset in order across each row. Second, Frame 4 sports a scrollbar because we told it to, even though the contents may otherwise fit the frame without scrolling. (Scrollbars automatically appear if the contents overflow the frame's dimensions, unless explicitly disabled with `scrolling=no`.)

Another item of interest is the `name` attribute in Frame 3. Once named, you can reference a particular frame in which to display a hypertext-linked document. To do that, you add a special `target` attribute to the anchor (`<a>`) tag of the source hypertext link. For instance, to link a document called "new.html" for display in our example window Frame 3, which we've named "fill_me", the anchor looks like this:

```
<a href="new.html" target="fill_me">
```

If the user selects this link, say in Frame 1, the *new.html* document replaces the original *frame3.html* contents in Frame 3.

Frame Layout

The `<frameset>` tag defines the collection of frames or other framesets in a document. Framesets may be nested, providing a richer set of layout capabilities. The `<frameset>` tag replaces the `<body>` tag in a document. You may not include any other content except valid `<head>` and `<frameset>` content.

The `<frameset>` tag uses two attributes to let you define the size and number of columns (`cols`) and rows (`rows`) of either frames or nested framesets to display in the document window. These attributes divide a frameset in a grid-like or tabular format. Both attributes accept a quote-enclosed, comma-separated list of values that specify either the absolute or relative width (for columns) or height (for rows) for the frames. The number of attribute values determines how many rows or columns of frames the browser displays in the document window.

Each value in the `rows` and `cols` attributes can be specified in one of three ways: as an absolute number of pixels, as a percentage of the total width or height of the frameset, or as a portion of the space remaining after setting aside room for adjacent elements.

The browser matches the size specifications as closely as possible. However, the browser will not extend the boundaries of the main document window or leave blank space outside of frames. Space is allocated to a particular frame in reference to all other frames across the row or down the column, and the entire document window is filled. Also, the main document window for a frame document does not have scrollbars.

Here is an example of setting row heights in pixels:

```
<frameset rows="150,300,150" >
```

This creates three frames, each stretching across the entire document window. The top and bottom rows are set to 150 pixels tall; the middle is set to 300 pixels. Unless the browser window is exactly 600 pixels tall, the browser automatically and proportionally stretches or compresses the top and bottom rows so that each occupies one-quarter of the window space. The middle row occupies the remaining half of the window. This frameset could be expressed with percentages like this:

```
<frameset rows="25%,50%,25%" >
```

The percentages should add up to 100%, of course. If they don't, the browser resizes the rows proportionally to make them fit.

To make row and column sizing easier, you can use the asterisk (*) character. The asterisk represents one equal portion of the remaining window space, whatever it is. For example:

```
<frameset cols="50,*" >
```

creates one fixed 50-pixel column down the left side of the window; the remaining space goes to the right column. The asterisk can also be used for more than one column or row. For example:

```
<frameset rows="*,100,*" >
```

creates a 100-pixel-tall row across the middle of a frameset and rows above and below it that are equal in height.

If you precede the asterisk with an integer value, the corresponding row or column gets proportionally more of the available space. For example:

```
<frameset cols="10%,3*,*,*" >
```

creates four columns: the first column occupies 10% of the overall width of the frameset. The second column then gets three-fifths of the remaining space, and the third and fourth columns each get one-fifth. Using the asterisk makes it easy to divide remaining space in a frameset.

Be aware that unless you explicitly tell it not to, the browser lets users manually resize the individual columns and rows in a frame document. To prevent this, use the noresize attribute for the <frame> tag.

Nested Framesets

You can achieve more complex layouts by using nested <frameset> tags. Any frame within a frameset can contain another frameset.

For example, Figure 4-2 shows a layout of two columns, the first with two rows and the second with three rows. This is created by nesting two <frameset> tags with row specifications within a top-level <frameset> that specifies the columns:

```
<frameset cols="50%,*" >
  <frameset rows="50%,*">
    <frame src="frame1.html">
    <frame src="frame2.html">
  </frameset>
  <frameset rows="33%,33%,*">
    <frame src="frame3.html">
    <frame src="frame4.html">
    <frame src="frame5.html">
  </frameset>
</frameset>
```

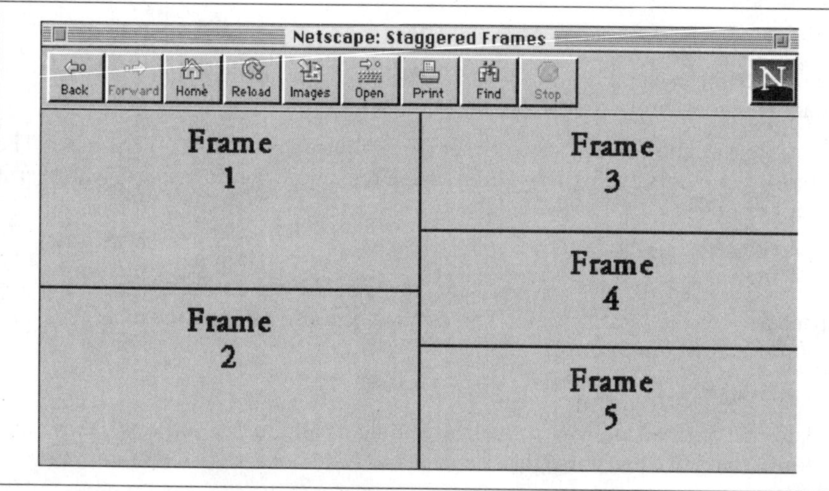

Figure 4-2. Staggered frame layouts using nested <frameset> tags

The <frame> Tag

A frame document contains no displayable content (except for the contents of the <noframes> tag, if applicable). The <frame> tags provide URL references to the individual documents that occupy each frame. <frame> tags are standalone elements, and therefore do not require a closing tag.

Frames are placed into a frameset column by column, from left to right, and then row by row, from top to bottom—so the sequence and number of <frame> tags inside a <frameset> are important.

Netscape displays empty frames for <frame> tags that do not contain an src document attribute and for those trailing ones in a frameset that do not have an associated <frame> tag. Such orphans, however, remain empty; you cannot put content into them later, even if they have a target name attribute for display redirection.

Listed below are the basic attributes that can be used in the <frame> tag.

src=*document_name*
: The value of the src attribute is a URL of the document that is to be displayed in the frame. The document may be any valid HTML document or displayable object, including images and multimedia. The referenced document may itself be another frame document.

name=*frame_name*
: The optional name attribute labels the frame for later reference by a target attribute in a hypertext link anchor <a> tag. If a link that targets a frame's name is selected, the document is displayed in the named frame. The value of the name attribute is a text string enclosed in quotes.

noresize
: Even though you may explicitly set their dimensions with attributes in the <frameset> tag, users can manually alter the size of a column or row of frames. To suppress this behavior, add the noresize attribute to the frame tags in the row or column whose relative dimensions you want to maintain.

scrolling=[yes,no,auto]
: Normally, the browser displays vertical and horizontal scrollbars for frames whose contents exceed the allotted space. If there is sufficient room for the content, no scrollbars appear. The scrolling attribute gives you explicit control over whether scrollbars appear. A value of yes turns the scrollbars on; no turns them off. The value of auto gives the default scrollbar behavior and is the same as not using the scrolling attribute at all.

marginheight=*height*
marginwidth=*width*
: The browser normally places a small amount of space between the edge of a frame and its contents. Those margins can be manually set with the marginheight and marginwidth attributes, whose values are given in pixels. A margin cannot be less than one pixel, nor so big that there is no room left for the frame's contents.

Frame Targets

The <frame> tag includes an attribute that allows you to name the frame. A hypertext link in another frame can load its referenced document into the named frame by using the target attribute in the <a> tag. For example:

```
<frame src="frame.html" name="display_frame">
```

describes a frame that displays *frame.html* and is named *display_frame*. If another frame or window (or even the same frame) contains this link:

```
<a href="file.html" target="display_frame">
```

and this link is selected, the file *file.html* replaces the file *frame.html* in the frame named *display_frame*. This is the basic use of targeting frames. A useful example is a book with a table of contents. The table of contents is loaded into a frame that occupies a narrow column on the left side of the browser window. The table of contents contains a list of links to each chapter in the book. Each chapter link targets the frame that occupies the rest of the window. You can then view the chapters while keeping the table of contents available for further navigation.

It can be tedious to specify a target for every hyperlink in your documents, especially when most are targeted at the same window or frame. To alleviate this problem, you can use the `target` attribute for the `<base>` tag in the `<head>` of your document. Adding a target to the `<base>` tag sets the default target for every hypertext link in the document that does not contain an explicit `target` attribute.

There are a couple of things to note about the use of targets and named frames:

- If a link without a target is contained within a frame, the referenced document replaces the current contents of the same frame if it is selected.
- If a link contains a target that does not exist, a new window is opened to display the referenced document, and the window is given the target's name. That window can thus be used by other links that target it.

Four reserved target names for special document redirection actions are listed below. They all begin with the underscore (_) character. You should not use the underscore character as the first letter of any name that you assign a frame, as it will be ignored by the browser.

`_blank`
: A linked document with `target="_blank"` is always loaded into a newly opened, unnamed window.

`_self`
: This target value is the default for all `<a>` tags that do not specify a target, causing the referenced document to be loaded in the same frame or window as the source document. The `_self` target is redundant and unnecessary unless used in combination with the `target` attribute of the `<base>` tag to override the default target value for all the links in the source document.

`_parent`
: The `_parent` target causes the document to load into the parent window or frameset containing the frame containing the hypertext reference. If the reference is in a window or top-level frame, it is equivalent to the target `_self`.

`_top`
: This target causes the document to load into the window containing the hypertext link, replacing any frames currently displayed in the window.

Frame Border Attributes

The recommended method for defining frame borders is to set the various border style attributes in the <frame> or <frameset> via a CSS stylesheet or inline style. Internet Explorer and Netscape Navigator both support attributes that adjust the style of the borders that surround frames. These attributes were introduced in earlier browsers prior to a standardized specification. Although they have the same functions, the attributes are slightly different for each browser.

Netscape uses the `frameborder` attribute to toggle between 3D borders and simple rules for borders. The default is to use 3D borders; a value of `no` gives simple borders. This attribute can be placed in either the <frameset> tag or in a <frame> tag. A setting in an individual <frame> overrides an outer <frameset> setting.

You can also set the color of the borders in both <frameset> and <frame> with the `bordercolor` attribute.

In the <frameset> tag, you can set the width of the borders in a whole frameset with the `border` attribute. The default width is 5 pixels. To achieve borderless frames in Netscape, set `border=0` and `frameborder=no`.

Internet Explorer does all the same things, only with different attributes. It also uses `frameborder` in the <frameset> and <frame> tags, but the values are `1` for 3D borders and `0` for simple ones. In the <frameset> tag, you can set the amount of space between frames with the `framespacing` attribute. By setting `framespacing=0` and `frameborder=0`, you can achieve borderless frames.

Another feature in Internet Explorer is the floating frame. This has all the abilities that a regular frame does, but it is placed within a document like an <img> would be. The tag for a floating frame is <iframe>, and it requires a closing tag. The attributes include all of the regular <frame> attributes, and the sizing, alignment, and placement attributes of <img>.

5
Tables

HTML tables offer a detailed way to present data, as well as a creative way to lay out the information in your web documents. The standard HTML model for tables is straightforward: a table is a collection of data arranged and related in rows and columns of cells. Most cells contain data values; others contain row and column headers that describe the data.

The HTML 4.01 table specification defines a number of tags and attributes for creating tables. Newly supported tags allow you to organize and display table data with great detail, and with the application of CSS-style elements, table styles can be standardized across your documents.

The main tags that describe tables are: `<table>`, `<caption>`, `<tr>`, `<th>`, and `<td>`. The `<table>` tag surrounds the table and gives default specifications for the entire table such as background color, border size, and spacing between cells. The optional `<caption>` tag is placed within the `<table>` tags and provides a caption for the table. `<tr>` tags denote each row of the table and contain the tags for each cell within a row. `<th>` and `<td>` describe the table cells themselves, `<th>` being a header cell and `<td>` being a regular cell. `<th>` and `<td>` tags surround the information that is displayed within each table cell.

Table cells are defined across each row of a table. The number of cells in a row is determined by the number of `<th>` or `<td>` tags contained within a `<tr>`. If a table cell spans more than one row (using the `rowspan` attribute), the affected rows below it automatically accommodate the cell, and no additional cell tag is needed to represent it in those rows.

Figure 5-1 shows an HTML table rendered in two different browsers. Note how differently each browser displays the same table. You should keep these differences in mind when designing tables and test to see how your table looks in different browsers (as with all of your HTML documents).

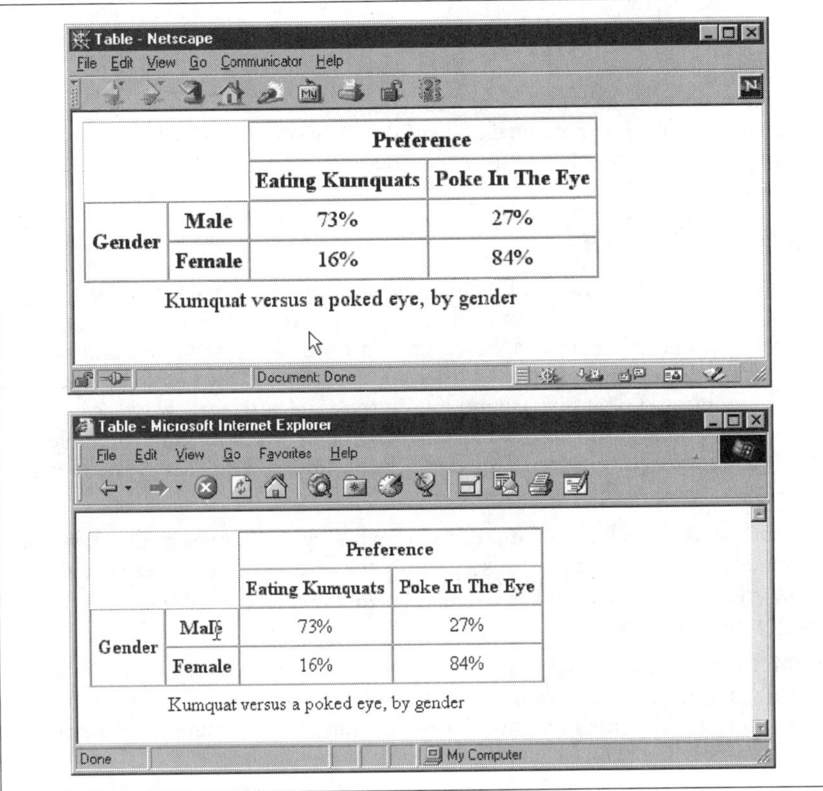

Figure 5-1. HTML table rendered by Navigator (top) and by Explorer (bottom)

Here is the code that renders the table:

```
<table border cellspacing=0 cellpadding=5>
  <caption align=bottom> Kumquat versus a poked
  eye, by gender</caption>
  <tr>
    <td colspan=2 rowspan=2></td>
    <th colspan=2 align=center>Preference</th>
  </tr>
  <tr>
    <th>Eating Kumquats</th>
    <th>Poke In The Eye</th>
  </tr>
  <tr align=center>
    <th rowspan=2>Gender</th>
    <th>Male</th>
    <td>73%</td>
    <td>27%</td>
  </tr>
  <tr align=center>
    <th>Female</th>
    <td>16%</td>
```

```
    <td>84%</td>
  </tr>
</table>
```

The contents of table cells may be any data that can be displayed in an HTML document. This can be plain text, images, tagged text, and other HTML structures. The table cells are sized according to their contents and in relation to other cells.

The <table> Tag

Tables are normally treated as floating objects within a browser window. They're aligned in the browser window to match the text flow, usually left-justified (or centered). Unlike inline images, however, text normally floats above and below a table but not beside it. Internet Explorer and Netscape allow you to set the alignment of a table and float text around it with the `align` attribute. `align` accepts two values, `left` and `right`. These values instruct the browser to align the table with either the left or right margin of the text flow around it. Text then flows along the opposite side of the table, if there is room.

The `hspace` and `vspace` attributes add extra space between the table and surrounding content. `hspace` adds space to the left and right sides of the table; `vspace` adds space above and below it. The value of each attribute is given as an integer number of pixels.

The `width` attribute can give you some control over the width of a table. Tables are normally rendered at the width that fits all the contents. The `width` attribute allows you to widen the table beyond the default size to occupy a set number of pixels or a percentage of the window's width. For example:

```
<table width="100%" >
```

always stretches the table to the full width of the browser window. This is a conditional instruction, however. The size of a table cell is always determined by the size of the biggest "fixed" content, such as an image or a nonbreaking line of text. Therefore, a table may need to be wider than you wish it. If the table cells contain mostly wrapping text elements such as paragraphs (`<p>`), the browser usually accommodates your request.

The `border` attribute to `<table>` controls the borders within and around the table. Simply using `border` with no attributes adds default borders to a table, which are not rendered the same in any two browsers. You can set border width by giving the attribute an integer number of pixels as a value. The `border=0` setting turns table borders off completely.

The amount of space around each cell is controlled by the `cellpadding` and `cellspacing` attributes to the `<table>` tag. Each accepts an integer number of pixels as a value. `cellpadding` sets the space between a cell's contents and its edges, whether borders are on or off. `cellspacing` sets the space between adjacent table cells. If borders are turned on, `cellspacing` will add the space outside of the border (half on one side, half on the other). The border width is not included or affected by `cellspacing` or `cellpadding`.

The additional attributes to the <table> tag are supported only by Internet Explorer. The rules and frames attributes tell the browser where to draw the rules (or borders) in the table. These settings depend on the use of other tags for the table such as <colgroup> or <tfoot>, which group table cells into distinct sections. There are many different values for rules and frames, making this feature quite versatile. It is, however, not supported in other browsers.

The other <table> attributes exclusive to Internet Explorer set backgrounds and colors for 3D borders. They are also usable in the lower-level <tr>, <th>, and <td> tags. They are discussed presently.

The <caption> Tag

You can add a title or caption to your table by using a <caption> tag within a <table>. The default placement of the caption for Netscape and Internet Explorer is above the table and centered with it. The placement and alignment of the caption is controlled by special alignment attributes that differ between the browsers.

In Netscape, the align attribute accepts two values: top and bottom. These allow you to put the caption above or below the table. The default value is top.

Internet Explorer, on the other hand, uses the align attribute for horizontal placement of the caption. It accepts values of left, right, and center (the default). The vertical positioning of the caption in Internet Explorer is controlled by a special valign attribute, which accepts either top (the default) or bottom. Each browser ignores the attributes and values it does not accept.

The <tr> Tag

Every row in a table is created with a <tr> tag. Within the <tr> tag are one or more cells containing either headers, each defined with the <th> tag, or data, each defined with the <td> tag.

Every row in a table has the same number of cells as the longest row; the browser automatically creates empty cells to pad rows with fewer defined cells.

Attributes to the <tr> tag control behavior for every cell it contains. There are two commonly used attributes for this tag:

- align is used differently in <tr> than it is in <table> (where it is now deprecated). In a table row, align lets you change the default horizontal alignment of the contents of the cells within the row. The attribute accepts values of left, right, center, or justify. HTML 4.01 also allows the value char, which aligns the contents to a specified character. However, this attribute is not yet supported in Navigator or Explorer. The default horizontal alignment for header cells (<th>) is centered; for data cells (<td>) it is left-justified.
- The valign attribute allows you to specify the vertical alignment of cell contents within a row. Four values are supported: top, bottom, baseline, and middle. The default vertical alignment is the same as specifying middle.

The browser treats each table cell as though it were its own browser window, fitting the contents to the size of the cell by breaking lines and flowing text. You can restrict line breaks with the nowrap attribute.

Background colors can be set for the cells in a row with `bgcolor`. Additional attributes for the `<tr>` tag that can specify a background image and set 3D border colors are specific to Internet Explorer.

The <th> and <td> Tags

The `<th>` (table header) and `<td>` (table data) tags go inside the `<tr>` tags of an HTML table to create the cells and contents of each cell within a row. The two tags operate similarly, except that header cells are typically rendered in bold text and centered by default. `<td>` cell contents are rendered in the regular base font, left-justified.

The `align`, `valign`, and other attributes work the same in the cell tags as they do in the row tag. When specified for `<th>` and `<td>`, these attributes override the same behavior set in the upper-level tags for their specific cell.

The other attributes to the cell tags are very important to the layout of your table. The `width` attribute can set the width of a table cell and all cells within its column. As with the `<table>` tag, a value may be given in an integer number of pixels or a percentage of the width of the table. A `width` value may be ignored by the browser if contents within the column have a fixed width larger than the value (i.e., an image or nonbreaking line of text). You should use only one `width` value in the cells of the same column. If two `width` values are specified in the same column of cells, the browser uses the larger value.

The `nowrap` attribute, when included in a cell tag, disables regular linebreaking of text within a table cell. With `nowrap`, the browser assembles the contents of a cell onto a single line, unless you insert a `<br>` or `<p>` tag, which forces a break.

Cell Spanning

It is common to have table cells span several columns or rows. This behavior is set within the `<th>` and `<td>` tags with the `colspan` and `rowspan` attributes. Each value is given in an integer number of columns or rows the cell is to stretch across. For example:

```
<td colspan=3>
```

tells the browser to make the cell occupy the same horizontal space as three cells in rows above or below it. The browser flows the contents of the cell to occupy the entire space.

If there aren't enough empty cells on the right, the browser just extends the cell over as many columns as exist to the right; it doesn't add extra empty cells to each row to accommodate an overextended `colspan` value.

Similar to the `colspan` attribute, `rowspan` stretches a cell down two or more rows in a table. You include the `rowspan` attribute in the `<th>` or `<td>` tag of the uppermost row of a table where you want the cell to begin and set its value equal to the number of rows you want it to span. The cell then occupies the same space as the current row and an appropriate number of cells below that row. The following code:

```
<td rowspan=3>
```

creates a cell that occupies the current row plus two more rows below that. The browser ignores overextended rowspan values and extends the current cell only down rows you've explicitly defined by other <tr> tags following the current row.

You may combine colspan and rowspan attributes to create a cell that spans both rows and columns. In our example table in Figure 5-1, the blank cell in the upper-left corner does this with the tag:

```
<td colspan=2 rowspan=2></td>
```

Border Color and Backgrounds

Previous versions of Internet Explorer introduced a number of additional attributes to its table tags that let you set images for the backgrounds and border colors of table elements. They can set values for the whole table, individual rows, and individual cells. Values can be set in a nested fashion, so that a specification for a single cell can override the broader setting for its row or the whole table.

Each attribute accepts a value specified as either an RGB color value or a standard color name, both of which are described in Chapter 8.

The recommended method for setting backgrounds is to define style attributes for table elements. See Chapter 9.

The background attribute allows you to set a background image for the entire table or individual cells. The image is tiled behind the appropriate table element automatically. The value of the background attribute is the URL of the image file.

Borders in Netscape and Internet Explorer create a 3D effect by using three differently colored strips. There is a thick center strip with much thinner strips on each side. One of the outer strips is colored darker than the center strip, and one is lighter, producing a shadowed effect. Internet Explorer allows you to set the colors for each of these elements when you have borders turned on with the border attribute in the <table> tag.

The bordercolor attribute sets the color of the main center strip of a border. The bordercolorlight attribute sets the color of the light strip of a border, the top- or left-most strip. bordercolordark sets the color of the dark strip, the bottom- or right-most strip.

You needn't specify all three border colors. The default for Internet Explorer's table borders sets the lighter and darker strips about 25% brighter and darker than the main border color.

Advanced Table Tags

While it is easy to build a simple table quickly with the tags we have described, you may desire more advanced table control such as varying border styles, running headers and footers, and column-based layout. HTML 4.0 adds new tags to accomplish these tasks, which originally appeared as extensions for Internet Explorer 3.0. Although they are defined in the latest standard, the latest browsers do not fully implement them. When making a table with these tags, make sure to test your tables on multiple browsers to ensure desired layout.

Table Section Tags

The three table section tags provide a way for you to break your table into logical sections: the header, body, and footer. You define the sections by placing the row tags (`<tr>`) within the `<thead>`, `<tbody>`, or `<tfoot>` tags. The usual attributes for controlling the placement of the contents can be used in these tags to set the alignment for the rows and cells they contain.

The main purpose for defining these sections is that when the table is printed or displayed in multiple sections, it will use consistent running headers and footers. Another benefit is that you can visibly delineate the sections by adjusting the size of the rules between them. Internet Explorer allows you to do this by supplying the `rules` attribute to the `<table>` tag with the values `groups`, `rows`, or `all`.

Column Grouping

Similar to the sectioning of tables by rows, you can also section tables by columns. You can define column groups to span a number of similar columns, or you can create them from dissimilar columns. Each column group is defined by the `<colgroup>` tag. `<colgroup>` tags should appear within `<table>` tags. They group columns specified by the table cell tags that appear in the rest of the table. Multiple column groups can be delineated with additional `<colgroup>` tags.

To create column groups of similar columns, use the `span` attribute to `<colgroup>`. For example:

```
<colgroup span=2 width="25%">
<colgroup span=4 width="75%">
```

Here we create two groups. The first has two columns; the second has four. We have also used the common width attribute to set the relative widths of the columns. Other common attributes can be used here as well.

For groups of similar columns, place a `<col>` element for each within a `<colgroup>`. This example creates the same groups as above:

```
<colgroup width="25%" >
 <col>
 <col>
</colgroup>
<colgroup width="75%">
 <col>
 <col>
 <col>
 <col>
</colgroup>
```

By specifying columns with `<col>`, you can set specific attributes for the cells contained in that column.

To make the distinction between column groups when your table is displayed, use the `rules` attribute to draw rules between your groups. The values can be either `groups`, `cols`, or `all`.

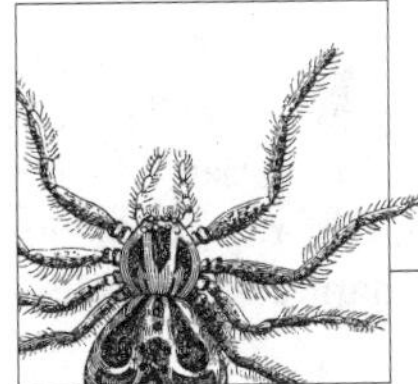

6
Forms

Most CGI programs use HTML forms to gather user input. Forms are comprised of one or more text-input boxes, clickable radio buttons, multiple-choice check-boxes, and even pull-down menus and clickable images, all placed inside the `<form>` tag. Within a form, you may also put regular body content, including text and images. The JavaScript event handlers can be used in various form elements as well, providing a number of effects such as testing and verifying form contents.

The <form> Tag

You place a form anywhere inside the body of an HTML document with its elements enclosed by the `<form>` tag and its respective end tag `</form>`. All of the form elements within a `<form>` tag comprise a single form. The browser sends all of the values of these elements—blank, default, or user-modified—when the user submits the form to the server.

The required `action` attribute for the `<form>` tag gives the URL of the application that is to receive and process the form's data. A typical `<form>` tag with the `action` attribute looks like this:

```
<form action="http://www.oreilly.com/cgi-bin/update" >
...
</form>
```

The example URL tells the browser to contact the server named *www.oreilly.com* and pass along the user's form values to the application named *update*, located in the *cgi-bin* directory.

The browser specially encodes the form's data before it passes the data to the server so it doesn't become scrambled or corrupted during the transmission. It's up to the server to decode the parameters or pass them, still encoded, to the application.

The standard encoding format is the media type named `application/x-www-form-urlencoded`. You can change that encoding with the optional `enctype` attribute in the <form> tag. If you do elect to use an alternative encoding, the only other supported format is multipart/form-data.

The standard encoding—application/x-www-form-urlencoded—converts any spaces in the form values to a plus sign (+), nonalphanumeric characters into a percent sign (%) followed by two hexadecimal digits that are the ASCII code of the character, and the line breaks in multiline form data into %0D%0A. (See Chapter 12 for more information on URL encoding.)

The multipart/form-data encoding encapsulates the fields in the form as several parts of a single MIME-compatible compound document.

The other required attribute for the <form> tag sets the method by which the browser sends the form's data to the server for processing. There are two ways: the POST method and the GET method. See Chapter 12 for more information on GET and POST.

The <input> Tag

Use the <input> tag to define any one of a number of common form elements, including text fields, multiple-choice lists, clickable images, and submission buttons. Although there are many attributes for this tag, only the type and name attributes are required for each element (only type for a submission button). Each type of input element uses only a subset of the allowed attributes. Additional <input> attributes may be required based on the specified form element.

You select the type of element to include in the form with the <input> tag's required type attribute and name the field (used during the form-submission process to the server) with the name attribute.

The most useful (as well as the most common) form-input element is the text-entry field. A text-entry field appears in the browser window as an empty box on one line and accepts a single line of user input that becomes the value of the element when the user submits the form to the server. To create a text entry field inside a form in your HTML document, set the type of the <input> form element to text. You must include a name attribute as well.

The size and maxlength attributes allow you to dictate the width, in characters, of the text-input display box and how many total characters to accept from the user, respectively. The default value for size is dependent on the browser; the default value for maxlength is unlimited.

A text-entry field is usually blank until the user types something into it. You may, however, specify an initial default value for the field with the value attribute.

Password Fields

Password fields behave like a regular text field in a form, except that the user-typed characters don't appear onscreen. Rather, the browser obscures the characters in masked text to keep such things as passwords and other sensitive codes from prying eyes.

To create a password field, set the value of the type attribute to password. All other attributes and semantics of the conventional text field apply to the masked field. Note that a masked text field is not all that secure, since the browser transmits it unencrypted when the form is submitted to the server.

File-Selection Fields

The file-selection form field (introduced by Netscape Navigator) lets users select a file stored on their computer and send it to the server when they submit the form. Browsers present the file-selection form field to the user like other text fields, but it's accompanied by a button labeled "Browse." Users either type the pathname directly as text into the field or, with the Browse option, select the name of a locally stored file from a system-specific dialog box.

Create a file-selection field in a form by setting the value of the type attribute to file. Like other text fields, the size and maxlength of a file-selection field should be set to appropriate values.

Checkboxes

The checkbox element gives users a way to quickly and easily select or deselect an item in your form. Checkboxes may also be grouped to create a set of choices, any of which may be selected or deselected by the user.

Create individual checkboxes by setting the type attribute for each <input> tag to checkbox. Include the required name and value attributes. If the item is selected, it contributes a value when the form is submitted. If it is not selected, that element doesn't contribute a value. The optional checked attribute (no value) tells the browser to display a checked checkbox and include the value when submitting the form to the server, unless the user specifically clicks the mouse to deselect (uncheck) the box.

The browsers include the value of selected (checked) checkboxes with other form parameters when they are submitted to the server. The value of the checked checkbox is the text string you specify in the required value attribute.

By giving several checkboxes the same name attribute value, you create a group of checkbox elements. The browser automatically collects the values of a checkbox group and submits their selected values as a comma-separated string to the server, significantly easing server-side form processing.

Radio Buttons

Radio buttons are similar in behavior to checkboxes, except only one in the group may be selected by the user. Create a radio button by setting the type attribute of the <input> element to radio. Like checkbox elements, radio buttons each require a name and value attribute; buttons with the same name value are members of a group. One of them may be initially checked by including the checked attribute with that element. If no element in the group is checked, the browser automatically checks the first element in the group.

You should give each radio button element a different value, so the server can sort them after submission of the form.

Submission Buttons

The submit button (`<input type=submit>`) does what its name implies, setting in motion the form's submission to the server from the browser. You may have more than one submit button in a form. You may also include `name` and `value` attributes with a submit button.

With the simplest submit button (that is, one without a `name` or `value` attribute), the browser displays a small rectangle or oval with the default label "Submit." Otherwise, the browser labels the button with the text you include with the tag's `value` attribute. If you provide a `name` attribute, the `value` attribute for the submit button is added to the parameter list the browser sends to the server.

Reset Buttons

The reset type of form `<input>` button is nearly self-explanatory: it lets the user reset—erase or set to some default value—all elements in the form. By default, the browser displays a reset button with the label "Reset" or "Clear." You can change that by specifying a `value` attribute with your own button label.

Custom Buttons

With the image type of `<input>` form element, you create a custom button, one that is a "clickable" image. It's a special button made out of your specified image that, when clicked by the user, tells the browser to submit the form to the server, and includes the x,y coordinates of the mouse pointer in the form's parameter list. Image buttons require a `src` attribute with the URL of the image file, and you can include a `name` attribute. You may also include the `align` attribute to control image alignment within the current line of text, much like the `align` attribute for the `<img>` tag.

Hidden Fields

The last type of form `<input>` element we describe in this chapter is a way to embed information into your forms that cannot be ignored or altered by the browser or user. Rather, the `<input type=hidden>` tag's required `name` and `value` attributes automatically get included in the submitted form's parameter list. These serve to "label" the form and can be invaluable when sorting out different forms or form versions from a collection of submitted and saved forms.

The <textarea> Tag

The `<textarea>` tag creates a multiline text-entry area in the user's browser display. In it, the user may type a nearly unlimited number of lines of text. When the form is submitted, the browser sends the text along with the name specified by the required `name` attribute.

You may include plain text between the <textarea> tag and its end tag </textarea>. The browser uses that text as the default value for the text area.

You can control the dimensions of a multiline text area by defining the cols and rows attributes for the visible rectangular area set aside by the browser for multiline input.

Normally, text typed in the text area by the user is transmitted to the server exactly as typed, with lines broken only where the user pressed the Enter key. With the wrap attribute set to virtual, the text is wrapped within the text area for presentation to the user, but the text is transmitted to the server as if no wrapping had occurred, except where the user pressed the Enter key. With the wrap attribute set to physical, the text is wrapped within the text area and is transmitted to the server as if the user had actually typed it that way. To obtain the default action, set the wrap attribute to off.

The <select> Tag

Checkboxes and radio buttons give you powerful means for creating multiple-choice questions and answers, but they can lead to long forms that are tedious to write and put a fair amount of clutter onscreen. The <select> tag gives you two compact alternatives: pull-down menus and scrolling lists.

By placing a list of <option> tagged items inside the <select> tag of a form, you create a pull-down menu of choices.

As with other form tags, the name attribute is required and used by the browser when submitting the <select> choices to the server. Unlike radio buttons, however, no item is preselected, so if the user doesn't select any, no values are sent to the server when the form is submitted. Otherwise, the browser submits the selected item or collects multiple selections, each separated with commas, into a single parameter list and includes the name attribute when submitting <select> form data to the server.

To allow more than one option selection at a time, add the multiple attribute to the <select> tag. This causes the <select> to behave like an <input type=checkbox> element. If multiple is not specified, exactly one option can be selected at a time, just like a group of radio buttons.

The size attribute determines how many options are visible to the user at one time. The value of size should be a positive integer. If size is set to 1 and multiple is not specified, the <select> list is typically implemented as a pop-up menu, while values greater than 1 or specifying the multiple attribute cause the <select> to be displayed as a scrolling list.

Use the <option> tag to define each item within a <select> form element. The browser displays the <option> tag's contents as an element within the <select> tag's menu or scrolling list, so the content must be plain text only, without any other sort of markup.

Use the value attribute to set a value for each option the browser sends to the server if that option is selected by the user. If the value attribute has not been specified, the value of the option is set to the content of the <option> tag.

By default, all options within a multiple-choice <select> tag are unselected. Include the selected attribute (no value) inside the <option> tag to preselect one or more options, which the user may then deselect. Single-choice <select> tags preselect the first option if no option is explicitly preselected.

An Example Form

Figure 6-1 presents an HTML form showing as many form features as we can fit in the example.

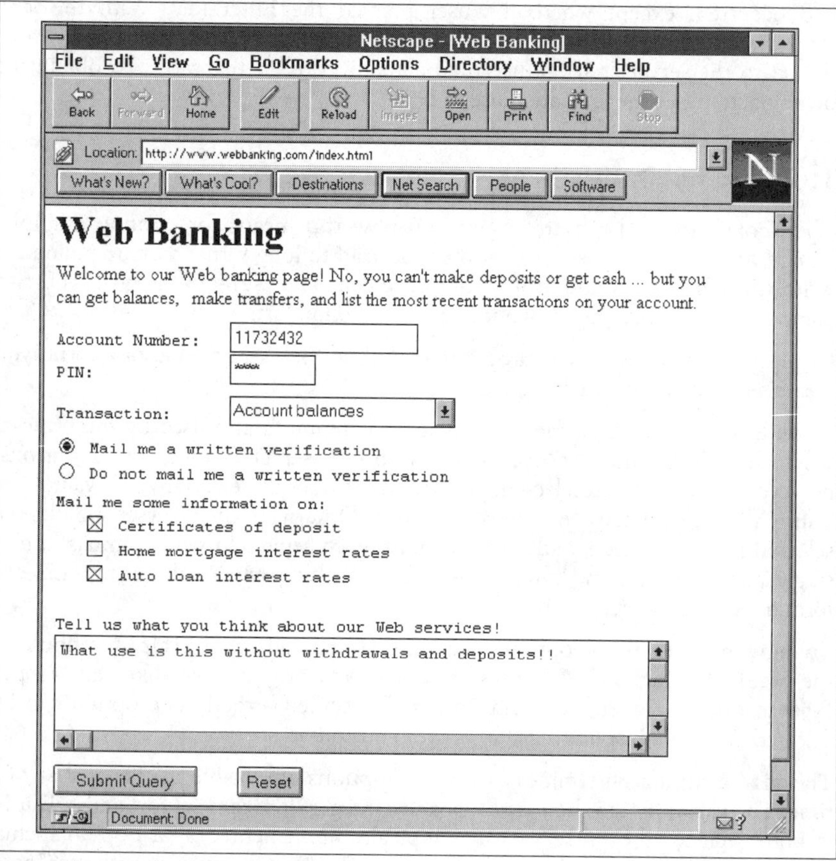

Figure 6-1. The completed form

The HTML used to create this form is shown here:

```
<html><head><title>Web Banking</title></head>
<body>
<h1>Web Banking</h1>
Welcome to our Web banking page!  No, you can't make
deposits or get cash ... but you can get balances, make
transfers, and list the most recent transactions on your account.
<form method="post" action="/cgi-bin/banking.pl">
```

```
<pre>
Account Number:    <input type="text" name="acct">
PIN:               <input type="password" name="pin" size=8>

Transaction:       <select name="transaction">
                   <option selected>Account balances
                   <option>Transfers
                   <option>Show recent transactions
                   <option>Stop payment on a check
                   </select>

<input type="radio" name="verify_by_mail" value="yes" checked> Mail me
a written verification
<input type="radio" name="verify_by_mail" value="no"> Do not mail me a
written verification

Mail me some information on:
   <input type="checkbox"name="info" value="cds"> Certificates of
deposit
   <input type="checkbox" name="info" value="mortgages"> Home mortgage
interest rates
   <input type="checkbox" name="info" value="autoloans"> Auto loan
interest rates


Tell us what you think about our Web services!
<textarea rows=5 cols=60 name="comments">
</textarea>

<input type="submit">    <input type="reset">
</form>
</body></html>
```

First, we use an <input> text field to get the user's bank account number. For the user's Personal Identification Number (PIN), we use an <input> password field so that the numbers don't appear on screen. (In real life, this wouldn't be considered sufficient for protecting someone's PIN, since the data entered is sent unencrypted across the Internet.)

Next, we use a selection box to have the user choose a transaction. The user can choose to get account balances, transfer money, see a listing of the most recent transactions on that account, or stop payment on a check.

We use a radio box to let the user choose whether to get a written verification of this transaction. The default is to send written verification. In a radio box, the user can choose exactly one of the options. Notice that with radio boxes, each item needs to have the same name but different value attributes.

Next, we use a series of checkboxes to find out what additional information a user might want us to send.

For any loose ends, we use a <textarea> box to allow the user a chance to blow off steam.

Finally, we provide submit and reset buttons.

When the user submits this query, the browser sends a request to the server similar to the following:

```
POST /cgi-bin/banking.pl HTTP/1.0
Content-Length: 154
Accept: image/gif
        ... (more headers )

acct=11732432&pin=0545&transaction=Account+balances&verify_by_mail=YES
&info=cds,autoloans&comments=What+use+is+this+without+withdrawals+and+
deposits%21%21
```

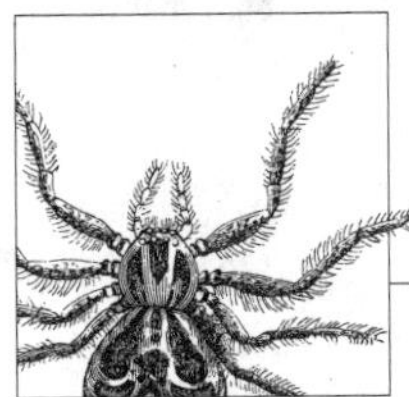

7
Character Entities

The following table lists the defined standard and proposed character entities for HTML, as well as several that are nonstandard but generally supported.

Entity names, if defined, appear for their respective characters and can be used in the character-entity sequence `&name;` to define any character for display by the browser. Otherwise, or alternatively for named characters, use the character's three-digit numeral value in the sequence `&#nnn;` to specially define a character entity. Actual characters, however, may or may not be displayed by the browser, depending on the computer platform and user-selected font for display.

Not all 256 characters in the ISO character set appear in the table. Missing ones are not recognized by the browser as either named or numeric entities.

To be sure that your documents are fully compliant with the HTML and XHTML standards, use only those named character entities with no entries in the conformance column. Characters with a value of "!!!" in the conformance column are not formally defined by the standards; use them at your own risk.

Numeric entity	Named entity	Symbol	Description	Conformance
			Horizontal tab	
		Line feed	
		Carriage return	
			Space	
!		!	Exclamation point	
"	"	"	Quotation mark	
#		#	Hash mark	
$		$	Dollar sign	
%		%	Percent sign	

Numeric entity	Named entity	Symbol	Description	Conformance
&	&	&	Ampersand	
'		'	Apostrophe	
(		(	Left parenthesis	
)		)	Right parenthesis	
*		*	Asterisk	
+		+	Plus sign	
,		,	Comma	
-		-	Hyphen	
.		.	Period	
/		/	Slash	
0 – 9		0–9	Digits 0–9	
:		:	Colon	
;		;	Semicolon	
<	<	<	Less than sign	
=		=	Equals sign	
>	>	>	Greater than sign	
?		?	Question mark	
@		@	Commercial at sign	
A – Z		A–Z	Letters A–Z	
[		[	Left square bracket	
\		\	Backslash	
]		]	Right square bracket	
^		^	Caret	
_		_	Underscore	
`		`	Grave accent	
a – z		a–z	Letters a–z	
{		{	Left curly brace	
			|	Vertical bar	
}		}	Right curly brace	
~		~	Tilde	
‚		‚	Low left single quote	!!!
ƒ		ƒ	Florin	!!!
„		„	Low left double quote	!!!
…		…	Ellipsis	!!!

Numeric entity	Named entity	Symbol	Description	Conformance
†		†	Dagger	!!!
‡		‡	Double dagger	!!!
ˆ		ˆ	Circumflex	!!!
‰		‰	Permil	!!!
Š		Š	Capital S, caron	!!!
‹		<	Less than sign	!!!
Œ		Œ	Capital OE ligature	!!!
Ž		Ž	Capital Z, caron	!!!
‘		‘	Left single quote	!!!
’		’	Right single quote	!!!
“		“	Left double quote	!!!
”		”	Right double quote	!!!
•		•	Bullet	!!!
–		–	En dash	!!!
—		—	Em dash	!!!
˜		~	Tilde	!!!
™		™	Trademark	!!!
š		š	Small s, caron	!!!
›		>	Greater than sign	!!!
œ		œ	Small oe ligature	!!!
ž		ž	Small z, caron	!!!
Ÿ		Ÿ	Capital Y, umlaut	!!!
			Nonbreaking space	
¡	¡	¡	Inverted exclamation point	
¢	¢	¢	Cent sign	
£	£	£	Pound sign	
¤	¤	¤	General currency sign	
¥	¥	¥	Yen sign	
¦	¦	¦	Broken vertical bar	
§	§	§	Section sign	
¨	¨	¨	Umlaut	
©	©	©	Copyright	
ª	ª	ª	Feminine ordinal	
«	«	«	Left angle quote	

Numeric entity	Named entity	Symbol	Description	Conformance
¬	¬	¬	Not sign	
		-	Soft hyphen	
®	®	®	Registered trademark	
¯	¯	¯	Macron accent	
°	°	°	Degree sign	
±	±	±	Plus or minus	
²	²	2	Superscript 2	
³	³	3	Superscript 3	
´	´	´	Acute accent	
µ	µ	µ	Micro sign (Greek mu)	
¶	¶	¶	Paragraph sign	
·	·	·	Middle dot	
¸	¸	¸	Cedilla	
¹	¹	1	Superscript 1	
º	º	º	Masculine ordinal	
»	»	»	Right angle quote	
¼	¼	1/4	Fraction-one-fourth	
½	½	1/2	Fraction one-half	
¾	¾	3/4	Fraction three-fourths	
¿	¿	¿	Inverted question mark	
À	À	À	Capital A, grave accent	
Á	Á	Á	Capital A, acute accent	
Â	Â	Â	Capital A, circumflex accent	
Ã	Ã	Ã	Capital A, tilde	
Ä	Ä	Ä	Capital A, umlaut	
Å	Å	Å	Capital A, ring	
Æ	Æ	Æ	Capital AE ligature	
Ç	Ç	Ç	Capital C, cedilla	
È	È	È	Capital E, grave accent	
É	É	É	Capital E, acute accent	
Ê	Ê	Ê	Capital E, circumflex accent	
Ë	Ë	Ë	Capital E, umlaut	
Ì	Ì	Ì	Capital I, grave accent	
Í	Í	Í	Capital I, acute accent	
Î	Î	Î	Capital I, circumflex accent	

Numeric entity	Named entity	Symbol	Description	Conformance
Ï	Ï	Ï	Capital I, umlaut	
Ð	Ð	Œ	Capital eth, Icelandic	
Ñ	Ñ	Ñ	Capital N, tilde	
Ò	Ò	Ò	Capital O, grave accent	
Ó	Ó	Ó	Capital O, acute accent	
Ô	Ô	Ô	Capital O, circumflex accent	
Õ	Õ	Õ	Capital O, tilde	
Ö	Ö	Ö	Capital O, umlaut	
×	×	×	Multiply sign	
Ø	Ø	Ø	Capital O, slash	
Ù	Ù	Ù	Capital U, grave accent	
Ú	Ú	Ú	Capital U, acute accent	
Û	Û	Û	Capital U, circumflex accent	
Ü	Ü	Ü	Capital U, umlaut	
Ý	Ý	Ý	Capital Y, acute accent	
Þ	Þ	Þ	Capital thorn, Icelandic	
ß	ß	ß	Small sz ligature, German	
à	à	à	Small a, grave accent	
á	á	á	Small a, acute accent	
â	â	â	Small a, circumflex accent	
ã	ã	ã	Small a, tilde	
ä	ä	ä	Small a, umlaut	
å	å	å	Small a, ring	
æ	æ	æ	Small ae ligature	
ç	ç	ç	Small c, cedilla	
è	è	è	Small e, grave accent	
é	é	é	Small e, acute accent	
ê	ê	ê	Small e, circumflex accent	
ë	ë	ë	Small e, umlaut	
ì	ì	ì	Small i, grave accent	
í	í	í	Small i, acute accent	
î	î	î	Small i, circumflex accent	
ï	ï	ï	Small i, umlaut	
ð	ð	ð	Small eth, Icelandic	

Numeric entity	Named entity	Symbol	Description	Conformance
ñ	ñ	ñ	Small n, tilde	
ò	ò	ò	Small o, grave accent	
ó	ó	ó	Small o, acute accent	
ô	ô	ô	Small o, circumflex accent	
õ	õ	õ	Small o, tilde	
ö	ö	ö	Small o, umlaut	
÷	÷	÷	Division sign	
ø	ø	ø	Small o, slash	
ù	ù	ù	Small u, grave accent	
ú	ú	ú	Small u, acute accent	
û	û	û	Small u, circumflex accent	
ü	ü	ü	Small u, umlaut	
ý	ý	y	Small y, acute accent	
þ	þ	þ	Small thorn, Icelandic	
ÿ	ÿ	ÿ	Small y, umlaut	

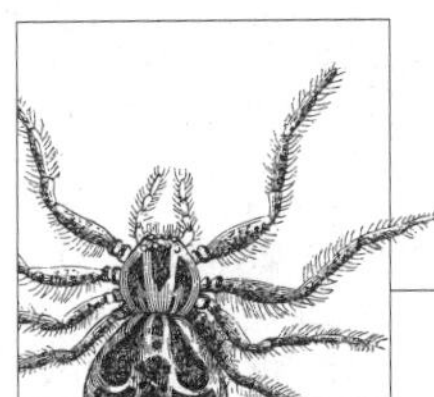

8
Color Names and Values

With the popular browsers, you can prescribe the colors of various elements of your document via tag attributes or CSS style definitions.

You may specify the color value as a six-digit hexadecimal number that represents the red, green, and blue (RGB) components of the color. The first two digits correspond to the red component of the color, the next two to the green component, and the last two to the blue component. A value of 00 corresponds to the component being completely off; a value of FF (255) corresponds to the component being completely on. Thus, bright red is FF0000, bright green is 00FF00, and bright blue is 0000FF. Other primary colors are mixtures of two components, such as yellow (FFFF00), magenta (FF00FF), and cyan (00FFFF). White (FFFFFF) and black (000000) are also easy to figure out.

You use these values in a tag by replacing the color with the RGB triple, preceded by a hash (#) symbol. To make all visited links display as magenta, use this body tag:

```
<body vlink="#FF00FF" >
```

Determining the hexadecimal value for more esoteric colors like "papaya whip" or "navajo white" is very difficult. You can go crazy trying to adjust the RGB triple for a color to get the shade just right, especially when each adjustment requires loading a document into your browser to view the result.

To make life easier, the HTML 4.0 standard defines 16 standard color names that can be used anywhere a numeric color value can be used. You can make all visited links in the display magenta with the following attribute for the body tag:

```
<body vlink="magenta" >
```

The color names and RGB values defined in the HTML standard are:

aqua (#00FFFF)	gray (#808080)	navy (#000080)	silver (#C0C0C0)
black (#000000)	green (#008000)	olive (#808000)	teal (#008080)
blue (#0000FF)	lime (#00FF00)	purple (#800080)	yellow (#FFFF00)
fuchsia (#FF00FF)	maroon (#800000)	red (#FF0000)	white (#FFFFFF)

The popular browsers go well beyond the HTML 4.0 standard and support the several hundred color names defined for use in the X Window System. Note that color names may contain no spaces; also, the word *gray* may be spelled *grey* in any color name.

Colors marked with an asterisk (*) represent a family of colors numbered one through four. Thus, there are actually four variants of blue, named blue1, blue2, blue3, and blue4, along with plain old blue. Blue1 is the lightest of the four; blue4 the darkest. The unnumbered color name is the same color as the first; thus, blue and blue1 are identical.

Finally, if all that isn't enough, there are 100 variants of gray (and grey) numbered 1 through 100. Gray1 is the darkest, gray100 is the lightest, and gray is very close to gray75.

The extended color names are:

aliceblue
antiquewhite*
aquamarine*
azure*
beige
bisque*
black
blanchedalmond
blue*
blueviolet
brown*
burlywood*
cadetblue*
chartreuse*
chocolate*
coral*
cornflowerblue
cornsilk*
cyan*
darkblue
darkcyan
darkgoldenrod*
darkgray
darkgreen
darkkhaki
darkmagenta
darkolivegreen*
darkorange*
darkorchid*
darkred
darksalmon
darkseagreen*
darkslateblue
darkslategray*
darkturquoise
darkviolet
deeppink*
deepskyblue*
dimgray
dodgerblue*
firebrick*
floralwhite
forestgreen
gainsboro
ghostwhite
gold*
goldenrod*
gray
green*
greenyellow
honeydew*
hotpink*
indianred*
ivory*
khaki*
lavender
lavenderblush*
lawngreen
lemonchiffon*
lightblue*
lightcoral
lightcyan*
lightgoldenrod*
lightgoldenrodyellow
lightgray
lightgreen
lightpink*
lightsalmon*
lightseagreen
lightskyblue*
lightslateblue
lightslategray
lightsteelblue*
lightyellow*
limegreen
linen
magenta*
maroon*
mediumaquamarine
mediumblue
mediumorchid*
mediumpurple*
mediumseagreen
mediumslateblue
mediumspringgreen
mediumturquoise
mediumvioletred
midnightblue
mintcream
mistyrose*
moccasin
navajowhite*
navy
navyblue
oldlace
olivedrab*
orange*
orangered*
orchid*
palegoldenrod
palegreen*
paleturquoise*
palevioletred*
papayawhip
peachpuff*
peru
pink*
plum*
powderblue
purple*
red*
rosybrown*
royalblue*
saddlebrown
salmon*
sandybrown
seagreen*
seashell*
sienna*
skyblue*
slateblue*
slategray*
snow*
springgreen*
steelblue*
tan*
thistle*
tomato*
turquoise*
violet
violetred*
wheat*
white
whitesmoke
yellow*
yellowgreen

CSS

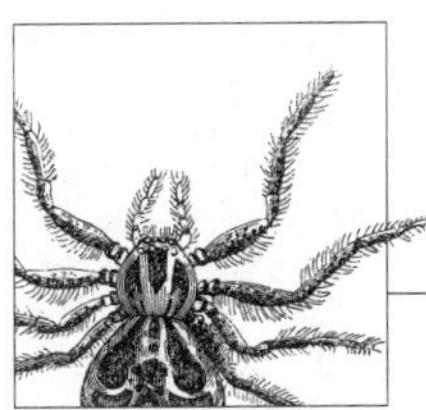

9

Cascading Style Sheets

Style sheets are the way publishing professionals manage the overall "look" of their publications—backgrounds, fonts, colors, etc. Most desktop publishing software supports style sheets, as do the popular word processors.

From its earliest origins, HTML focused on content over style. Authors were encouraged to provide high quality information, and leave it to the browser to worry about presentation. We strongly urge you to adopt that philosophy in your HTML documents. However, while use of the HTML `<font>` tag and related attributes like `Wcolor` produce acute presentation effects, style sheets, when judiciously applied, bring consistency and order to documents. Style sheets let the HTML author control the presentation attributes for all the tags in a document or a whole collection of many documents, and from a single master style sheet.

In early 1996, the World Wide Web Consortium put together a draft proposal defining Cascading Style Sheets (CSS) for HTML. This draft proposal quickly matured into a recommended standard, which the commercial browser manufacturers were quick to exploit. Style is fast achieving parity with content on the World Wide Web.

Since we realize that eventual compliance with the W3C standard is likely, we'll cover all the components of the standard in this section, even if they are not yet supported by any browser. We'll denote clearly what is real, what is proposed, and what is actually supported.

The Elements of Styles

At the simplest level, a style is nothing more than a rule that tells the browser how to display a particular HTML tag. Each tag has a number of properties associated with it, whose values define how that tag is rendered by the browser. A rule defines a specific value for one or more properties of a tag. For example, most tags have a color property, the value of which defines the color used to display that tag. Other properties include font attributes, line spacing, margins, and borders.

There are three ways to attach a style to a tag

- Inline styles
- Document-level styles
- External style sheets

You may use one or more style types in your documents. The browser either merges the style definitions from each style or redefines the style characteristic for a tag's contents. Styles from these various sources are applied to your document, combining and defining style properties that cascade from external style sheets through local document styles, ending with inline styles.

Inline Styles

The inline style is the simplest way to attach a style to a tag—just include a `style` attribute with the tag, with a list of properties and their values. The browser uses the style properties and values to render the contents of just this instance of the tag.

For instance, the following style tells the browser to display the level-one header text, "This is blue," in the `<h1>` tag style characteristic of the browser and also in the color blue and italicized:

```
<h1 style="color: blue; font-style: italic" >This is blue</h1>
```

This type of style definition is called "inline" because it occurs with the tag as it appears in the document. The scope of the style covers the contents of that tag only. Since inline styles are sprinkled throughout your document, they can be difficult to maintain. Use the style attribute sparingly and only in those rare circumstances when you cannot achieve the same effects otherwise.

Style definitions are created with the name of the style attribute—`color`, for example—followed by a colon and then the style's value. You will commonly supply a list of style definitions for a single element. In the list, each style definition is separated by a semicolon.

Document-Level Styles

The real power of style sheets dawns when you place a list of presentation rules within the head of an HTML document. Enclosed within their own `<style>` and `</style>` tags, "document-level" style sheets affect all the same tags within that document, except for tags that contain an overriding inline style attribute.

The `<style>` tag must appear within the `<head>` of a document. Everything between the `<style>` and `</style>` tags is considered part of the style rules to be applied to the document. To be perfectly correct, the content of the `<style>` tag is not HTML and is not bound by the normal rules for HTML content. The `<style>` tag, in effect, lets you insert foreign content into your HTML document that the browser uses to format your tags. Older browsers may not know how to handle this content, so it is common practice to place your style definitions inside an HTML comment (`<!-- -->`) within the style tag.

Style definitions in a style sheet begin with the name of the tag you are defining a style for. The style definitions are contained in braces following the tag name. For example, this document-level style sheet displays the contents of all `<h1>` tags as blue, italic text:

```
<head>
<title>All True Blue</title>

<style type="text/css">
  <!--
  /* make all H1 headers blue */

  H1 {color: blue; font-style: italic}

  -->
</style>
</head>

<body>
<h1>This is blue</h1>
...
<h1>Ever so blue</h1>
```

One important attribute for the `style` tag is the `type` attribute. The `type` attribute defines the types of styles you are including within the tag. Cascading style sheets always carry the type `text/css`; JavaScript style sheets use the type `text/javascript`. We prefer to include the `type` attribute so that there is no opportunity for confusion.

Comments are welcome inside the `<style>` tag and in external style sheets, but don't use a standard HTML comment; style sheets aren't HTML. Rather, enclose style comments beginning with the sequence `/*` and ending with `*/`. Use this comment syntax for both document-level and external style sheets. Comments may not be nested.

We recommend documenting your styles whenever possible, especially in external style sheets. Whenever the possibility exists that your styles may be used by other authors, comments make it much easier to understand your styles.

External Style Sheets

You may also place style definitions, like our document-level style sheet example for the `<h1>` tags, into a text file with the MIME type of `text/css` and import this style sheet into your HTML documents. Because an external style sheet is a file separate from the HTML document and is loaded by the browser over the network, you can store it anywhere, reuse it often, and even use others' style sheets. But most important, external style sheets give you the power to influence the display styles not only of all related tags in a single document, but for an entire collection of documents.

For example, suppose we create a file named *gen_styles.css* containing the style rule:

```
H1 {color: blue; font-style: italic}
```

For each and every one of the HTML documents in our collections, we can tell the browser to read the contents of the *gen_styles.css* file, which, in turn, colors all the `<h1>` tag contents blue and renders the text in italic. Of course, since style definitions cascade by nature, the style can be overridden by a document-level or inline style definition.

You can load external style sheets into your HTML document in two different ways: with the <link> tag for the @import style command.

Linked external style sheets

One way to load an external style sheet is to use the <link> tag:

```
<head>
<title>Linked Style</title>

<link rel=stylesheet type="text/css"
      href="http://www.kumquats.com/styles/gen_styles.css"
      title="The blues"/>

</head>
```

The <link> tag creates a relationship between the current document and some other document on the Web. In the example, we tell the browser that the document named in the href attribute is a style sheet, and that its contents conform to the CSS standard, as indicated by the type attribute. We also provide a title for the style sheet, making it available for later reference by the browser.

The <link> tag must appear in the <head> of a document. The URL of the style sheet may be absolute or relative to the document's base URL.

Imported external style sheets

The second technique for loading an external style sheet imports the files with a special command within the <style> tag:

```
<head>
<title>Imported style sheet</title>

<style type="text/css">
  <!--

    @import url(http://www.oreilly.com/styles/gen_styles.css);
    @import url(http://www.oreilly.com/styles/spec_styles.css);
    BODY: {background: url(backgrounds/marble.gif)}

  -->
</style>

</head>
```

The @import command expects a single URL parameter that names the network path to the external style sheet. The url keyword, parentheses, and trailing semicolon are all required elements of the @import command. The URL may be absolute or relative to the document's base URL. The @import command must appear before any conventional style rules, either in the <style> tag or in an external style sheet. Otherwise, the browser ignores the preceding style definitions. This ordering also means that subsequent style rules can override rules in the imported sheet, and indeed they do.

The @import command can appear in a document-level style definition or even in another external style sheet, letting you create nested style sheets.

> **Linked Versus Imported Style Sheets**
>
> At first glance, it may appear that linked and imported style sheets are equivalent, using different syntax for the same functionality. This is true if you use just one `<link>` tag in your document. However, special rules come into play if you include two or more `<link>` tags within a single document.
>
> With one `<link>` tag, the browser loads the styles in the referenced style sheet and formats the document accordingly, with any document-level and inline styles overriding the external definitions. With two or more `<link>` tags, the browser presents the user with a list of all the linked style sheets. The user can then select one of the sheets, which is used to format the document. The other linked style sheets are ignored.
>
> On the other hand, the styles-conscious browser merges, as opposed to separate, multiple imported style sheets to form a single set of style rules for your document. The last imported style sheet takes precedence if there are duplicate definitions among the style sheets. Imported styles also override linked external styles, just as document-level and inline styles override external style definitions.

Style Syntax

The syntax of a style, as you may have gleaned from our previous examples, is fairly straightforward. A style rule is made up of at least three basic parts: a tag selector, which identifies the name of the tag that the style rule affects, followed by a curly brace ({ }) enclosed, semicolon-separated list of one or more style `property:value` declaration pairs:

```
tag-selector {property1:value1; property2:value1 value2 value3; ...}
```

Properties require at least one value but may include two or more values. Separate multiple values with a space, as is done for the three values that define `property2` in the example. Some properties require that multiple values be separated with commas.

Styles-conscious browsers ignore letter case in any element of a rule. Hence, H1 and h1 are the same selector, and COLOR, color, ColOR, and cOLor are equivalent properties. Convention dictates, however, that tag names be all uppercase, and that properties and values be lowercase. We'll abide by those conventions throughout this book.

Any valid HTML tag name (a tag minus its enclosing < and > characters and attributes) can be a selector. You may include more than one tag name in the list of selectors, as we explain in the following sections.

Multiple Selectors

When separated by commas, all the tags named in the selector list are affected by the property values in the style rule. This can make life very easy for the HTML author. For instance:

```
H1, H2, H3, H4, H5, H6 {text-align: center}
```

tells the browser to center the contents of the header tag levels 1–6. Clearly, one line is easier to type, understand, and modify than six. And it takes less time and fewer resources to transmit across a network, as well.

Contextual Selectors

Normally, the browser applies styles to tags wherever they appear in your document, without regard to context. However, the CSS standard does define a way to have a style applied only when a tag occurs within a certain context within a document, such as when it is nested within other tags.

To create a contextual selector, list the tags in the order in which they should be nested in your document, outermost tag first, with *no* commas separating them. When that nesting order is encountered by the browser, the style property is applied to the last tag in the list.

For example, here's how you might use contextual styles to define the classic numbering sequence used for outlines: capital letters for the outer level, uppercase Roman numerals for the next level, lowercase letters for the next, and Arabic numerals for the innermost level:

```
OL LI {list-style: upper-alpha}
OL OL LI {list-style: upper-roman}
OL OL OL LI {list-style: lower-alpha}
OL OL OL OL LI {list-style: decimal}
```

According to the example style sheet, when the styles-conscious browser encounters the `<li>` tag nested within one `<ol>` tag, it uses the upper-alpha value for the list-style property of the `<li>` tag. When it sees an `<li>` tag nested within two `<ol>` tags, the same browser uses the upper-roman list style. Nest an `<li>` tag within three and four `<ol>` tags, and you'll see the lower-alpha and decimal list-style used, respectively.

Similarly, you may impose a specific style on tags related only by context. For instance, this contextual style definition colors the emphasis tag's (`<em>`) contents red only when it appears inside a level-one header tag (`<h1>`), not elsewhere in the document:

```
H1 EM {color: red}
```

If there is potential ambiguity between two contextual styles, the more specific context prevails. Like individual tags, you may also have several contextual selectors mixed with individual selectors, each and all separated by commas, sharing the same list of style declarations. For example:

```
H1 EM, P STRONG, ADDRESS {color: red}
```

means that you'll see red whenever the `<em>` tag appears within an `<h1>` tag, or when the `<strong>` tag appears within a `<p>` tag, and for the contents of the `<address>` tag.

The nesting need not be exact to match the rule. For example, if you nest the `<strong>` tag within a `<ul>` tag within a `<p>` tag, you'll still match the rule for P STRONG that we defined above. If a particular nesting matches several style rules, the most specific rule is used.

Style Classes

There is one more feature of style sheets that we haven't mentioned yet: classes. Classes let you create, at the document level or in an external style sheet, several different styles for a single tag, each distinguished by a class name. To apply the style class, name it as the value of the class attribute in the tag.

Regular classes

In a technical paper you might want to define one paragraph style for the abstract, another for equations, and a third for centered quotations. None of the paragraph tags may have an explicit context in the HTML document so you could distinguish it from the others. Rather, you may define each as a different style class:

```
<style type="text/css">
<!--

P.abstract {font-style: italic;
            left-margin: 0.5cm;
            right-margin: 0.5cm}

P.equation {font-family: Symbol;
            text-align: center}

H1, P.centered {text-align: center;
                left-margin: 0.5cm;
                right-margin: 0.5cm}

-->
</style>
```

Notice first in the example that defining a class is simply a matter of appending a period-separated class name as a suffix to the tag name as the selector in a style rule. The class name can be any sequence of letters, numbers, and hyphens but must begin with a letter. And classes, like all selectors, may be included with other selectors, separated by commas, as in the third example. The only restriction on classes is that they can't be nested: e.g., `P.equation.centered` is not allowed.

Accordingly, the first rule in the example creates a class of paragraph styles named "abstract" whose text is italic and indented from the left and right margins by a half centimeter. Similarly, the second paragraph style class "equation" instructs the browser to center the text and to use the Symbol typeface to display the text. The last style rule creates a style with centered text and half-centimeter margins, applying this style to all level-one headers, as well as creating a class of the `<p>` tag named centered with that style.

To use a particular class of a tag, you add the class attribute to the tag, as in this example:

```
<p class="abstract">
This is the abstract paragraph.  See how the margins are indented?
</p>

<h3>The equation paragraph follows</h3>
```

```
<p class="equation">
a = b + 1
</p>

<p class="centered">
This paragraph's text should be centered.
</p>
```

For each paragraph, the value of the class attribute is the name of the class to be used for that tag.

Generic classes

You may also define a class without associating it with a particular tag, and apply that class selectively through your documents for a variety of tags. For example:

```
.italic {font-style: italic}
```

creates a generic class named *italic*. To use it, simply include its name with the class attribute. So, for instance, use `<p class="italic">` or `<h1 class="italic">` to create an italic paragraph or header.

Generic classes are quite handy and make it easy to apply a particular style to a broad range of tags.

Using IDs as classes

Almost all HTML tags accept the `id` attribute, which assigns an identifier to the element that is unique within the document. This identifier can be the target of a URL, used by automated document processing tools, and can specify a style rule for the element.

To create a style class that can be applied with the `id` attribute, follow the same syntax used for style classes, except with a `#` character before the class name instead of a period. This style creates such classes:

```
<style type="text/css">
<!--

#yellow { color : yellow}
H1#blue { color : blue}

-->
</style>
```

Within your document, you could use `<h1 id="blue">` to create a blue heading, or add `id="yellow"` to almost any tag to turn it yellow. You can mix and match both `class` and `id` attributes, giving you a limited ability to apply two independent style rules to a single element.

There is a dramatic drawback to using classes defined this way: the value of the `id` attribute must be unique to exactly one tag within the document. You cannot legally reuse the class, although the browser might let you get away with it.

For this reason, we discourage creating and using these kinds of classes. Stick to the conventional style of classes to create correct, robust HTML documents.

Style pseudo-classes

In addition to conventional style classes, the CSS standard defines pseudo-classes, which allow you to define the display style for certain tag states. Pseudo-classes are like regular classes, with two notable differences: they are attached to the tag name with a colon instead of a period, and they have predefined names, not arbitrary ones you may give them.

There are five pseudo-classes, three of which are associated with the `<a>` tag. The other two can be used on any text element.

The browsers distinguish three special states for the hyperlinks created by the `<a>` tag: not visited, being visited, and visited. The browser may change the appearance of the tag's contents to indicate its state, such as underlining or changing the colors. Through pseudo-classes, the HTML author can control how these states get displayed by defining styles for `A:link`, `A:active`, and `A:visited`. The *link* pseudo-class controls the appearance of links that are not selected by the user and have not yet been visited. The *active* pseudo-class defines the appearance of links that are currently selected by the user and are being processed by the browser. The *visited* pseudo-class defines those links that have already been visited by the user.

To completely define all three states of the `<a>` tag, you might write:

```
A:link {color: blue}
A:active {color: red; font-weight: bold}
A:visited {color: green}
```

The two other pseudo-classes usually apply to the `<p>` element, and are named *first-letter* and *first-line*. As you might expect, these pseudo-classes control the appearance of the first letter and first line, respectively, of a paragraph and create effects commonly found in printed media, such as initial drop-caps and bold first lines. For example:

```
P:first-line {font-style: small-caps}
```

converts the first line of a paragraph to small capital letters. Similarly:

```
P:first-letter {font-size: 200%; float: left}
```

tells the browser to make the first letter of a paragraph twice as large as the remaining text and float the letter to the left, allowing the first two lines of the paragraph to float around the larger initial letter.

You may mix pseudo-classes with regular classes by appending the pseudo-class name to the selector's class name.

Class inheritance

Classes inherit the style properties of their generic base tag. For instance, all the properties of the plain `<p>` tag apply to a specially defined paragraph class, except where the class overrides a particular property.

Classes cannot inherit from other classes, only from the unclassed version of the tag they represent. In general, therefore, you should put as many common styles into the rule for the basic version of a tag, and create classes only for those properties that are unique to that class. This makes maintenance and sharing of your style classes easier, especially for large document collections.

Style Properties

At the heart of the CSS specification are 53 properties that let you control how the styles-conscious browser presents your documents to the user. The standard collects these properties into six groups: fonts, colors and backgrounds, text, boxes and layout, lists, and tag classification. You'll find a summary of the style properties later in this chapter.

Property Values

There are five distinct kinds of property values: keywords, length values, percentage values, URLs, and colors.

Keyword property values

A property may have a keyword value that expresses action or dimension. For instance, the effects of underline and line-through are obvious property values. And you can express property dimensions with keywords like `small` and `xx-large`. Some keywords are even relational: `bolder`, for instance, is an acceptable value for the font-weight property. Keyword values are not case-sensitive: Underline, UNDERLINE, and underline are all acceptable keyword values. Keywords also cover such properties as font-family names.

Length property values

So-called length values (a term taken from the CSS standard) explicitly state the size of a property. They are numbers, some with decimals, too. Length values may have a leading + or - sign to indicate that the value is to be added to or subtracted from the immediate value of the property. Length values must be followed immediately by a two-letter unit abbreviation—with no intervening spaces.

There are three kinds of length-value units: relative, pixels, and absolute. Relative units specify a size that is relative to the size of some other property of the content. Currently, there are only two relative units: `em`, which is the height of the current font, and `x-height`, which is the height of the letter "x" in the current font (abbreviated `ex`). The pixels unit, abbreviated `px`, is equal to the size of a pixel on the browser's display. Absolute property value units are more familiar to us all. They include inches (`in`), centimeters (`cm`), millimeters (`mm`), points (`pt`, 1/72 of an inch), and picas (`pc`, 12 points).

All of the following are valid length values, although not all units are recognized by all browsers:

```
1in
1.5cm
+0.25mm
-3pt
-2.5pc
+100em
-2.75ex
250px
```

Since CSS in this instance is mostly used for screen display, you should generally use pixels (`px`) as the length property.

Percentage property values

Similar to the relative length-value type, a percentage value describes a property size relative to some other aspect of the content. It has an optional sign and decimal portion to its numeric value and must have the percent sign (%) suffix. For example:

```
line-height: 120%
```

computes the separation between lines to be 120% of the current line height (usually relative to the text font height). Note that this value is not dynamic, though: changes made to the font height after the rule has been processed by the browser will not affect the computed line height.

URL property values

Some properties expect a URL as a value. The syntax for using a URL in a style property is different from conventional HTML:

```
url(service://server.com/pathname)
```

The keyword `url` is required, as are the opening and closing parentheses. Do not leave any spaces between `url` and the opening parenthesis. The `url` value may contain either an absolute or a relative URL. However, note that the URL is relative to the immediate style sheet's URL, the one in which it is declared. This means that if you use a `url` value in a document-level or inline style, the URL is relative to the HTML document containing the style document. Otherwise, the URL is relative to the imported or linked external style sheet's URL.

Color property values

Color values specify colors in a property. You can specify a color as a color name or a hexadecimal RGB triple, as is done for common HTML attributes, or as a decimal RGB triple unique to style properties. Both color names and hexadecimal RGB triple notation are described in Chapter 8.

Style sheets accept three-digit hexadecimal color values. The single digit is doubled to create a conventional six-digit triple. Thus, the color #78C is equivalent to #7788CC. In general, three-digit color values are handy only for simple colors.

The decimal RGB triple notation is a bit different:

```
rgb(red, green, blue)
```

The red, green, and blue intensity values are integers in the range 0 to 255 or integer percentages. As with a URL value, do not leave any spaces between `rgb` and the opening parenthesis.

For example, in decimal RGB convention, the color white is `rgb(255, 255, 255)` or `rgb(100%, 100%, 100%)`, and a medium yellow is `rgb(127, 127, 0)` or `rgb(50%, 50%, 0%)`.

Property Inheritance

In lieu of a specific rule for a particular tag, properties and their values for tags within tags are inherited from the parent tag. Thus, setting a property for the `<body>` tag effectively applies that property to every tag in the body of your document, except for those that specifically override it. So, to make all the text in your document blue, you need only say:

```
BODY {color: blue}
```

rather than create a rule for every tag you use in your document.

This inheritance extends to any level. If you later created a `<div>` tag with text of a different color, the styles-conscious browser displays all the text contents of the `<div>` tag and all its enclosed tags in that new color. When the `<div>` tag ends, the color reverts to that of the containing `<body>` tag.

CSS Reference

The remainder of this chapter lists all the properties defined in the World Wide Web Consortium's Recommended Specification for Cascading Style Sheets, Level 1 (*http://www.w3.org/pub/WWW/TR/REC-CSS1*). All browsers do not implement all properties fully, and some simply do not work correctly. As in the HTML reference, we use the Netscape and Internet Explorer icons to show which browser supports that property. Properties with no icons are not currently supported by these browsers.

The following list includes each property's possible values, defined as either an explicit keyword (shown in constant width) or as one of these values:

color

Either a color name or hexadecimal RGB value, as defined in Chapter 8, or an RGB triple of the form:

```
rgb(red, green, blue)
```

where red, green, and blue are either numbers in the range 0 to 255 or percentage values indicating the brightness of that color component. Values of 255 or 100% indicate that the corresponding color component is at its brightest; values of 0 or 0% indicate that the corresponding color component is turned off completely. For example:

```
rgb(27, 119, 207)
rgb(50%, 75%, 0%)
```

are both valid color specifications.

length

An optional sign (either + or -), immediately followed by a number (with or without a decimal point) immediately followed by a two-character unit identifier. For values of zero, the unit identifier may be omitted. The unit identifiers `em` and `ex` refer to the overall height of the font and to the height of the letter "x", respectively. The unit identifier `px` is equal to a single pixel on the display device. The unit identifiers `in`, `cm`, `mm`, `pt`, and `pc` refer to inches, centimeters, millimeters, points, and picas, respectively. There are 72.27 points per inch and 12 points in a pica.

number

An optional sign, immediately followed by a number (with or without a decimal point).

percent

An optional sign, immediately followed by a number (with or without a decimal point), immediately followed by a percent sign. The actual value is computed as a percentage of some other element property, usually the element's size.

url

The keyword `url`, immediately followed (no spaces) by a left parenthesis, followed by a URL optionally enclosed in single or double quotes, followed by a matching right parenthesis. This is a valid URL, for example:

```
url("http://members.aol.com/htmlguru")
```

Finally, some values are lists of other values and are described as a "list of" some other value. In these cases, a list consists of one or more of the allowed values, separated by commas. The standard defines a default value for most properties. The default property is listed in the top syntax line for the property. Additional allowed values are listed beneath each description.

background

`background:`*`list`*

Composite property for the background-attachment, background-color, background-image, background-position, and background-repeat properties; *list* is any of these properties' values, in any order.

background-attachment

`background-attachment: scroll`

Determines if the background image is fixed in the window or scrolls as the document scrolls. Accepted values: `fixed`, `scroll`

background-color

`background-color: transparent`

Sets the background color of an element. Accepted values: *`color`*, `transparent`.

background-image

`background-image: none`

Sets the background image of an element. Accepted values: *`url`*, `transparent`.

background-position

`background-position:` *`percent`*

Sets the initial position of the element's background image, if specified; values are normally paired to provide x, y positions. Default position is `0% 0%`. Accepted values: *`length`*, *`percent`*, `top`, `center`, `bottom`, `left`, `right`.

background-repeat

`background-repeat: repeat`

Determines how the background image is repeated (tiled) across an element. Accepted values: `repeat`, `repeat-x`, `repeat-y`, `no-repeat`.

border

`border: list`

Sets all four borders on an element; value is one or more of a color, a value for border-width, and a value for border-style.

border-bottom

`border-bottom: list`

Sets the bottom border on an element; value is one or more of a color, a value for border-bottom-width, and a value for border-style.

border-bottom-width

`border-bottom-width: medium`

Sets the thickness of an element's bottom border. Accepted values: `medium`, *`length`*, `thin`, `thick`.

border-color

`border-color: color`

Sets the color of all four of an element's borders; default is the color of the element.

border-left

`border-left: list`

Sets the left border on an element; value is one or more of a color, a value for border-left-width, and a value for border-style.

border-left-width

`border-left-width: medium`

Sets the thickness of an element's left border. Accepted values: *`length`*, `medium`, `thin`, `thick`.

border-right

`border-right: list`

Sets the right border on an element; value is one or more of a color, a value for border-right-width, and a value for border-style.

border-right-width

`border-right-width: medium`

Sets the thickness of an element's right border. Accepted values: *`length`*, `medium`, `thin`, `thick`.

border-style

`border-style: none`

Sets the style of all four of an element's borders. Accepted values: `none`, `dashed`, `dotted`, `double`, `groove`, `inset`, `outset`, `ridge`, `solid`.

border-top

`border-top: list`

Sets the top border on an element; value is one or more of a color, a value for border-top-width, and a value for border-style.

border-top-width `border-top-width: medium`

Sets the thickness of an element's top border. Accepted values: *length*, `medium`, `thin`, `thick`.

border-width `border-width: medium`

Sets the thickness of all four of an element's borders. Accepted values: *length*, `medium`, `thin`, `thick`.

clear `clear: none`

Sets which margins of an element must not be adjacent to a floating element; the element will be moved down until that margin is clear. Accepted values: `none`, `both`, `left`, `right`.

color `color:` *color*

Sets the color of an element.

display `display: block`

Controls how an element is displayed. Accepted values: `block`, `inline`, `list-item`, `none`.

float `float: none`

Determines if an element floats to the left or right, allowing text to wrap around it, or be displayed inline (using none). Accepted values: `left`, `right`, `none`.

font `font:` *list*

Sets all the font attributes for an element; value is any of the values for font-style, font-variant, font-weight, font-size, line-height, and font-family, in that order.

font-family `font-family:` *list of font names*

Defines the font for an element, either as a specific font or as one of the generic fonts serif, sans-serif, cursive, fantasy, or monospace.

font-size `font-size:` *size*

Defines the font size. Accepted values: *length*, *percent*, `xx-small`, `x-small`, `small`, `medium`, `large`, `x-large`, `xx-large`, `larger`, `smaller`.

font-style

`font-style: normal`

Defines the style of the face, either normal or some type of slanted style. Accepted values: `italic`, `oblique`, `normal`.

font-variant

`font-variant: normal`

Defines a font to be in small caps. Accepted values: `smallcaps`, `normal`.

font-weight

`font-weight: normal`

Defines the font weight. If a number is used, it must be a multiple of 100 between 100 and 900; 400 is normal, 700 is the same as the keyword bold. Accepted values: `bold`, `bolder`, `lighter`, *`number`*, `normal`.

height

`height: auto`

Defines the height of an element. Accepted values: *length*, `auto`.

letter-spacing

`letter-spacing: normal`

Inserts additional space between text characters. Accepted values: *`length`*, `normal`.

line-height

`line-height: normal`

Sets the distance between adjacent text baselines. Accepted values: *`length`*, *`number`*, *`percent`*, `normal`.

list-style

`list-style: list`

Defines list-related styles using any of the values for list-style-image, list-style-position, and list-style-type.

list-style-image

`list-style-image: none`

Defines an image to be used as a list item's marker, in lieu of the value for list-style-type. Accepted values: *url*, `none`.

list-style-position

`list-style-position: outside`

Indents or extends (default) a list item's marker with respect to the item's content. Accepted values: `inside`, `outside`.

list-style-type

`list-style-type: disc`

Defines a list item's marker for either unordered lists (`circle`, `disc`, or `square`) or ordered lists (the rest). Accepted values: `circle`, `square`, `decimal`, `disc`, `lower-alpha`, `lower-roman`, `none`, `upper-alpha`, `upper-roman`.

margin

`margin: length`

Defines all four of an element's margins. Accepted values: *length*, *percent*, auto.

margin-bottom

`margin-bottom: length`

Defines the bottom margin of an element; default value is 0. Accepted values: *length*, *percent*, auto.

margin-left

`margin-left: length`

Defines the left margin of an element; default value is 0. Accepted values: *length*, *percent*, auto.

margin-right

`margin-right: length`

Defines the right margin of an element; default value is 0. Accepted values: *length*, *percent*, auto.

margin-top

`margin-top: length`

Defines the top margin of an element; default value is 0. Accepted values: *length*, *percent*, auto.

padding

`padding:list`

Defines all four padding amounts around an element.

padding-bottom

`padding-bottom: length`

Defines the bottom padding of an element; default value is 0. Accepted values: *length*, *percent*.

padding-left

`padding-left: length`

Defines the left padding of an element; default value is 0. Accepted values: *length*, *percent*.

padding-right

`padding-right: length`

Defines the right padding of an element; default value is 0. Accepted values: *length*, *percent*.

padding-top

`padding-top: length`

Defines the top padding of an element; default value is 0. Accepted values: *length*, *percent*.

text-align

`text-align: style`

Sets the text alignment style for an element. The default value is dependent on the element. Accepted values: `center`, `justify`, `left`, `right`.

text-decoration

`text-decoration: none`

Defines any decoration for the text; values may be combined. Accepted values: `blink`, `line-through`, `none`, `overline`, `underline`.

text-indent

`text-indent: length`

Defines the indentation of the first line of text in an element; default value is 0. Accepted values: *`length`*, *`percent`*.

text-transform

`text-transform: none`

Transforms the text in the element accordingly. Accepted values: `capitalize`, `lowercase`, `none`, `uppercase`.

vertical-align

`vertical-align: position`

Sets the vertical positioning of an element. The default setting is dependent on the element. Accepted values: *`percent`*, `baseline`, `bottom`, `middle`, `sub`, `super`, `text-bottom`, `text-top`, `top`.

word-spacing

`word-spacing: normal`

Inserts additional space between words. Accepted values: *`length`*, `normal`.

white-space

`white-space: normal`

Defines how whitespace within an element is handled. Accepted values: `normal`, `nowrap`, `pre`.

width

`width: auto`

Defines the width of an element. Accepted values: *`length`*, *`percent`*, `auto`.

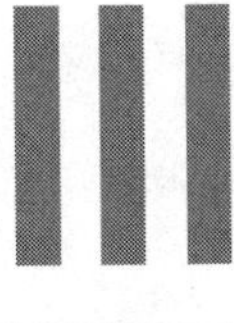

XML

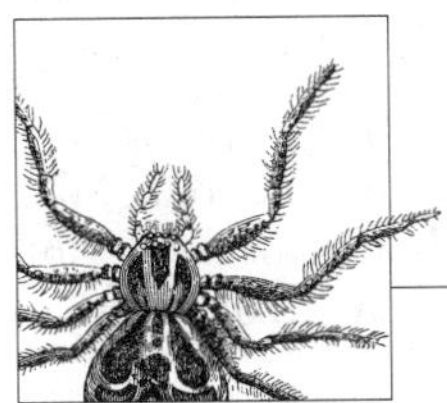

10
XML

The *Extensible Markup Language* (XML) is a document-processing standard that is an official recommendation of the World Wide Web Consortium (W3C), the same group responsible for overseeing the HTML standard. Many expect XML and its sibling technologies to become the markup language of choice for dynamically generated content, including nonstatic web pages. Many companies are already integrating XML support into their products.

XML is actually a simplified form of *Standard Generalized Markup Language* (SGML), an international documentation standard that has existed since the 1980s. However, SGML is extremely complex, especially for the Web. Much of the credit for XML's creation can be attributed to Jon Bosak of Sun Microsystems, Inc., who started the W3C working group responsible for scaling down SGML to a form more suitable for the Internet.

Put succinctly, XML is a *metalanguage* that allows you to create and format your own document markups. With HTML, existing markup is static: `<HEAD>` and `<BODY>`, for example, are tightly integrated into the HTML standard and cannot be changed or extended. XML, on the other hand, allows you to create your own markup tags and configure each to your liking—for example, `<HeadingA>`, `<Sidebar>`, `<Quote>`, or `<ReallyWildFont>`. Each of these elements can be defined through your own *document type definitions* and *stylesheets* and applied to one or more XML documents. XML schemas provide another way to define elements. Thus, it is important to realize that there are no correct tags for an XML document, except those you define yourself.

While many XML applications currently support *Cascading Style Sheets* (CSS), a more extensible style sheet specification exists, called the *Extensible Stylesheet Language* (XSL). With XSL, you ensure that XML documents are formatted the same way no matter which application or platform they appear on.

XSL consists of two parts: XSLT (*transformations*) and XSL-FO (*formatting objects*). Transformations, as discussed in this book, allow you to work with XSLT and convert XML documents to other formats such as HTML. Formatting objects is described briefly later in this chapter.

This chapter offers a quick overview of XML, as well as some sample applications that allow you to get started in coding. We won't cover everything about XML. Some XML-related specifications are still in flux as this book goes to print. However, after reading this book, we hope that the components that make up XML will seem a little less foreign.

XML Terminology

Before we move further, we need to standardize some terminology. An XML document consists of one or more *elements*. An element is marked with the following form:

```
<Body>
This is text formatted according to the Body element
</Body>.
```

This element consists of two *tags*: an opening tag, which places the name of the element between a less-than sign (<) and a greater-than sign (>), and a closing tag, which is identical except for the forward slash (/) that appears before the element name. Like HTML, the text between the opening and closing tags is considered part of the element and is processed according to the element's rules.

Elements can have *attributes* applied, such as the following:

```
<Price currency="Euro">25.43</Price>
```

Here, the attribute is specified inside of the opening tag and is called `¤cy;`. It is given a value of `Euro`, which is placed inside quotation marks. Attributes are often used to further refine or modify the default meaning of an element.

In addition to the standard elements, XML also supports *empty elements*. An empty element has no text between the opening and closing tags. Hence, both tags can (optionally) be combined by placing a forward slash before the closing marker. For example, these elements are identical:

```
<Picture src="blueball.gif"></Picture>
<Picture src="blueball.gif"/>
```

Empty elements are often used to add nontextual content to a document or provide additional information to the application that parses the XML. Note that while the closing slash may not be used in single-tag HTML elements, it is *mandatory* for single-tag XML empty elements.

Unlearning Bad Habits

Whereas HTML browsers often ignore simple errors in documents, XML applications are not nearly as forgiving. For the HTML reader, there are a few bad habits from which we should dissuade you:

XML is case-sensitive
: Element names must be used exactly as they are defined. For example, `<Paragraph>` and `<paragraph>` are not the same.

Attribute values must be in quotation marks

You can't specify an attribute value as &<picture src=/images/blueball.gif/>;, an error that HTML browsers often overlook. An attribute value must always be inside single or double quotation marks, or else the XML parser will flag it as an error. Here is the correct way to specify such a tag:

```
<picture src="/images/blueball.gif"/>
```

A non-empty element must have an opening and a closing tag

Each element that specifies an opening tag must have a closing tag that matches it. If it does not, and it is not an empty element, the XML parser generates an error. In other words, you cannot do the following:

```
<Paragraph>
This is a paragraph.
<Paragraph>
This is another paragraph.
```

Instead, you must have an opening and a closing tag for each paragraph element:

```
<Paragraph>This is a paragraph.</Paragraph>
<Paragraph>This is another paragraph.</Paragraph>
```

Tags must be nested correctly

It is illegal to do the following:

```
<Italic><Bold>This is incorrect</Italic></Bold>
```

The closing tag for the <Bold> element should be inside the closing tag for the <Italic> element to match the nearest opening tag and preserve the correct element nesting. It is essential for the application parsing your XML to process the hierarchy of the elements:

```
<Italic><Bold>This is correct</Bold></Italic>
```

These syntactic rules are the source of many common errors in XML, especially because some of this behavior can be ignored by HTML browsers. An XML document adhering to these rules (and a few others that we'll see later) is said to be *well-formed*.

An Overview of an XML Document

Generally, two files are needed by an XML-compliant application to use XML content:

The XML document

This file contains the document data, typically tagged with meaningful XML elements, any of which may contain attributes.

Document Type Definition (DTD)

This file specifies rules for how the XML elements, attributes, and other data are defined and logically related in the document.

There's another type of file commonly used to help display XML data: the *style sheet*.

The style sheet dictates how document elements should be formatted when they are displayed. Note that you can apply different stylesheets to the same document, depending on the environment, thus changing the document's appearance without affecting any of the underlying data. The separation between content and formatting is an important distinction in XML.

A Simple XML Document

Example 10-1 shows a simple XML document.

Example 10-1. sample.xml

```
<?xml version="1.0" encoding="UTF-8"?>
<!DOCTYPE OReilly:Books SYSTEM "sample.dtd">
<!-- Here begins the XML data -->
<OReilly:Books xmlns:OReilly=http://www.oreilly.com>
   <OReilly:Product>Webmaster in a Nutshell</OReilly:Product>
   <OReilly:Price>24.95</OReilly:Price>
</OReilly:Books>
```

Let's look at this example line by line.

In the first line, the code between the `<?xml` and the `?>` is called an XML declaration. This declaration contains special information for the XML processor (the program reading the XML), indicating that this document conforms to Version 1.0 of the XML standard and uses UTF-8 (Unicode optimized for ASCII) encoding.

The second line is as follows:

```
<!DOCTYPE OReilly:Books SYSTEM "sample.dtd">
```

This line points out the *root element* of the document, as well as the DTD validating each of the document elements that appear inside the root element. The root element is the outermost element in the document that the DTD applies to; it typically denotes the document's starting and ending point. In this example, the `<OReilly:Books>` element serves as the root element of the document. The `SYSTEM` keyword denotes that the DTD of the document resides in an external file named *sample.dtd*. On a side note, it is possible to simply embed the DTD in the same file as the XML document. However, this is not recommended for general use because it hampers reuse of DTDs.

Following that line is a comment. Comments always begin with `<!--` and end with `-->`. You can write whatever you want inside comments; they are ignored by the XML processor. Be aware that comments, however, cannot come before the XML declaration and cannot appear inside an element tag. For example, this is illegal:

```
<OReilly:Books <!-- This is the tag for a book -->>
```

Finally, the elements `<OReilly:Product>`, `<OReilly:Price>`, and `<OReilly:Books>` are XML elements we invented. Like most elements in XML, they hold no special significance except for whatever document rules we define for them. Note that these elements look slightly different than those you may have seen previously because we are using namespaces. Each element tag can be divided into two parts. The portion before the colon (:) identifies the tag's namespace; the portion after the colon identifies the name of the tag itself.

Let's discuss some XML terminology. The <OReilly:Product> and <OReilly:Price> elements would both consider the <OReilly:Books> element their *parent*. In the same manner, elements can be *grandparents* and *grandchildren* of other elements. However, we typically abbreviate multiple levels by stating that an element is either an *ancestor* or a *descendant* of another element.

Namespaces

Namespaces were created to ensure uniqueness among XML elements. They are not mandatory in XML, but it's often wise to use them.

For example, let's pretend that the <OReilly:Books> element was simply named <Books>. When you think about it, it's not out of the question that another publisher would create its own <Books> element in its own XML documents. If the two publishers combined their documents, resolving a single (correct) definition for the <Books> tag would be impossible. When two XML documents containing identical elements from different sources are merged, those elements are said to *collide*. Namespaces help to avoid element collisions by scoping each tag.

In Example 10-1, we scoped each tag with the OReilly namespace. Namespaces are declared using the &xmlns:;*something* attribute, where *something* defines the prefix of the namespace. The attribute value is a unique identifier that differentiates this namespace from all other namespaces; the use of a URI is recommended. In this case, we use the O'Reilly URI *http://www.oreilly.com* as the default namespace, which should guarantee uniqueness. A namespace declaration can appear as an attribute of any element, in which case the namespace remains inside that element's opening and closing tags. Here are some examples:

```
<OReilly:Books xmlns:OReilly=http://www.oreilly.com>
  ...
</OReilly:Books>

<xsl:stylesheet xmlns:xsl=http://www.w3.org>
  ...
</xsl:stylesheet>
```

You are allowed to define more than one namespace in the context of an element:

```
<OReilly:Books xmlns:OReilly=http://www.oreilly.com
    xmlns:Songline=http://www.songline.com>
  ...
</OReilly:Books>
```

If you do not specify a name after the xmlns prefix, the namespace is dubbed the *default namespace* and is applied to all elements inside the defining element that do not use a namespace prefix of their own. For example:

```
<Books xmlns=http://www.oreilly.com
       xmlns:Songline=http://www.songline.com>
    <Book>
        <Title>Webmaster in a Nutshell</Title>
        <ISBN>0-596-00357-9</ISBN>
    </Book>
    <Songline:CD>18231</Songline:CD>
</Books>
```

Here, the default namespace (represented by the URI *http://www.oreilly.com*) is applied to the elements <Books>, <Book>, <Title>, and <ISBN>. However, it is not applied to the <Songline:CD> element, which has its own namespace.

Finally, you can set the default namespace to an empty string. This ensures that there is no default namespace in use within a specific element:

```
<header xmlns=
        xmlns:OReilly=http://www.oreilly.com
        xmlns:Songline=http://www.songline.com>
   <entry>Learn XML in a Week</entry>
   <price>10.00</price>
</header>
```

Here, the <entry> and <price> elements have no default namespace.

A Simple Document Type Definition (DTD)

Example 10-2 creates a simple DTD for our XML document.

Example 10-2. sample.dtd

```
<?xml version="1.0"?>
<!ELEMENT OReilly:Books (OReilly:Product, OReilly:Price)>
<!ATTLIST OReilly:Books
      xmlns:OReilly CDATA "http://www.oreilly.com">
<!ELEMENT OReilly:Product (#PCDATA)>
<!ELEMENT OReilly:Price (#PCDATA)>
```

The purpose of this DTD is to declare each of the elements used in our XML document. All document-type data is placed inside a construct with the characters <!*something*>.

Each <!ELEMENT> construct declares a valid element for our XML document. With the second line, we've specified that the <OReilly:Books> element is valid:

```
<!ELEMENT OReilly:Books
    (OReilly:Product, OReilly:Price)>
```

The parentheses group together the required child elements for the element <OReilly:Books>. In this case, the <OReilly:Product> and <OReilly:Price> elements *must* be included inside our <OReilly:Books> element tags, and they must appear in the order specified. The elements <OReilly:Product> and <OReilly:Price> are therefore considered *children* of <OReilly:Books>.

Also, the <OReilly:Product> and <OReilly:Price> elements are declared in our DTD:

```
<!ELEMENT OReilly:Product (#PCDATA)>
<!ELEMENT OReilly:Price (#PCDATA)>
```

Again, parentheses specify required elements. In this case, they both have a single requirement, represented by #PCDATA. This is shorthand for *parsed character data*, which means that any characters are allowed, as long as they do not include other element tags or contain the characters < or &, or the sequence]]>. These characters are forbidden because they could be interpreted as markup. (We'll see how to get around this shortly.)

The line <!ATTLIST OReilly:Books xmlns:OReilly CDATA "http://www.oreilly.com"> indicates that the <xmlns:OReilly> attribute of the <OReilly:Books> element defaults to the URI associated with O'Reilly & Associates if no other value is explicitly specified in the element.

The XML data shown in Example 10-1 adheres to the rules of this DTD: it contains an <OReilly:Books> element, which in turn contains an <OReilly:Product> element followed by an <OReilly:Price> element inside it (in that order). Therefore, if this DTD is applied to the data with a <!DOCTYPE> statement, the document is said to be *valid*.

A Simple XSL Style Sheet

XSL allows developers to describe transformations using XSL Transformations (XSLT), which can convert XML documents into XSL Formatting Objects, HTML, or other textual output.

As this book goes to print, the XSL Formatting Objects specification is still changing; therefore, this book covers only the XSLT portion of XSL. The examples that follow, however, are consistent with the W3C specification.

Let's add a simple XSL style sheet to the example:

```
<?xml version="1.0"?>
<xsl:stylesheet version="1.0"
    xmlns:xsl="http://www.w3.org/1999/XSL/Transform">
    <xsl:output method="html"/>
    <xsl:template match="/">
        <font size="+1">
            <xsl:apply-templates/>
        </font>
    </xsl:template>
</xsl:stylesheet>
```

The first thing you might notice when you look at an XSL style sheet is that it is formatted in the same way as a regular XML document. This is not a coincidence. By design, XSL stylesheets are themselves XML documents, so they must adhere to the same rules as well-formed XML documents.

Breaking down the pieces, you should first note that all XSL elements must be contained in the appropriate <xsl:stylesheet> outer element. This tells the XSLT processor that it is describing style sheet information, not XML content itself. After the opening <xsl:stylesheet> tag, we see an XSLT directive to optimize output for HTML. Following that are the rules that will be applied to our XML document, given by the <xsl:template> elements (in this case, there is only one rule).

Each rule can be further broken down into two items: a *template pattern* and a *template action*. Consider the line:

```
<xsl:template match="/">
```

This line forms the template pattern of the style sheet rule. Here, the target pattern is the root element, as designated by match="/". The / is shorthand to represent the XML document's root element.

The contents of the `<xsl:template>` element:

```
<font size="+1">
    <xsl:apply-templates/>
</font>
```

specify the template action that should be performed on the target. In this case, we see the empty element `<xsl:apply-templates/>` located inside a `<font>` element. When the XSLT processor transforms the target element, every element inside the root element is surrounded by the `<font>` tags, which will likely cause the application formatting the output to increase the font size.

In our initial XML example, the `<OReilly:Product>` and `<OReilly:Price>` elements are both enclosed inside the `<OReilly:Books>` tags. Therefore, the font size will be applied to the contents of those tags. Example 10-3 displays a more realistic example.

Example 10-3. sample.xsl

```
<?xml version="1.0"?>
<xsl:stylesheet version="1.0"
   xmlns:xsl="http://www.w3c.org/1999/XSL/Transform"
   xmlns:OReilly="http://www.oreilly.com">

   <xsl:output method="html">

   <xsl:template match="/">
      <html>
         <body>
            <xsl:apply-templates/>
         </body>
      </html>
   </xsl:template>

   <xsl:template match="OReilly:Books">
      <font size="+3">
         <xsl:text>Books: </xsl:text>
         <br/>
            <xsl:apply-templates/>
      </font>
   </xsl:template>

   <xsl:template match="OReilly:Product">
      <font size="+0">
         <xsl:apply-templates/>
         <br/>
      </font>
   </xsl:template>

   <xsl:template match="OReilly:Price">
      <font size="+1">
         <xsl:text>Price: $</xsl:text>
            <xsl:apply-templates/>
         <xsl:text> + tax</xsl:text>
         <br/>
```

Example 10-3. sample.xsl (continued)

```
      </font>
   </xsl:template>
</xsl:stylesheet>
```

In this example, we target the `<OReilly:Books>` element, printing the word `Books:` before it in a larger font size. In addition, the `<OReilly:Product>` element applies the default font size to each of its children, and the `<OReilly:Price>` tag uses a slightly larger font size to display its children, overriding the default size of its parent, `<OReilly:Books>`. (Of course, neither one has any children elements; they simply have text between their tags in the XML document.) The text `Price: $` will precede each of `<OReilly:Price>`'s children, and the characters `+ tax` will come after it, formatted accordingly.

Here is the result after we pass *sample.xsl* through an XSLT processor:

```
<html xmlns:OReilly="http://www.oreilly.com">
   <body>
      <font size="+3">
   Books: <br>
         <font size="+0">
Webmaster in a Nutshell<br>
         </font>
         <font size="+1">
Price $34.95 + tax
         </font>
      </font>
   </body>
</html>
```

And that's it: everything needed for a simple XML document! Running the result through an HTML browser, you should see something similar to Figure 10-1.

Books:
Webmaster in a Nutshell
Price $34.95 + tax

Figure 10-1. Sample XML output

XML Reference

Now that you have had a quick taste of working with XML, here is an overview of the more common rules and constructs of the XML language.

Well-Formed XML

These are the rules for a well-formed XML document:

- All element attribute values must be in quotation marks.
- An element must have both an opening and a closing tag, unless it is an empty element.

- If a tag is a standalone empty element, it must contain a closing slash (/) before the end of the tag.
- All opening and closing element tags must nest correctly.
- Isolated markup characters are not allowed in text; < or & must use entity references. In addition, the sequence]]> must be expressed as]]> when used as regular text. (Entity references are discussed in further detail later.)
- Well-formed XML documents without a corresponding DTD must have all attributes of type CDATA by default.

Special Markup

XML uses the following special markup constructs.

<?xml ...?>

Although they are not required to, XML documents typically begin with an XML declaration, which must start with the characters `<?xml` and end with the characters `?>`. Attributes include:

Attributes

`version`
: The `version` attribute specifies the correct version of XML required to process the document, which is currently `1.0`. This attribute cannot be omitted.

`encoding`
: The `encoding` attribute specifies the character encoding used in the document (e.g., `UTF-8` or `iso-8859-1`). UTF-8 and UTF-16 are the only encodings that an XML processor is required to handle. This attribute is optional.

`standalone`
: The optional `standalone` attribute specifies whether an external DTD is required to parse the document. The value must be either yes or no (the default). If the value is no or the attribute is not present, a DTD must be declared with an XML `<!DOCTYPE>` instruction. If it is yes, no external DTD is required.

For example:

```
<?xml version="1.0"?>
<?xml version="1.0" encoding="UTF-8" standalone="yes"?>
<?xml version="number"
[encoding="encoding"]
[standalone="yes|no"] ?>
```

<?...?>

A processing instruction allows developers to place attributes specific to an outside application within the document. Processing instructions always begin with the characters `<?` and end with the characters `?>`. For example:

```
<?works document="hello.doc" data="hello.wks"?>
```

You can create your own processing instructions if the XML application processing the document is aware of what the data means and acts accordingly.

```
<?target attribute1="value"
attribute2="value"
... ?>
```

<!DOCTYPE>

The `<!DOCTYPE>` instruction allows you to specify a DTD for an XML document. This instruction currently takes one of two forms:

```
<!DOCTYPE root-element SYSTEM "URI_of_DTD">
<!DOCTYPE root-element PUBLIC "name" "URI_of_DTD">
```

Keywords

`SYSTEM`
: The `SYSTEM` variant specifies the URI location of a DTD for private use in the document. For example:

```
<!DOCTYPE Book SYSTEM
   "http://mycompany.com/dtd/mydoctype.dtd">
```

`PUBLIC`
: The `PUBLIC` variant is used in situations in which a DTD has been publicized for widespread use. In these cases, the DTD is assigned a unique name, which the XML processor may use by itself to attempt to retrieve the DTD. If this fails, the URI is used:

```
<!DOCTYPE Book PUBLIC "-//O'Reilly//DTD//EN"
   "http://www.oreilly.com/dtd/xmlbk.dtd">
```

Public DTDs follow a specific naming convention. See the XML specification for details on naming public DTDs.

```
<!DOCTYPE root-element SYSTEM|PUBLIC
["name"] "URI_of_DTD">
```

<!-- ... -->

You can place comments anywhere in an XML document, except within element tags or before the initial XML processing instructions. Comments in an XML document always start with the characters `<!--` and end with the characters `-->`. In addition, they may not include double hyphens within the comment. The contents of the comment are ignored by the XML processor. For example:

```
<!-- Sales Figures Start Here -->
<Units>2000</Units>
<Cost>49.95</Cost>
<!-- comments -->
```

CDATA

You can define special sections of character data, or CDATA, which the XML processor does not attempt to interpret as markup. Anything included inside a CDATA section is treated as plain text.

CDATA sections begin with the characters `<![CDATA[` and end with the characters `]]>`. For example:

```
<![CDATA[
   Im now discussing the <element> tag of documents
   5 & 6: "Sales" and "Profit and Loss". Luckily,
   the XML processor wont apply rules of formatting
   to these sentences!
]]>
```

Note that entity references inside a CDATA section will not be expanded.

```
<![CDATA[ ... ]]>
```

Element and Attribute Rules

An element is either bound by its start and end tags or is an empty element. Elements can contain text, other elements, or a combination of both. For example:

```
<para>
   Elements can contain text, other elements, or
   a combination. For example, a chapter might
   contain a title and multiple paragraphs, and
   a paragraph might contain text and
   <emphasis>emphasis elements</emphasis>.
</para>
```

An element name must start with a letter or an underscore. It can then have any number of letters, numbers, hyphens, periods, or underscores in its name. Elements are *case-sensitive*: `<Para>`, `<para>`, and `<pArA>` are considered three different element types.

Element type names may not start with the string `xml` in any variation of upper- or lowercase. Names beginning with `xml` are reserved for special uses by the W3C XML Working Group. Colons (:) are permitted in element type names only for specifying namespaces; otherwise, colons are forbidden. For example:

Example	Comment
`<Italic>`	Legal
`<_Budget>`	Legal
`<Punch line>`	Illegal: has a space
`<205Para>`	Illegal: starts with number
`<repair@log>`	Illegal: contains @ character
`<xmlbob>`	Illegal: starts with `xml`

Element type names can also include accented Roman characters, letters from other alphabets (e.g., Cyrillic, Greek, Hebrew, Arabic, Thai, Hiragana, Katakana, or Devanagari), and ideograms from the Chinese, Japanese, and Korean languages. Valid element type names can therefore include <são>, <peut-être>, <più>, and <niño>, plus a number of others our publishing system isn't equipped to handle.

If you use a DTD, the content of an element is constrained by its DTD declaration. Better XML applications inform you which elements and attributes can appear inside a specific element. Otherwise, you should check the element declaration in the DTD to determine the exact semantics.

Attributes describe additional information about an element. They always consist of a name and a value, as follows:

```
<price currency="Euro">
```

The attribute value is always quoted, using either single or double quotes. Attribute names are subject to the same restrictions as element type names.

XML Reserved Attributes

The following are reserved attributes in XML.

xml:lang

The `&xml:lang;` attribute can be used on any element. Its value indicates the language of the body of the element. This is useful in a multilingual context. For example, you might have:

```
<para xml:lang="en">Hello</para>
<para xml:lang="fr">Bonjour</para>
```

This format allows you to display one element or the other, depending on the user's language preference.

The syntax of the `&xml:lang;` value is defined by ISO-639. A two-letter language code is optionally followed by a hyphen and a two-letter country code. Traditionally, the language is given in lowercase and the country in uppercase (and for safety, this rule should be followed), but processors are expected to use the values in a case-insensitive manner.

In addition, ISO-3166 provides extensions for nonstandardized languages or language variants. Valid `&xml:lang;` values include notations such as `en`, `en-US`, `en-UK`, `en-cockney`, `i-navajo`, and `x-minbari`.

```
xml:lang="iso_639_identifier"
```

xml:space

The `&xml:space;` attribute indicates whether any whitespace inside the element is significant and should not be altered by the XML processor. The attribute can take one of two enumerated values:

`preserve`
: The XML application preserves all whitespace (newlines, spaces, and tabs) present within the element.

`default`
: The XML processor uses its default processing rules when deciding to preserve or discard the whitespace inside the element.

You should set &xml:space; to preserve only if you want an element to behave like the HTML <pre> element, such as when it documents source code.

```
xml:space="default|preserve"
```

Entity and Character References

Entity references are used as substitutions for specific characters (or any string substitution) in XML. A common use for entity references is to denote document symbols that might otherwise be mistaken for markup by an XML processor. XML predefines five entity references for you, which are substitutions for basic markup symbols. However, you can define as many entity references as you like in your own DTD. (See the next section.)

Entity references always begin with an ampersand (&) and end with a semicolon (;). They cannot appear inside a CDATA section but can be used anywhere else. Predefined entities in XML are shown in the following table:

Entity	Char	Notes
`&`	&	Do not use inside processing instructions.
`<`	<	Use inside attribute values quoted with ".
`>`	>	Use after]] in normal text and inside processing instructions.
`"`	"	Use inside attribute values quoted with ".
`'`	'	Use inside attribute values quoted with '.

In addition, you can provide character references for Unicode characters with a numeric character reference. A decimal character reference consists of the string &#, followed by the decimal number representing the character, and finally, a semicolon (;). For hexadecimal character references, the string &#x is followed first by the hexadecimal number representing the character and then a semicolon. For example, to represent the copyright character, you could use either of the following lines:

```
This document is &#169; 2001 by OReilly and Assoc.
This document is &#xA9; 2001 by OReilly and Assoc.
```

The character reference is replaced with the "circled-C" (©) copyright character when the document is formatted.

Document Type Definitions

A DTD specifies how elements inside an XML document should relate to each other. It also provides grammar rules for the document and each of its elements. A document adhering to the XML specifications and the rules outlined by its DTD is considered to be *valid*. (Don't confuse this with a well-formed document, which adheres only to the XML syntax rules outlined earlier.)

Element Declarations

You must declare each of the elements that appear inside your XML document within your DTD. You can do so with the `<!ELEMENT>` declaration, which uses this format:

```
<!ELEMENT elementname rule>
```

This declares an XML element and an associated rule called a *content model*, which relates the element logically to the XML document. The element name should not include <> characters. An element name must start with a letter or an underscore. After that, it can have any number of letters, numbers, hyphens, periods, or underscores in its name. Element names may not start with the string `xml` in any variation of upper- or lowercase. You can use a colon in element names only if you use namespaces; otherwise, it is forbidden.

ANY and PCDATA

The simplest element declaration states that between the opening and closing tags of the element, anything can appear:

```
<!ELEMENT library ANY>
```

The `ANY` keyword allows you to include other valid tags and general character data within the element. However, you may want to specify a situation where you want only general characters to appear. This type of data is better known as *parsed character data*, or PCDATA. You can specify that an element contain only PCDATA with a declaration such as the following:

```
<!ELEMENT title (#PCDATA)>
```

Remember, this declaration means that any character data that is *not* an element can appear between the element tags. Therefore, it's legal to write the following in your XML document:

```
<title></title>
<title>Webmaster in a Nutshell</title>
<title>Java Network Programming</title>
```

However, the following is illegal with the previous `PCDATA` declaration:

```
<title>
Webmaster <emphasis>in a Nutshell</emphasis>
</title>
```

On the other hand, you may want to specify that another element *must* appear between the two tags specified. You can do this by placing the name of the element in the parentheses. The following two rules state that a `<books>` element must contain a `<title>` element, and a `<title>` element must contain parsed character data (or null content) but not another element:

```
<!ELEMENT books (title)>
<!ELEMENT title (#PCDATA)>
```

Multiple sequences

If you wish to dictate that multiple elements must appear in a specific order between the opening and closing tags of a specific element, you can use a comma (,) to separate the two instances:

```
<!ELEMENT books (title, authors)>
<!ELEMENT title (#PCDATA)>
<!ELEMENT authors (#PCDATA)>
```

In the preceding declaration, the DTD states that within the opening <books> and closing </books> tags, there must first appear a <title> element consisting of parsed character data. It must be immediately followed by an <authors> element containing parsed character data. The <authors> element cannot precede the <title> element.

Here is a valid XML document for the DTD excerpt defined previously:

```
<books>
   <title>Webmaster in a Nutshell, Third Edition</title>
   <authors>Stephen Spainhour and Robert Eckstein</authors>
</books>
```

The previous example showed how to specify both elements in a declaration. You can just as easily specify that one or the other appear (but not both) by using the vertical bar (|):

```
<!ELEMENT books (title|authors)>
<!ELEMENT title (#PCDATA)>
<!ELEMENT authors (#PCDATA)>
```

This declaration states that either a <title> element or an <authors> element can appear inside the <books> element. Note that it must have one or the other. If you omit both elements or include both elements, the XML document is not considered valid. You can, however, use a recurrence operator to allow such an element to appear more than once. Let's talk about that now.

Grouping and recurrence

You can nest parentheses inside your declarations to give finer granularity to the syntax you're specifying. For example, the following DTD states that inside the <books> element, the XML document must contain either a <description> element or a <title> element immediately followed by an <author> element. All three elements must consist of parsed character data:

```
<!ELEMENT books ((title, author)|description)>
<!ELEMENT title (#PCDATA)>
<!ELEMENT author (#PCDATA)>
<!ELEMENT description (#PCDATA)>
```

Now for the fun part: you are allowed to dictate inside an element declaration whether a single element (or a grouping of elements contained inside parentheses) must appear zero or one times, one or more times, or zero or more times. The characters used for this appear immediately after the target element (or element grouping) that they refer to and should be familiar to Unix shell programmers. Occurrence operators are shown in the following table:

Attribute	Description
?	Must appear once or not at all (zero or one times)
+	Must appear at least once (one or more times)
*	May appear any number of times or not at all (zero or more times)

If you want to provide finer granularity to the <author> element, you can redefine the following in the DTD:

```
<!ELEMENT author (authorname+)>
<!ELEMENT authorname (#PCDATA)>
```

This indicates that the <author> element must have at least one <authorname> element under it. It is allowed to have more than one as well. You can define more complex relationships with parentheses:

```
<!ELEMENT reviews (rating, synopsis?, comments+)*>
<!ELEMENT rating ((tutorial|reference)*, overall)>
<!ELEMENT synopsis (#PCDATA)>
<!ELEMENT comments (#PCDATA)>
<!ELEMENT tutorial (#PCDATA)>
<!ELEMENT reference (#PCDATA)>
<!ELEMENT overall (#PCDATA)>
```

Mixed content

Using the rules of grouping and recurrence to their fullest allows you to create very useful elements that contain *mixed content*. Elements with mixed content contain child elements that can intermingle with PCDATA. The most obvious example of this is a paragraph:

```
<para>
This is a <emphasis>paragraph</emphasis> element. It
contains this <link ref="http://www.w3.org">link</link>
to the W3C. Their website is <emphasis>very</emphasis>
helpful.
</para>
```

Mixed content declarations look like this:

```
<!ELEMENT quote (#PCDATA|name|joke|soundbite)*>
```

This declaration allows a <quote> element to contain text (#PCDATA), <name> elements, <joke> elements, and/or <soundbite> elements in any order. You can't specify things such as:

```
<!ELEMENT memo (#PCDATA, from, #PCDATA, to, content)>
```

Once you include #PCDATA in a declaration, any following elements must be separated by or bars (|), and the grouping must be optional and repeatable (*).

Empty elements

You must also declare each of the empty elements that can be used inside a valid XML document. This can be done with the EMPTY keyword:

```
<!ELEMENT elementname EMPTY>
```

For example, the following declaration defines an element in the XML document that can be used as `<statuscode/>` or `<statuscode></statuscode>`:

```
<!ELEMENT statuscode EMPTY>
```

Entities

Inside a DTD, you can declare an *entity*, which allows you to use an *entity reference* to substitute a series of characters for another character in an XML document—similar to macros.

General entities

A *general entity* is an entity that can substitute other characters inside the XML document. The declaration for a general entity uses the following format:

```
<!ENTITY name "replacement_characters">
```

We have already seen five general entity references, one for each of the characters <, >, &, ', and ". Each of these can be used inside an XML document to prevent the XML processor from interpreting the characters as markup. (Incidentally, you do not need to declare these in your DTD; they are always provided for you.)

Earlier, we provided an entity reference for the copyright character. We could declare such an entity in the DTD with the following:

```
<!ENTITY copyright "&#xA9;">
```

Again, we have tied the `©right;` entity to Unicode value 169 (or hexadecimal 0xA9), which is the circled-C (©) copyright character. You can then use the following in your XML document:

```
<copyright>
&copyright; 2001 by MyCompany, Inc.
</copyright>
```

There are a couple of restrictions to declaring entities:

- You cannot make circular references in the declarations. For example, the following is invalid:

  ```
  <!ENTITY entitya "&entityb; is really neat!">
  <!ENTITY entityb "&entitya; is also really neat!">
  ```

- You cannot substitute nondocument text in a DTD with a general entity reference. The general entity reference is resolved only in an XML document, not a DTD document. (If you wish to have an entity reference resolved in the DTD, you must instead use a *parameter entity reference*.)

Parameter entities

Parameter entity references appear only in DTDs and are replaced by their entity definitions in the DTD. All parameter entity references begin with a percent sign, which denotes that they cannot be used in an XML document—only in the DTD in which they are defined. Here is how to define a parameter entity:

```
<!ENTITY % name "replacement_characters">
```

Here are some examples using parameter entity references:

```
<!ENTITY % pcdata "(#PCDATA)">
<!ELEMENT authortitle %pcdata;>
```

As with general entity references, you can't make circular references in declarations. In addition, parameter entity references must be declared before they can be used.

External entities

XML allows you to declare an *external entity* with the following syntax:

```
<!ENTITY quotes SYSTEM
      "http://www.oreilly.com/stocks/quotes.xml">
```

This allows you to copy the XML content (located at the specified URI) into the current XML document using an external entity reference. For example:

```
<document>
   <heading>Current Stock Quotes</heading>
   &quotes;
</document>
```

This example copies the XML content located at the URI *http://www.oreilly.com/stocks/quotes.xml* into the document when it's run through the XML processor. As you might guess, this works quite well when dealing with dynamic data.

Unparsed entities

By the same token, you can use an *unparsed entity* to declare non-XML content in an XML document. For example, if you want to declare an outside image to be used inside an XML document, you can specify the following in the DTD:

```
<!ENTITY image1 SYSTEM
      "http://www.oreilly.com/ora.gif" NDATA GIF89a>
```

Note that we also specify the `NDATA` (notation data) keyword, which tells exactly what type of unparsed entity the XML processor is dealing with. You typically use an unparsed entity reference as the value of an element's attribute, one defined in the DTD with the type `ENTITY` or `ENTITIES`. Here is how you should use the unparsed entity declared previously:

```
<image src="image1"/>
```

Note that we did not use an ampersand (`&`) or a semicolon (`;`). These are only used with parsed entities.

Notations

Finally, *notations* are used in conjunction with unparsed entities. A notation declaration simply matches the value of an `NDATA` keyword (`GIF89a` in our example) with more specific information. Applications are free to use or ignore this information as they see fit:

```
<!NOTATION GIF89a SYSTEM "-//CompuServe//NOTATION
      Graphics Interchange Format 89a//EN">
```

Attribute Declarations in the DTD

Attributes for various XML elements must be specified in the DTD. You can specify each of the attributes with the <!ATTLIST> declaration, which uses the following form:

```
<!ATTLIST target_element attr_name attr_type default>
```

The <!ATTLIST> declaration consists of the target element name, the name of the attribute, its datatype, and any default value you want to give it.

Here are some examples of legal <!ATTLIST> declarations:

```
<!ATTLIST box length CDATA "0">
<!ATTLIST box width CDATA "0">
<!ATTLIST frame visible (true|false) "true">
<!ATTLIST person marital
     (single | married | divorced | widowed) #IMPLIED>
```

In these examples, the first keyword after ATTLIST declares the name of the target element (i.e., <box>, <frame>, <person>). This is followed by the name of the attribute (i.e., length, width, visible, marital). This, in turn, is generally followed by the datatype of the attribute and its default value.

Attribute modifiers

Let's look at the default value first. You can specify any default value allowed by the specified datatype. This value must appear as a quoted string. If a default value is not appropriate, you can specify one of the modifiers listed in the following table in its place.

Modifier	Description
#REQUIRED	The attribute value must be specified with the element.
#IMPLIED	The attribute value is unspecified, to be determined by the application.
#FIXED "*value*"	The attribute value is fixed and cannot be changed by the user.
"*value*"	The default value of the attribute.

With the #IMPLIED keyword, the value can be omitted from the XML document. The XML parser must notify the application, which can take whatever action it deems appropriate at that point. With the #FIXED keyword, you must specify the default value immediately afterwards:

```
<!ATTLIST date year CDATA #FIXED "2001">
```

Datatypes

The following table lists legal datatypes to use in a DTD.

Type	Description
CDATA	Character data
enumerated	A series of values from which only one can be chosen
ENTITY	An entity declared in the DTD

Type	Description
ENTITIES	Multiple whitespace-separated entities declared in the DTD
ID	A unique element identifier
IDREF	The value of a unique ID type attribute
IDREFS	Multiple whitespace-separated IDREFs of elements
NMTOKEN	An XML name token
NMTOKENS	Multiple whitespace-separated XML name tokens
NOTATION	A notation declared in the DTD

The CDATA keyword simply declares that any character data can appear, although it must adhere to the same rules as the PCDATA tag. Here are some examples of attribute declarations that use CDATA:

```
<!ATTLIST person name CDATA #REQUIRED>
<!ATTLIST person email CDATA #REQUIRED>
<!ATTLIST person company CDATA #FIXED "OReilly">
```

Here are two examples of enumerated datatypes where no keywords are specified. Instead, the possible values are simply listed:

```
<!ATTLIST person marital
   (single | married | divorced | widowed) #IMPLIED>
<!ATTLIST person sex (male | female) #REQUIRED>
```

The ID, IDREF, and IDREFS datatypes allow you to define attributes as IDs and ID references. An ID is simply an attribute whose value distinguishes the current element from all others in the current XML document. IDs are useful for applications to link to various sections of a document that contain an element with a uniquely tagged ID. IDREFs are attributes that reference other IDs. Consider the following XML document:

```
<?xml version="1.0" standalone="yes"?>
<!DOCTYPE sector SYSTEM sector.dtd>
<sector>
   <employee empid="e1013">Jack Russell</employee>
   <employee empid="e1014">Samuel Tessen</employee>
   <employee empid="e1015" boss="e1013">
      Terri White</employee>
   <employee empid="e1016" boss="e1014">
      Steve McAlister</employee>
</sector>
```

and its DTD:

```
<!ELEMENT sector (employee*)>
<!ELEMENT employee (#PCDATA)>
<!ATTLIST employee empid ID #REQUIRED>
<!ATTLIST employee boss IDREF #IMPLIED>
```

Here, all employees have their own identification numbers (e1013, e1014, etc.), which we define in the DTD with the ID keyword using the empid attribute. This attribute then forms an ID for each <employee> element; no two <employee> elements can have the same ID.

Attributes that only reference other elements use the IDREF datatype. In this case, the boss attribute is an IDREF because it uses only the values of other ID attributes as its values. IDs will come into play when we discuss XLink and XPointer.

The IDREFS datatype is used if you want the attribute to refer to more than one ID in its value. The IDs must be separated by whitespace. For example, adding this to the DTD:

```
<!ATTLIST employee managers IDREFS #REQUIRED>
```

allows you to legally use the XML:

```
<employee empid="e1016" boss="e1014"
          managers="e1014 e1013">
    Steve McAllister
</employee>
```

The NMTOKEN and NMTOKENS attributes declare XML name tokens. An *XML name token* is simply a legal XML name that consists of letters, digits, underscores, hyphens, and periods. It can contain a colon if it is part of a namespace. It may not contain whitespace; however, any of the permitted characters for an XML name can be the first character of an XML name token (e.g., .profile is a legal XML name token, but not a legal XML name). These datatypes are useful if you enumerate tokens of languages or other keyword sets that match these restrictions in the DTD.

The attribute types ENTITY and ENTITIES allow you to exploit an entity declared in the DTD. This includes unparsed entities. For example, you can link to an image as follows:

```
<!ELEMENT image EMPTY>
<!ATTLIST image src ENTITY #REQUIRED>
<!ENTITY chapterimage SYSTEM "chapimage.jpg" NDATA "jpg">
```

You can use the image as follows:

```
<image src="chapterimage">
```

The ENTITIES datatype allows multiple whitespace-separated references to entities, much like IDREFS and NMTOKENS allow multiple references to their datatypes.

The NOTATION keyword simply expects a notation that appears in the DTD with a <!NOTATION> declaration. Here, the player attribute of the <media> element can be either mpeg or jpeg:

```
<!NOTATION mpeg SYSTEM "mpegplay.exe">
<!NOTATION jpeg SYSTEM "netscape.exe">
<!ATTLIST media player
      NOTATION (mpeg | jpeg) #REQUIRED>
```

Note that you must enumerate each of the notations allowed in the attribute. For example, to dictate the possible values of the player attribute of the <media> element, use the following:

```
<!NOTATION mpeg SYSTEM "mpegplay.exe">
<!NOTATION jpeg SYSTEM "netscape.exe">
<!NOTATION mov SYSTEM "mplayer.exe">
```

```
<!NOTATION avi SYSTEM "mplayer.exe">
<!ATTLIST media player
      NOTATIONS (mpeg | jpeg | mov) #REQUIRED>
```

Note that according the rules of this DTD, the `<media>` element is not allowed to play AVI files. The NOTATION keyword is rarely used.

Finally, you can place all the ATTLIST entries for an element inside a single ATTLIST declaration, as long as you follow the rules of each datatype:

```
<!ATTLIST person
          name CDATA #REQUIRED
          number IDREF #REQUIRED
          company CDATA #FIXED "OReilly">
```

Included and Ignored Sections

Within a DTD, you can bundle together a group of declarations that should be ignored using the IGNORE directive:

```
<![IGNORE[
   DTD content to be ignored
]]>
```

Conversely, if you wish to ensure that certain declarations are included in your DTD, use the INCLUDE directive, which has a similar syntax:

```
<![INCLUDE[
   DTD content to be included
]]>
```

Why you would want to use either of these declarations is not obvious until you consider replacing the INCLUDE or IGNORE directives with a parameter entity reference that can be changed easily on the spot. For example, consider the following DTD:

```
<?xml version="1.0" encoding="iso-8859-1"?>
<![%book;[
   <!ELEMENT text (chapter+)>
]]>
<![%article;[
   <!ELEMENT text (section+)>
]]>
<!ELEMENT chapter (section+)>
<!ELEMENT section (p+)>
<!ELEMENT p (#PCDATA)>
```

Depending on the values of the entities book and article, the definition of the text element will be different:

- If book has the value INCLUDE and article has the value IGNORE, then the text element must include chapters (which in turn may contain sections that themselves include paragraphs).
- But if book has the value IGNORE and article has the value INCLUDE, then the text element must include sections.

When writing an XML document based on this DTD, you may write either a book or an article simply by properly defining `book` and `article` entities in the document's *internal subset.*

Internal subsets

You can place parts of your DTD declarations inside the `DOCTYPE` declaration of the XML document, as shown:

```
<!DOCTYPE boilerplate SYSTEM "generic-inc.dtd" [
   <!ENTITY corpname "Acme, Inc.">
]>
```

The region between brackets is called the DTD's internal subset. When a parser reads the DTD, the internal subset is read first, followed by the *external subset*, which is the file referenced by the `DOCTYPE` declaration.

There are restrictions on the complexity of the internal subset, as well as processing expectations that affect how you should structure it:

- Conditional sections (such as `INCLUDE` or `IGNORE`) are not permitted in an internal subset.
- Any parameter entity reference in the internal subset must expand to zero or more declarations. For example, specifying the following parameter entity reference is legal:

  ```
  %paradecl;
  ```

  as long as `%paradecl;` expands to the following:

  ```
  <!ELEMENT para CDATA>
  ```

  However, if you simply write the following in the internal subset, it is considered illegal because it does not expand to a whole declaration:

  ```
  <!ELEMENT para (%paracont;)>
  ```

Nonvalidating parsers aren't required to read the external subset and process its contents, but they are required to process any defaults and entity declarations in the internal subset. However, a parameter entity can change the meaning of those declarations in an unresolvable way. Therefore, a parser must stop processing the internal subset when it comes to the first external parameter entity reference that it does not process. If it's an internal reference, it can expand it, and if it chooses to fetch the entity, it can continue processing. If it does not process the entity's replacement, it must not process the attribute list or entity declarations in the internal subset.

Why use this? Since some entity declarations are often relevant only to a single document (for example, declarations of chapter entities or other content files), the internal subset is a good place to put them. Similarly, if a particular document needs to override or alter the DTD values it uses, you can place a new definition in the internal subset. Finally, in the event that an XML processor is nonvalidating (as we mentioned previously), the internal subset is the best place to put certain DTD-related information, such as the identification of ID and IDREF attributes, attribute defaults, and entity declarations.

The Extensible Stylesheet Language

The Extensible Stylesheet Language (XSL) is one of the most intricate specifications in the XML family. XSL can be broken into two parts: XSLT, which is used for transformations, and XSL Formatting Objects (XSL-FO). While XSLT is currently in widespread use, XSL-FO is still maturing; both, however, promise to be useful for any XML developer.

This section will provide you with a firm understanding of how XSL is meant to be used. For the very latest information on XSL, visit the home page for the W3C XSL working group at *http://www.w3.org/Style/XSL/*.

As we mentioned, XSL works by applying element-formatting rules that you define for each XML document it encounters. In reality, XSL simply transforms each XML document from one series of element types to another. For example, XSL can be used to apply HTML formatting to an XML document, which would transform it from:

```
<?xml version="1.0"?>
<OReilly:Book title="XML Comments">
 <OReilly:Chapter title="Working with XML">
  <OReilly:Image src="http://www.oreilly.com/1.gif"/>
  <OReilly:HeadA>Starting XML</OReilly:HeadA>
  <OReilly:Body>
    If you havent used XML, then ...
  </OReilly:Body>
 </OReilly:Chapter>
</OReilly:Book>
```

to the following HTML:

```
<HTML>
  <HEAD>
   <TITLE>XML Comments</TITLE>
  </HEAD>
  <BODY>
   <H1>Working with XML</H1>
   <img src="http://www.oreilly.com/1.gif"/>
   <H2>Starting XML</H2>
   <P>If you havent used XML, then ...</P>
  </BODY>
</HTML>
```

If you look carefully, you can see a predefined hierarchy that remains from the source content to the resulting content. To venture a guess, the <OReilly:Book> element probably maps to the <HTML>, <HEAD>, <TITLE>, and <BODY> elements in HTML. The <OReilly:Chapter> element maps to the HTML <H1> element, the <OReilly:Image> element maps to the <img> element, and so on.

This demonstrates an essential aspect of XML: each document contains a hierarchy of elements that can be organized in a tree-like fashion. (If the document uses a DTD, that hierarchy is well defined.) In the previous XML example, the <OReilly:Chapter> element is a leaf of the <OReilly:Book> element, while in the HTML document, the <BODY> and <HEAD> elements are leaves of the <HTML>

element. XSL's primary purpose is to apply formatting rules to a *source tree*, rendering its results to a *result tree*, as we've just done.

However, unlike other style sheet languages such as CSS, XSL makes it possible to transform the structure of the document. XSLT applies transformation rules to the document source and by changing the tree structure, produces a new document. It can also amalgamate several documents into one or even produce several documents starting from the same XML file.

Formatting Objects

One area of the XSL specification that is gaining steam is the idea of *formatting objects*. These objects serve as universal formatting tags that can be applied to virtually any arena, including both video and print. However, this (rather large) area of the specification is still in its infancy, so we will not discuss it further in this reference. For more information on formatting objects, see *http://www.w3.org/TR/XSL/*. The remainder of this section discusses XSL transformations.

XSLT Style Sheet Structure

The general order for elements in an XSL style sheet is as follows:

```
<xsl:stylesheet version="1.0"
    xmlns:xsl="http://www.w3.org/1999/XSL/Transform">
  <xsl:import/>
  <xsl:include/>
  <xsl:strip-space/>
  <xsl:preserve-space/>
  <xsl:output/>
  <xsl:key/>
  <xsl:decimal-format/>
  <xsl:namespace-alias/>
  <xsl:attribute-set>...</xsl:attribute-set>
  <xsl:variable>...</xsl:variable>
  <xsl:param>...</xsl:param>

  <xsl:template match="...">
    ...
  </xsl:template>

  <xsl:template name="...">
    ...
  </xsl:template>

</xsl:stylesheet>
```

Essentially, this ordering boils down to a few simple rules. First, all XSL stylesheets must be well-formed XML documents, and each <XSL> element must use the namespace specified by the xmlns declaration in the <stylesheet> element (commonly xsl:). Second, all XSL stylesheets must begin with the XSL root element tag, <xsl:stylesheet>, and close with the corresponding tag, </xsl:stylesheet>. Within the opening tag, the XSL namespace must be defined:

```
<xsl:stylesheet
   version="1.0"
   xmlns:xsl="http://www.w3.org/1999/XSL/Transform">
```

After the root element, you can import external stylesheets with `<xsl:import>` elements, which must always be first within the `<xsl:stylesheet>` element. Any other elements can then be used in any order and in multiple occurrences if needed.

Templates and Patterns

An XSLT style sheet transforms an XML document by applying *templates* for a given type of node. A template element looks like this:

```
<xsl:template match="pattern">
   ...
</xsl:template>
```

where *pattern* selects the type of node to be processed.

For example, say you want to write a template to transform a `<para>` node (for paragraph) into HTML. This template will be applied to all `<para>` elements. The tag at the beginning of the template will be:

```
<xsl:template match="para">
```

The body of the template often contains a mix of template instructions and text that should appear literally in the result, although neither are required. In the previous example, we want to wrap the contents of the `<para>` element in `<p>` and `</p>` HTML tags. Thus, the template would look like this:

```
<xsl:template match="para">
   <p><xsl:apply-templates/></p>
</xsl:template>
```

The `<xsl:apply-templates/>` element recursively applies all other templates from the style sheet against the `<para>` element (the current node) while this template is processing. Every style sheet has at least two templates that apply by default. The first default template processes text and attribute nodes and writes them literally in the document. The second default template is applied to elements and root nodes that have no associated namespace. In this case, no output is generated, but templates are applied recursively from the node in question.

Now that we have seen the principle of templates, we can look at a more complete example. Consider the following XML document:

```
<?xml version="1.0" encoding="iso-8859-1"?>

<!DOCTYPE text SYSTEM "example.dtd">

<chapter>
   <title>Sample text</title>
   <section title="First section">
      <para>This is the first section of the text.</para>
   </section>
   <section title="Second section">
      <para>This is the second section of the text.</para>
   </section>
</chapter>
```

To transform this into HTML, we use the following template:

```
<?xml version="1.0" encoding="iso-8859-1"?>
<xsl:stylesheet version="1.0"
   xmlns:xsl="http://www.w3.org/1999/XSL/Transform">

   <xsl:output method="html"/>

   <xsl:template match="chapter">
      <html>
         <head>
            <title><xsl:value-of select="title"/></title>
         </head>
         <body>
            <xsl:apply-templates/>
         </body>
      </html>
   </xsl:template>

   <xsl:template match="title">
      <center>
         <h1><xsl:apply-templates/></h1>
      </center>
   </xsl:template>

   <xsl:template match="section">
      <h3><xsl:value-of select="@title"/></h3>
      <xsl:apply-templates/>
   </xsl:template>

   <xsl:template match="para">
      <p><xsl:apply-templates/></p>
   </xsl:template>

</xsl:stylesheet>
```

Let's look at how this style sheet works. As processing begins, the current node is the document root (not to be confused with the `<chapter>` element, which is its only descendant), designated as `/` (like the root directory in a Unix filesystem). The XSLT processor searches the style sheet for a template with a matching pattern in any children of the root. Only the first template matches (`<xsl:template match="chapter">`). The first template is then applied to the `<chapter>` node, which becomes the current node.

The transformation then takes place: the `<html>`, `<head>`, `<title>`, and `<body>` elements are simply copied into the document because they are not XSL instructions. Between the tags `<head>` and `</head>`, the `<xsl:value-of select="title"/>` element copies the contents of the `<title>` element into the document. Finally, the `<xsl:apply-templates/>` element tells the XSL processor to apply the templates recursively and insert the result between the `<body>` and `</body>` tags.

This time through, the title and section templates are applied because their patterns match. The title template inserts the contents of the `<title>` element between the HTML `<center>` and `<h1>` tags, thus displaying the document title.

The section template works by using the <xsl:value-of select="@title"> element to recopy the contents of the current element's title attribute into the document produced. We can indicate in a pattern that we want to copy the value of an attribute by placing the at symbol (@) in front of its name.

The process continues recursively to produce the following HTML document:

```
<html>
   <head>
      <title>Sample text</title>
   </head>
   <body>
      <center>
         <h1>Sample text</h1>
      </center>
      <h3>First section</h3>
      <p>This is the first section of the text.</p>
      <h3>Second section</h3>
      <p>This is the second section of the text.</p>
   </body>
</html>
```

As you will see later, patterns are XPath expressions for locating nodes in an XML document. This example includes very basic patterns, and we have only scratched the surface of what can be done with templates. More information will be found in the section on XPath later in this chapter.

In addition, the <xsl:template> element has a &mode; attribute that can be used for conditional processing. An <xsl:template match="*pattern*" mode="*mode*"> template is tested only when it is called by an <xsl:apply-templates mode="*mode*"> element that matches its mode. This functionality can be used to change the processing applied to a node dynamically.

Parameters and Variables

To finish up with templates, we should discuss the name attribute. These templates are similar to functions and can be called explicitly with the <xsl:call-template name="*name*"/> element, where *name* matches the name of the template you want to invoke. When you call a template, you can pass it parameters. Let's assume we wrote a template to add a footer containing the date the document was last updated. We could call the template, passing it the date of the last update this way:

```
<xsl:call-template name="footer">
<xsl:with-param name="date" select="@lastupdate"/>
</xsl:call-template>
```

The call-template declares and uses the parameter this way:

```
<xsl:template name="footer">
   <xsl:param name="date">today</xsl:param>
   <hr/>
   <xsl:text>Last update: </xsl:text>
   <xsl:value-of select="$date"/>
</xsl:template>
```

The parameter is declared within the template with the `<xsl:param name="date">` element whose content (today) provides a default value. We can use this parameter inside the template by placing a dollar sign ($) in front of the name.

We can also declare variables using the `<xsl:variable name="*name*">` element, where the content of the element gives the variable its value. The variables are used like parameters by placing a dollar sign ($) in front of their names. Note that even though they are called variables, their values are constant and cannot be changed. A variable's visibility also depends on where it is declared. A variable that is declared directly as a child element of `<xsl:stylesheet>` can be used throughout the style sheet as a global variable. Conversely, when a variable is declared in the body of the template, it is visible only within that same template.

Style Sheet Import and Rules of Precedence

Style sheets may be imported using the `<xsl:import href= "*uri*">` element, where the `&href;` attribute indicates the path of the style sheet to be imported. Note that an `<xsl:import>` statement must be a direct child of the `<xsl:stylesheet>` element.

Imported style sheet templates have lower precedence than templates contained in the file into which they are incorporated. This means that if two templates compete for the processing of an element, the template of the original file takes precedence over the template of the imported file. Thus, imported templates can be overridden by redefining them in the original style sheet.

The rules of precedence can be changed in two ways:

- The `<xsl:apply-imports/>` element can be used to give imported templates precedence in the body of a template.
- The `priority="*level*"` attribute can be given in the opening `<xsl:template>` tag. Therefore, the level of precedence defined for the template is a real number. The larger the number, the more precedence the template has. A value of +1 ensures that the template has precedence over other templates for which no precedence has been defined (0 is the default). A value of –1 guarantees that any other unprioritized template has precedence. Priority values overrule import precedence.

Style sheets can also be included in an XSL file with the `<xsl:include href="*uri*"/>` element. The precedence of an included template is the same as that of the calling style sheet templates.

Loops and Tests

To process an entire list of elements at the same time, use the `<xsl:for-each>` loop. For example, the following template adds a table of contents to our example:

```
<xsl:template name="toc">
<xsl:for-each select="section">
<xsl:value-of select="@title"/>
<br/>
</xsl:for-each>
</xsl:template>
```

The body of this <xsl:for-each> loop processes all the <section> elements that are children of the current node. Within the loop, we output the value of each section's title attribute, followed by a line break.

XSL also defines elements that can be used for tests:

<xsl:if test="*expression*">
: The body of this element is executed only if the test expression is true.

<xsl:choose>
: This element allows for several possible conditions. It is comparable to switch in the C and Java languages. The <xsl:choose> element is illustrated as follows:

```
<xsl:choose>
   <xsl:when test="case-1">
      <!-- executed in case 1 -->
   </xsl:when>
   <xsl:when test="case-2">
      <!-- executed in case 2 -->
   </xsl:when>

   <xsl:otherwise>
      <!-- executed by default -->
   </xsl:otherwise>
</xsl:choose>
```

The body of the first <xsl:when> element whose test expression is true will be executed. The XSL processor then moves on to the instructions following the closing </xsl:choose> element tag, skipping the remaining tests. The <xsl:otherwise> element is optional; its body is executed only if none of the preceding elements were executed.

Numbering Elements

XSL provides a simple method for numbering elements with the <xsl:number> element. Let's assume we want to number the sections and paragraphs in a document. We can do this by adding the following code before displaying the section titles and the content of the paragraphs:

```
<xsl:number count="sect|para"
   level="multiple" format="1.1"/>
<xsl:text>- </xsl:text>
```

The result is:

```
1 - First section
1.1 - This is the first section of text.
2 - Second section
2.1 - This is the second section of text.
```

The count attribute decides which elements should be numbered. Elements must be separated by a |. The level attribute specifies the level of numbering and may take one of three string values: single, multiple, or any. single tells the processor to number only one level. In this case, paragraph numbers will not indicate the section number. multiple numbers several levels, meaning that the first part of the paragraph number is the section number in our previous example. any tells the processor to add numbering without regard to level. Here, the numbers of the sections and paragraphs are consecutive.

The format attribute indicates the style of numbering. Letters or numbers may be used, with a separator in between. The letters may be `A` or `a` (for alphabetical numbering in upper- or lowercase), `I` or `i` (for numbering in upper- or lowercase Roman numerals), or `1` (for numbering in Arabic numerals). For example, to number sections with Roman numerals and paragraphs with lowercase letters, use this format attribute:

```
format="I.a"
```

Output Method

An XSLT processor can be instructed to produce a specific type of output with the `<xsl:output/>` element. For example, `<xsl:output method="html"/>` causes the processor to execute certain transformations needed for the resulting document to be valid HTML. Specifically, it transforms empty tags. For example, the XML `<hr/>` tag is converted to the HTML `<hr>` tag (for horizontal rules) without a closing slash.

It is also possible to indicate an XML output method (`method="xml"`), where the XSLT processor adds the standard XML header (`<?xml version="1.0"?>`). It may seem strange to produce an XML document from another XML document, yet it is often helpful to convert a document from one DTD to a valid document for another DTD. Thus, XSLT is also a language for inter-DTD conversions.

Finally, you can specify a text output method (`method="text"`) to produce pure text. XSLT has built-in outputs for XML, HTML, and text, but some processors may support other output methods (sometimes identified by URLs).

We should point out that when you choose the HTML or XML output method, the processor may remove or rearrange whitespace in blocks of text (spaces, tabs, and carriage returns). However, there are several solutions for preserving whitespace. The first is to indicate the list of elements to be preserved in the `<xsl:preserve-space elements="`*`list`*`">` element. The second is to add the `&indent="no";` attribute to the `<xsl:output>` element to indicate that you do not want the resulting document to be indented. Note, however, that spaces are no longer preserved in `<xsl:text>` elements where content is written as-is in the resulting document. No indenting is produced for the text output method.

XSLT Elements

The following list is an enumeration of XSLT elements.

<xsl:apply-imports>

This styles the current node and each of its children using the imported style sheet rules, ignoring those in the style sheet that performed the import. Note that the rules don't apply to the current node's siblings or ancestors.

```
<xsl:apply-imports/>
```

<xsl:apply-templates>

This specifies that the immediate children (default) or the selected nodes of the source element should be processed further. For example:

```
<xsl:template match="section">
     <B><xsl:apply-templates/><B>
</xsl:template>
```

This example processes the children of the selected `<section>` element after applying a bold tag. The optional `select` attribute determines which nodes should be processed:

```
<xsl:template match="section">
   <HR>
   <xsl:apply-templates
      select="paragraph (@indent)//sidebar"/>
   <HR>
   <xsl:apply-templates
      select="paragraph (@indent)/quote"/>
   <HR>
</xsl:template>
```

This example processes only specific children of the selected `<section>` element. In this case, the first target is a `<sidebar>` element that is a descendant of a `<paragraph>` element that has defined an `indent` attribute. The second target is a `<quote>` element that is the direct child of a `<paragraph>` element that has defined an `indent` attribute. The optional `mode` attribute causes only templates with a matching `mode` to be applied.

```
<xsl:apply-templates
   [select="node-set-expression"]
   [mode="mode"]/>
```

<xsl:attribute>

This adds an attribute with the given name to an element in the result tree. Only one attribute with a particular name can be added to a specific element. The contents of the `<xsl:attribute>` element form the value of the attribute:

```
<xsl:element name="book">
<xsl:attribute name="title">Moby Dick</xsl:attribute>
<xsl:text>This is about a whale</xsl:text>
</xsl:element>
```

This creates the following element in the result tree:

```
<book title="Moby Dick">This is about a whale</book>
```

The optional `namespace` attribute specifies a namespace for the new attribute.

```
<xsl:attribute name="name"
   [namespace="namespace"]>
   ...
</xsl:attribute>
```

<xsl:attribute set>

This allows the naming of a collection of attributes that can be applied to elements.

The following example creates an attribute set for images and applies them with a template:

```
<xsl:attribute-set name="image">
   <xsl:attribute name="border">0</xsl:attribute>
   <xsl:attribute name="width">120</xsl:attribute>
   <xsl:attribute name="height">60</xsl:attribute>
</xsl:attribute-set>
<xsl:template match="image">
   <img src="{@url}" xsl:use-attribute-sets="image"/>
</xsl:template>
```

The use-attribute-sets option allows you to include a list of other attribute sets in the one being defined.

```
<xsl:attribute-set
   name="name"
   [use-attribute-sets="list"]/>
```

<xsl:call template>

This function invokes a template by its name. It is possible to specify parameters in the body of this element. The following example calls the template image while passing the parameters width and height:

```
<xsl:call-template name="image">
   <xsl:with-param name="width">120</xsl:with-param>
   <xsl:with-param name="height">60</xsl:with-param>
</xsl:call-template>
<xsl:call-template
   name="name">
   ...
</xsl:call-template>
```

<xsl:choose>

The <xsl:choose> element, in conjunction with the elements <xsl:when> and <xsl:otherwise>, offers the ability to perform multiple condition tests. For example:

```
<xsl:template match="chapter/title">
   <xsl:choose>
      <xsl:when test="[position()=1]">
         Start Here:
      </xsl:when>
      <xsl:otherwise>
         Then Read:
       </xsl:otherwise>
   </xsl:choose>
   <xsl:apply-templates/>
</xsl:template>
```

This example matches against each of the qualifying <title> elements, but it must test each <title> element to determine how to format it. Here, formatting depends on whether the element is first. The string `Start Here:` is applied before the first `<title>` element, and the string `Then Read:` is placed before the others.

```
<xsl:choose>
   ...
</xsl:choose>
```

<xsl:comment>

This inserts a comment into the XML document. For example:

```
<xsl:comment>English material below</xsl:comment>
```

is translated into a comment in the XML result tree when it is processed:

```
<!-- English material below -->
<xsl:comment>
   ...
</xsl:comment>
```

<xsl:copy>

This element copies the current node from the source document into the output document. This copies the node itself, as well as any namespace nodes the node possesses. However, it does not copy the node's content or attributes.

The `&use-attribute-sets;` attribute contains a whitespace-separated list with names of `<xsl:attribute-set>` elements. These attribute sets are merged, and all attributes in the merged set are added to the copied element. The `&use-attribute-sets;` attribute can only be used when the node copied is an element node.

```
<xsl:copy
   [use-attribute-sets="list"]>
   ...
</xsl:copy>
```

<xsl:copy-of>

The `<xsl:copy-of>` instruction inserts the result tree fragment identified by the `select` attribute into the output document. This copies not only the specific node or nodes identified by the expression, but also all those nodes' children, attributes, namespaces, and descendants. (This is how it differs from `xsl:copy`.) If the expression selects something other than a node set or a result tree fragment (e.g., a number), then the expression is converted to its string value, and the string is output.

```
<xsl:copy-of
   select="expression"/>
```

<xsl:decimal format>

The `<xsl:decimal-format>` element defines a pattern by which the XPath `format-number()` function can convert floating-point numbers into text strings. The attributes are specified as follows:

`name`
: The string by which the `format-number()` function identifies which `<xsl:decimal-format>` element to use. If this attribute is omitted, then the element establishes the default decimal format used by the `format-number()` function.

`decimal-separator`
: The character that separates the integer part from the fractional part in a floating-point number. This is a period (decimal point) in English and a comma in French. It may be something else again in other languages.

`grouping-separator`
: The character that separates groups of digits (e.g., the comma that separates every three digits in English).

`infinity`
: The string that represents IEEE 754 infinity; infinity by default.

`minus-sign`
: The character prefixed to negative numbers; a hyphen by default.

`NaN`
: The string that represents IEEE 754 Not a Number; NaN by default.

`percent`
: The character that represents a percent; % by default.

`per-mille`
: The character that represents a per mille; #x2030 by default.

`zero-digit`
: The character that represents zero in a format pattern; 0 by default.

`digit`
: The character that represents a digit in a format pattern; # by default.

`pattern-separator`
: The character that separates positive and negative subpatterns in a format pattern; a semicolon (;) by default.

```
<xsl:decimal-format
   [name ="name"]
   [decimal-separator = "char"]
   [grouping-separator = "char"]
   [infinity = "string"]
   [minus-sign = "char"]
   [NaN = "string"]
   [percent = "char"]
   [per-mille = "char"]
   [zero-digit = "char"]
   [digit = "char"]
   [pattern-separator = "char"]/>
```

<xsl:element> This inserts the element <name> into the result document. For example:

```
<xsl:element name="book">
   <xsl:element name="chapter">
      <xsl:text>The Opening of Pandoras Box</xsl:text>
   </xsl:element>
</xsl:element>
```

This creates the following in the result tree:

```
<book>
   <chapter>The Opening of Pandoras Box</chapter>
</book>
```

Elements without explicit namespaces use the default namespace of their current context. Also, you can create a namespace for the element yourself:

```
<xsl:element name="OReilly:Book"
   namespace="http://www.oreilly.com">
```

This employs the namespace associated with the URI *http://www.oreilly.com* with the element. If no namespaces are associated with the URI, it becomes the default namespace.

The `&use-attribute-sets;` attribute contains a whitespace-separated list with names of `<xsl:attribute-set>` elements. These attribute sets are merged, and all attributes in the merged set are added to the element.

```
<xsl:element
   name="name"
   [namespace="URI"]
   [use-attribute-sets="list"]>
   ...
</xsl:element>
```

<xsl:fallback> This element is used in conjunction with *extension elements* that aren't a part of XSLT 1.0. `<xsl:fallback>` defines a template to be invoked if the enclosing element is undefined. It's possible to test the availability of an element with `element-available()`.

```
<xsl:fallback> ... </xsl:fallback>
```

<xsl:for-each> The `<xsl:for-each>` directive allows you to select any number of nodes in an XML document that match the same expression given by `select`. For example, consider the following XML document:

```
<book>
   <chapter>
      <title>A Mystery Unfolds</title>
      <paragraph>
      It was a dark and stormy night...
      </paragraph>
   </chapter>
```

```
    <chapter>
      <title>A Sudden Visit</title>
      <paragraph>
      Marcus found himself sleeping...
      </paragraph>
    </chapter>
  </book>
```

Note there are two <chapter> siblings in the document. Let's assume we want to provide an HTML numbered list for each <title> element that is the direct child of a <chapter> element, which in turn has a <book> element as a parent. The following template performs the task:

```
<xsl:template match="book>
  <ol>
  <xsl:for-each select="chapter">
    <li><xsl:process select="title"></li>
  </xsl:for-each>
  </ol>
</xsl:template>
```

After formatting, here is what the result looks like:

```
<ol>
<li>A Mystery Unfolds</li>
<li>A Sudden Visit</li>
</ol>
```

The XSLT processor processes a <title> element in each <chapter> element that is the child of a <book> element. The result is a numbered list of chapters that could be used for a table of contents.

```
<xsl:for-each select="node-set-expression"/>
```

<xsl:if>

You can use the <xsl:if> conditional to select a specific element while inside a template. The <xsl:if> element uses the test attribute to determine whether to include the contents of an element. The test attribute takes an expression that tests for a specific element or attribute. For example:

```
<xsl:template match="chapter/title">
  <xsl:apply-templates/>
  <xsl:if test="not([last()])">, </xsl:if>
</xsl:template>
```

This template matches each qualifying <title> element but inserts commas only after those that are not the last <title> element. The result is a standard comma-separated list.

```
<xsl:if
  test="expression">
  ...
</xsl:if>
```

<xsl:import>

This specifies the URI of an XSL style sheet whose rules should be imported into this style sheet. The `import` statement must occur before any other elements in the style sheet. If a conflict arises between matching rules, rules in the XSL style sheet performing the import take precedence over rules in the imported style sheet. In addition, if more than one style sheet is imported into this document, the most recently imported style sheet takes precedence over stylesheets imported before it:

```
<xsl:import href="webpage.xsl"/>
```

This example imports the style sheet found in the *webpage.xsl* file.

```
<xsl:import href="address"/>
```

<xsl:include>

This specifies the name of an XSL style sheet that is to be included in the document. The `include` processing will replace the `<xsl:include>` statement with the contents of the file. Because the included document has been inserted in the referring style sheet, any included rules have the same preference as those in the referring style sheet (compare to `<xsl:import>`):

```
<xsl:include href="chapterFormats.xsl"/>
<xsl:include href="address"/>
```

<xsl:key>

Keys are comparable to identifiers in XML. This element is used in `<xsl:stylesheet>` to create a reference to elements specified by the pattern and expression values. For example:

```
<xsl:key name="chap" match="chapter" use="@title"/>
```

This element creates a key named `chap` to identify chapters by title. You can then reference a chapter with an XPath function such as:

```
key("chap", "The XSL Language")
<xsl:key name="name"
   match="pattern"
   use="expression"/>
```

<xsl:message>

The `<xsl:message>` instruction asks the XSLT processor to send a message to the user or calling program. Exactly what it does with those messages depends on the processor. One common use of `<xsl:message>` is to print debugging information.

If the `terminate` attribute is present and has the value yes, then the XSLT processor should halt after the message has been delivered and acted on.

```
<xsl:message [terminate="yes|no"]>
   ...
</xsl:message>
```

<xsl:namespace-alias>

The `<xsl:namespace-alias>` element declares that one namespace URI (*prefix1*) in the style sheet should be replaced by a different namespace URI (*prefix2*) in the result tree. Either attribute value can be set to `#default` to indicate that the nonprefixed default namespace is to be used.

```
<xsl:namespace-alias
   stylesheet-prefix="prefix1"
   result-prefix="prefix2"/>
```

<xsl:number>

This element inserts a formatted integer into the result tree. The value of this number can be determined by the attributes or generated by the XSLT processor. The attributes are described as follows:

`value`
: This attribute contains an XPath expression returning the number to be formatted. If necessary, the number is rounded to the nearest integer. Most commonly, the `value` attribute is omitted, in which case the number is calculated from the position of the current node in the source document. The position is calculated as specified by the `level`, `count`, and `from` attributes.

`count`
: This attribute contains a pattern that specifies which nodes should be counted at those levels. The default is to count all nodes of the same node type (element, text, attribute, etc.) and name as the current node.

`from`
: This attribute contains a pattern identifying the node from which counting starts; that is, it says which node is number 1.

`level`
: This attribute can be set to `single` (all preceding siblings of the ancestor of the current node that match the `count` pattern), `multiple` (for nested counting of each type of ancestor of the current node that match the `count` pattern), or `any` (count all nodes in the document that match the `count` pattern and precede the current node). The default is `single`.

`format`
: This attribute determines how the list will be numbered. Format tokens include:

- 1, 2, 3, 4, 5, 6
- 01, 02, 03, 04, 05, 06, 07, 08, 09, 10, 11, 12
- A, B, C, D...Z, AA, AB, AC...
- a, b, c, d...z, aa, ab, ac...
- i, ii, iii, iv, v, vi, vii, viii, ix, x, xi...
- I, II, III, IV, V, VI, VII, VIII, IX, X, XI, XII...

You can change the starting point as well. For instance, setting the format token to 5 would create the sequence 5, 6, 7, 8, 9.

`lang`
: This contains the RFC 1766 language code describing the language in which the number should be formatted (e.g., `en` or `fr`).

`letter-value`
: The default is `traditional`. However, you can set this to `alphabetic` to indicate that a format of I should start the sequence I, J, K, L, M, N rather than I, II, III, IV, V, VI.

`grouping-separator`
: This specifies the character that separates groups of digits. For instance, in English this is customarily the comma that separates every three digits, as in 2,987,667,342. In French a space is used instead so this number would be written as 2 987 667 342.

`grouping-size`
: This specifies the number of digits in each group. In most languages, including English, digits are divided into groups of three. However, a few languages use groups of four instead.

```
<xsl:number
   [value = "expression"]
   [count = "pattern"]
   [from = "pattern"]
   [level = "single|multiple|any"]
   [format = "letter/digit"]
   [lang = "langcode"]
   [letter-value = "alphabetic|traditional"]
   [grouping-separator = "char"]
   [grouping-size = "number"] />
```

<xsl:otherwise>

This attribute specifies the default case in an `<xsl:choose>` element. See the “<xsl:choose>” entry earlier in this reference section.

```
<xsl:otherwise>...</xsl:otherwise>
```

<xsl:output>

The `<xsl:output>` element helps determine the exact formatting of the XML document produced when the result tree is stored in a file, written onto a stream, or otherwise serialized into a sequence of bytes. It has no effect on the production of the result tree itself. The following attributes are defined:

`method`
: The default method is `xml`, which simply implies that the serialized output document will be a well-formed parsed entity or XML document. If `method` is set to `html`, or if the method attribute is not present and the root element of the output tree is `<html>`, then empty element tags such as `<br/>` are converted to `<br>` when output, and a variety of other changes are to attempt to generate HTML that is more compatible with existing browsers. The `text` method only outputs the contents of the text nodes in the output tree. It strips all markup. XSLT

processors are also allowed to recognize and support other values such as TeX or RTF.

`version`
: This contains a name token that identifies the version of the output method. In practice, this has no effect on the output.

`encoding`
: This contains the name of the encoding the outputter should use, such as `ISO-8859-1` or `UTF-16`.

`omit-xml-declaration`
: If this has the value yes, then no XML declaration is included. If it has the value no or is not present, then an XML declaration is included.

`standalone`
: This sets the value of the `standalone` attribute in the XML declaration. Like that attribute, it must have the value yes or no.

`doctype-public`
: This specifies the public identifier used in the document type declaration.

`doctype-system`
: This specifies the system identifier used in the document type declaration.

`cdata-section-elements`
: This is a whitespace-separated list of the qualified element names in the result tree whose contents should be emitted using a CDATA section rather than a character reference.

`indent`
: If this has the value yes, the processor is allowed (but not required) to insert extra whitespace to attempt to "pretty-print" the output tree. The default is no.

`media-type`
: This specifies the media type of the output, such as `text/html` or `text/xml`.

```
<xsl:output
   [method = "xml|html|text"]
   [version = "nmtoken"]
   [encoding = "encoding_name"]
   [omit-xml-declaration = "yes|no"]
   [standalone = "yes|no"]
   [doctype-public = "public_id"]
   [doctype-system = "system_id"]
   [cdata-section-elements = "element1 element2 ..."]
   [indent = "yes|no"]
   [media-type = "string"]/>
```

<xsl:param> An `<xsl:param>` element binds its contents to the specified name, which can be called from and included in a template. As a top-level element, <xsl:param> provides a default value used if the named parameter is not supplied when a style sheet is called. An <xsl:param> element may also appear inside an <xsl:template> element to receive the values of the parameters passed in with <xsl:with-param>, and to provide a default value good only inside that template for the case where a proper <xsl:with-param> element is not used. If the select attribute is included, its value becomes the default value of the parameter, in which case the value of the content should be empty.

```
<xsl:param
   name="name"
   [select="expression"]>
   ...
</xsl:param>
```

<xsl:preserve-space>

This declares one or more XML elements in which all whitespace located between the opening and closing tags is preserved; hence, the XML processor will not remove it. By default, whitespace is not removed from elements; <xsl:preserve-space> can override any elements declared in the <xsl:strip-space> directive:

```
<xsl:preserve-space elements="title"/>
<xsl:preserve-space
   elements="element1 element2 ..."/>
```

<xsl:processing-instruction>

The <xsl:processing-instruction> element inserts a processing instruction into the result tree. This element cannot be used to generate an XML declaration; use <xsl:output> for that. The name attribute specifies the target of the processing instruction.

```
<xsl:processing-instruction
   name="name">
   ...
<xsl:processing-instruction>
```

<xsl:sort>

The <xsl:sort> instruction appears as a child of either <xsl:apply-templates> or <xsl:for-each>. It changes the order of the context node list from document order to some other order, such as alphabetic. Multiple-key sorts (for example, sort by last name, then by first name, then by middle name) can be performed with multiple <xsl:sort> elements in descending order of importance of the keys. The following attributes are defined:

`select`
: This contains the key to sort by.

`data-type`
: By default, sorting is purely alphabetic. However, alphabetic sorting leads to strange results with numbers. For instance, 10, 100, and 1000 all sort before 2, 3, and 4. You can specify numeric sorting by setting the data-type attribute to number.

`lang`
: Sorting is language dependent. The language can be adjusted by setting the `lang` attribute to an RFC 1766 language code. The default language is system dependent.

`order`
: This specifies the order by which strings are sorted. The value can be either `descending` or `ascending`. The default is `ascending`.

`case-order`
: The `case-order` attribute can be set to `upper-first` or `lower-first` to specify whether uppercase letters sort before lowercase letters or vice versa. The default depends on the language.

```
<xsl:sort
   select = "expression"
   [data-type = "text|number"]
   [lang = "langcode"]
   [order = "ascending|descending"]
   [case-order = "upper-first|lower-first"]/>
```

<xsl:strip-space> This declares an XML element or list of elements in which all whitespace located between the opening and closing tags is insignificant and should be removed by the XSL processor:

```
<xsl:strip-space elements="title"/>
```

Note that this is not necessarily the same as the `xml:space="default"` attribute, which allows the XSL processor more freedom to decide how to handle whitespace.

```
<xsl:strip-space
   elements="element1 element2 ..."/>
```

<xsl:stylesheet> The `<xsl:stylesheet>` element is the root element for XSLT stylesheets. The contents of this element must first contain any `<xsl:import>` elements, followed by any other top-level elements in any order. `<xsl:stylesheet>` uses the following attributes:

`version`
: The version number of XSLT used by the style sheet.

`xmlns:xsl`
: This attribute contains a standard namespace declaration that maps the prefix `xsl` to the namespace URI *http://www.w3.org/1999/XSL/Transform*. The prefix can be changed if necessary. This attribute is technically optional, but de facto required.

`id`
: Any XML name that's unique within the style sheet and is of type `ID`.

`extension-element-prefixes`
: A whitespace-separated list of namespace prefixes used by extension elements in this document.

`exclude-result-prefixes`
A whitespace-separated list of namespace prefixes whose declarations should not be copied into the output document. If a namespace is needed in the output, it will be copied regardless.

```
<xsl:stylesheet
   version = "number"
   xmlns:xsl="http://www.w3.org/1999/XSL/Transform"
   [id = "id"]
   [extension-element-prefixes = "prefix1 prefix2..."]
   [exclude-result-prefixes = "prefixa prefixb..."]>
   ...
</xsl:stylesheet>
```

<xsl:template>

The `<xsl:template>` top-level element is the key to all of XSLT. The `match` attribute contains a pattern against which nodes are compared as they're processed. If the pattern is the best match for a node, then the contents are instantiated and inserted into the output tree. This element uses the following attributes:

`match`
A pattern against which nodes can be compared. This pattern is a location path that uses the abbreviated XPath syntax. Only the child and attribute axes may be used. The `//` separator may also be used.

`priority`
A number. In the event that more than one template matches a given node, the one that most specifically matches the node is chosen. If several templates match a node with the same level of specificity, then the template with the highest value of the `priority` attribute is instantiated. If several matching templates have equal priorities, then the last one in the style sheet is chosen (the processor may also throw an error in this situation).

`name`
A name by which this template can be invoked from an `<xsl:call-template>` element rather than by node matching.

`mode`
The template's mode. If the `<xsl:template>` element has a mode, then this template is only matched when the `mode` attribute of the calling instruction matches the value of this `mode` attribute.

```
<xsl:template
   [match = "pattern"]
   [priority = "number"]
   [name = "name"]
   [mode = "mode"]>
   ...
</xsl:template>
```

<xsl:text>

This inserts text verbatim into the document. For example:

```
<xsl:text>The price is $20.00.</xsl:text>
```

is inserted into the XML document as:

```
The price is $20.00.
```

XML special characters (such as & and <) included in the content of this element are escaped (i.e., replaced by character entities) in the output by default. The attribute disable-output-escaping can be set to yes to disable this behavior.

```
<xsl:text>
   [disable-output-escaping="yes|no"]>
   ...
</xsl:text>
```

<xsl:value-of>

This extracts a specific value from a source tree. The select attribute is a single pattern-matching expression that resolves to the value of a string, an element, or an attribute:

```
<xsl:template match="index">
   This index is <xsl:value-of select="@(type)">
   <xsl:apply-templates/>
</xsl:template>
```

The select attribute extracts the value of an element or attribute in the source tree and prints it verbatim in the result tree. XML special characters (such as & and <) included in the content of this element are escaped (i.e., replaced by character entities) in the output by default. The attribute disable-output-escaping can be set to yes to disable this behavior.

```
<xsl:value-of select="expression">
   [disable-output-escaping="yes|no"]/>
```

<xsl:variable>

The top-level <xsl:variable> element binds a name to a value of any type (string, number, node set, etc.). The value can then be dereferenced elsewhere in the style sheet using the form $*name* in attribute value templates. Once a variable name has been assigned a value, it cannot change. The select attribute is an optional expression that sets the value of the variable. If <xsl:variable> has a select attribute, then it must be an empty element.

```
<xsl:variable
   name="name"
   [select="expression"]>
   ...
</xsl:variable>
```

<xsl:when>

This is a conditional for testing in an <xsl:choose> element. See the "<xsl:choose>" entry earlier in this reference section.

```
<xsl:when
   test="expression">
   ...
</xsl:when>
```

<xsl:with-param> The `<xsl:with-param>` element passes a named parameter to a template that expects it. It can be a child either of `<xsl:apply-templates>` or `<xsl:call-template>`. The parameter is received in the `<xsl:template>` by an `<xsl:param>` element with the same name. If a template expects to receive a particular parameter and doesn't get it, then it can take the default from the value of the `<xsl:param>` element instead.

```
<xsl:with-param
   name="name"
   [select="expression"]>
   ...
</xsl:with-param>
```

XPath

XPath is a recommendation of the World Wide Web Consortium (W3C) for locating nodes in an XML document tree. XPath is not designed to be used alone but in conjunction with other tools, such as XSLT or XPointer. These tools use XPath intensively and extend it for their own needs through new functions and new basic types.

XPath provides a syntax for locating a node in an XML document. It takes its inspiration from the syntax used to denote paths in filesystems such as Unix. This node, often called the *context node*, depends on the context of the XPath expression. For example, the context of an XSLT expression found in an `<xsl:template match="para">` template will be the selected `<para>` element (recall that XSLT templates use XPath expressions). This node can be compared to a Unix shell's current directory.

Given our earlier XML examples, it is possible to write the following expressions:

`chapter`
: Selects the `<chapter>` element descendants of the context node

`chapter/para`
: Selects the `<para>` element descendants of the `<chapter>` element children of the context node

`../chapter`
: Selects the `<chapter>` element descendants of the parent of the context node

`./chapter`
: Selects the `<chapter>` element descendants of the context node

`*`
: Selects all element children of the context node

`*/para`
: Selects the <para> grandchildren of the context node

`.//para`
: Selects the <para> element descendants (children, children of children, etc.) of the context node

`/para`
: Selects the <para> element children of the document root element

In addition, XPath recognizes the at symbol (@) for selecting an attribute instead of an element. Thus the following expressions can be used to select an attribute:

`para/@id`
: Selects the `id` attribute of the <para> element descendants of the context node

`@*`
: Selects all the attributes in the context node

Paths can be combined using the | operator. For example, `intro | chapter` selects the <intro> and <chapter> elements of the children of the context node.

Certain functions can also be included in the path. The functions must return a node or set of nodes. The functions available are:

Function	Selection
`node( )`	Any node (of any type)
`text( )`	Text node
`comment( )`	Comment node
`processing-instruction( )`	Processing-instruction node
`id(`*`id`*`)`	Node whose unique identifier is *`id`*

The `id( )` function is especially helpful for locating a node by its unique identifier (recall that identifiers are attributes defined by the DTD). For example, we can write the expression `id("xml-ref")/title` to select the <title> element whose parent has the `xml-ref` identifier.

The preceding examples show that the analogy with file paths is rather limited. However, this syntax for writing an XPath expression is a simplification of the more complete XPath syntax where an axis precedes each step in the path.

Axes

Axes indicate the direction taken by the path. In the previous examples, the syntactic qualifiers such as `/` for root, `..` for parent, and `//` for descendant, are abbreviations that indicate the axis of the node search. These are some of the simple axes on which to search for a node.

XPath defines other search axes that are indicated by a prefix separated from the rest of the XPath expression (called *location-steps*) by a double colon. For example, to indicate that we require a para node to be the parent of the context node in the document, we could write the expression preceding::para. XPath defines 13 axes:

Axis	Selection
self	The context node itself (abbreviated as .)
child	The children of the context node (by default)
descendant	The descendants of the context node; a descendant is a child, or a child of a child, and so on
descendant-or-self	Same as the descendant, but also contains the context node (abbreviated as //)
parent	The parent of the context node (abbreviated as ..)
ancestor	The ancestors of the context node
ancestor-or-self	The same nodes as the ancestor, plus the context node
following-sibling	Siblings (having the same parent as the context node) in the same document that are after the context node
preceding-sibling	Siblings in the same document that are before the context node
following	All nodes in the same document that are after the context node
preceding	All nodes in the same document that are before the context node
attribute	The attributes of the context node (abbreviated as @)
namespace	The namespace nodes of the context node

It is possible to write the following expressions:

`ancestor::chapter`
: Selects the <chapter> elements that are ancestors of the context node

`following-sibling::para/@title`
: Selects the title attributes of <para> elements in siblings of the context node that follow it in document order

`id(xpath)/following::chapter/node()`
: Selects all the nodes in the <chapter> element following the element with the xpath identifier in document order

The result of an XPath expression is a node-set. It may be helpful to filter a node-set with predicates.

Predicates

A predicate is an expression in square brackets that filters a node-set. For example, we could write the following expressions:

`//chapter[1]`
: Selects the first <chapter> element in the document

`//chapter[@title=XPath]`
: Selects the <chapter> element in the document where the value of the title attribute is the string XPath

`//chapter[section]`
: Selects the <chapter> elements in the document with a <section> child

<para[last()]>
: Selects the last <para> element child of the context node

Note that a path in a predicate does not change the path preceding the predicate, but only filters it. Thus, the following expression:

```
/book/chapter[conclusion]
```

selects a <chapter> element that is a child of the <book> element at the root of the document with a descendant of type conclusion, but not a <conclusion> element itself.

There may be more than one predicate in an expression. The following expression:

```
/book/chapter[1]/section[2]
```

selects the second section of the first chapter. In addition, the order of the predicates matters. Thus, the following expressions are not the same:

chapter[example][2]
: Selects the second <chapter> that includes <example> elements

chapter[2][example]
: Selects the second <chapter> element if it includes at least one <example> element

An expression can include logical or comparison operators. The following operators are available:

Operator	Meaning
or	Logical or
and	Logical and
not()	Negation
= !=	Equal to and different from
< <=	Less than and less than or equal to
> >=	More than and more than or equal to

The character < must be entered as < in expressions. Parentheses may be used for grouping. For example:

chapter[@title = XPath]
: Selects <chapter> elements where the title attribute has the value XPath

chapter[position() < 3]
: Selects the first two <chapter> elements

chapter[position() != last()]
: Selects <chapter> elements that are not in the last position

chapter[section/@title=examples or subsection/@title= examples]
: Selects <chapter> elements that include <section> or <subsection> elements with the title attribute set to examples

XPath also defines operators that act on numbers. The numeric operators are +, -, *, div (division of real numbers), and mod (modulo).

Functions

In the previous examples we saw such XPath functions as `position()` and `not()`. XPath defines four basic types of functions that return: booleans (true or false), numbers (real numbers), strings (strings of characters), and node-sets. The functions are grouped based on the datatypes they act upon.

The following functions deal with node-sets (optional arguments are followed by a question mark):

`last()`
: Returns the total number of nodes of which the context node is a part

`position()`
: Returns a number that is the position of the context node (in document order or after sorting)

`count(`*node-set*`)`
: Returns the number of nodes contained in the specified *node-set*

`id(`*name*`)`
: Returns the node with the identifier *name*

`local-name([`*node-set*`])`
: Returns a string that is the name (without the namespace) of the first node in document order of the *node-set*, or the context-node, if the argument is omitted

`namespace-uri([`*node-set*`])`
: Returns a string that is the URI for the namespace of the first node in document order of the *node-set*, or the context node, if the argument is omitted

`name([`*node-set*`])`
: Returns a string that is the full name (with namespace) of the first node in document order of the *node-set*, or the context node, if the argument is omitted

The following functions deal with strings:

`string(`*object*`)`
: Converts its argument *object*, which can be of any type, to a string.

`concat(`*str1, str2, ...*`)`
: Returns the concatenation of its arguments.

`starts-with(`*str1, str2*`)`
: Returns true if the first argument string (*str1*) starts with the second argument string (*str2*).

`contains(`*str1, str2*`)`
: Returns true if the first argument string (*str1*) contains the second argument string (*str2*).

`substring-before (str1, str2)`
: Returns the substring of the first argument string (*str1*) that precedes the first occurrence of the second argument string (*str2*).

`substring-after (str1, str2)`
: Returns the substring of the first argument string (*str1*) that follows the first occurrence of the second argument string (*str2*).

`substring(str, num[, length])`
: Returns the substring of the first argument (*str*) starting at the position specified by the second argument (*num*) with the *length* specified in the third. If the third argument is not specified, the substring continues to the end of the string.

`string-length(str)`
: Returns the number of characters in the string.

`normalize-space(str)`
: Returns the argument string with whitespace normalized by stripping any leading and trailing whitespace and replacing sequences of whitespace characters by a single space.

`translate(str1, str2, str3)`
: Returns the first argument string (*str1*) with occurrences of characters in the second argument string (*str2*) replaced by the character at the corresponding position in the third argument string (*str3*).

The following functions deal with boolean operations:

`boolean(object)`
: Converts its argument (*object*), which can be of any type, to a boolean

`not(boolean)`
: Returns `true` if its argument evaluates as false

`true()`
: Returns `true`

`false()`
: Returns `false`

`lang(str)`
: Returns `true` if the language of the document (or the closest ancestor indicating the language) is the language passed in the argument (*str*)

The following functions deal with numbers:

`number([obj])`
: Converts its argument (*obj*), which can be of any type, to a number (using the context node if the argument is omitted).

`sum(node-set)`
: Returns the sum of the result of converting every node in the *node-set* to a number. If any node is not a number, the function returns `NaN` (not a number).

`floor(num)`
: Returns the largest integer that is not greater than the argument (*num*).

`ceiling(num)`
: Returns the smallest integer that is not less than the argument (*num*).

`round(num)`
: Returns the integer that is closest to the argument (*num*).

These functions can be used not only in XPath expressions, but in XSLT elements as well. For example, to count the number of sections in a text, we could add the following to a style sheet:

```
<xsl:text>The number of sections is </xsl:text>
<xsl:value-of select="count(//section)"/>
```

Additional XSLT Functions and Types

XSLT defines additional functionality for its own needs. One feature is a new datatype (in addition to the four datatypes defined by XPath): the *result tree fragment*. This datatype is comparable to a node-set, except that its nodes are in a tree rather than an unorganized collection. All the operations that are permitted for node-sets are permitted for tree fragments. However, you cannot use the `/`, `//`, or `[ ]` operators on result tree fragments.

XSLT also defines additional functions:

`document(obj[, node-set])`
: Returns a node-set that comprises the document whose URI (related to the second, optional argument) was passed as the first argument *obj*. If the second argument is omitted, the context node is used.

`key(str, obj)`
: Returns the node-set of the nodes keyed by *obj* in the key named *str*.

`format-number(num, str1[, str2])`
: Returns a string containing the formatted value of *num*, according to the format-pattern string in *str1* and the decimal-format string in *str2* (or the default decimal- format if there is no third argument).

`current()`
: Returns the current node.

`unparsed-entity-uri(str)`
: Returns the URI of the unparsed entity given by *str*.

`generate-id(node-set)`
: Generates a unique ID for the first node in the given *node-set*.

`system-property(str)`
: Returns the value of the system property passed as a string *str*. The system properties are: `xsl:version` (the version of XSLT implemented by the processor), `xsl:vendor` (a string identifying the vendor of the XSL processor), and `xsl:vendor-url` (the vendor's URL).

XPointer and XLink

The final pieces of XML we cover are XPointer and XLink. These are separate standards in the XML family dedicated to working with XML links. Before we delve into them, however, we should warn you that the standards described here are not final as of publication time.

It's important to remember that an XML link is only an *assertion* of a relationship between pieces of documents; how the link is actually presented to a user depends on a number of factors, including the application processing the XML document.

Unique Identifiers

To create a link, we must first have a labeling scheme for XML elements. One way to do this is to assign an identifier to specific elements we want to reference using an ID attribute:

```
<paragraph id="attack">
Suddenly the skies were filled with aircraft.
</paragraph>
```

You can think of IDs in XML documents as street addresses: they provide a unique identifier for an element within a document. However, just as there might be an identical address in a different city, an element in a different document might have the same ID. Consequently, you can tie together an ID with the document's URI, as shown here:

```
http://www.oreilly.com/documents/story.xml#attack
```

The combination of a document's URI and an element's ID should uniquely identify that element throughout the universe. Remember that an ID attribute does not need to be named `id`, as shown in the first example. You can name it anything you want, as long as you define it as an XML ID in the document's DTD. (However, using `id` is preferred in the event that the XML processor does not read the DTD.)

Should you give an ID to every element in your documents? No. Odds are that most elements will never be referenced. It's best to place IDs on items that a reader would want to refer to later, such as chapter and section divisions, as well as important items, such as term definitions.

ID References

The easiest way to refer to an ID attribute is with an ID reference, or IDREF. Consider this example:

```
<?xml version="1.0" standalone="yes"?>
<DOCTYPE document [
    <!ELEMENT document (employee*)>
    <!ELEMENT employee (#PCDATA)>
    <!ATTLIST employee empnumber ID #REQUIRED>
    <!ATTLIST employee boss IDREF #IMPLIED>
]>
<employee empnumber="emp123">Jay</employee>
```

```
<employee empnumber="emp124">Kay</employee>
<employee empnumber="emp125" boss="emp123">Frank</employee>
<employee empnumber="emp126" boss="emp124">Hank</employee>
```

As with ID attributes, an IDREF is typically declared in the DTD. However, if you're in an environment where the processor might not read the DTD, you should call your ID references IDREF.

The chief benefit of using an IDREF is that a validating parser can ensure that every one points to an actual element; unlike other forms of linking, an IDREF is guaranteed to refer to something within the current document.

As we mentioned earlier, the IDREF only asserts a relationship of some sort; the style sheet and the browser will determine what is to be done with it. If the referring element has some content, it might become a link to the target. But if the referring element is empty, the style sheet might instruct the browser to perform some other action.

As for the linking behavior, remember that in HTML a link can point to an entire document (which the browser will download and display, positioned at the top) or to a specific location in a document (which the browser will display, usually positioned with that point at the top of the screen). However, linking changes drastically in XML. What does it mean to have a link to an entire element, which might be a paragraph (or smaller) or an entire group of chapters? The XML application attempts some kind of guess, but the display is best controlled by the style sheet. For now, it's best to simply make a link as meaningful as you can.

XPointer

XPointer is designed to resolve the problem of locating an element or range of elements in an XML document. It is possible to do this in HTML if the element is referenced by an `<a name="`*`name`*`">` tag. Here, a link is made for the section of the document using the `<a href="`*`url#name`*`">` tag.

Fragment-identifier syntax

As we saw earlier, XML has this type of functionality through its unique identifiers. It is possible to locate an element with an identifier using a link such as the following:

```
document.xml#identifier
```

where *`identifier`* is a valid XPointer fragment identifier. However, this form is a simplification that is tolerated for compatibility with previous versions. The most common syntax for an XPointer fragment identifier is:

```
document.xml#xpointer(xpath)
```

Here *`xpath`* is an expression consistent with the XPath specification. It is the right thing to do in this case because it can be used to locate a node-set within a document. The link *`document.xml#identifier`* can be rewritten as:

```
document.xml#xpointer(id("identifier"))
```

There is a third possible form made up of a whole number separated by slashes. Each whole number selects an *n*th child from its predecessor in the expression.

Several fragment identifiers can be combined by placing them one after the other. For example:

```
document.xml#xpointer(...)xpointer(...)...
```

The application must evaluate the fragments, from left to right, and use the first valid fragment. This functionality is useful for two reasons:

- It offers several solutions, the first of which is based on suppositions that may prove to be false (and produce an error). For example, we can try to locate a fragment in a document using an identifier, then (if no ID was defined) using the attribute value with the name `id`. We would write the fragment:

  ```
  xpointer(id("conclusion"))xpointer(//*[@id=conclusion])
  ```

- It also allows for future specifications. If an XPointer application encounters an expression that does not begin with `xpointer`, it will simply ignore it and move on to the next expression.

As we mentioned earlier, the XPointer application is responsible for link rendering, but it is also responsible for error handling. If the link's URL is wrong or if the fragment identifier is not valid, it is up to the application to manage the situation (by displaying an error message, for example).

XPointer datatypes

Earlier we showed you how to locate an XML node within a document. XPointer goes even further by defining the *point*, *range*, and *position* (location) types:

Point
: Can precede or follow a node (point of type `node`) or a character (thus, a point of type `character`).

Range
: Is defined as the content of a document between two points (where the starting point cannot be located after the ending point within a document). A range cannot be reduced to a set of nodes and characters because it can include fragments of the former.

Position
: Is a generalized concept of the node. It can be a node, a point, or a range.

Equipped with these new datatypes, XPointer can set out to locate a resource in an XML document.

Manipulation of points, ranges, and positions

A range is defined using the `to` operator. This operator is enclosed in starting points (to the left) and ending points (to the right). The second point is calculated using the first point as a reference. For example, to make a range from the beginning of the first paragraph to the end of the last paragraph in a section where the ID is `XPointer`, you would write:

```
xpointer(id("XPointer")/para[1] to
id("XPointer")/para[last( )])
```

or:

```
xpointer(id("XPointer")/para[1] to
following-sibling::para[last( )])
```

A range defined this way may be compared with the selection a user can make in a document with a mouse.

Naturally, XPointer also has functions to manipulate points and ranges. The available functions are:

`string-range(`*`positions, string[, offset][, length]`*`)`
: This function can be used to search for strings in a document and return a set of positions where they appear. The first argument is an XPath expression—a set of positions where the search must take place. The second is the string being searched. To search for the string `XML` in `<chapter>` elements where the `title` attribute is `XPointer`, we would write the expression:

```
string-range(//chapter[@title=XPointer], "XML")
```

To index the word `XML` by pointing to the first occurrence of the word in an element such as `<para>`, use the following expression:

```
string-range(//para, "XML")[1]
```

This function takes two other optional arguments. The third argument, *`offset`*, is a number that indicates the first character to be included in the result range offset from the beginning of the string searched for. The fourth argument, *`length`*, gives the length of the result range. By default, *`offset`* has a value of 1, thus the result range begins before the first character in the string. *`length`* has a default value such that the result range covers the entire string searched.

`range(`*`positions`*`)`
: This function takes an XPath expression and returns a set of ranges (a location set) where each includes the positions passed as parameters. It can be used to convert a set of positions (which may be nodes) to a set comprising ranges only.

`range-inside(`*`positions`*`)`
: This function takes an XPath expression and returns a set of ranges (a location set) for each of the positions passed as arguments.

`start-point(`*`positions`*`)`
: This function takes an XPath expression and returns the starting point of the range for each of the positions passed as arguments. The result is a set of points.

`end-point(`*`positions`*`)`
: This function takes an XPath expression and returns the end point of the range for each of the positions passed as arguments. The result is a set of points.

`here()`
: This function is defined only within an XML document. It returns a unique position comprising the element containing the XPointer expression or the attribute that contains it.

`origin()`
: This function can be used only for links triggered by the user. It returns the element's position to the original link.

XLink

Now that we know about XPointer, let's take a look at some inline links:

```
<?xml version="1.0"?>
<simpledoc xmlns:xlink="http://www.w3.org/1999/xlink">
<title>An XLink Demonstration</title>
<section id="target-section">
   <para>This is a paragraph in the first section.</para>
   <para>More information about XLink can be found at
      <reference xlink:type="simple"
      xlink:href="http://www.w3.org">
      the W3C
      </reference>.
   </para>
</section>
<section id="origin-section">
   <para>
   This is a paragraph in the second section.
   </para>
   <para>
   You should go read
      <reference xlink:type="simple"
      xlink:href="#target-section">
      the first section
      </reference>
   first.
   </para>
</section>
</simpledoc>
```

The first link states that the text the W3C is linked to the URL *http://www.w3.org*. How does the browser know? Simple. An HTML browser knows that every `<a>` element is a link because the browser has to handle only one document type. In XML, you can make up your own element type names, so the browser needs some way of identifying links.

XLink provides the `&xlink:type;` attribute for link identification. A browser knows it has found a simple link when any element sets the `&xlink:type;` attribute to a value of `simple`. A simple link is like a link in HTML—one-way and beginning at the point in the document where it occurs. (In fact, HTML links can be recast as XLinks with minimal effort.) In other words, the content of the link element can be selected for traversal at the other end. Returning to the source document is left to the browser.

Once an XLink processor has found a simple link, it looks for other attributes that it knows:

`&xlink:href;`
: This attribute is deliberately named to be familiar to anyone who has used the Web before. Its value is the URI of the other end of the link; it can refer to an entire document or to a point or element within that document. If the target is in an XML document, the fragment part of the URI is an XPointer.

  This attribute must be specified, since without it, the link is meaningless. It is an error not to include it.

`&xlink:role;`
: This describes the nature of the object at the other end of the link. XLink doesn't predefine any roles; you might use a small set to distinguish different types of links in your documents, such as cross-references, additional reading, and contact information. A style sheet might take a different action (such as presenting the link in a different color) based on the role, but the application won't do anything automatically.

`&xlink:title;`
: A title for the resource at the other end of the link can be provided, identical to HTML's `title` attribute for the `<a>` element. A browser might display the title as a tool tip; an aural browser might read the title when the user pauses at the link before selecting it. A style sheet might also make use of the information, perhaps to build a list of references for a document.

`&xlink:show;`
: This attribute suggests what to do when the link is traversed. It can take the following values:

  `embed`
  : The content at the other end of the link should be retrieved and displayed where the link is. An example of this behavior in HTML is the `<img>` element, whose target is usually displayed within the document.

  `replace`
  : When the link is activated, the browser should replace the current view with a view of the resource targeted by the link. This is what happens with the `<a>` element in HTML: the new page replaces the current one.

  `new`
  : The browser should somehow create a new context, if possible, such as opening a new window.

  `other`
  : This value specifies behavior that isn't described by the other values. It is up to the application to determine how to display the link.

  `none`
  : This specifies no behavior.

  You do not need to give a value for this attribute. Remember that a link primarily *asserts* a relationship between data; behavior is best left to a style sheet. So unless the behavior is paramount (as it might be in some cases of `embed`), it is best not to use this attribute.

`&xlink:actuate;`
: The second of the behavioral attributes specifies when the link should be activated. It can take the following values:

  `onRequest`
  : The application waits until the user requests that the link be followed, as the `<a>` element in HTML does.

  `onLoad`
  : The link should be followed immediately when it is encountered by the application; this is what most HTML browsers do with `<img>` elements, unless the user has turned off image loading.

  `other`
  : The link is activated by other means, not specified by XLink. This is usually defined by other markup in the document.

  `none`
  : This indicates no information about the activation of the link and may be used when the link has no current meaningful target or action.

Building Extended Links

XLink has much more to offer, including links to multiple documents and links between disparate documents (where the XML document creating the links does not even contain any links).

Extended links

An XLink application recognizes extended links by the presence of an `&xlink:type="extended";` attribute that distinguishes it from a simple link (such as those used in HTML). An extended link may have semantic attributes (`&xlink:role;` and `&xlink:title;`) that function just as they do for a simple link.

In addition, an extended link may be one of four types as defined by its `xlink:type="`*`type`*`"` attribute:

`resource`
: Supplies the local resource for the link (generally the text used to materialize the link)

`locator`
: Supplies a URI for the remote document participating in the link

`arc`
: Supplies a description of the potential paths among the documents participating in the extended link

`title`
: Supplies a label for the link

Consider this example of an extended link supplying an XML bibliography:

```
<biblio xlink:type="extended">
   <text xlink:type="resource"
      xlink:role="text">XML Bibliography</text>
   <book xlink:type="locator" xlink:role="book"
      xlink:href="xmlgf.xml"
         xlink:title="XML Pocket Reference"/>
   <book xlink:type="locator" xlink:role="book"
      xlink:href="lxml.xml"
         xlink:title="Learning XML"/>
   <author xlink:type="locator" xlink:role="author"
      xlink:href="robert-eckstein.xml"
         xlink:title="Robert Eckstein"/>
   <author xlink:type="locator" xlink:role="author"
      xlink:href="erik-ray.xml"
         xlink:title="Erik Ray"/>
   <arc xlink:type="arc"/>
</biblio>
```

The extended link will probably be represented graphically as a menu with an entry for each element, except for the last one (`arc`), which has no graphical representation. However, the graphical representation of the link is the application's responsibility. Let's look at the role of each of the elements.

Resource elements

Resource elements, which include the &`xlink:type="resource"`; attribute, define a local resource that participates in a link. An extended link that includes a resource is considered inline because the file in which it is found participates in a link. A link that has no resource is called out-of-line.

XLink applications use the following attributes:

Attribute	Description
`xlink:type`	`resource` (fixed value)
`xlink:role`	Role of this resource in the link (used by arcs)
`xlink:title`	Text used by the XLink application to represent this resource

In our example, the <text> element supplies the text to be displayed to represent the link.

Locator elements

Locator elements have the &`xlink:type="locator"`; attribute and use a URI to point to a remote resource. XLink applications use the following locator attributes:

Attribute	Description
`xlink:type`	`locator` (fixed value)
`xlink:href`	URI of the resource pointed to
`xlink:role`	Role resource pointed to (used by arcs)
`xlink:title`	Text the XLink application uses to graphically represent the resource

In our example, we use two kinds of locators: those with a role of book that point to documents describing publications, and those with a role of author that point to a biography. Here, the role is important because it tells the XLink application the potential traversals among resources.

Arc elements

Arc elements have the &xlink:type="arc"; attribute and determine the potential traversals among resources, as well as the behavior of the XLink application during such traversals. Arc elements may be represented as arrows in a diagram, linking resources that participate in an extended link.

XLink applications use the following arc attributes:

Attribute	Description
xlink:type	arc (fixed value)
xlink:from	Indicates the role of the resource of the originating arc
xlink:to	Indicates the role of the resource of the destination arc
xlink:show	new, replace, embed, other, or none: tells the XLink application how to display the resource to which the arc is pointing
xlink:actuate	onLoad, onRequest, other, or none: tells the XLink application the circumstances under which the traversal is made
xlink:arcrole	Role of the arc
xlink:title	Text that may be used to represent the arc

The values of the &xlink:show; and &xlink:actuate; attributes have the same meaning as they do with simple links.

Let's go back to our example of the bibliography, where we could define the following arc:

```
<arc xlink:from="text" xlink:to="book"
   xlink:show="new" xlink:actuate="onRequest"/>
```

The arc creates a link from the text displayed by the navigator (a resource where the role is text) to the descriptive page from the book (remote resource where the role is book). The page must be displayed in a new window (&xlink:show="new";) when the user clicks the mouse button (&xlink:actuate="onRequest";).

To include the author's biography in the card for the book, we will define the following arc:

```
<arc xlink:from="book" xlink:to="author"
   xlink:show="embed" xlink:actuate="onLoad"/>
```

&xlink:show="embed"; indicates that the destination of the arc (the biography) must be included in the card for the book (origin of the arc) and that the destination must be included when the book page is loaded (&xlink:actuate="onLoad";).

Finally, we need to indicate that the absence of the &xlink:from; or &xlink:to; attribute indicates that the origin or destination of the arc corresponds to all the roles defined in the link. Thus, the arc in our example (<arc xlink:type="arc"/>) authorizes all the traversals possible among the resources of the extended link.

Title elements

Elements with a type of <title> tell the XLink application the title of the extended link. This element is needed when you want titles to have markers (for example, to put the text in bold) or if you want to provide titles in multiple languages. A <title> element must have the &xlink:type="title"; attribute.

As there may be a large number of attributes for the elements participating in an extended link, we recommend using the default values in the DTD. This eliminates the need to include fixed-value attributes for an element.

For example, because the &xlink:type; attribute of the <biblio> element always has extended as the value, we could declare the <biblio> element in the DTD as follows:

```
<!ELEMENT biblio (text, book+, author+, arc+)>
<!ATTLIST biblio xlink:type (extended) #FIXED "extended">
```

We would not need to indicate the type, and if we proceed the same way for the other elements in the extended link, we could write the following link:

```
<biblio>
   <text>XML Bibliography</text>
   <book xlink:href="xmlgf.xml"
      xlink:title="XML Pocket Reference"/>
   <book xlink:href="lxml.xml"
      xlink:title="Learning XML"/>
   <author xlink:href="robert-eckstein.xml"
      xlink:title="Robert Eckstein"/>
   <author xlink:href="erik-ray.xml"
      xlink:title="Erik Ray"/>
   <arc/>
</biblio>
```

By limiting ourselves to the strict minimum (attributes where the value is fixed do not need to be written), we gain readability.

Linkbases

As indicated earlier, an extended link with no resource-type element (local resource) is described as being out-of-line. Therefore, this type of link is not defined in any files to which it points. It may be convenient to regroup extended links in XML files called *linkbases*.

This raises the question of the location of such XML files. If we have no way of finding the linkbases associated with a given file (not provided in the W3C specification), we must indicate the URI in one of the files participating in the link. This is possible with the &xlink:role; attribute with the value &xlink:extended-linkset;.

The XLink application recognizes the attribute and can look for the associated linkbase where the URI is indicated by the &xlink:href; attribute. For example, to link the linkbase of the URI *linkbase.xml* to an XML file, we could use an element with the following syntax:

```
<linkbase>
<uri xlink:role="XLink:extended-linkset"
   xlink:href="linkbase.xml"/>
</linkbase>
```

We can indicate as many linkbases in a file as we want. A linkbase can itself contain a reference to another linkbase. It is up to the XLink application to manage circular references and limit the depth of the search for linkbases.

XBase

XBase is a W3C specification currently in development. XBase can be used to change the base of URIs in an XML document (which, by default, is the document's directory). XLink processors take XBase into consideration in order to manage URIs, using the `xml:base="URI"` attribute as follows:

```
<base xml:base="http://www.oreilly.com/bdl/"/>
<linkbase>
   <uri xlink:role="xlink:extended-linkset"
       xlink:href="linkbase.xml"/>
</linkbase>
```

The *linkbase.xml* linkbase is searched for in the *http://www. oreilly.com/bdl/* directory, not in the directory of the document where the request was made to load the linkbase.

Loading of the base continues in the nodes that descend from the node in which the base is defined (this is the same behavior as the `&xml:lang;` and `&xml:space;` attributes).

IV

JavaScript

11
JavaScript

JavaScript is a lightweight, object-based scripting language. The general-purpose core of the language has been embedded in Netscape Navigator, Microsoft Internet Explorer, and other web browsers and embellished for web programming with the addition of objects that represent the web browser window and its contents. This client-side version of JavaScript allows executable content to be included in web pages. With JavaScript, you can move beyond static HTML to write web pages that include programs that interact with the user, control the browser, and dynamically create HTML content. JavaScript is the most popular scripting language for client-side web development.

This chapter starts with coverage of the core JavaScript language, followed by material on client-side JavaScript, as used in web browsers. The final portion of this chapter is a quick-reference for the core and client-side JavaScript APIs. For complete coverage of JavaScript, we recommend *JavaScript: The Definitive Guide*, by David Flanagan (O'Reilly).

Versions of JavaScript

The name JavaScript is owned by Netscape. Microsoft's implementation of the language is officially known as JScript, but very few people actually make a distinction between JavaScript and JScript. Versions of JScript are more or less compatible with the equivalent versions of JavaScript, although JScript skipped a version and went directly from JavaScript 1.0 compatibility to JavaScript 1.2 compatibility.

JavaScript has been standardized by ECMA (the organization formerly known as the European Computer Manufacturers Association) and is on the fast track for standardization by the International Standards Organization (ISO). The relevant standards are ECMA-262 and, when standardized by ISO, ISO-16262. These standards define a language officially known as ECMAScript, which is approximately equivalent to JavaScript 1.1, although not all implementations of JavaScript currently conform to all details of the ECMA standard. The name ECMAScript is universally regarded as ugly and cumbersome and was chosen precisely for this reason: it favors neither Netscape's JavaScript nor Microsoft's JScript.

In this chapter, we universally use the term JavaScript to refer to the scripting language. Where certain functionality is implemented only by either Navigator or Internet Explorer, we've noted that fact. When necessary, we use the term ECMA-262 to refer to the standardized version of the language.

The following table specifies what versions of client-side JavaScript are supported by various versions of Netscape Navigator and Microsoft Internet Explorer:

Version	Navigator	Internet Explorer
2	JavaScript 1.0	
3	JavaScript 1.1	JavaScript 1.0
4	JavaScript 1.2; not fully ECMA-262 compliant prior to Version 4.5	JavaScript 1.2;EMCA-262 compliant

Syntax

JavaScript syntax is modeled on Java syntax; Java syntax, in turn, is modeled on C and C++ syntax. Therefore, C, C++, and Java programmers should find that JavaScript syntax is comfortably familiar.

Case-Sensitivity

JavaScript is a case-sensitive language. All keywords are in lowercase. All variables, function names, and other identifiers must be typed with a consistent capitalization.

Whitespace

JavaScript ignores whitespace between tokens. You may use spaces, tabs, and newlines to format and indent your code in a readable fashion.

Semicolons

JavaScript statements are terminated by semicolons. When a statement is followed by a newline, however, the terminating semicolon may be omitted. Note that this places a restriction on where you may legally break lines in your JavaScript programs: you may not break a statement across two lines if the first line can be a complete legal statement on its own.

Comments

JavaScript supports both C and C++ comments. Any amount of text, on one or more lines, between /* and */ is a comment, and is ignored by JavaScript. Also, any text between // and the end of the current line is a comment, and is ignored. Examples:

```
// This is a single-line, C++-style comment.
/*
```

```
 * This is a multi-line, C-style comment.
 * Here is the second line.
 */
/* Another comment. */ // This too.
```

Identifiers

Variable, function, and label names are JavaScript *identifiers*. Identifiers are composed of any number of letters and digits, and _ and $ characters. The first character of an identifier must not be a digit, however. The following are legal identifiers:

```
i
my_variable_name
v13
$str
```

Keywords

The following keywords are part of the JavaScript language, and have special meaning to the JavaScript interpreter. Therefore, they may not be used as identifiers.

```
break       do          if          switch      typeof
case        else        in          this        var
catch       false       instanceof  throw       void
continue    finally     new         true        while
default     for         null        try         with
delete      function    return
```

JavaScript also reserves the following words for possible future extensions. You may not use any of these words as identifiers either.

```
abstract    enum         int          short
boolean     export       interface    static
byte        extends      long         super
char        final        native       synchronized
class       float        package      throws
const       goto         private      transient
debugger    implements   protected    volatile
double      import       public
```

In addition, you should avoid creating variables that have the same name as global properties and methods: see the Global, Object, and Window reference pages. Within functions, do not use the identifier `arguments` as an argument name or local variable name.

Variables

Variables are declared and initialized with the var statement:

```
var i = 1+2+3;
var x = 3, message = 'hello world';
```


JavaScript

Variable declarations in top-level JavaScript code may be omitted, but they are required to declare local variables within the body of a function.

JavaScript variables are *untyped*: they can contain values of any data type.

Global variables in JavaScript are implemented as properties of a special Global object. Local variables within functions are implemented as properties of the Argument object for that function. Global variables are visible throughout a JavaScript program. Variables declared within a function are only visible within that function. Unlike C, C++, and Java, JavaScript does not have block-level scope: variables declared within the curly braces of a compound statement are not restricted to that block and are visible outside of it.

Data Types

JavaScript supports three primitive data types: numbers, booleans, and strings; and two compound data types: object and arrays. In addition, it defines specialized types of objects that represent functions, regular expressions, and dates.

Numbers

Numbers in JavaScript are represented in 64-bit floating-point format. JavaScript makes no distinction between integers and floating-point numbers. Numeric literals appear in JavaScript programs using the usual syntax: a sequence of digits, with an optional decimal point and an optional exponent. For example:

```
1
3.14
0001
6.02e23
```

Integers may also appear in hexadecimal notation. A hexadecimal literal begins with `0x`:

```
0xFF // The number 255 in hexadecimal
```

When a numeric operation overflows, it returns a special value that represents positive or negative infinity. When an operation underflows, it returns zero. When an operation such as taking the square root of a negative number yields an error or meaningless result, it returns the special value `NaN`, which represents a value that is not-a-number. Use the global function `isNaN()` to test for this value.

The Number object defines useful numeric constants. The Math object defines various mathematical functions such as `Math.sin()`, `Math.pow()`, and `Math.random()`.

Booleans

The boolean type has two possible values, represented by the JavaScript keywords `true` and `false`. These values represent truth or falsehood, on or off, yes or no, or anything else that can be represented with one bit of information.

Strings

A JavaScript string is a sequence of arbitrary letters, digits, and other characters from the 16-bit Unicode character set.

String literals appear in JavaScript programs between single or double quotes. One style of quotes may be nested within the other:

```
'testing'
"3.14"
'name="myform"'
"Wouldn't you prefer O'Reilly's book?"
```

When the backslash character (\) appears within a string literal, it changes, or escapes, the meaning of the character that follows it. The following table lists these special escape sequences:

Escape	Represents
`\b`	Backspace
`\f`	Form feed
`\n`	Newline
`\r`	Carriage return
`\t`	Tab
`\'`	Apostrophe or single quote that does not terminate the string
`\"`	Double-quote that does not terminate the string
`\\`	Single backslash character
`\x`*dd*	Character with Latin-1 encoding specified by two hexadecimal digits *dd*
`\u`*dddd*	Character with Unicode encoding specified by four hexadecimal digits *dddd*

The String class defines many methods that you can use to operate on strings. It also defines the `length` property, which specifies the number of characters in a string.

The addition (+) operator concatenates strings. The equality (==) operator compares two strings to see if they contain exactly the same sequences of characters. (This is compare-by-value, not compare-by-reference, as C, C++, or Java programmers might expect.) The inequality operator (`!=`) does the reverse. The relational operators(<, <=, >, and >=) compare strings using alphabetical order.

JavaScript strings are *immutable*, which means that there is no way to change the contents of a string. Methods that operate on strings typically return a modified copy of the string.

Objects

An *object* is a compound data type that contains any number of properties. Each property has a name and a value. The . operator is used to access a named property of an object. For example, you can read and write property values of an object o as follows:

```
o.x = 1;
o.y = 2;
o.total = o.x + o.y;
```

Object properties are not defined in advance as they are in C, C++, or Java; any object can be assigned any property. JavaScript objects are associative arrays: they associate arbitrary data values with arbitrary names. Because of this fact, object properties can also be accessed using array notation:

```
o["x"] = 1;
o["y"] = 2;
```

Objects are created with the `new` operator. You can create a new object with no properties as follows:

```
var o = new Object();
```

Typically, however, you use predefined constructors to create objects that are members of a class of objects and have suitable properties and methods automatically defined. For example, you can create a Date object that represents the current time with:

```
var now = new Date();
```

You can also define your own object classes and corresponding constructors; doing this is documented later in this section.

In JavaScript 1.2 and later, you can use object literal syntax to include objects literally in a program. An object literal is a comma-separated list of name/value pairs, contained within curly braces. For example:

```
var o = {x:1, y:2, total:3};
```

See Object (and Date) in the reference section.

Arrays

An array is a type of object that contains numbered values rather than named values. The [ ] operator is used to access the numbered values of an array:

```
a[0] = 1;
a[1] = a[0] + a[0];
```

The first element of a JavaScript array is element 0. Every array has a `length` property that specifies the number of elements in the array. The last element of an array is element `length-1`. Array elements can hold any type of value, including objects and other arrays, and the elements of an array need not all contain values of the same type.

You create an array with the `Array()` constructor:

```
var a = new Array();      // Empty array
var b = new Array(10);    // 10 elements
var c = new Array(1,2,3); // Elements 1,2,3
```

As of JavaScript 1.2, you can use array literal syntax to include arrays directly in a program. An array literal is a comma-separated list of values enclosed within square brackets. For example:

```
var a = [1,2,3];
var b = [1, true, [1,2], {x:1, y:2}, "Hello"];
```

See Array in the reference section for a number of useful array manipulation methods.

Functions and methods

A function is a piece of JavaScript code that is defined once and can be executed multiple times by a program. A function definition looks like this:

```
function sum(x, y) {
  return x + y;
}
```

Functions are invoked using the () operator and passing a list of argument values:

```
var total = sum(1,2);  // Total is now 3
```

In JavaScript 1.1, you can create functions using the Function() constructor:

```
var sum = new Function("x", "y", "return x+y;");
```

In JavaScript 1.2 and later, you can define functions using function literal syntax, which makes the Function() constructor obsolete:

```
var sum = function(x,y) { return x+y; }
```

When a function is assigned to a property of an object, it is called a *method* of that object. Within the body of a method, the keyword this refers to the object for which the function is a property.

Within the body of a function, the arguments[] array contains the complete set of arguments passed to the function. See Function and Arguments in the reference section.

null and undefined

There are two JavaScript values that are not of any of the types described above. The JavaScript keyword null is a special value that indicates "no value". If a variable contains null, you know that it does not contain a valid value of any other type. The other special value in JavaScript is the undefined value. This is the value of uninitialized variables and the value returned when you query object properties that do not exist. In JavaScript 1.5, there is a pre-defined global variable named undefined that holds this special undefined value. null and undefined serve similar purposes and the == operator considers them equal; if you need to distinguish between them, use the === operator.

Expressions and Operators

JavaScript expressions are formed by combining values (which may be literals, variables, object properties, array elements, or function invocations) using JavaScript operators. Parentheses can be used in an expression to group subexpressions and alter the default order of evaluation of the expression. Some examples:

```
1+2
total/n
sum(o.x, a[3])++
```

JavaScript defines a complete set of operators, most of which should be familiar to C, C++, and Java programmers. They are listed in the table below, and a brief explanation of the nonstandard operators follows. The P column specifies operator precedence and the A column specifies operator associativity: L means left-to-right associativity, and R means right-to-left associativity.

P	A	Operator	Operation performed
15	L	.	Access an object property
	L	[]	Access an array element
	L	()	Invoke a function
	R	new	Create new object
14	R	++	Pre-or-post increment (unary)
	R	--	Pre-or-post decrement (unary)
	R	-	Unary minus (negation)
	R	+	Unary plus (no-op)
	R	~	Bitwise complement (unary)
	R	!	Logical complement (unary)
	R	delete	Undefine a property (unary) (JS 1.2)
	R	typeof	Return data type (unary) (JS 1.1)
	R	void	Return undefined value (unary) (JS 1.1)
13	L	*, /, %	Multiplication, division, remainder
12	L	+, -	Add, subtract
	L	+	Concatenate strings
11	L	<<	Integer shift left
	L	>>	Shift right, sign-extension
	L	>>>	Shift right, zero extension
10	L	<, <=	Less than, less than or equal
	L	>, >=	Greater than, greater than or equal
	L	instanceof	Check object type (JS 1.5)
	L	in	Check whether property exists (JS 1.5)
9	L	==	Test for equality
	L	!=	Test for inequality
	L	===	Test for identity (JS 1.3)
	L	!==	Test for non-identity (JS 1.3)
8	L	&	Integer bitwise AND
7	L	^	Integer bitwise XOR
6	L	|	Integer bitwise OR
5	L	&&	Logical AND
4	L	||	Logical OR
3	R	?:	Conditional operator (3 operands)
2	R	=	Assignment
	R	*=, +=, -=, etc.	Assignment with operation
1	L	,	Multiple evaluation

JavaScript operators that are not familiar from C, C++, and Java are the following:

=== and !==
: The JavaScript equality operator, `==`, defines equality loosely and allows type conversions. For example, it considers the number `3` and the string `"3"` to be equal, it considers `false` to be equal to `0`, and it considers `null` and `undefined` to be equal. The identity operator, `===`, written with three equals signs, is stricter: it only evaluates to `true` if its operands are identical: i.e., if they have the same type and are equal. Similarly, the JavaScript non-identity operator `!==` is stricter than the non-equality `!=` operator.

String operators
: In JavaScript, the `+` operator concatenates string arguments in addition to adding numeric arguments. The `==` and `===` operators compare strings by value by testing to see whether they contain exactly the same characters. The relational operators `<`, `<=`, `>`, and `>=` compare strings based on alphabetical order.

`typeof`
: Return the type of the operand as a string. Evaluates to "number", "string", "boolean", "object", "function", or "undefined". Evaluates to "object" if the operand is `null`.

`instanceof`
: Evaluates to `true` if the object on the left was created with the constructor function (such as Date or RegExp) on the right.

`in`
: Evaluates to `true` if the object on the right has (or inherits) a property with the name on the left.

`delete`
: Deletes an object property. Note that this is not the same as simply setting the property to `null`. Evaluates to `false` if the property could not be deleted, or `true` otherwise.

`void`
: Ignores the operand and evaluates to `undefined`.

Statements

A JavaScript program is a sequence of JavaScript statements. Most JavaScript statements have the same syntax as the corresponding C, C++, and Java statements.

Expression statements

Every JavaScript expression can stand alone as a statement. Assignments, method calls, increments, and decrements are expression statements. For example:

```
s = "hello world";
x = Math.sqrt(4);
x++;
```

Compound statements

When a sequence of JavaScript statements is enclosed within curly braces, it counts as a single compound statement. For example, the body of a `while` loop consists of a single statement. If you want the loop to execute more than one statement, use a compound statement. This is a common technique with `if`, `for`, and other statements described later.

Empty statements

The empty statement is simply a semicolon by itself. It does nothing, and is occasionally useful for coding empty loop bodies.

Labeled statements

As of JavaScript 1.2, any statement can be labeled with a name. Labeled loops can then be used with the labeled versions of the `break` and `continue` statements:

```
label : statement
```

Alphabetical statement reference

The following paragraphs document all JavaScript statements, in alphabetical order.

`break`
: The `break` statement terminates execution of the innermost enclosing loop, or, in JavaScript 1.2 and later, the named loop:

```
break ;
break label ;
```

`case`
: `case` is not a true statement. Instead it is a keyword used to label statements within a JavaScript 1.2 or later `switch` statement:

```
case constant-expression :
    statements
    [ break ; ]
```

Because of the nature of the `switch` statement, a group of statements labeled by `case` should usually end with a `break` statement.

`continue`
: The `continue` statement restarts the innermost enclosing loop, or, in JavaScript 1.2 and later, restarts the named loop:

```
continue ;
continue label ;
```

`default`
: Like `case`, `default` is not a true statement, but instead a label that may appear within a JavaScript 1.2 or later `switch` statement:

```
default:
    statements
    [ break ; ]
```

`do/while`

The `do/while` loop repeatedly executes a statement while an expression is `true`. It is like the `while` loop, except that the loop condition appears (and is tested) at the bottom of the loop. This means that the body of the loop is executed at least once:

```
do
    statement
while ( expression ) ;
```

This statement was introduced in JavaScript 1.2. In Netscape 4, the `continue` statement does not work correctly within `do/while` loops.

`for`

The `for` statement is an easy-to-use loop that combines the initialization and increment expressions with the loop condition expression:

```
for (initialize ; test ; update )
    statement
```

The `for` loop repeatedly executes *`statement`* as long as the *`test`* expression is `true`. It evaluates the *`initialize`* expression once before starting the loop and evaluates the *`update`* expression at the end of each iteration.

`for/in`

The `for/in` statement loops through the properties of a specified object:

```
for (variable in object)
    statement
```

The `for/in` loop executes a statement once for each property of an object. Each time through the loop, it assigns the name of the current property to the specified variable. Some properties of pre-defined JavaScript objects are not enumerated by the `for/in` loop. User-defined properties are always enumerated.

`function`

The `function` statement defines a function in a JavaScript program:

```
function funcname ( args ) {
    statements
}
```

This statement defines a function named *`funcname`*, with a body that consists of the specified statement, and arguments as specified by *`args`*. *`args`* is a comma-separated list of zero or more argument names. These arguments can be used in the body of the function to refer to the parameter values passed to the function.

`if/else`

The `if` statement executes a statement if an expression is `true`:

```
if ( expression )
    statement
```

When an `else` clause is added, the statement executes a different statement if the expression is `false`:

```
if ( expression )
    statement
```

```
else
    statement2
```

Any else clause may be combined with a nested if/else statement to produce an else if statement:

```
if ( expression )
    statement
else if ( expression2 )
    statement2
else
    statement3
```

`return`
: The return statement causes the currently executing function to stop executing and return to its caller. If followed by an expression, the value of that expression is used as the function return value:

```
return ;
return expression ;
```

`switch`
: The switch statement is a multi-way branch. It evaluates an expression and then jumps to a statement that is labeled with a case clause that matches the value of the expression. If no matching case label is found, the switch statement jumps to the statement, if any, labeled with default:

```
switch ( expression ) {
    case constant-expression: statements
    [ case constant-expression: statements ]
    [ . . . ]
    default: statements
}
```

Each set of *statements* within a switch statement is usually terminated with a break or return so that execution does not fall through from one case to the next one.

`throw`
: The throw statement signals an error, or throws an exception. It causes program control to jump immediately to the nearest enclosing exception handler (see the try/catch/finally statement). The throw statement is defined by ECMAv3 and implemented in JavaScript 1.5. Its syntax is:

```
throw expression ;
```

The *expression* may evaluate to any type. (See Error in the reference section.)

`try/catch/finally`
: The try/catch/finally statement is JavaScript's exception handling mechanism. It is defined by ECMAv3 and implemented in JavaScript 1.5. Its syntax is:

```
try {
    statements
}
catch ( argument ) {
    statements
}
```

```
finally {
    statements
}
```

The try clause of this statement defines a block of code for which exceptions and errors are to be handled. If a program error occurs, or an exception is thrown within the try block, control jumps to the exception-handling statements in the catch clause. This clause includes a single argument or local variable; the value that was thrown by the exception is assigned to this local variable so that it can be referred to by the statements of the catch clause. The finally clause contains statements that are executed after the try or catch clauses, whether or not an exception is thrown. The catch and finally clauses are optional, but you cannot omit both of them.

JavaScript

var
: The var statement declares and optionally initializes one or more variables. Variable declaration is optional in top-level code, but is required to declare local variables within function bodies:

```
var name [ = value ] [ , name2 [ = value2 ] . . . ] ;
```

while
: The while statement is a basic loop. It repeatedly executes a statement while an expression is true:

```
while ( expression )
    statement ;
```

with
: The with statement adds an object to the scope chain, so that a statement is interpreted in the context of the object:

```
with ( object )
    statement ;
```

The with statement has some complex and nonintuitive side effects; its use is strongly discouraged.

Object-Oriented JavaScript

JavaScript objects are associative arrays that associate values with named properties. JavaScript provides a simple inheritance mechanism, and it is possible to define new classes of objects for use in your own programs. To define a new class, start by writing a constructor function. A constructor is like any other function, except it is invoked with the new operator and it uses the this keyword to refer to and initialize the newly created object. For example, here is a constructor to create objects of a new class named Point.

```
function Point(x,y) { // Constructor for Point
  this.x = x;  // Initialize X coordinate
  this.y = y;  // Initialize Y coordinate
}
```

Every JavaScript function used as a constructor has a property named prototype. This property refers to a special prototype object for the class of objects created by the constructor. Any properties you define on this prototype object are inherited by all objects created with the constructor function. The prototype object is commonly used to make methods available to all instances of a class. Defining a method named toString allows instances of your class to be converted to strings. For example:

```
// Define function literals and assign them
// to properties of the prototype object.
Point.prototype.distanceTo = function(that) {
  var dx = this.x - that.x;
  var dy = this.y - that.y;
  return Math.sqrt(dx*dx + dy*dy);
}
Point.prototype.toString = function () {
  return '(' + this.x + ',' + this.y + ')';
}
```

If you want to define static (or class) methods or properties, you can assign them directly to the constructor function, rather than to the prototype object. For example:

```
// Define a commonly used Point constant
Point.ORIGIN = new Point(0,0);
```

The preceding code fragments define a simple Point class that we can use with code like this:

```
// Call constructor to create a new Point object
var p = new Point(3,4);
// Invoke a method of the object, using a static
// property as the argument.
var d = p.distanceTo(Point.ORIGIN);
// Adding the object to a string implicitly
// invokes toString().
var msg = "Distance to " + p + " is " + d;
```

Regular Expressions

JavaScript supports regular expressions for pattern matching with the same syntax as the Perl programming language. JavaScript 1.2 supports Perl 4 regular expressions, and JavaScript 1.5 adds supports for some of the additional features of Perl 5 regular expressions. A regular expression is specified literally in a JavaScript program as a sequence of characters within slash (/) characters, optionally followed by one or more of the modifier characters g (global search), i (case-insensitive search), and m (multi-line mode; a JavaScript 1.5 feature). In addition to this literal syntax, RegExp objects can be created with the RegExp() constructor, which accepts the pattern and modifier characters as string arguments, without the slash characters.

A full explanation of regular expression syntax is beyond the scope of this chapter, but the tables in the following subsections offer brief syntax summaries.

Literal characters

Letters, numbers, and most other characters are literals in a regular expression: they simply match themselves. As we'll see in the sections that follow, however, there are a number of punctuation characters and escape sequences (beginning with \) that have special meanings. The simplest of these escape sequences provide alternative ways of representing literal characters.

Character	Meaning
\n, \r, \t	Match literal newline, carriage return, tab
\\, \/, *, \+, \?, etc.	Match a punctuation character literally, ignoring or escaping its special meaning
\x*nn*	The character with hexadecimal encoding *nn*
\u*xxxx*	The Unicode character with hexadecimal encoding *xxxx*

Character classes

Regular expression syntax uses square brackets to represent character sets or classes in a pattern. In addition, escape sequences define certain commonly-used character classes, as shown in the following table.

Character	Meaning
[...]	Match any one character between brackets
[^...]	Match any one character not between brackets
.	Match any character other than newline
\w, \W	Match any word/non-word character
\s, \S	Match any whitespace/non-whitespace
\d, \D	Match any digit/non-digit

Repetition

The following table shows regular expression syntax that controls the number of times that a match may be repeated.

Character	Meaning
?	Optional term; match zero or one time
+	Match previous term one or more times
*	Match previous term zero or more times
{*n*}	Match previous term exactly *n* times
{*n*,}	Match previous term *n* or more times
{*n*,*m*}	Match at least *n* but no more than *m* times

In JavaScript 1.5, any of the repetition characters may be followed by a question mark to make them non-greedy, which means they match as few repetitions as possible while still allowing the complete pattern to match.

Grouping and alternation

Regular expressions use parentheses to group subexpressions, just as mathematical expressions do. Parentheses are useful, for example, to allow a repetition character to be applied to an entire subexpression. They are also useful with the | character, which is used to separate alternatives. Parenthesized groups have a special behavior: when a pattern match is found, the text that matches each group is saved and can be referred to by group number. The following table summarizes this syntax.

Character	Meaning
a | *b*	Match either *a* or *b*
(*sub*)	Group subexpression *sub* into a single term, and remember the text that it matched
(?:*sub*)	Group subexpression *sub* but do not number the group or remember the text it matches (JS 1.5)
n	Match exactly the same characters that were matched by group number *n*
$*n*	In replacement strings, substitute the text that matched the *n*th subexpression

Anchoring match position

An *anchor* in a regular expression matches a position in a string (such as the beginning or the end of the string) without matching any of the characters of a string. It can be used to anchor a match to a position.

Character	Meaning
^, $	Require match at beginning/end of a string, or in multiline mode, beginning/end of a line
\b, \B	Require match at a word boundary/non-boundary
(?=*p*)	Look-ahead assertion: require that the following characters match the pattern *p*, but do not include them in the match (JS 1.5)
(?!*p*)	Negative look-ahead assertion: require that the following characters do not match the pattern *p* (JS 1.5)

Versions of JavaScript

Netscape has defined numerous versions of JavaScript. Microsoft has released more-or-less compatible versions under the name "JScript," and the ECMA standards body has released three versions of a JavaScript standard named "ECMAScript". The following paragraphs describe these various versions, and explain how they relate to each other. Each entry in the reference section contains availability information that documents the version of JavaScript in which a feature was introduced.

JavaScript 1.0
: The original version of the language. It was buggy and is now essentially obsolete. Implemented by Netscape 2.

JavaScript 1.1
: Introduced a true Array object; most serious bugs resolved. Implemented by Netscape 3.

JavaScript 1.2
: Introduced the `switch` statement, regular expressions, and a number of other features. Almost compliant with ECMA v1, but has some incompatibilities. Implemented by Netscape 4.

JavaScript 1.3
: Fixed incompatibilities of JavaScript 1.2. Compliant with ECMA v1. Implemented by Netscape 4.5.

JavaScript 1.4
: Only implemented in Netscape server products.

JavaScript 1.5
: Introduced exception handling. Compliant with ECMA v3. Implemented by Mozilla and Netscape 6.

JScript 1.0
: Roughly equivalent to JavaScript 1.0. Implemented by early releases of IE 3.

JScript 2.0
: Roughly equivalent to JavaScript 1.1. Implemented by later releases of IE 3.

JScript 3.0
: Roughly equivalent to JavaScript 1.3. Compliant with ECMA v1. Implemented by IE 4.

JScript 4.0
: Not implemented by any web browser.

JScript 5.0
: Supported exception handling; partial ECMA v3 compliance. Implemented by IE 5.

JScript 5.5
: Roughly equivalent to JavaScript 1.5. Fully compliant with ECMA v3. Implemented by IE 5.5 and IE 6.

ECMA v1
: The first standard version of the language. Standardized the basic features of JavaScript 1.1 and added a few new features. Did not standardize the `switch` statement or regular expression support. Conformant implementations are JavaScript 1.3 and JScript 3.0.

ECMA v2
: A maintenance release of the standard that included clarifications but defined no new features.

ECMA v3
: Standardized the `switch` statement, regular expressions, and exception handling. Conformant implementations are JavaScript 1.5 and JScript 5.5.

Client-Side JavaScript

Client-side JavaScript is the name given to JavaScript code that is embedded within an HTML file and executed by a web browser. In addition to the core objects described in the previous section, client-side JavaScript code has access to a number of other objects that represent the web browser, the document displayed in the browser, and the contents of that document. Client-side JavaScript programs are usually event-based, which means that JavaScript *event handlers* are executed in response to user interactions with the browser and the document. The client-side JavaScript scripting framework is powerful enough to open substantial security holes in web browsers. For this reason, web browsers typically restrict the actions of client-side scripts. This section starts by explaining how JavaScript code is embedded in HTML files, then goes on to introduce the client-side JavaScript objects, JavaScript events and event handling, and JavaScript security restrictions.

JavaScript in HTML

JavaScript code may be embedded in HTML files in the form of scripts, event handlers and URLs, as detailed below.

The <script> tag

Most JavaScript code appears in HTML files between a `<script>` tag and a `</script>` tag. For example:

```
<script>
document.write("The time is: " + new Date());
</script>
```

In JavaScript 1.1 and later you can use the `src` attribute of the `<script>` tag to specify the URL of an external script to be loaded and executed. Files of JavaScript code typically have a *.js* extension. Note that the `</script>` tag is still required when this attribute is used:

```
<script src="library.js"></script>
```

HTML allows scripts to be written in languages other than JavaScript, and some browsers, such as Internet Explorer, support languages such as VBScript. You can use the `language` attribute to specify what language a script is written in. This attribute defaults to "`JavaScript`" in all browsers, so you do not usually have to set it. You can also use attribute values such as "JavaScript1.3" and "JavaScript1.5" to specify the version of JavaScript your code uses. Browsers that do not support the specified version of the language simply ignore the script.

HTML 4 doesn'tt actually recognize the `language` attribute of the `<script>` tag. Instead, the official way to specify the language a script is written in is with the type attribute. For JavaScript, set this attribute to the MIME type "text/javascript":

```
<script src="functions.js"
        language="JavaScript1.5"
        type="text/javascript"></script>
```

Event handlers

JavaScript code may also appear as the value of an event handler attribute of an HTML tag. Event handler attribute names always begin with "on". The code specified by one of these attributes is executed when the named event occurs. For example, the following HTML creates a button, and the `onclick` attribute specifies an event handler that displays an alert (a dialog box) when the user clicks the button:

```
<input type="button" value="Press Me"
       onclick="alert('Hello World!');">
```

A list of other available event handler attributes is included later in this section.

JavaScript URLs

JavaScript code may appear in a URL that uses the special `javascript:` pseudo-protocol. The content of such a URL is determined by evaluating the JavaScript code and converting the resulting value to a string. If you want to use a JavaScript URL to execute JavaScript code without returning any document content that would overwrite the current document, use the `void` operator:

```
<form action="javascript:void validate()">
```

The Window Object

The Window object represents a web browser window. In client-side JavaScript, the Window object is the global object that defines all top-level properties and methods. The properties and methods of the Window object are therefore global properties and global functions and you can refer to them by their property names without any object prefix. One of the properties of the Window object is named `window` and refers back to the Window object itself:

```
window        // The global Window object
window.status // The status property of the window
status        // Or omit the object prefix
```

See the Window object in the reference section for a full list of its properties and methods. The following sections summarize the most important of these properties and methods and demonstrate key client-side programming techniques using the Window object. Note that the most important property of the Window object is `document`, which refers to the Document object that describes the document displayed by the browser window. The Document object is described in a section of its own following these window-related subsections.

Simple dialog boxes

Three methods allow you to display simple dialog boxes to the user. `alert()` lets you display a message to the user, `confirm()` lets you ask the user a yes-or-no question, and `prompt()` lets you ask the user to enter a single line of text. For example:

```
alert("Welcome to my home page!");
if (confirm("Do you want to play?")) {
    var n = prompt("Enter your name");
}
```

The status line

Most web browser include a status line at the bottom of the window that is used to display the destination of links and other information. You can specify text to appear in the status line with the status property. The text you set on this property appears in the status area until you or the browser overwrites it with some new value. You can also set defaultStatus to specify text to appear by default when the browser is not displaying any other information in the status line. Here is an HTML hyperlink that uses JavaScript in an event handler to set the status text to something other than the URL of the link:

```
<a href="help.html"
   onmouseover="status='Help'; return true;">
Help</a>
```

Timers

Client-side JavaScript uses event handlers to specify code to be run when a specific event occurs. You can also use timers to specify code to be run when a specific number of milliseconds has elapsed. To run a string of JavaScript code after a specified amount of time, call the setTimeout() method, passing the string of code and the number of milliseconds. If you want to run a string of code repeatedly, use setInterval() to specify the code to run and the number of milliseconds between invocations. Both functions return a value that you can pass to clearTimeout() or clearInterval(), respectively, to cancel the pending execution of code. For example:

```
var count = 0;
// Update status line every second
var timer = setInterval("status=++count",1000);
// But stop updating after 5 seconds;
setTimeout("clearInterval(timer)", 5000);
```

System information

The navigator and screen properties of the Window object refer to the Navigator and Screen objects, which themselves define properties that contain system information, such as the name and version of the web browser, the operating system it is running on, and the resolution of the user's screen. See Navigator and Screen in the reference section for details. The Navigator object is commonly used when writing code specific to a particular web browser or web browser version:

```
if (navigator.appName == "Netscape" &&
    parseInt(navigator.appVersion) == 4) {
  // Code for Netscape 4 goes here.
}
```

Browser navigation

The location property of the Window object refers to the contents of the browser's location bar (the field that you type URLs into). Reading the value of this property gives you the URL that is currently being displayed. More importantly, setting the location property to a new URL tells the browser to load and display the document referred to by that URL:

```
// In old browsers, load a different page
if (parseInt(navigator.appVersion) <= 4)
    location = "staticpage.html";
```

Note that any script or event handler that sets the location property of its own window (we'll discuss multiple windows and multiple frames later in this section) is overwritten when the new document is loaded and will not continue running!

Although the location property can be queried and set as if it were a string, it actually refers to a Location object. The Location object has properties that allow you to query and set individual portions of the currently displayed URL:

```
// Get the substring of the URL following ?
var query = location.search.substring(1);
// Scroll to a named portion of the document
location.hash = "#top";
```

In addition, the reload() method makes the browser reload the currently displayed URL.

The history property of the Window object refers to the History object for the browser window. This object defines methods that allow you to move the browser backward and forward through its browsing history, just as the user can with the browser's **Back** and **Forward** buttons:

```
history.back();    // Go back once
history.forward(); // Go forward
history.go(-3);    // Go back three times
```

Window control

The Window object defines methods to move, resize, and scroll windows, and methods to give keyboard focus to and take focus away from windows. For example:

```
// Automatically scroll 10 pixels a second
setInterval("scrollBy(0,1)", 100);
```

See moveTo(), moveBy(), resizeTo(), resizeBy(), scrollTo() scrollBy(), focus() and blur() in the Window object entry of the reference section for more information.

More important than these methods that manipulate an existing window are the open() method that creates a new browser window and the close() method that closes a script-created window. The open() method takes three arguments. The first is the URL to be displayed in the new window. The second is an optional name for the window. If a window by that name already exists, it is reused and no new window is created. The third argument is an optional string that specifies the size of the new window and the features, or chrome, that it should display. For example:

```
// Open a new window
w = open("new.html", "newwin", // URL and name
         "width=400,height=300," + // size
         "location,menubar," +     // chrome
         "resizable,scrollbars,status,toolbar");
// And close that new window
w.close();
```

Note that most browsers only allow scripts to close windows that they have opened themselves. Also, because of the recent proliferation of nuisance pop-up advertisements on the Web, some browsers do not allow scripts to open new windows at all.

Multiple windows and frames

As discussed previously, the open() method of the Window object allows you to create new browser windows that are represented by new Window objects. The window that a script is running in is the global object for that script, and you can use all the properties and methods of that Window object as if they were globally defined. When a script running in one window needs to control or interact with a different window, however, you must explicitly specify the Window object:

```
// Create a new window and manipulate it.
var w = open("newdoc.html");
w.alert("Hello new window");
w.setInterval("scrollBy(0,1)",50);
```

HTML allows a single window to have multiple frames. Many web designers choose to avoid frames, but they are still in fairly common use. JavaScript treats each frame as a separate Window object, and scripts in different frames run independently of each other. The frames property of the Window object is an array of Window objects, representing the subframes of a window:

```
// Scripts in framesets refer to frames like this:
frames[0].location = "frame1.html";
frames[1].location = "frame2.html";
// With deeply nested frames, you can use:
frames[1].frames[2].location = "frame2.3.html";
// Code in a frame refers to the top-level window:
top.status = "Hello from the frame";
```

The parent property of a Window object refers to the containing frame or window. The top property refers to the top-level browser window that is at the root of the frame hierarchy. (If the Window object represents a top-level window rather than a frame, the parent and top properties simply refer to the Window object itself.)

Each browser window and frame has a separate JavaScript execution context, and in each context, the Window object is the global object. This means that any variables declared or functions defined by scripts in the window or frame become properties of the corresponding Window object. This allows a script in one window or frame to use variables and functions defined in another window or frame. It is common, for example, to define functions in the <head> of a top-level window, and then have scripts and event handlers in nested frames call those functions using the top property:

```
// Code in a frame calls code in the window.
top.stop_scrolling();
```

The Document Object

Every Window object has a document property that refers to a Document object. The Document object is arguably more important than the Window object itself: while the Window represents the browser window, the Document object represents the HTML document that is displayed in that window. The Document object has various properties that refer to other objects which allow access to and modification of document content. The way that document content is accessed and modified is called the document object model, or DOM, and there are several DOMs in existence:

Legacy DOM
The original legacy document object model evolved along with early versions of the JavaScript language. It is well supported by all browsers, but allows access only to certain key portions of documents, such as forms, form elements, and images.

W3C DOM
This document object model allows access and modification of all document content and is standardized by the World Wide Web Consortium (W3C). It is at least partially supported by Netscape 6 and later, Internet Explorer 5 and later, and other modern browsers. The W3C DOM is not closely compatible with the IE 4 DOM, but it does standardize many of the legacy features of the original DOM. This chapter covers the core features of the standard, and presents a simplified subset of the DOM relevant for JavaScript programmers working with HTML documents. You can find complete coverage in *JavaScript: The Definitive Guide*.

IE 4 DOM
Microsoft's Internet Explorer Version 4 extended the legacy DOM with powerful new features for accessing and modifying all content of a document. These features were never standardized, but some of them are supported in non-Microsoft browsers.

The following sections explain each of these DOMs in more detail and describe how you can use them to access and modify document content.

The Legacy DOM

The original client-side JavaScript DOM defines provides access to document content through properties of the Document object. Several read-only properties, such as `title`, `URL`, and `lastModified` provide information about the document as a whole. See the reference section for further details on these and all Document properties and methods. Other properties are arrays that refer to specific types of document content:

`forms[]`
An array of Form objects representing the forms in a document.

`images[]`
An array of Image objects representing the images that appear in a document.

`applets[]`
An array of objects that represent the Java applets embedded in a document. JavaScript can actually be used to script Java and control these applets, but doing so is beyond the scope of this pocket reference.

`links[]`
An array of Link objects representing the hyperlinks in the document.

`anchors[]`
An array of Anchor objects representing the anchors (named positions created with the `name` attribute of the HTML `<a>` tag) in the document.

The arrays contain objects in the order they appear in the document. The first form in a document is document.forms[0]; the third image is document.images[2]. Another way to refer to document forms, images, and applets is to give them names with the HTML name attribute:

```
<form name="address">...</form>
```

When an form, image, or applet is given a name like this, you can use the name to look it up in the array, or to look it up directly as a property of the document itself:

```
document.forms["address"]  // A named form
document.address           // The same thing
```

The Form object is particularly interesting. It has an elements[] array that contains objects representing the elements of the form, in the order they appear in the form. See Input, Select, and Textarea in the reference section for details on these form elements.

The elements[] array of a Form works much like the forms[] array of a Document: it holds form elements in the order they appear in the form, but it also allows them to be referred to by name. Consider this HTML excerpt:

```
<form name='address'><input name='street'></form>
```

You can refer to the input element of the form in several ways:

```
document.forms[0].elements[0]
document.address.elements['street']
document.address.street
```

The legacy DOM does not provide any way to refer to document content other than forms, form elements, images, applets, links, and anchors. There is no array that provides a list of all <h1> tags, for example, nor is there any way for a script to obtain the actual text of a document. This is a shortcoming that is addressed by the W3C and IE 4 DOMs, as we'll see later. Although it is limited, the legacy DOM does allow scripts to dynamically alter some document content, as we'll see in the following subsections.

Dynamically generated documents

In addition to the properties already described, the Document object defines several important methods for dynamically generating document content. Use the write() method to output text into the document at the location of the <script> that contains the method calls. For example:

```
document.write("<p>Today is: " + new Date());
document.write("<p>Document updated: " +
  document.lastModified);
```

Note that text output in this way may contain arbitrary HTML tags; the browser parses and displays any such text after executing the script that output it.

The write() method can be used from a <script> tag only while a document is still loading. If you try to use it within an event handler that is triggered after the document has loaded, it erases the document and the event handler it contains. It is legal, however, to use an event handler in one window or frame to trigger a document.write() call into another window. When you do this, however, you must write the complete contents of the new document, and remember to call the document.close() method when you are done:

```
var clock = open("", "", "width=400,height=30");
var d = clock.document; // Save typing below
setInterval("d.write(new Date());d.close();", 1000);
```

Dynamic forms

As we've seen, the `elements[]` array of a Form object contains objects that represent the input elements of the form. Many of these objects have properties that you can use to query or set the value displayed in the form element. This provides another way to dynamically change document content. For example, the following code sets the `value` property of a Text object to display the current local time:

```
<form><input size=10></form>  // An HTML form
<script>  /* Display a clock in the form */
// The Text element we're working with.
var e = document.forms[0].elements[0];
// Code to display the time in that element
var s="e.value=(new Date()).toLocaleTimeString();"
setInterval(s, 1000); // Run it every second
</script>
```

Form validation

The `<form>` tag supports an `onsubmit` event handler, which is triggered when the user tries to submit a form. You can use this event handler to perform *validation*: checking that all required fields have been filled in, for example. If the `onsubmit` handler returns `false`, the form is not submitted. For example:

```
<form name="address" onsubmit="checkAddress()">
<!-- form elements go here -->
</form>
<script>
// A simple form validation function
function checkAddress() {
  var f = document.address; // The form to check
  // Loop through all elements
  for(var i = 0; i < f.elements.length; i++) {
    // Ignore all but text input elements
    if (f.elements[i].type != "text") continue;
    // Get the user's entry
    var text = f.elements[i].value;
    // If it is not filled in, alert the user
    if (text == null || text.length == 0) {
      alert("Please fill in all form fields.");
      return false;
    }
  }
}
</script>
```

Image rollovers

The legacy DOM allows you to accomplish one common special effect: dynamically replacing one image on the page with another. This is often done for image rollovers, in which an image changes when the mouse moves over it. The `images[]` array of the Document object contains Image objects that represent the document's images. Each Image object has a `src` property that specifies the URL of the image to be displayed. To change the image that is displayed, simply set this property to a new URL:

```
document.images[0].src = "newbanner.gif";
```

To use this technique for an image rollover, you must use it in conjunction with the `onmouseover` and `onmouseout` event handlers that are triggered when the mouse moves on to and off of the image. Here is some basic HTML code with JavaScript event handlers to accomplish a rollover:

```
<img name="button" src="b1.gif"
     onmouseover="document.button.src='b2.gif';"
     onmouseout="document.button.src='b1.gif';">
```

When an image is going to be dynamically displayed, it is helpful to preload it into the browser cache so that there is no network delay before it appears. You can do this with a dynamically created off-screen Image object:

```
var i = new Image(); // Create Image object
i.src="b2.gif";      // Load, but don't display image
```

Working with cookies

The `cookie` property of the Document object is a peculiar one that allows you to set and query the cookies associated with your document. To associate a transient cookie with the document, simply set the `cookie` property to a string of the form:

```
name=value
```

This creates a cookie with the specified *name* and *value* for this document. If you want to create a cookie that is stored even when the user quits the browser, add an expiration date using a string of the form:

```
name=value; expires=date
```

The expiration *date* should be in the form returned by `Date.toGMTString()`. If you want the cookie to be accessible to other documents from your web site, you can specify a path prefix:

```
name=value; expires=date; path=prefix
```

A single document may have more than one cookie associated with it. To query a document's cookies, simply read the value of the `cookie` property. This string contains *name=value* strings separated from each other by a semicolon and a space. When reading cookies, you'll never see a "path=" or "expires=" clause; you'll just get the cookie name and value. Here's a function that retrieves the value of a single named cookie from the `cookie` property. It assumes that cookie values never contain semicolons.

```
function getCookie(name) {
  // Split cookies into an array
  var cookies = document.cookie.split('; ');
  for(var i = 0; i < cookies.length; i++) {
    var c = cookies[i];          // One cookie
```

```
    var pos = c.indexOf('=');   // Find = sign
    var n = c.substring(0,pos); // Get name
    if (n == name)              // If it matches
      return c.substring(pos+1);  // Return value
  }
  return null;  // Can't find the named cookie
}
```

The W3C DOM

The W3C DOM standardizes most of the features of the legacy DOM, but also adds important new ones. In addition to supporting `forms[]`, `images[]`, and other array properties of the Document object, it defines methods that allow scripts to access and manipulate any document element, not just special-purpose elements like forms and images.

Finding elements by ID

When creating a document that contains special elements that will be manipulated by a script, you can identify each special element by giving it an `id` attribute with a unique value. Then, you can use the `getElementById()` method of the Document object to look up those elements by their ID:

```
<h1 id="title">Title</h1>
<script>
var t = document.getElementById("title");
</script>
```

Finding elements by tag name

Another way to access document elements is to look them up by tag name. The `getElementsByTagName()` method of the Document object returns an array of all elements of that type. Each document element also supports the same method, so you can obtain an array of specific types of tags that are descendants of an element:

```
// Get an array of all <ul> tags
var lists = document.getElementsByTagName("ul");
// Find the 3rd <li> tag in the second <ul>
var item = lists[1].getElementsByTagName("li")[2];
```

Traversing a document tree

The W3C DOM represents every document as a tree. The nodes of this tree represent the HTML tags, the strings of text, and the HTML comments that comprise the document. Each node of the tree is represented by a JavaScript object, and each has properties that allow you to traverse the tree, as illustrated by the following code fragment:

```
// Look up a node in the document
var n = document.getElementById("mynode");
var p = n.parentNode;  // The containing tag
var c0 = n.firstChild;     // First child of n
var c1 = c0.nextSibling;  // 2nd child of n
var c2 = n.childNodes[2]; // 3rd child of n
var last = n.lastChild;    // last child of n
```

See Node in the reference section for further details.

The Document object itself is a kind of node, and supports these same properties. The `documentElement` property of the Document object refers to the single `<html>` tag element at the root of all HTML documents, and the `body` property refers to the `<body>` tag.

Node types

Every node in a document tree has a `nodeType` property that specifies what type of node it is. Different types of nodes are represented by different subclasses of the Node object. The following `nodeType` values are relevant to JavaScript programmers working with HTML documents (other values exist for XML documents):

nodeType	Represents
1	Element: an HTML tag
2	Text: text in a document
8	Comment: an HTML comment
9	Document: the HTML document

Use the `nodeName` property of an Element node to determine the name of the HTML tag it represents. Use the `nodeValue` property of Text and Comment nodes to obtain the document text or comment text represented by the node. See Element, Text, Comment, and Document in the reference section for details on each of these node types. Also see Node for information on the common properties and methods they all share.

HTML attributes

As we've seen above, HTML tags in a document tree are represented by Element objects. In HTML documents, each Element object has properties that correspond directly to the attributes of the HTML tag. For example, you can query or set the value of the `caption` attribute of a `<table>` tag by setting the `caption` property of the corresponding Element object. See Element in the reference section for details.

Manipulating document elements

One easy way to manipulate HTML documents with the W3C DOM is simply to set the properties that correspond to HTML attributes. As we saw in the legacy DOM, this allows you to change images by setting the `src` property of the document element that represents an `<img>` tag, for example. It also allows you to set colors, sizes, and alignments of document elements. One particularly fruitful way to manipulate document elements is through the `style` property which controls CSS styles. We'll cover this important topic in more detail later in this chapter.

Changing document text

You can change the textual content of a document simply by setting the `nodeValue` property of a Text node:

```
// Find the first <h1> tag in the document
var h1 = document.getElementsByTagName("h1")[0];
```

```
// Set new text of its first child
h1.firstChild.nodeValue = "New heading";
```

In addition to manipulating the nodeValue property, the Text object also allows you to modify the data property, or to use methods to append, insert, delete, or replace text.

Note that the problem with the previous code is that it assumes that the content of the <h1> tag is plain text. The code would fail for a document with the following heading because the text of the heading is a grandchild of the <h1> tag rather than a direct child:

```
<h1><i>Original Heading</i></h1>
```

One way around this problem is to set the innerHTML property of the heading node. This property is part of the IE 4 DOM, not the W3C DOM, but it is supported by most modern browsers because it is so useful. We'll see it again when we consider the IE 4 DOM. Another way around the problem is to replace the heading node with a newly created <h1> tag and text node containing the desired text, as shown in the next section.

Changing document structure

In addition to changing document text and the attributes of document elements, the W3C DOM allows you to alter the tree structure of the document itself. This is done with Node methods that allow you to insert, append, remove, and replace children of a node and with Document methods that allow you to create new Element and Text nodes. The following code illustrates:

```
// Find a <ol> element by name:
var list = document.getElementById("mylist");
// Create a new <li> element
var item = document.createElement("li");
// Append it to the list
list.appendChild(item);
// Create a Text node
var text = document.createTextNode("new item");
// Append it to the new <li> node
item.appendChild(text);
// Remove the new item from the list
list.removeChild(item);
// Place the new item at the start of the list
list.insertBefore(item,list.firstChild);
```

As a further example, here is a JavaScript function that uses the W3C DOM to embolden an arbitrary document node by reparenting it within a newly created <b> tag:

```
function embolden(node) {  // Embolden node n
  var b = document.createElement("b");
  var p = n.parentNode; // Get parent of n
  p.replaceChild(b, n); // Replace n with <b>
  b.appendChild(n);     // Insert n into <b> tag
}
```

IE 4 DOM

The IE 4 DOM was introduced in Version 4 of Microsoft's Internet Explorer browser. It is a powerful but nonstandard DOM with capabilities similar to those of the W3C DOM. IE 5 and later include support for most basic W3C DOM features, but this documentation on the IE 4 DOM is included because IE 4 is still commonly used. The following subsections document the IE 4 DOM in terms of its differences from the W3C DOM, so you should be familiar with the W3C DOM first.

Accessing document elements

The IE 4 DOM does not support the `getElementById()` method. Instead, it allows you to look up arbitrary document elements by `id` attribute within the `all[]` array of the document object:

```
var list = document.all["mylist"];
list = document.all.mylist;  // this also works
```

Instead of supporting the `getElementsByTagName()` method, the IE 4 DOM takes the unusual step of defining a `tags()` method on the `all[]` array, which exists on document elements as well as the Document object itself. Here's how to find all `<li>` tags within the first `<ul>` tag:

```
var lists = document.all.tags("UL");
var items = lists[0].all.tags("LI");
```

Note that you must specify the desired HTML tag name in uppercase with the `all.tags()` method.

Traversing the document tree

You can traverse an IE 4 document tree in much the same way that you can traverse a W3C document tree. The difference is in the names of the relevant properties: instead of `childNodes[]`, IE 4 uses `children[]`, and instead of `parentNode`, IE 4 uses `parentElement`. IE 4 does not have any analogs to `firstChild`, `nextSibling`, and related W3C properties. One important difference between the IE 4 and W3C DOMs is that the IE 4 document tree only include HTML tags: comments are ignored and document text is not part of the tree itself. Instead, the text contained by any element is available through the `innerHTML` and `innerText` properties of the element object. (We'll see more about `innerHTML` in the next section.)

Modifying document content and structure

The nodes of an IE 4 document tree are Element objects that are similar to the Element node of the W3C DOM. Like the Element nodes of a W3C document tree, these objects have properties that correspond to the attributes of the HTML tags, and you can query and set the properties as desired. To change the textual content of a document element, set its `innerText` property to the desired text. This deletes any existing tags or text within the element and replaces it with the specified text.

The IE 4 DOM does not have any methods for explicitly creating, inserting, removing, or replacing nodes of the document tree. However, it does support the very important innerHTML property, which allows you to replace the content of any document element with an arbitrary string of HTML. Doing this requires an invocation of the HTML parser, making it less efficient than manipulating the nodes directly. On the other hand, it is tremendously convenient, so much so that Mozilla, Netscape 6 and later, and other modern browsers have implemented innerHTML despite the fact that it is nonstandard .

The IE 4 DOM also includes the related outerHTML property, which replaces the element and its content, and the insertAdjacentHTML() and insertAdjacentText() methods. These are not as commonly used, nor as commonly implemented outside of IE as innerHTML; you can read about them in the reference section under Element.

DOM compatibility

If you want to write a script that uses the W3C DOM when it is available, and otherwise uses the IE 4 DOM if it is available, you can use a capability-testing approach that first checks for the existence of a method or property to determine whether the browser has the capability you desire. For example:

```
if (document.getElementById) {
  // If the W3C method exists, use it
}
else if (document.all) {
  // If the all[] array exists, use it
}
else {
  // Otherwise use the legacy DOM
}
```

DHTML: Scripting CSS Styles

DHTML, or Dynamic HTML, is the result of combining HTML, CSS, and JavaScript: it uses scripts to dynamically modify the style—which may include the position and visibility—of document elements. In the W3C and the IE 4 DOMs, every document element has a style property that corresponds to the HTML style attribute that specifies inline styles. Instead of referring to a simple string, however, the style property refers to a Style object that has properties corresponding to each of the CSS attributes of the style.

For example, if an element e has a style attribute that specifies the CSS color attribute, you can query the value of that attribute as e.style.color. When a CSS attribute name contains hyphens, the corresponding JavaScript property name removes the hyphens and uses mixed-case capitalization. Thus, to set the background-color CSS attribute of an element e, you set e.style.backgroundColor. There is one special case: the CSS float attribute is a reserved word in JavaScript, so the corresponding JavaScript property is cssFloat.

The CSS standard defines many properties that you can use to fine-tune the visual appearance of your documents. The Style entry in the reference section includes a table that lists them all. The positioning and visibility properties are particularly relevant for dynamic scripting. If the position property is set to absolute, you can use the top and left properties to specify the absolute position (in pixels, percentages, or other units) of the document element. Similarly, the width and height properties specify the size of the element. The visibility property can initially be set to hidden to make a document element invisible, and then dynamically set to visible to make the element appear when appropriate.

Note that the values of all Style properties are always strings, even for properties like left and width which represent numbers. When setting these length and dimension properties, be sure to convert your numbers to strings and to add the appropriate units specification (usually the string px for pixels.) The following table summarizes these positioning and visibility properties.

Property	Description/values
position	How the element is positioned: absolute, relative, fixed, or static (the default).
left, top	The X and Y coordinates of the left and top edges of the element.
width	The width of the element.
height	The height of the element.
zIndex	The stacking order. Values are integers; higher values are drawn on top of lower values.
display	How to display the element. Common values are block, inline, and none for elements that don't get laid out at all.
visibility	Whether the element is visible or hidden. Space is still allocated for non-positioned hidden elements.
overflow	What to do when element content exceeds element size. Values: visible (content overflows); hidden (excess content hidden); scroll (display permanent scrollbar); auto (scrollbars only when needed).
clip	What portion of element content to display. Syntax: rect(*top right bottom left*).

The following code shows a simple DHTML animation. Each time it is called, the function nextFrame() moves an element 10 pixels to the right and uses setTimeout() to tell JavaScript to call it again in 50 milliseconds. After 20 invocations, the function uses the visibility property to hide the element and stops calling itself.

```
<h1 id='title'>DHTML Animation<h1>
<script>
// Look up the element to animate
var e = document.getElementById("title");
// Make it position-able.
e.style.position = "absolute";
var frame = 0;  // Initialize frame counter.
// This function moves the element one frame
// at a time, then hides it when done.
function nextFrame() {
  if (frame++ < 20) { // Only do 20 frames
    e.style.left = (10 * frame) + "px";
    // Call ourselves again in 50ms.
    setTimeout("nextFrame()", 50);
  }
  else e.style.visibility="hidden"; // Hide it.
}
nextFrame();  // Start animating now!
</script>
```

Events and Event Handling

We saw at the beginning of this section that one way to embed client-side JavaScript into HTML documents is to use event handler attributes of HTML tags. The table below lists the standard event handler attributes and the HTML tags to which they may be applied. The first column of the table gives the event handler attribute name: these names always begin with "on". The second column of the table lists the HTML tags to which these attributes can be applied, and explains, when necessary, what events trigger the handler code to be executed.

Handler	Supported by/triggered when
`onabort`	`<img>`; image load aborted
`onblur`	`<body>` and form elements; window or element loses keyboard focus
`onchange`	Form elements; displayed value changes
`onclick`	All elements; mouse press and release; return `false` to cancel
`ondblclick`	All elements; mouse double-click
`onerror`	`<img>`; image loading fails
`onfocus`	`<body>` and form elements; window or element gets keyboard focus
`onkeydown`	`<body>` and form elements; key pressed; return `false` to cancel
`onkeypress`	`<body>` and form elements; key pressed and released; return `false` to cancel
`onkeyup`	`<body>` and form elements; key released
`onload`	`<body>`, `<frameset>`, `<img>`, `<iframe>`, `<object>`; document, image, or object completely loaded
`onmousedown`	All elements; mouse button pressed
`onmousemove`	All elements; mouse pointer moved
`onmouseout`	All elements; mouse moves off element
`onmouseover`	All elements; mouse moves over element; return `true` to prevent link URL display in status bar
`onmouseup`	All elements; mouse button released
`onreset`	`<form>`; form reset requested; return `false` to prevent reset
`onresize`	`<body>`, `<frameset>`; window size changes
`onsubmit`	`<form>`; form submission requested; return `false` to prevent submission
`onunload`	`<body>`, `<frameset>`; document unloaded

Note that when the browser triggers certain event handlers, such as `onclick`, `onmouseover` and `onsubmit`, it examines the return value of the handler (if there is one) to determine whether it should perform the default action associated with the event or not. Typically, if an event handler returns `false`, the default action (such as following a hyperlink or submitting a form) is not performed. The one exception is for the `onmouseover` handler: when the mouse moves over a hyperlink, the browser displays the link's URL in the status line unless the event handler returns `true`.

Event handlers as JavaScript functions

We've seen that the various document object models represent HTML tags as JavaScript objects, with the attributes of those tags as properties of the objects.

The same is true of event handlers. If your HTML document includes a single `<form>` tag with an `onsubmit` event handler attribute, that event handler is available as:

```
document.forms[0].onsubmit
```

Although HTML event handler attributes are written as strings of JavaScript code, the value of the corresponding JavaScript properties are not strings of code, but actual JavaScript functions. You can create a new event handler simply by assigning a function to the appropriate property:

```
function validate() { // Form validation function
  // check validity here
  return valid;        // return true or false
}
// Now check user input before submitting it
document.forms[0].onsubmit = validate;
```

Advanced event handling

The previous sections describe the basic event-handling model for client-side JavaScript. Advanced event handling features are also available, but unfortunately, there are three incompatible event models: the standard W3C DOM model, the Internet Explorer model (Microsoft has not adopted the W3C standard), and the Netscape 4 model. These event models are complex, so the following list simply summarizes the advanced features supported by these models. For details consult *JavaScript: The Definitive Guide*.

Event details
: In the advanced event handling models, event details such as event type, mouse buttons and coordinates, modifier key state, and so on, are provided through the properties of an Event object. In the W3C and Netscape event models, this Event object is passed as an argument to the event handler. In the IE model, the Event object is not an argument but is instead stored in the event property of the Window on which the event occurs. Unfortunately, each of the three advanced event models use different property names to store event details, so cross-browser compatibility is difficult. See Event in the reference section for documentation of each of the three types of Event objects.

Event propagation
: In the basic event model, event handlers are triggered only for the document element on which the event occurred. In the advanced models, events can propagate up and/or down the element hierarchy and be handled by one or more event handlers. In the Netscape and W3C models, events start at the document object and propagate down through the document tree to the element on which they occurred. If any of the containing elements have special capturing event handlers registered, these event handlers capture the event and get first crack at handling it. In the IE and W3C models, certain types of events (such as mouse clicks) bubble up the document tree after being handled at their source. Thus, you might register an `onclick` event handler on a `<div>` object in order to handle all mouse clicks that occur on elements within that `<div>`. Capturing, bubbling, and normal event handlers

have the option of preventing the event from propagating any further, although the way this is done is different in each model.

Event handler registration

In the W3C event model, event handlers are not simply assigned to properties of document objects. Instead, each document object has an `addEventListener()` method that you call to register an event handler function for a named type of event. This allows advanced applications to register more than one handler for the same event type.

JavaScript

JavaScript Security Restrictions

For security reasons, client-side JavaScript implementations typically impose restrictions on the tasks that scripts can perform. The most obvious restrictions are omissions of dangerous capabilities: there is no way for client-side JavaScript to delete files on a user's local hard disk, for example. Other restrictions exist to prevent the disclosure of private information or to keep scripts from annoying users. There is no standard set of security restrictions, but the following are restrictions found in typical browser implementations. Don't attempt to write scripts that do these things: even if they work for your browser, they probably won't work in others.

Same origin policy

Scripts can only read properties of windows and documents that were loaded from the same web server. This is a substantial and pervasive restriction on cross-window scripting, and prevents scripts from reading information from other unrelated documents that the user is viewing. This restriction also prevents scripts from registering event handlers or spoofing events on unrelated documents.

File uploads

Scripts cannot set the `value` property of the FileUpload form element.

Sending email and posting news

Scripts cannot submit forms to `mailto:` or `news:` URLs without user confirmation.

Closing windows

A script can only close browser windows that it created itself, unless it gets user confirmation.

Snooping in the cache

A script cannot load any `about:` URLs, such as `about:cache`.

Hidden windows and window decorations

A script cannot create small or offscreen windows or windows without a titlebar.

Note that this list of security restrictions is not static. As the use of JavaScript has grown, advertisers and unsavory characters have started doing annoying things with it. As a result, newer browsers, such as Mozilla 1.0, allow user-configurable security restrictions that can prevent scripts from opening new windows (such as pop-up ads), or from moving or resizing existing windows.

JavaScript API Reference

The rest of this chapter contains a quick-reference for the core and client-side JavaScript APIs. It documents the complete core JavaScript API, covers the legacy (Level 0) DOM API, and presents a simplified view of the W3C Level 2 DOM API. Portions of that API not relevant to JavaScript programmers working with HTML documents have been omitted. The upper-right corner of the title block for each reference entry contains information that states whether a feature is part of the core or client-side API, and further indicates which version of JavaScript, which browsers, or which version of the DOM introduced the feature.

Because JavaScript is a loosely-typed language, there is not an official set of class names for the classes and objects of the JavaScript API, and they sometimes appear under different names in different references. The following table summarizes the reference entries that follow, and allows you to quickly scan for the class or object you are interested in.

Anchor	A named position in a document
Applet	A Java applet
Arguments	The arguments of a function
Array	Array creation and manipulation
Attr	An attribute of a document element
Boolean	A wrapper object for boolean values
Comment	An HTML comment
DOMException	Signals DOM errors
DOMImplementation	Creates documents, checks DOM features
Date	Manipulates dates and times
Document	An HTML document
DocumentFragment	Nodes to be manipulated together
Element	An HTML tag in a document
Error	Predefined exception types
Event	Event details
Form	An HTML input form
Function	A JavaScript function
Global	Global properties and functions
History	Browsing history
Image	An HTML image
Input	A form input element
Layer	An independent document layer
Link	An `<a>` or `<area>` link
Location	Current browser location
Math	Mathematical functions and constants
Navigator	Information about the browser
Node	A node in a document tree
Number	Support for numbers
Object	The superclass of all JavaScript objects
Option	A selectable option
RegExp	Regular expressions for pattern matching
Screen	Information about the display
Select	A graphical selection list
String	String manipulation

Style	Inline CSS properties of an element
Text	A run of text in a document
Textarea	Multiline text input
Window	Browser window or frame

Anchor

Client-Side JavaScript 1.2

A named position in a document

Inherits From: Element

```
document.anchors[index]
document.anchors[name]
```

Description

An Anchor object represents an <a> tag with a `name` attribute, which serves to create a named position in a document.

Properties

`name`

The value of the `name` attribute of the <a> tag.

See Also

`Document.anchors[]`, Link, `Location.hash`

Applet

Client-Side JavaScript 1.1

A Java applet

```
document.applets[i]
document.applets[appletName]
document.appletName
```

Properties & Methods

The properties and methods of an Applet object are the same as the public fields and methods of the Java applet it represents. JavaScript code can query and set the Java fields and invoke the Java methods of the applet.

Arguments

Core JavaScript 1.1; JScript 2.0; ECMA v1

The arguments of a function

```
arguments[n]
arguments.length
```

Description

The Arguments object is defined only within a function body, and within every function body, the local variable `arguments` refers to the Arguments object for that function. The Arguments object is an array whose elements are the values that were passed as arguments to the function. Element 0 is the first argument, element 1 is the second argument, and so on. All values passed as arguments become array elements of the Arguments object, whether or not those arguments are given names in the function declaration.

Properties

`callee`

A reference to the function that is currently executing. Useful for recursion in unnamed functions. JS 1.2; JScript 5.5; ECMA v1; only defined within a function body.

`length`

The number of arguments passed to the function. JS 1.1; JScript 2; ECMA v1; only defined within a function body.

See Also

Function

Array

Core JavaScript 1.1; JScript 2.0; ECMA v1

Array creation and manipulation

Constructor

```
new Array()              // empty
new Array(n)             // n undefined elements
new Array(e0, e1,...)    // specified elements
```

Literal Syntax

In JavaScript 1.2, JScript 3.0, and ECMA v3, you can create and initialize an array by placing a comma-separated list of expressions within square brackets. The values of these expressions become the elements of the array. For example:

```
var a = [1, true, 'abc'];
var b = [a[0], a[0]*2, f(x)];
```

Properties

`length`

A read/write integer specifying the number of elements in the array, or, when the array does not have contiguous elements, a number one larger than the index of the last element in the array. Changing the value of this property truncates or extends the array.

Methods

`concat(`*`value, ...`*`)`

Returns a new array, which is formed by concatenating each of the specified arguments to this one. If any arguments to `concat()` are themselves arrays, their elements are concatenated, rather than the arrays themselves. JS 1.2; JScript 3.0; ECMA v3.

`join(`*`separator`*`)`

Returns the string that results from converting each element of an array to a string and then concatenating the strings together, with the *separator* string between elements.

`pop()`

Removes and returns the last element of the array, decrementing the array length. JS 1.2; JScript 5.5; ECMA v3.

`push(value, ...)`
: Appends the specified value or values to the end of the array, and returns the new length of the array. JS 1.2; JScript 5.5; ECMA v3.

`reverse()`
: Reverses the order of the elements of an array. Returns nothing.

`shift()`
: Removes and returns the first element of the array, shifting subsequent elements down one and decrementing the array length. JS 1.2; JScript 5.5; ECMA v3.

`slice(start, end)`
: Returns a new array that contains the elements of the array from the element numbered *start*, up to, but not including, the element numbered *end*. JS 1.2; JScript 3.0; ECMA v3.

`sort(orderfunc)`
: Sorts the elements of an array, and returns a reference to the array. Note that the array is sorted in place and no copy is made. The optional *orderfunc* argument may specify a function that defines the sorting order. The function should expect two arguments and should return a value that is less than 0 if the first argument is less than the second, 0 if they are equal, and a value greater that 0 if the first is greater than the second.

`splice(start, deleteCount, value,...)`
: Deletes the specified number of elements from the array starting at the specified index, then inserts any remaining arguments into the array at that location. Returns an array containing the deleted elements. JS 1.2; JScript 5.5; ECMA v3.

`toLocaleString()`
: Returns a localized string representation of the array. JS 1.5; JScript 5.5; ECMA v1.

`toString()`
: Returns a string representation of *array*.

`unshift(value, ...)`
: Inserts the argument or arguments as new elements at the beginning of an array, shifting existing array elements up to make room. Returns the new length of the array. JS 1.2; JScript 5.5; ECMA v3.

Attr — DOM Level 1

An attribute of a document element — Inherits From: Node

Properties

`name`
: The name of the attribute. Read-only.

`ownerElement`
: The Element object that contains this attribute. Read-only. DOM Level 2.

`specified`
: `true` if the attribute was explicitly specified in the document source or set by a script. `false` otherwise. Read-only.

`value`
: The value of the attribute as a string. Read/write.

See Also

`Document.createAttribute()`, `Element.getAttributeNode()`, `Element.setAttributeNode()`

Boolean

Core JavaScript 1.1; JScript 2.0; ECMA v1

A wrapper object for boolean values

Constructor

```
new Boolean(value)
Boolean(value)
```

Invoked as a function, without the `new` operator, `Boolean()` converts *`value`* to a boolean value (not a Boolean object) and returns it. All values convert to `true` except for 0, NaN, `null`, `undefined`, and the empty string, "". When invoked with the `new` operator, the `Boolean()` constructor performs the same conversion and wraps the result in a Boolean object.

Methods

`toString()`
: Returns "true" or "false", depending on the value of the Boolean object.

`valueOf()`
: Returns the primitive boolean value wrapped by the Boolean object.

Comment

DOM Level 1

An HTML comment

Inherits From: Node

Properties

Comment nodes have exactly the same properties as Text nodes.

Methods

Comment nodes support all of the methods of Text nodes except for `splitText()`.

See Also

Text

DOMException

DOM Level 1

Signals DOM errors

Properties

`code`
: An error code that provides some detail about what caused the exception. Some possible values (and their meanings) for this property are defined by the constants listed below.

Constants

The following constants define the code values that may be encountered by when working with HTML documents. Note that these constants are static properties of DOMException, not properties of individual exception objects.

`DOMException.INDEX_SIZE_ERR = 1`
: Out-of-bounds error for an array or string index.

`DOMException.HIERARCHY_REQUEST_ERR = 3`
: An attempt was made to place a node somewhere illegal in the document tree hierarchy.

`DOMException.WRONG_DOCUMENT_ERR = 4`
: An attempt was made to use a node with a document other than the document that created the node.

`DOMException.INVALID_CHARACTER_ERR = 5`
: An illegal character was used (in an element name, for example).

`DOMException.NOT_FOUND_ERR = 8`
: A node was not found where it was expected.

`DOMException.NOT_SUPPORTED_ERR = 9`
: A method or property is not supported in the current DOM implementation.

`DOMException.INUSE_ATTRIBUTE_ERR = 10`
: An attempt was made to associate an Attr with an Element when that Attr node was already associated with a different Element node.

`DOMException.SYNTAX_ERR = 12`
: A syntax error occurred, such as in a CSS property specification.

DOMImplementation — DOM Level 1

Creates documents, checks DOM features

document.implementation

Methods

`createHTMLDocument(`*title*`)`
: Creates and returns a new HTML Document object and populates it with `<html>`, `<head>`, `<title>`, and `<body>` elements. *title* is the text to appear in the `<title>` element. DOM Level 2.

`hasFeature(`*feature*, *version*`)`
: Returns `true` if the implementation supports the specified version of the specified feature, or `false` otherwise. If no version number is specified, the method returns `true` if the implementation completely supports any version of the specified feature. Both *feature* and *version* are strings; for example, "core", "1.0" or "html", "2.0".

Date

Core JavaScript 1.0; JScript 1.0; ECMA v1

Manipulates dates and times

Constructor

```
new Date();             // current time
new Date(milliseconds) // from timestamp
new Date(datestring);  // parse string
new Date(year, month, day, hours, minutes, seconds, ms)
```

With no arguments, the `Date()` constructor creates a Date object set to the current date and time. When one numeric argument is passed, it is taken as the internal numeric representation of the date in milliseconds, as returned by the `getTime()` method. When one string argument is passed, it is taken as a string representation of a date. Otherwise, the constructor is passed between two and seven numeric arguments that specify the individual fields of the local date and time. All but the first two arguments—the year and month fields—are optional. See the static `Date.UTC()` method for an alternative that uses universal time instead of local time.

When called as a function without the `new` operator, `Date()` ignores any arguments passed to it and returns a string representation of the current date and time.

Methods

The Date object has no properties; instead, all access to date and time values is done through methods. Most methods come in two forms: one that operates using local time, and one that has "UTC" in its name and operates using universal (UTC or GMT) time. These pairs of methods are listed here. Note that the return values and optional arguments described below for most `set()` methods are not supported prior to ECMA standardization. See the various `get()` methods for the legal ranges of each of the various date fields.

`get[UTC]Date()`
: Returns the day of the month, in local or universal time. Return values are between 1 and 31.

`get[UTC]Day()`
: Returns the day of the week, in local or universal time. Return values are between 0 (Sunday) and 6 (Saturday).

`get[UTC]FullYear()`
: Returns the year in full four-digit form, in local or universal time. JS 1.2; JScript 3.0; ECMA v1.

`get[UTC]Hours()`
: Returns the hours field, in local or universal time. Return values are between 0 (midnight) and 23 (11 p.m.).

`get[UTC]Milliseconds()`
: Returns the milliseconds field, in local or universal time. JS 1.2; JScript 3.0; ECMA v1.

`get[UTC]Minutes()`
: Returns the minutes field, in local or universal time. Return values are between 0 and 59.

`get[UTC]Month()`
: Returns the month field, in local or universal time. Return values are between 0 (January) and 11 (December).

`get[UTC]Seconds()`
: Returns the seconds field, in local or universal time. Return values are between 0 and 59.

`getTime()`
: Returns the internal millisecond representation of the date; that is, returns the number of milliseconds between midnight (UTC) of January 1st, 1970 and the date and time represented by the Date object. Note that this value is independent of time zone.

`getTimezoneOffset()`
: Returns the difference, in minutes, between the local and UTC representations of this date. Note that the value returned depends on whether daylight savings time is or would be in effect at the specified date.

`getYear()`
: Returns the year field minus 1900. Deprecated in favor of `getFullYear()`.

`set[UTC]Date(`*`day_of_month`*`)`
: Sets the day of the month field, using local or universal time. Returns the millisecond representation of the adjusted date.

`set[UTC]FullYear(`*`year, month, day`*`)`
: Sets the year (and optionally the month and day), using local or universal time. Returns the millisecond representation of the adjusted date. JS 1.2; JScript 3.0; ECMA v1.

`set[UTC]Hours(`*`hours, mins, secs, ms`*`)`
: Sets the hour (and optionally the minutes, seconds, and milliseconds fields), using local or universal time. Returns the millisecond representation of the adjusted date.

`set[UTC]Milliseconds(`*`millis`*`)`
: Sets the milliseconds field of a date, using local or universal time. Returns the millisecond representation of the adjusted date. JS 1.2; JScript 3.0; ECMA v1.

`set[UTC]Minutes(`*`minutes, seconds, millis`*`)`
: Sets the minutes field (and optionally the seconds and milliseconds fields) of a date, using local or universal time. Returns the millisecond representation of the adjusted date.

`set[UTC]Month(`*`month, day`*`)`
: Sets the month field (and optionally the day of the month) of a date using local or universal time. Returns the millisecond representation of the adjusted date.

`set[UTC]Seconds(`*`seconds, millis`*`)`
: Sets the seconds field (and optionally the milliseconds field) of a date, using local or universal time. Returns the millisecond representation of the adjusted date.

`setTime(`*`milliseconds`*`)`
: Sets the internal millisecond date representation. Returns the *`milliseconds`* argument.

`setYear(`*`year`*`)`
: Sets the 2-digit year field. Deprecated in favor of `set[UTC]FullYear()`.

`toDateString()`
: Returns a string that represents the date portion of the date, expressed in the local timezone. JS 1.5; JScript 5.5; ECMA v3.

`toGMTString()`
: Converts a Date to a string, using the GMT timezone, and returns the string. Deprecated in favor of `toUTCString()`.

`toLocaleDateString()`
: Returns a string that represents the date portion of the date, expressed in the local time zone, using the local date formatting conventions. JS 1.5; JScript 5.5; ECMA v3.

`toLocaleString()`
: Converts a Date to a string, using the local timezone and the local date formatting conventions.

`toLocaleTimeString()`
: Returns a string that represents the time portion of the date, expressed in the local time zone, using the local time formatting conventions. JS 1.5; JScript 5.5; ECMA v3.

`toString()`
: Returns a string representation of the date using the local time zone.

`toTimeString()`
: Returns a string that represents the time portion of the date, expressed in the local time zone. JS 1.5; JScript 5.5; ECMA v3.

`toUTCString()`
: Converts a Date to a string, using universal time, and returns the string. JS 1.2; JScript 3.0; ECMA v1.

`valueOf()`
: Returns the millisecond representation of the date, exactly as `getTime()` does. JS 1.1; ECMA v1.

Static Functions

In addition to the previously listed instance method, the Date object defines two static methods. These methods are invoked through the `Date()` constructor itself, not through individual Date objects:

`Date.parse(`*`date`*`)`
: Parses a string representation of a date and time and returns the internal millisecond representation of that date.

`Date.UTC(`*`yr, mon, day, hr, min, sec, ms`*`)`
: Returns the millisecond representation of the specified UTC date and time.

Document

Client-Side JavaScript 1.0; DOM Level 1

An HTML document

Inherits From: Node (in DOM Level 1)

```
window.document
document
```

Description

The Document object represents an HTML document and is one of the most important objects in client-side JavaScript. It was introduced in JavaScript 1.0, and a number of methods and properties were added in JavaScript 1.1. Netscape and Internet

Explorer each add nonstandard methods and properties to the Document object, and the W3C DOM standardizes additional properties and methods.

Common Properties

All implementations of the Document object support the following properties. This list is followed by separate lists of properties defined by the W3C DOM Document object and by the IE 4 and Netscape 4 Document objects.

`alinkColor`
: A string that specifies the color of activated links. Deprecated.

`anchors[]`
: An array of Anchor objects, one for each anchor that appears in the document. JS 1.2.

`applets[]`
: An array of Applet objects, one for each applet that appears in the document. JS 1.1.

`bgColor`
: A string that specifies the background color of the document. Deprecated.

`cookie`
: A string-valued property with special behavior that allows the cookies associated with this document to be queried and set.

`domain`
: A string that specifies the Internet domain the document is from. Used for security purposes. JS 1.1.

`embeds[]`
: An array of objects that represent data embedded in the document with the `<embed>` tag. A synonym for `plugins[]`. Some plugins and ActiveX controls can be controlled with JavaScript code. The API depends on the specific control. JS 1.2.

`fgColor`
: A string that specifies the default text color for the document. Deprecated.

`forms[]`
: An array of Form objects, one for each HTML form that appears in the document.

`images[]`
: An array of Image objects, one for each image that is embedded in the document with the HTML `<img>` tag. JS 1.1.

`lastModified`
: A read-only string that specifies the date of the most recent change to the document (as reported by the web server). JS 1.0.

`linkColor`
: A string that specifies the color of unvisited links. Deprecated.

`links[]`
: An array of Link objects, one for each hypertext link that appears in the document.

`location`
: The URL of the document. Deprecated in favor of the `URL` property.

`plugins[]`
: A synonym for the `embeds[]` array. JS 1.1.

`referrer`
: A read-only string that contains the URL of the document, if any, from which the current document was linked.

`title`
: The text contents of the `<title>` tag. Read-only prior to DOM Level 1.

`URL`
: A read-only string that specifies the URL of the document. JS 1.1.

`vlinkColor`
: A string that specifies the color of visited links. Deprecated.

W3C DOM Properties

In DOM-compliant browsers, the Document object inherits the properties of Node, and defines the following additional properties.

`body`
: A reference to the Element object that represents the `<body>` tag of this document.

`defaultView`
: The Window in which the document is displayed. Read-only. DOM Level 2.

`documentElement`
: A read-only reference to the `<html>` tag of the document.

`implementation`
: The DOMImplementation object that represents the implementation that created this document. Read-only.

IE 4 Properties

The following nonstandard (and nonportable) properties are defined by Internet Explorer 4 and later versions.

`activeElement`
: A read-only property that refers to the input element that is currently active (i.e., has the input focus).

`all[ ]`
: An array of all Element objects within the document. This array may be indexed numerically to access elements in source order, or it may be indexed by element `id` or `name`.

`charset`
: The character set of the document.

`children[ ]`
: An array that contains the HTML elements that are direct children of the document. Note that this is different than the `all[ ]` array that contains all elements in the document, regardless of their position in the containment hierarchy.

`defaultCharset`
: The default character set of the document.

`expando`
: This property, if set to `false`, prevents client-side objects from being expanded. That is, it causes a runtime error if a program attempts to set the value of a nonexistent property of a client-side object. Setting `expando` to `false` can sometimes help to catch bugs caused by property misspellings, which can otherwise be difficult to detect. This property can be particularly helpful for programmers who

are switching to JavaScript after becoming accustomed to case-insensitive languages. Although `expando` only works in IE, it can be safely (but ineffectively) set in Netscape.

`parentWindow`
The window that contains the document.

`readyState`
Specifies the loading status of a document. It has one of the following four string values:

`uninitialized`
The document has not started loading.

`loading`
The document is loading.

`interactive`
The document has loaded sufficiently for the user to interact with it.

`complete`
The document is completely loaded.

Netscape 4 Properties

The following nonstandard (and nonportable) properties are defined by Netscape 4.

`height`
The height, in pixels, of the document.

`layers[]`
An array of Layer objects that represents the layers contained within a document. This property is only available in Netscape 4; it is discontinued as of Netscape 6.

`width`
The width, in pixels, of the document.

Common Methods

All implementations of the Document object support the following methods. This list is followed by separate lists of methods defined by the W3C DOM standard and by the IE 4 and Netscape 4 Document objects.

`clear()`
Erases the contents of the document and returns nothing. This method is deprecated in JavaScript 1.1. JS 1.0; deprecated.

`close()`
Closes a document stream opened with the `open()` method and returns nothing. JS 1.0.

`open()`
Deletes existing document content and opens a stream to which new document contents may be written. Returns nothing. JS 1.0.

`write(`*`value`*`, ...)`
Inserts the specified string or strings into the document currently being parsed or appends to document opened with `open()`. Returns nothing. JS 1.0.

`writeln(`*`value`*`, ...)`
Identical to `write()`, except that it appends a newline character to the output. Returns nothing. JS 1.0

W3C DOM Methods

In DOM-compliant browsers, the Document object inherits the methods of Node, and defines the following additional methods.

`createAttribute(name)`
: Returns a newly-created Attr node with the specified name.

`createComment(text)`
: Creates and returns a new Comment node containing the specified text.

`createDocumentFragment()`
: Creates and returns an empty DocumentFragment node.

`createElement(tagName)`
: Creates and returns a new Element node with the specified tag name.

`createTextNode(text)`
: Creates and returns a new Text node that contains the specified `text`.

`getElementById(id)`
: Returns the Element of this document that has the specified value for its `id` attribute, or `null` if no such Element exists in the document.

`getElementsByName(name)`
: Returns an array of nodes of all elements in the document that have a specified value for their `name` attribute. If no such elements are found, returns a zero-length array.

`getElementsByTagName(tagname)`
: Returns an array of all Element nodes in this document that have the specified tag name. The Element nodes appear in the returned array in the same order they appear in the document source.

`importNode(importedNode, deep)`
: Creates and returns a copy of a node from some other document that is suitable for insertion into this document. If the *deep* argument is `true`, it recursively copies the children of the node too. DOM Level 2.

Netscape 4 Methods

`getSelection()`
: Returns the currently selected document text with HTML tags removed.

IE 4 Methods

`elementFromPoint(x,y)`
: Returns the Element located at a specified point.

Event Handlers

In DOM-compliant browsers and IE 4, the Document object supports the same list of generic event handlers that the Element object does. Although the `onload` and `onunload` handlers logically belong to the Document object, they are implemented as properties of the Window object.

See Also

Anchor, Applet, Element, Form, Image, Layer, Link, Window

DocumentFragment

DOM Level 1

Nodes to be manipulated together

Inherits From: Node

Description

DocumentFragment inherits the methods and properties of Node, and defines no new method or properties of its own. It has one important behavior, however: when a DocumentFragment is inserted into a document tree, it is not the DocumentFragment node itself that is inserted, but the children of the DocumentFragment. This makes DocumentFragment useful as a temporary placeholder for nodes you want to insert, all at once, into a document.

See Also

`Document.createDocumentFragment()`

Element

DOM Level 1, IE 4

An HTML tag in a document

Inherits From: Node (in DOM Level 1)

Description

The Element object represents an HTML element or tag. IE 4 and later, DOM-compliant browsers such as IE 5 and later, and Netscape 6 and later allow access to every element of a document. They also define the properties and methods listed here on each of those elements. Unfortunately, the methods and properties defined by the IE 4 DOM are not the same as the methods and properties defined by the W3C DOM standard. Because of this incompatibility, they are grouped separately in the following lists.

W3C DOM Properties

In web browsers that support the W3C DOM, all elements in an HTML document have properties that correspond to their HTML attributes, including such universal attributes such as `dir`, `id`, `lang`, and `title`. When an HTML attribute name consists of multiple words, the corresponding JavaScript property name uses mixed case. Otherwise the JavaScript property is in lowercase (e.g., `id` and `href`, but `tagIndex` and `accessKey`). Two HTML attributes have names that are reserved words in JavaScript or Java, and special property names are required. JavaScript uses the property `className` to refer to the `class` attribute of all HTML tags and uses `htmlFor` to refer to the `for` attribute of `<label>` and `<script>` tags. In addition to their HTML attributes, all elements define the following properties. Remember also that in DOM-compliant browsers, all HTML elements inherit the properties of the Node object.

`className`
: The string value of the `class` attribute of the element, which specifies one or more CSS classes. Note that this property is not named "class" because that name is a reserved word in JavaScript.

`style`
: A Style object that represents the `style` attribute of the HTML element.

`tagName`
: The read-only tag name of the element. For HTML documents, the tag name is returned in uppercase, regardless of its capitalization in the document source. In XHTML documents, the value is in lowercase.

IE DOM Properties

Internet Explorer 4 and later versions define a proprietary DOM. In the IE 4 DOM, as in the W3C DOM, each HTML element has JavaScript properties that correspond to its HTML attributes. In addition, the IE 4 DOM defines the following properties for each element:

`all[]`
: An array of all Element objects that are descendants of this element. This array may be indexed numerically to access elements in source order. Or it may be indexed by element `id` or `name`. See also `Document.all[]`.

`children[]`
: An array of Element objects that are direct children of this element. Note that the IE 4 DOM has no equivalent of the Text or Comment nodes, so the children of an element can only be other Element objects.

`className`
: A read/write string that specifies the value of the `class` attribute of an element.

`document`
: A reference to the containing Document object.

`innerHTML`
: The HTML text contained within the element, not including the opening and closing tags of the element itself. Setting this property replaces the content of the element. Because this nonstandard property is powerful and widely used, it has been implemented by other browsers including Netscape 6 and later and Mozilla.

`innerText`
: The plain text contained within the element, not including the opening and closing tags of the element itself. Setting this property replaces the content of the element with unparsed plain text.

`offsetHeight`
: The height, in pixels, of the element and all its content.

`offsetLeft`
: The X-coordinate of the element relative to the `offsetParent` container element.

`offsetParent`
: Specifies the container element that defines the coordinate system in which `offsetLeft` and `offsetTop` are measured. For most elements, `offsetParent` is the Document object that contains them. However, if an element has a dynamically positioned ancestor, that ancestor is the `offsetParent`. Table cells are positioned relative to the row in which they are contained.

`offsetTop`
: The Y-coordinate of the element, relative to the `offsetParent` container element.

`offsetWidth`
: The width, in pixels, of the element and all its content.

`outerHTML`
: The HTML text of an element, including its start tags, end tags, and content. Setting this property completely replaces the element and its content.

`outerText`
: The plain text of an element, including its start and end tags. Setting this property replaces the element and its contents with unparsed plain text.

`parentElement`
The element that is the direct parent of this one. This property is read-only.

`sourceIndex`
The index of the element in the `Document.all[]` array of the document that contains it.

`style`
A Style object that represents the inline CSS style attributes for this element. Setting properties of this object changes the display style of the element.

`tagName`
A read-only string that specifies the name of the HTML tag that this element represents.

W3C DOM Methods

In web browsers that support the W3C DOM, all elements in an HTML document support the following methods, and also inherit the methods of Node. Many of these methods are used to get and set attribute values, and are rarely used because Element objects have properties that mirror all their HTML attributes.

`getAttribute(`*`name`*`)`
Returns the value of a named attribute as a string.

`getAttributeNode(`*`name`*`)`
Returns the value of a named attribute as an Attr node.

`getElementsByTagName(`*`name`*`)`
Returns an array of all descendants of this element that have the specified tag name, in the order in which they appear in the document.

`hasAttribute(`*`name`*`)`
Returns `true` if this element has an attribute with the specified name, or `false` if it does not. DOM Level 2.

`removeAttribute(`*`name`*`)`
Deletes the named attribute from this element and returns nothing.

`removeAttributeNode(`*`oldAttr`*`)`
Removes the specified Attr node from the list of attributes for this element. Returns the Attr node that was removed.

`setAttribute(`*`name, value`*`)`
Sets the named attribute to the specified string value and returns nothing.

`setAttributeNode(`*`newAttr`*`)`
Adds the specified Attr node to the list of attributes for this element. If an attribute with the same name already exists, its value is replaced. Returns the Attr node that was replaced by *`newAttr`*, or `null` if no attribute was replaced.

IE DOM Methods

Internet Explorer 4 and later versions support the following nonstandard methods for all document elements.

`contains(`*`target`*`)`
Returns `true` if this element contains the Element *`target`*, or `false` if it does not.

`getAttribute(`*`name`*`)`
Returns the value of the named attribute of this element as a string, or `null` if there is no such attribute.

`insertAdjacentHTML(`*`where, text`*`)`
: Inserts the HTML *text* into the document near this element at a position specified by *where*. *where* must be one of the strings "BeforeBegin", "AfterBegin", "BeforeEnd" or "AfterEnd". Returns nothing.

`insertAdjacentText(`*`where, text`*`)`
: Inserts plain text *text* into the document near this element, at the position specified by *where*. Returns nothing.

`removeAttribute(`*`name`*`)`
: Deletes the named attribute and its value from the element. Returns `true` on success; `false` on failure.

`scrollIntoView(`*`top`*`)`
: Scrolls the document so this element is visible at the top or bottom of the window. If *top* is `true` or is omitted, the element appears at the top of the window. If `false`, the element appears at the bottom.

`setAttribute(`*`name, value`*`)`
: Sets the named attribute to the specified string value and returns nothing.

Event Handlers

Elements of an HTML document define the following event handlers to respond to raw mouse and keyboard events. Particular types of elements (such as the Form and Input objects) may define more specialized event handlers (such as `onsubmit` and `onchange`) that impose an interpretation upon the raw input events.

`onclick`
: Invoked when the user clicks on the element.

`ondblclick`
: Invoked when the user double-clicks on the element.

`onhelp`
: Invoked when the user requests help. IE only.

`onkeydown`
: Invoked when the user presses a key.

`onkeypress`
: Invoked when the user presses and releases a key.

`onkeyup`
: Invoked when the user releases a key.

`onmousedown`
: Invoked when the user presses a mouse button.

`onmousemove`
: Invoked when the user moves the mouse.

`onmouseout`
: Invoked when the user moves the mouse off the element.

`onmouseover`
: Invoked when the user moves the mouse over an element.

`onmouseup`
: Invoked when the user releases a mouse button.

See Also

Form, Input, Node, Select, Textarea

Error

Core JavaScript 1.5; JScript 5.5; ECMA v3

Predefined exception types

Inherits From: Object

Constructor

```
new Error(message)
new EvalError(message)
new RangeError(message)
new ReferenceError(message)
new SyntaxError(message)
new TypeError(message)
new URIError(message)
```

These constructors create an instance of the Error class or of one of its subclasses. The *message* argument is optional.

Properties

Error and all of its subclasses define the same two properties:

`message`
: An error message that provides details about the exception. This property holds the string passed to the constructor, or an implementation-defined default string.

`name`
: A string that specifies the type of the exception. This property is always the name of the constructor used to create the exception object.

Methods

`toString()`
: Returns a string representation of the Error (or subclass) object.

Event

DOM Level 2, IE 4, Netscape 4

Event details

Description

The Event object serves to provide both details about an event and control over the propagation of an event. DOM Level 2 defines a standard Event object, but Internet Explorer 4, 5, and 6 use a proprietary object instead. Netscape 4 has its own proprietary object that is different from the other two. DOM Level 2 does not standardize keyboard events, so the Netscape 4 Event object may be still useful to programmers interested in key events in Netscape 6 and later. The properties of the DOM, IE, and Netscape 4 Event objects are listed in separate sections below.

In the DOM and Netscape event models, an Event object is passed as an argument to the event handler. In the IE event model, the Event object that describes the most recent event is instead stored in the `event` property of the Window object.

DOM Constants

These constants are the legal values of the `eventPhase` property; they represent the current phase of event propagation for this event.

`Event.CAPTURING_PHASE = 1`
: The event is in its capturing phase.

`Event.AT_TARGET = 2`
: The event is being handled by its target node.

`Event.BUBBLING_PHASE = 3`
: The event is bubbling.

DOM Properties

All properties of this object are read-only.

`altKey`
: `true` if the **Alt** key was held down when an event occurred. Defined for mouse events.

`bubbles`
: `true` if the event is of a type that bubbles; `false` otherwise. Defined for all events.

`button`
: Specifies which mouse button changed state during a mousedown, mouseup, or click event. 0 indicates the left button, 1 indicates the middle button, and 2 indicates the right button. Note that this property is only defined when a button changes state: it is not used to report whether a button is held down during a mousemove event, for example. Also, this property is not a bitmap: it cannot tell you if more than one button is held down. Netscape 6.0 uses the values 1, 2, and 3 instead of 0, 1, and 2. This is fixed in Netscape 6.1.

`cancelable`
: `true` if the default action associated with the event can be canceled with `preventDefault()`, `false` otherwise. Defined for all events.

`clientX, clientY`
: These properties specify the X and Y coordinates of the mouse pointer, relative to the client area of the browser window. Note that these coordinates do not take document scrolling into account. Defined for mouse events.

`ctrlKey`
: `true` if the **Ctrl** key was held down when the event occurred. Defined for mouse events.

`currentTarget`
: The document node that is currently handling this event. During capturing and bubbling, this is different than `target`. Defined for all events.

`detail`
: The click count: 1 for a single click, 2 for a double-click, 3 for a triple click, and so on. Defined for click, mousedown and mouseup events.

`eventPhase`
: The current phase of event propagation. The constants above define the three legal values for this property. Defined for all events.

`metaKey`
: `true` if the **Meta** key was held down when the event occurred. Defined for mouse events.

`relatedTarget`
: For mouseover events, this is the document node that the mouse left when it moved over the target. For mouseout events, it is the node that the mouse entered when leaving the target. It is undefined for other types of events.

`screenX, screenY`
: These properties specify the X and Y coordinates of the mouse pointer relative to the upper-left corner of the user's screen. Defined for mouse events.

`shiftKey`
: `true` if the **Shift** key was held down when the event occurred. Defined for mouse events.

`target`
: The target for this event; the document node that generated the event. Note that this may be any node, including Text nodes; it is not restricted to Element nodes. Defined for all events.

`timeStamp`
: A Date object that specifies the date and time at which the event occurred. Defined for all events, but implementations are not required to provide a valid timestamp.

`type`
: The type of event that occurred. This is the name of the event handler property with the leading "on" removed. For example, "click", "load", or "mousedown". Defined for all events.

`view`
: The Window object in which the event was generated.

DOM Methods

`preventDefault()`
: Tells the web browser not to perform the default action (if there is one) associated with this event. If the event is not of a type that is cancelable, this method has no effect. Returns nothing.

`stopPropagation()`
: Stops the event from propagating any further through the capturing, target, or bubbling phases of event propagation. Returns nothing.

IE 4 Properties

`altKey`
: A boolean value that specifies whether the **Alt** key was held down when the event occurred.

`button`
: For mouse events, `button` specifies which mouse button or buttons were pressed. This read-only integer is a bitmask: the 1 bit is set if the left button was pressed. The 2 bit is set if the right button was pressed. The 4 bit is set if the middle button (of a three button mouse) was pressed.

`cancelBubble`
: If an event handler wants to stop an event from being propagated up to containing objects, it must set this property to `true`.

`clientX, clientY`
: The X and Y coordinates, relative to the web browser page, at which the event occurred.

`ctrlKey`
: A boolean value that specifies whether the **Ctrl** key was held down when the event occurred.

`fromElement`
: For mouseover and mouseout events, `fromElement` refers to the object from which the mouse pointer is moving.

`keyCode`
: For keyboard events, `keyCode` specifies the Unicode character code generated by the key that was struck.

`offsetX, offsetY`
: The X and Y coordinates at which the event occurred, within the coordinate system of the event's source element (see `srcElement`).

`returnValue`
: If this property is set, its value takes precedence over the value actually returned by an event handler. Set this property to `false` to cancel the default action of the source element on which the event occurred.

`screenX, screenY`
: The X and Y coordinates, relative to the screen, at which the event occurred.

`shiftKey`
: A boolean value that specifies whether the **Shift** key was held down when the event occurred.

`srcElement`
: The Window, Document, or Element object that generated the event.

`toElement`
: For mouseover and mouseout events, `toElement` refers to the object into which the mouse pointer is moving.

`type`
: A string property that specifies the type of the event. Its value is the name of the event handler, minus the "on" prefix. So, when the `onclick()` event handler is invoked, the `type` property of the Event object is "click".

`x, y`
: The X and Y coordinates at which the event occurred. These properties specify coordinates relative to the innermost containing element that is dynamically positioned using CSS.

Netscape 4 Properties

`height`
: Set only in resize events. Specifies the new height of the window or frame that was resized.

`layerX, layerY`
: Specify the X and Y coordinates, relative to the enclosing layer, at which an event occurred.

`modifiers`
: Specifies which keyboard modifier keys were held down when the event occurred. This numeric value is a bitmask consisting of any of the constants `Event.ALT_MASK`, `Event.CONTROL_MASK`, `Event.META_MASK`, or `Event.SHIFT_MASK`. Due to a bug, this property is not defined in Netscape 6 or 6.1.

`pageX, pageY`
: The X and Y coordinates, relative to the web browser page, at which the event occurred. Note that these coordinates are relative to the top-level page, not to any enclosing layers.

`screenX`, `screenY`
The X and Y coordinates, relative to the screen, at which the event occurred.

`target`
The Window, Document, Layer, or Element object on which the event occurred.

`type`
A string property that specifies the type of the event. Its value is the name of the event handler, minus the "on" prefix. So, when the `onclick()` event handler is invoked, the `type` property of the Event object is "click".

`which`
For keyboard and mouse events, `which` specifies which key or mouse button was pressed or released. For keyboard events, this property contains the character encoding of the key that was pressed. For mouse events, it contains 1, 2, or 3, indicating the left, middle, or right buttons.

`width`
Set only in resize events. Specifies the new width of the window or frame that was resized.

`x`, `y`
The X and Y coordinates at which the event occurred. These properties are synonyms for `layerX` and `layerY` and specify the position relative to the containing layer (if any).

Form — Client-Side JavaScript 1.0

An HTML input form — **Inherits From: Element**

document.forms[*form_number*]
document.forms[*form_name*]
document.*form_name*

Properties

The Form object defines properties for each of the attributes of the HTML `<form>` element, such as `action`, `encoding`, `method`, `name`, and `target`. In addition, it defines the following properties:

`elements[]`
A read-only array of Input objects representing the elements that appear in the form. The array can be indexed numerically, or by element name for elements that have HTML `name` attributes defined.

`length`
The number of elements in the form. Equivalent to `elements.length`.

Methods

`reset()`
Resets each of the input elements of the form to their default values. Returns nothing. JS 1.1.

`submit()`
Submits the form, but does not trigger the `onsubmit` event handler. Returns nothing.

Event Handlers

`onreset`
: Invoked just before the elements of the form are reset. Return `false` to prevent reset.

`onsubmit`
: Invoked just before the form is submitted. This event handler allows form entries to be validated before being submitted. Return `false` to prevent submission.

See Also

Element, Input, Select, Textarea

Function — Core JavaScript 1.0; JScript 1.0; ECMA v1

A JavaScript function

Constructor

`new Function(`*`argument_names...`*`, `*`body`*`)`

This constructor was introduced in JavaScript 1.1, and has been obsoleted by the function literal syntax of JavaScript 1.2.

Properties

`length`
: The number of named arguments specified when the function was declared. See `Arguments.length` for the number of argument actually passed. JS 1.1; JScript 2.0; ECMA v1.

`prototype`
: An object which, for a constructor function, defines properties and methods shared by all objects created with that constructor function. JS 1.1; JScript 2.0; ECMA v1.

Methods

`apply(`*`thisobj`*`, `*`args`*`)`
: Invokes the function as a method of *`thisobj`*, passing the elements of the array *`args`* as arguments to the function. Returns whatever value is returned by the invocation of the function. JS 1.2; JScript 5.5; ECMA v3.

`call(`*`thisobj`*`, `*`args...`*`)`
: Invokes the function as a method of *`thisobj`*, using any subsequent arguments as arguments to the function. Returns the value that is returned by the invocation of the function. JS 1.5; JScript 5.5; ECMA v3.

`toString()`
: Returns a string representation of the function. In some implementations, this is the actual source code of the function. JS 1.0; JScript 2.0; ECMA v1.

See Also

Arguments

Global

Core JavaScript 1.0; JScript 1.0; ECMA v1

Global properties and functions

`this`

Description

The Global object holds the global properties and methods listed. These properties and methods do not need to be referenced or invoked through any other object. Any variables and functions you define in your own top-level code become properties of the Global object. The Global object has no name, but you can refer to it in top-level code (i.e., outside of methods) with the `this` keyword. In client-side JavaScript, the Window object serves as the Global object. It has quite a few additional properties and methods, and can be referred to as `window`.

Global Properties

`Infinity`
: A numeric value that represents positive infinity. JS 1.3; JScript 3.0; ECMA v1.

`NaN`
: The not-a-number value. JS 1.3; JScript 3.0; ECMA v1.

`undefined`
: The undefined value. JS 1.5; JScript 5.5; ECMA v3.

Global Functions

`decodeURI(`*`uri`*`)`
: Returns a decoded copy of *`uri`*, with any hexadecimal escape sequences replaced with the characters they represent. JS 1.5; JScript 5.5; ECMA v3.

`decodeURIComponent(`*`s`*`)`
: Returns a decoded copy of *`s`*, with any hexadecimal escape sequences replaced with the characters they represent. JS 1.5; JScript 5.5; ECMA v3.

`encodeURI(`*`uri`*`)`
: Returns an encoded copy of *`uri`*, with certain characters replaced by hexadecimal escape sequences. Does not encode characters such as `#`, `?`, and `@` that are used to separate the components of a URI. JS 1.5; JScript 5.5; ECMA v3.

`encodeURIComponent(`*`s`*`)`
: Returns an encoded copy of *`s`*, with certain characters replaced by hexadecimal escape sequences. Encodes any punctuation characters that could be used to separate components of a URI. JS 1.5; JScript 5.5; ECMA v3.

`escape(`*`s`*`)`
: Returns an encoded copy of *`s`* in which certain characters have been replaced by hexadecimal escape sequences. JS 1.0; JScript 1.0; ECMA v1; deprecated in ECMA v3: use `encodeURI()` and `encodeURIComponent()` instead.

`eval(`*`code`*`)`
: Evaluates a string of JavaScript code and returns the result.

`isFinite(`*`n`*`)`
: Returns `true` if *`n`* is (or can be converted to) a finite number. Returns `false` if *`n`* is (or converts to) `NaN` (not a number) or positive or negative infinity. JS 1.2; JScript 3.0; ECMA v1.

`isNaN(x)`
: Returns `true` if *x* is (or can be converted to) the not-a-number value. Returns `false` if *x* is (or can be converted to) any numeric value. JS 1.1; JScript 1.0; ECMA v1.

`parseFloat(s)`
: Converts the string *s* (or a prefix of *s*) to a number and returns that number. Returns `NaN` (0 in JS 1.0) if *s* does not begin with a valid number. JS 1.0; JScript 1.1; ECMA v1.

`parseInt(s, radix)`
: Converts the string *s* (or a prefix of *s*) to an integer and returns that integer. Returns `NaN` (0 in JS 1.0) if *s* does not begin with a valid number. The optional *radix* argument specifies the radix (between 2 and 36) to use. If omitted, base 10 is the default or base 16 if *s* begins with the hexadecimal prefix "0x" or "0X". JS 1.0; JScript 1.1; ECMA v1.

`unescape(s)`
: Decodes a string encoded with `escape()`. Returns a decoded copy of *s*. JS 1.0; JScript 1.0; ECMA v1; deprecated in ECMA v3; use `decodeURI()` and `decodeURIComponent()` instead.

See Also

Window

History — Client-Side JavaScript 1.0

Go back or forward in browsing history

window.history
history

Methods

`back()`
: Goes back to a previously visited URL in the browsing history. Returns nothing.

`forward()`
: Goes forward in the browsing history. Returns nothing.

`go(n)`
: Goes to the *n*th URL relative to the currently displayed URL. Calling this method with –1 is the same as calling the `back()` method. Returns nothing.

Image — Client-Side JavaScript 1.1

An HTML image — Inherits From: Element

document.images[*i*]
document.images[*image-name*]
document.*image-name*

Constructor

```
new Image(width, height);
```

This constructor creates an off-screen Image object that cannot be displayed. The *width* and *height* arguments are optional. Setting the `src` attribute of the resulting object causes the browser to preload an image into its cache.

Properties

The Image object defines properties for each of the attributes of the HTML `<img>` element, such as `src`, `border`, `width`, `height`, `vspace`, and `hspace`. In addition, it defines or provides special behavior for the following properties:

`complete`
: `false` if the image is still loading. `true` if it has finished loading or if there was an error while loading. Read-only.

`src`
: A read/write string that specifies the URL of the image to be displayed by the browser. This property simply mirrors the `src` attribute of the `<img>` tag, but is detailed here because many important DHTML effects are created by dynamically setting the `src` property of an Image object, to replace one image with another.

Event Handlers

Image inherits event handlers from Element and also defines the following:

`onabort`
: Invoked if the user aborts the download of an image.

`onerror`
: Invoked if an error occurs while downloading the image.

`onload`
: Invoked when the image successfully finishes loading.

Input — Client-Side JavaScript 1.0

A form input element — **Inherits From: Element**

form.elements[*i*]
form.elements[*name*]
form.*name*

Properties

The Input object defines properties for each of the attributes of the HTML `<input>` tag, such as `maxLength`, `readOnly`, `size`, and `tabIndex`. In addition, it defines the following properties:

`checked`
: A read/write boolean that specifies whether an input element of type "checkbox" or "radio" is checked (`true`) or not (`false`).

`defaultChecked`
: A boolean that specifies whether an input element of type "checkbox" or "radio" is checked when first created or when it is reset to its initial state.

`defaultValue`
: A string that specifies the text that appears in an input element of type "text" or "password" when it is first created or when it is reset to its initial state. For security reasons, this property does not affect input elements of type file.

`form`
: A read-only reference to the Form object that contains the element. This property is defined for input elements of all types.

`name`
: The name of this input element, as specified by the HTML `name` attribute. This property is defined for input elements of all types.

`type`
: A string that specifies the type of the form element. This property mirrors the HTML type attribute. Legal values are listed in the following table; the default is text. Submit and Textarea objects also have a `type` property, with possible values select-one, select-multiple, and textarea. JS 1.1.

Type	Description
"button"	Push button
"checkbox"	Checkbox element
"file"	File upload element
"hidden"	Hidden element
"image"	Graphical form submit button
"password"	Masked text entry field
"radio"	Mutually-exclusive radio button
"reset"	Form reset button
"text"	Single-line text entry field
"submit"	Form submission button

`value`
: The string value that is sent when the form is submitted. For input elements of type "text", "password", and "file", this is the editable text displayed in the element. You can set this property to change that displayed text. For input elements of type "button", "submit", and "reset", `value` is the label that appears in the button. For other types, the value string is not displayed. Note that for security reasons, the `value` property of elements of type "file" is usually read-only.

Methods

`blur()`
: Yields the keyboard focus and returns nothing. Defined for all element types except "hidden".

`click()`
: Simulates a mouse click on the form element and returns nothing. Defined for button element types: "button", "checkbox", "radio", "reset", and "submit".

`focus()`
: Takes the keyboard focus and returns nothing. Defined for all element types except "hidden".

`select()`
: Selects the text that appears in the element and returns nothing. Works for elements of type "text", "password", and "file". Also defined by the Textarea object.

Event Handlers

`onblur`
: Invoked when the element loses keyboard focus. Defined for all element types except "hidden".

`onchange`
: For text-entry elements of type "text", "password", and "file", this event handler is invoked when the user changes the displayed text and then transfers keyboard focus away from the element, signaling that text entry is complete. It is not invoked for each keystroke.

`onclick`
: For button elements of type "button", "checkbox", "radio", "reset", and "submit", this event handler is invoked when the user clicks the button. Return `false` to prevent form submission or reset for elements of type "submit" and "reset", respectively.

`onfocus`
: Invoked the element gains keyboard focus. Defined for all element types except "hidden".

See Also

Form, Option, Select, Textarea

Layer — Client-Side Netscape 4 only

An independent document layer

```
document.layers[i]
document.layers[layer-name]
document.layer-name
```

Constructor

```
new Layer(width, parent_layer)
```

Description

The Layer object is supported only in Netscape 4 and was discontinued in Netscape 6. It is entirely nonstandard, but is documented here because it provides the only way to work with dynamically positioned objects in Netscape 4. Any HTML element with a CSS `position` attribute of `absolute` is represented by a Layer object in JavaScript. You can also create layers with the nonstandard `<layer>` tag, or with the `Layer()` constructor.

Properties

`above`
: The layer above this one, if any. Read-only.

`background`
: The background image of the layer.

`below`
: The layer below this one, if any. Read-only.

`bgColor`
: The background color of the layer.

`clip.bottom`
: The Y-coordinate of the bottom edge of the layer's clipping area, relative to `top`.

`clip.height`
: The height of the layer's clipping area. Setting this property also sets the value of `clip.bottom`.

`clip.left`
: The X-coordinate of the left edge of the layer's clipping area, relative to `left`.

`clip.right`
: The X-coordinate of the right edge of the layer's clipping area, relative to `left`.

`clip.top`
: The Y-coordinate of the top edge of the layer's clipping area, relative to `top`.

`clip.width`
: The width of the layer's clipping area. Setting this property also sets the value of `clip.right`.

`document`
: A read-only reference to the Document object contained within the layer.

`hidden`
: Specifies whether a layer is hidden or visible. Setting this property to `true` hides the layer, and setting it to `false` makes the layer visible.

`layers[]`
: An array that contains any child Layer objects of this layer. It is the same as the `document.layers[]` array of a layer.

`left`
: The X-coordinate of this layer, relative to the containing layer or document. Setting this property moves the layer to the left or right. `left` is a synonym for `x`.

`name`
: The `name` attribute of the HTML tag represented by this layer.

`pageX, pageY`
: The X and Y-coordinates of this layer relative to the top-level document. Note that these coordinates are relative to the top-level page, not relative to any containing layer.

`parentLayer`
: A read-only reference to the Layer or Window object that contains (is the parent of) this layer.

`siblingAbove, siblingBelow`
: These properties refer to the sibling Layer object (i.e., a child of the same parent Layer) immediately above or below this layer in the stacking order. If there is no such layer, these properties are `null`.

`src`
: A read/write string that specifies the URL, if any, of the contents of a layer. Setting this property to a new URL causes the browser to read the contents of that URL and display them in the layer.

`top`
: The Y-coordinate of this layer relative to the containing layer or document. Setting this property moves the layer up or down. `top` is a synonym for `y`.

`visibility`
: A read/write string that specifies the visibility of the layer. The three legal values are: "show", "hide", and "inherit".

`window`
: The Window object that contains the layer, regardless of how deeply nested the layer is within other layers.

`x, y`
: The X and Y-coordinates of the layer. `x` is a synonym for the `left` property and `y` is a synonym for the `top` property.

`zIndex`
: The position of the layer in the z-order, or stacking order, of layers. When two layers overlap, the one with the higher `zIndex` appears on top and obscures the one with the lower `zIndex`. If two sibling layers have the same `zIndex`, the one that appears later in the `layers[]` array of the containing document is displayed later and overlaps the one that appears earlier.

Methods

`load(`*`src, width`*`)`
: Loads a new URL into the layer, sets the layer width, and returns nothing.

`moveAbove(`*`other_layer`*`)`
: Moves this layer above another and returns nothing.

`moveBelow(`*`other_layer`*`)`
: Moves this layer below another and returns nothing.

`moveBy(`*`dx, dy`*`)`
: Moves the layer relative to its current position and returns nothing.

`moveTo(`*`x, y`*`)`
: Moves the layer to the point (*x*,*y*) relative to its containing layer or window and returns nothing.

`moveToAbsolute(`*`x, y`*`)`
: Moves the layer to a position relative to the page and returns nothing.

`resizeBy(`*`dw, dh`*`)`
: Resizes the layer by the specified amounts and returns nothing.

`resizeTo(`*`width, height`*`)`
: Resizes the layer to the specified size returns nothing.

Link — Client-Side JavaScript 1.0

An <a> or <area> link — Inherits From: Element

`document``.links[`*`i`*`]`

Properties

Many of the properties of a Link object represent portions of its URL. For each such property below, the example given is a portion of the following (fictitious) URL:

```
http://www.oreilly.com:1234/catalog/search.html
?q=JavaScript&m=10#results
```

`hash`
: A read/write string property that specifies the anchor portion of the Link's URL, including the leading hash (#) mark. For example: "#result".

`host`
: A read/write string property that specifies the hostname and port portions of a Link's URL. For example: "www.oreilly.com:1234".

`hostname`
: A read/write string property that specifies the hostname portion of a Link's URL. For example: "www.oreilly.com".

`href`
: A read/write string property that specifies the complete text of the Link's URL.

`pathname`
: A read/write string property that specifies the pathname portion of a Link's URL. For example: "/catalog/search.html".

`port`
: A read/write string (not a number) property that specifies the port portion of a Link's URL. For example: "1234".

`protocol`
: A read/write string property that specifies the protocol portion of a Link's URL, including the trailing colon. For example: "http:".

`search`
: A read/write string property that specifies the query portion of a Link's URL, including the leading question mark. For example: "?q=JavaScript&m=10".

`target`
: A read/write string property that specifies the name of a Window object (i.e., a frame or a top-level browser window) in which the linked document should be displayed. This property is the standard `target` HTML attribute. The special names "_blank", "_top", "_parent", and "_self" are allowed.

Event Handlers

`onclick`
: Invoked when the user clicks on the link. In JavaScript 1.1, this event handler may prevent the link from being followed by returning `false`.

`onmouseout`
: Invoked when the user moves the mouse off the link. JS 1.1.

`onmouseover`
: Invoked when the user moves the mouse over the link. The `status` property of the current window may be set here. Return `true` to tell the browser not to display the URL of the link in the status line.

See Also

Anchor, Location

Location

Client-Side JavaScript 1.0

Current browser location

```
location
window.location
```

Properties

The Location object defines the same URL-related properties that the Link object does, with the exception of the `target`. See the Link object for a description of the `hash`, `host`, `hostname`, `href`, `pathname`, `port`, `protocol`, and `search` properties. Setting any of these properties causes the browser to load and display the document from the new URL. As a shortcut, you can also load a new document by assigning a URL string to the `location` property of the Window.

Methods

`reload(`*`force`*`)`
: Reloads the current document from the cache or the server. The *force* argument is optional. If `true`, it forces a complete reload, even if the document has not been modified. Returns nothing. JS 1.1.

`replace(`*`url`*`)`
: Replaces the current document with a new one, without generating a new entry in the browsing history. Returns nothing. JS 1.1.

See Also

Link, `Window.location`

Math

Core JavaScript 1.0; JScript 1.0; ECMA v1

Mathematical functions and constants

```
Math.constant
Math.function()
```

Description

The Math object is a placeholder for grouping mathematical constants and functions. It does not define a class of objects as Date and String do. There is no `Math()` constructor, and functions like `Math.sin()` are simply functions, not methods that operate on an object.

Constants

`Math.E`
: The constant *e*, the base of the natural logarithm.

`Math.LN10`
: The natural logarithm of 10.

`Math.LN2`
: The natural logarithm of 2.

`Math.LOG10E`
: The base-10 logarithm of *e*.

`Math.LOG2E`
: The base-2 logarithm of *e*.

`Math.PI`
: The constant π.

`Math.SQRT1_2`
: 1 divided by the square root of 2.

`Math.SQRT2`
: The square root of 2.

Functions

`Math.abs(x)`
: Returns the absolute value of *x*.

`Math.acos(x)`
: Returns the arc cosine of *x*; the return value is between 0 and π radians.

`Math.asin(x)`
: Returns the arc sine of *x*; the return value is between -π/2 and π/2 radians.

`Math.atan(x)`
: Returns the arc tangent of *x*; the return value is between -π/2 and π/2 radians.

`Math.atan2(y, x)`
: Returns a value between -π and π radians that specifies the counterclockwise angle between the positive X-axis and the point (*x*, *y*). Note the order of the arguments to this function.

`Math.ceil(x)`
: Returns the nearest integer greater than or equal to *x*.

`Math.cos(x)`
: Returns the cosine of the specified value *x*.

`Math.exp(x)`
: Returns the constant *e* raised to the power of *x*.

`Math.floor(x)`
: Returns the nearest integer less than or equal to *x*.

`Math.log(x)`
: Returns the natural logarithm of *x*.

`Math.max(args...)`
: Returns the largest of the arguments. Returns `-Infinity` if there are no arguments. Returns `NaN` if any of the arguments is `NaN` or is a non-numeric value that cannot be converted to a number. Prior to ECMA v3, this function requires exactly 2 arguments.

`Math.min(args...)`
: Returns the smallest of the arguments. Returns `Infinity` if there are no arguments. Returns `NaN` if any argument is `NaN` or is a non-numeric value that cannot be converted to a number. Prior to ECMA v3, this function requires exactly 2 arguments.

`Math.pow(x, y)`
: Returns *x* to the power of *y*.

`Math.random()`
: Returns a pseudorandom number between 0.0 and 1.0. JS 1.1; JScript 1.0; ECMA v1.

`Math.round(x)`
: Returns the integer closest to *x*.

`Math.sin(x)`
: Returns the sine of *x*.

`Math.sqrt(x)`
: Returns the square root of *x*. Returns `NaN` if *x* is less than zero.

`Math.tan(x)`
: Returns the tangent of *x*.

See Also

Number

Navigator

Client-Side JavaScript 1.0

Information about the browser

`navigator`

Properties

`appCodeName`
: A read-only string that specifies a nickname for the browser. In all Netscape browsers, this is "Mozilla". For compatibility, this property is "Mozilla" in Microsoft browsers as well.

`appName`
: A read-only string property that specifies the name of the browser. For Netscape, the value of this property is "Netscape". In IE, the value of this property is "Microsoft Internet Explorer".

`appVersion`
: A read-only string that specifies version and platform information for the browser. The first part of this string is a version number. Pass the string to `parseInt()` to obtain the major version number only or to `parseFloat()` to obtain the major and minor version numbers as a floating-point value. The remainder of the string value of this property provides other details about the browser version, including the operating system it is running on. Unfortunately, however, the format of this information varies widely from browser to browser.

`cookieEnabled`
: A read-only boolean that is `true` if the browser has cookies enabled, and `false` if they are disabled. IE 4, Netscape 6.

`language`
: A read-only string that specifies the default language of the browser version. The value of this property is a standard two-letter language code such as "en" for English or "fr" for French. It can also be a five-letter string indicating a language and a regional variant, such as "fr_CA" for French, as spoken in Canada. Netscape 4; note that IE 4 provides two different language-related properties.

`platform`
: A read-only string that specifies the operating system and/or hardware platform the browser is running under. Although there is not standard set of values for this property, some typical values are "Win32", "MacPPC", and "Linux i586". JS 1.2.

`systemLanguage`
: A read-only string that specifies the default language of the operating system using the same standard codes used by the Netscape-specific `language` property. IE 4.

`userAgent`
: A read-only string that specifies the value the browser uses for the user-agent header in HTTP requests. Typically, this is the value of `navigator.appCodeName` followed by a slash and the value of `navigator.appVersion`.

`userLanguage`
: A read-only string that specifies the preferred language of the user using the same standard codes used by the Netscape-specific `language` property. IE 4.

Methods

`javaEnabled()`
: Returns `true` if Java is supported and enabled in the current browser, or `false` if it is not. JS 1.1.

See Also

Screen

Node — DOM Level 1

A node in a document tree

Subclasses

Attr, Comment, Document, DocumentFragment, Element, Text

Constants

All nodes in an HTML document are instances of one of the Node subclasses listed above. Every Node object has a `nodeType` property that specifies which of the subclasses it is an instance of. The following constants are the legal values for `nodeType`. Note that these are static properties of `Node`, not properties of individual Node objects. They are not defined in Internet Explorer 4, 5, or 6; in those browsers you must use the corresponding integer literals.

```
Node.ELEMENT_NODE = 1;            // Element
Node.ATTRIBUTE_NODE = 2;          // Attr
Node.TEXT_NODE = 3;               // Text
Node.COMMENT_NODE = 8;            // Comment
Node.DOCUMENT_NODE = 9;           // Document
Node.DOCUMENT_FRAGMENT_NODE=11;   // DocumentFragment
```

Properties

`attributes[]`
: If this Node is an Element, the `attributes` property is a read-only array of Attr objects that represent the attributes of the element. The array can be indexed by number or by attribute name. All HTML attributes have corresponding Element properties, however, so it is uncommon to use the `attributes[]` array.

`childNodes[]`
: This read-only array of Node objects contains the children of this node. If the node has no children, this property is a zero-length array.

`firstChild`
: This read-only property refers to the first child Node of this node, or `null` if the node has no children.

`lastChild`
: This read-only property refers to the last child Node of this node, or `null` if the node has no children.

`nextSibling`
: The sibling Node that immediately follows this one in the `childNodes[]` array of the `parentNode`, or `null` if there is no such node. Read-only.

`nodeName`
: The name of the node. For Element nodes, this property specifies the tag name of the element, which can also be retrieved with the `tagName` property of Element. For Attr nodes, this property specifies the attribute name. For other types of nodes, the value is a constant string that specifies the node type. Read-only.

`nodeType`
: The type of the node. The legal values for this property are defined by the constants listed above.

`nodeValue`
: The string value of a node. For Text and Comment nodes, this property holds the text content. For Attr nodes, it holds the attribute value. This property is read/write.

`ownerDocument`
: The Document object of which this Node is a part. For Document nodes, this property is `null`. Read-only.

`parentNode`
: The parent or container Node of this node, or `null` if there is no parent. Note that Document and Attr nodes never have parent nodes. Nodes that have been removed from the document or are newly created and have not yet been inserted into the document tree have a `parentNode` of `null`. Read-only.

`previousSibling`
: The sibling Node that immediately precedes this one in the `childNodes[]` array of the `parentNode`, or `null`, if there is no such node.

Methods

`addEventListener(`*`type`*`, `*`listener`*`, `*`useCapture`*`)`
: Registers an event listener for this node. *`type`* is a string that specifies the event type minus the "on" prefix (e.g., "click" or "submit"). *`listener`* is the event handler function. When triggered, it is invoked with an Event object as its argument. If *`useCapture`* is `true`, this is a capturing event handler. If `false` or omitted, it is a regular event handler. Returns nothing. DOM Level 2; not supported in IE 4, 5, or 6.

`appendChild(`*`newChild`*`)`
: Adds the *`newChild`* Node to the document tree by appending it to the `childNodes[]` array of this node. If the node is already in the document tree, it is first removed before being reinserted at its new position. Returns the *`newChild`* argument.

`cloneNode(`*`deep`*`)`
: Returns a copy of this node. If `deep` is `true`, the descendents of the node are recursively copied as well.

`hasAttributes()`
: Returns `true` if this node is an Element and has any attributes. DOM Level 2.

`hasChildNodes()`
: Returns true if this node has any children.

`insertBefore(`*`newChild, refChild`*`)`
: Inserts the *`newChild`* Node into the document tree immediately before the *`refChild`* Node, which must be a child of this node. If the node being inserted is already in the tree, it is first removed. Returns *`newChild`*.

`isSupported(`*`feature, version`*`)`
: Returns true if the specified version number of a named feature is supported by this node. See also `DOMImplementation.hasFeature()`. DOM Level 2.

`normalize()`
: Normalizes all Text node descendants of this node by deleting empty Text nodes and merging adjacent Text nodes. Returns nothing.

`removeChild(`*`oldChild`*`)`
: Removes the *`oldChild`* Node from the document tree. *`oldChild`* must be a child of this node. Returns `oldChild`.

`removeEventListener(`*`type, listener, useCapture`*`)`
: Removes the specified event listener. Returns nothing. DOM Level 2; not supported in IE 4, 5, or 6.

`replaceChild(`*`newChild, oldChild`*`)`
: Replaces the *`oldChild`* Node (which must be a child of this node) with the *`newChild`* Node. If *`newChild`* is already in the document tree, it is first removed from its current location. Returns *`oldChild`*.

See Also

Attr, Comment, Document, DocumentFragment, Element, Text

Number — Core JavaScript 1.1; JScript 2.0; ECMA v1

Support for numbers

Constructor

```
new Number(value)
Number(value)
```

With the `new` operator, the `Number()` constructor converts its argument to a numeric value and returns a new Number object wrapped around that value. Without `new`, `Number()` is a conversion function that converts its argument to a number and returns that value.

Constants

These constants are properties of `Number` itself, not of individual Number objects.

`Number.MAX_VALUE`
: The largest representable number. Approximately 1.79E + 308.

`Number.MIN_VALUE`
: The smallest representable number. Approximately 5E – 324.

`Number.NaN`
: Not-a-number value. Same as the global `NaN`.

`Number.NEGATIVE_INFINITY`
    Negative infinite value.

`Number.POSITIVE_INFINITY`
    Infinite value. Same as global `Infinity`.

Methods

`toExponential(`*`digits`*`)`
    Returns a string representation of the number, in exponential notation, with one digit before the decimal place and *`digits`* digits after the decimal place. The fractional part of the number is rounded, or padded with zeros so that it has the specified length. *`digits`* must be between 0 and 20, and if omitted, as many digits as necessary are used. JS 1.5; JScript 5.5; ECMA v3.

`toFixed(`*`digits`*`)`
    Returns a string representation of the number that does not use exponential notation, and has exactly *`digits`* digits after the decimal place. *`digits`* must be between 0 and 20. The number is rounded or padded with zeros if necessary. JS 1.5; JScript 5.5; ECMA v3.

`toLocaleString()`
    Returns an implementation-dependent string representation of the number, formatted according to local conventions. This may affect things such as the punctuation characters used for the decimal point and the thousands separator. JS 1.5; JScript 5.5; ECMA v3.

`toPrecision(`*`precision`*`)`
    Returns a string representation of *`number`* that contains *`precision`* significant digits. *`precision`* must be between 1 and 21. The returned string uses fixed-point notation where possible, or exponential notation otherwise. The number is rounded or padded with zeros if necessary. JS 1.5; JScript 5.5; ECMA v3.

`toString(`*`radix`*`)`
    Converts a number to a string, using a specified radix (base), and returns the string. *`radix`* must be between 2 and 36. If omitted, base 10 is used.

See Also

Math

Object   **Core JavaScript 1.0; JScript 1.0; ECMA v1**

The superclass of all JavaScript objects

Constructor

```
new Object();
```

This constructor creates an empty object to which you can add arbitrary properties.

Properties

All JavaScript objects, however they are created, have the following properties.

`constructor`
    A reference to the JavaScript function that was the constructor for the object. JS 1.1; JScript 2.0; ECMA v1.

Methods

All JavaScript objects, however they are created, have the following methods.

`hasOwnProperty(`*propname*`)`
: Returns `true` if the object has a non-inherited property with the specified name. Returns `false` if the object does not have a property with the specified name, or if it inherits that property from its prototype object. JS 1.5; JScript 5.5; ECMA v3.

`isPrototypeOf(`*o*`)`
: Returns `true` if this object is the prototype of *o*. Returns `false` if *o* is not an object or if this object is not its prototype. JS 1.5; JScript 5.5; ECMA v3.

`propertyIsEnumerable(`*propname*`)`
: Returns `true` if this object has a non-inherited enumerable property with the specified name, and returns `false` otherwise. Enumerable properties are those that are enumerated by `for/in` loops. JS 1.5; JScript 5.5; ECMA v3.

`toLocaleString()`
: Returns a localized string representation of the object. The default implementation of this method simply calls `toString()`, but subclasses may override it to provide localization. JS 1.5; JScript 5.5; ECMA v3.

`toString()`
: Returns a string representation of the object. The implementation of this method provided by the Object class is quite generic and does not provide much useful information. Subclasses of Object typically override this method by defining their own `toString()` method that produces more useful output. JS 1.0; JScript 2.0; ECMA v1.

`valueOf()`
: Returns the primitive value of the object, if any. For objects of type Object, this method simply returns the object itself. Subclasses of Object, such as Number and Boolean, override this method to return the primitive value associated with the object. JS 1.1; JScript 2.0; ECMA v1.

See Also

Array, Boolean, Function, Number, String

Option — Client-Side JavaScript 1.0

A selectable option — Inherits From: Element

select`.options[`*i*`]`

Constructor

In JavaScript 1.1 and later, Option objects can be created dynamically with the `Option()` constructor:

```
new Option(text, value, defaultSelected, selected)
```

Properties

`defaultSelected`
: A read/write boolean that specifies whether the option is initially selected when the Select object that contains it is created or reset.

`index`
: A read-only integer that specifies the index of the option within the `options[]` array of the Select object that contains it.

`selected`
: A read/write boolean value that specifies whether an option is currently selected. You can use this property to test whether a given option is selected. You can also set it to select or deselect an option. Note that when you select or deselect an option in this way, the `Select.onchange()` event handler is not invoked.

`text`
: A read/write string that specifies the text that appears to the user for the option.

`value`
: A read/write string that specifies the text that is passed to the web server if the option is selected when the form is submitted.

See Also

Select

RegExp

Core JavaScript 1.2; JScript 3.0; ECMA v3

Regular expressions for pattern matching

`/`*`pattern`*`/`*`attributes`*

Constructor

`new RegExp(`*`pattern`*`, `*`attributes`*`)`

Regular expression patterns are expressed using a complex grammar that is summarized earlier in this chapter.

Instance Properties

`global`
: A read-only boolean that specifies whether the RegExp has the `g` attribute and therefore performs global matching.

`ignoreCase`
: A read-only boolean that specifies whether the RegExp has the `i` attribute and therefore performs case-insensitive matching.

`lastIndex`
: For global RegExp objects, this read/write property specifies the character position immediately following the last match; this is the first character examined for the next match.

`multiline`
: A read-only boolean that specifies whether the RegExp has the `m` attribute and therefore performs multi-line matching.

`source`
: A read-only string that holds the source text of the regular expression *`pattern`*, excluding slashes and attributes.

Methods

`exec(string)`
: Matches *string* against this RegExp and returns an array containing the results of the match, or `null` if no match was found. Element 0 of the array is the matching text. Subsequent elements of the array contain the substrings that matched the subexpressions within the RegExp. The returned array also has an `index` property that specifies the start position of the match.

`test(string)`
: Returns `true` if *string* contains text matching this RegExp, or `false` otherwise.

See Also

`String.match()`, `String.replace()`, `String.search()`

Screen — Client-Side JavaScript 1.2

Information about the display

`screen`

Properties

`availHeight`
: The available height, in pixels, of the screen.

`availWidth`
: Specifies the available width, in pixels, of the screen.

`colorDepth`
: The depth of the browser's color palette, or the number of bits-per-pixel for the screen.

`height`
: Specifies the total height, in pixels, of the screen.

`width`
: Specifies the total width, in pixels, of the screen.

See Also

Navigator

Select — Client-Side JavaScript 1.0

A graphical selection list — Inherits From: Element

form.elements[*i*]
form.elements[*element_name*]
form.*element_name*

Properties

The Select object defines properties for each of the attributes of the HTML `<select>` tag, such as `disabled`, `multiple`, `name`, and `size`. In addition, it defines the following properties:

`form`
: The Form object that contains this Select object. Read-only.

`length`
: A read-only integer that specifies the number of elements in the `options[]` array. The value of this property is the same as `options.length`.

`options[]`
: An array of Option objects, each describing one of the options displayed within the Select element. You can shorten the set of options by setting the `options.length` property to a smaller value (or remove all options by setting it to zero). You can remove individual options by setting an element of the array to `null`—this shifts the elements above it down, shortening the array. You can append options to the Select object by using the `Option()` constructor to create a new Option and assigning it to `options[options.length]`.

`selectedIndex`
: A read/write integer that specifies the index of the selected option within the Select object. If no option is selected, `selectedIndex` is `-1`. If more than one option is selected, `selectedIndex` specifies the index of the first one only. Setting this property causes all other options to become deselected. Setting it to `-1` causes all options to be deselected.

`type`
: A read-only string property that specifies the type of the element. If the Select object allows only a single selection (i.e., if the `multiple` attribute does not appear in the object's HTML definition), this property is "select-one". Otherwise, the value is "select-multiple". See also `Input.type`. JS 1.1.

Methods

`add(`*`new, old`*`)`
: Inserts the Option object *new* into the `options[]` array at the position immediately before the Option object *old*. If *old* is `null`, the *new* Option is appended to the array. Returns nothing. DOM Level 1.

`blur()`
: Yields the keyboard focus and returns nothing.

`focus()`
: Grabs the keyboard focus and returns nothing.

`remove(`*`n`*`)`
: Removes the *n*th element from the `options[]` array. Returns nothing. DOM Level 1.

Event Handlers

`onblur`
: Invoked when input focus is lost.

`onchange`
: Invoked when the user selects or deselects an item.

`onfocus`
: Invoked when input focus is gained.

See Also

Form, Input, Option

String

Core JavaScript 1.0; JScript 1.0; ECMA v1

String manipulation

Inherits From: Object

Constructor

`String(s)`
`new String(s)`

Without the `new` operator, the `String()` function converts its argument to a string. With the `new` operator, it is a constructor that wraps the converted value in a String object.

Properties

`length`
: The number of characters in the string. Read-only.

Methods

`charAt(n)`
: Returns the character at position *n* in the string.

`charCodeAt(n)`
: Returns the Unicode encoding of the character at position *n* in the string. JS 1.2; JScript 5.5; ECMA v1.

`concat(value, ...)`
: Returns a new string that results from converting each of the arguments to a string and concatenating the resulting strings. JS 1.2; JScript 3.0; ECMA v3.

`indexOf(substring, start)`
: Returns the position of the first occurrence of *substring* within this string that appears at or after the *start* position or –1 if no such occurrence is found. If *start* is omitted, 0 is used.

`lastIndexOf(substring, start)`
: Returns the position of the last occurrence of *substring* within *string* that appears before the *start* position, or –1 if no such occurrence is found. If `start` is omitted, the string length is used.

`match(regexp)`
: Matches this string against the specified regular expression and returns an array containing the match results or `null` if no match is found. If *regexp* is not a global regular expression, the returned array is the same as for the `RegExp.exec()` method. If *regexp* is global (has the "g" attribute), the elements of the returned array contain the text of each match found. JS 1.2; JScript 3.0; ECMA v3.

`replace(regexp, replacement)`
: Returns a new string, with text matching *regexp* replaced with *replacement*. *regexp* may be a regular expression or a plain string. *replacement* may be a string, containing optional regular expression escape sequences (such as `$1`) that are replaced with portions of the matched text. It may also be a function that computes the replacement string based on match details passed as arguments. JS 1.2; JScript 3.0; ECMA v3.

`search(regexp)`
: Returns the position of the start of the first substring of this string that matches *regexp*, or –1 if no match is found. JS 1.2; JScript 3.0; ECMA v3.

`slice(start, end)`
: Returns a new string that contains all the characters of *string* from and including the position *start* and up to but not including *end*. If *end* is omitted, the slice extends to the end of the string. Negative arguments specify character positions measured from the end of the string. JS 1.2; JScript 3.0; ECMA v3.

`split(delimiter, limit)`
: Returns an array of strings, created by splitting *string* into substrings at the boundaries specified by *delimiter*. *delimiter* may be a string or a RegExp. If *delimiter* is a RegExp with a parenthesized subexpression, the delimiter text that matches the subexpression is included in the returned array. See also `Array.join()`. JS 1.1; JScript 3.0; ECMA v1.

`substring(from, to)`
: Returns a new string that contains characters copied from positions *from* to *to-1* of *string*. If to is omitted, the substring extends to the end of the string. Negative arguments are not allowed.

`substr(start, length)`
: Returns a copy of the portion of this string starting at *start* and continuing for *length* characters, or to the end of the string, if *length* is not specified. JS 1.2; JScript 3.0; nonstandard: use `slice()` or `substring()` instead.

`toLowerCase()`
: Returns a copy of the string, with all uppercase letters converted to their lowercase equivalent, if they have one.

`toUpperCase()`
: Returns a copy of the string, with all lowercase letters converted to their uppercase equivalent, if they have one.

Static Functions

`String.fromCharCode(c1, c2, ...)`
: Returns a new string containing characters with the encodings specified by the numeric arguments. JS 1.2; JScript 3.0; ECMA v1.

Style — DOM Level 2; IE 4

Inline CSS properties of an element

element`.style`

Properties

The Style object defines a large number of properties: one property for each CSS attribute defined by the CSS2 specification. The property names correspond closely to the CSS attribute names, with minor changes required to avoid syntax errors in JavaScript. Multiword attributes that contain hyphens, such as `font-family` are written without hyphens in JavaScript, and each word after the first is capitalized: `fontFamily`. Also, the `float` attribute conflicts with the reserved word `float`, so it translates to the property `cssFloat`.

The visual CSS properties are listed in the following table. Since the properties correspond directly to CSS attributes, no individual documentation is given for each property. See a CSS reference (such as *Cascading Style Sheets: The Definitive Guide* by

Eric A. Meyer, published by O'Reilly) for the meaning and legal values of each. Note that current browsers do not implement all of these properties.

All of the properties are strings, and care is required when working with properties that have numeric values. When querying such a property, you must use `parseFloat()` to convert the string to a number. When setting such a property you must convert your number to a string, which you can usually do by adding the required units specification, such as "px".

```
background              counterIncrement        orphans
backgroundAttachment    counterReset            outline
backgroundColor         cssFloat                outlineColor
backgroundImage         cursor                  outlineStyle
backgroundPosition      direction               outlineWidth
backgroundRepeat        display                 overflow
border                  emptyCells              padding
borderBottom            font                    paddingBottom
borderBottomColor       fontFamily              paddingLeft
borderBottomStyle       fontSize                paddingRight
borderBottomWidth       fontSizeAdjust          paddingTop
borderCollapse          fontStretch             page
borderColor             fontStyle               pageBreakAfter
borderLeft              fontVariant             pageBreakBefore
borderLeftColor         fontWeight              pageBreakInside
borderLeftStyle         height                  position
borderLeftWidth         left                    quotes
borderRight             letterSpacing           right
borderRightColor        lineHeight              size
borderRightStyle        listStyle               tableLayout
borderRightWidth        listStyleImage          textAlign
borderSpacing           listStylePosition       textDecoration
borderStyle             listStyleType           textIndent
borderTop               margin                  textShadow
borderTopColor          marginBottom            textTransform
borderTopStyle          marginLeft              top
borderTopWidth          marginRight             unicodeBidi
borderWidth             marginTop               verticalAlign
bottom                  markerOffset            visibility
captionSide             marks                   whiteSpace
clear                   maxHeight               widows
clip                    maxWidth                width
color                   minHeight               wordSpacing
content                 minWidth                zIndex
```

Text

DOM Level 1

A run of text in a document

Inherits From: Node

Description

A Text object represents a run of plain text without markup in a DOM document tree. Do not confuse it with the single-line text input element of HTML, which is represented by the Input object.

JavaScript

Properties

`data`
: The string of text contained by this node.

`length`
: The number of characters contained by this node. Read-only.

Methods

`appendData(`*`text`*`)`
: Appends the specified *text* to this node and returns nothing.

`deleteData(`*`offset, count`*`)`
: Deletes text from this node, starting with the character at the specified *offset*, and continuing for *count* characters. Returns nothing.

`insertData(`*`offset, text`*`)`
: Inserts the specified *text* into this node at the specified character *offset*. Returns nothing.

`replaceData(`*`offset, count, text`*`)`
: Replaces the characters starting at the specified *offset* and continuing for *count* characters with the specified *text*. Returns nothing.

`splitText(`*`offset`*`)`
: Splits this Text node into two at the specified character position, inserts the new Text node into the document after the original, and returns the new node.

`substringData(`*`offset, count`*`)`
: Returns a string that consists of the *count* characters starting with the character at position *offset*.

See Also

`Node.normalize()`

Textarea — Client-Side JavaScript 1.0

Multiline text input — Inherits From: Element

`form``.elements[`*`i`*`]`
`form``.elements[`*`name`*`]`
`form.name`

Description

The Textarea object is very similar to the Input object.

Properties

The Textarea object defines properties for each of the attributes of the HTML `<textarea>` tag, such as `cols`, `defaultValue`, `disabled`, `name`, `readOnly`, and `rows`. In addition, it defines the following properties:

`form`
: The Form object that contains this Textarea object. Read-only.

`type`
: A read-only string property that specifies the type of the element. For Textarea objects, this property is always "textarea".

`value`
A read/write string that specifies the text contained in the Textarea. The initial value of this property is the same as the `defaultValue` property.

Methods

`blur()`
Yields the keyboard focus and returns nothing.

`focus()`
Grabs the keyboard focus and returns nothing.

`select()`
Selects the entire contents of the text area. Returns nothing.

Event Handlers

`onblur`
Invoked when input focus is lost.

`onchange`
Invoked when the user changes the value in the Textarea element and moves the keyboard focus elsewhere. This event handler is invoked only when the user completes an edit in the Textarea element.

`onfocus`
Invoked when input focus is gained.

See Also

Element, Form, Input

Window — Client-Side JavaScript 1.0

Browser window or frame

```
self
window
window.frames[i]
```

Properties

The Window object defines the following properties. Nonportable, browser-specific properties are listed separately after this list. Note that the Window object is the Global object for client-side JavaScript; therefore, the Window object also has the properties listed on the Global reference page.

`closed`
A read-only boolean value that specifies whether the window has been closed.

`defaultStatus`
A read/write string that specifies a persistent message to appear in the status line whenever the browser is not displaying another message.

`document`
A read-only reference to the Document object contained in this window or frame. See Document.

`frames[]`
: An array of Window objects, one for each frame contained within the this window. Note that frames referenced by the `frames[]` array may themselves contain frames and may have a `frames[]` array of their own.

`history`
: A read-only reference to the History object of this window or frame. See History.

`length`
: Specifies the number of frames contained in this window or frame. Same as `frames.length`.

`location`
: The Location object for this window or frame. See Location. This property has special behavior: if you assign a URL string to it, the browser loads and displays that URL.

`name`
: A string that contains the name of the window or frame. The name is specified with the `Window.open()` method, or with the `name` attribute of a `<frame>` tag. Read-only in JS 1.0; read/write in JS 1.1.

`navigator`
: A read-only reference to the Navigator object, which provides version and configuration information about the web browser. See Navigator.

`opener`
: A read/write reference to the Window that opened this window. JS 1.1.

`parent`
: A read-only reference to the Window object that contains this window or frame. If this window is a top-level window, `parent` refers to the window itself.

`screen`
: A read-only reference to the Screen object that specifies information about the screen the browser is running on. See Screen. JS 1.2.

`self`
: A read-only reference to this window itself. This is a synonym for the `window` property.

`status`
: A read/write string that can be set to display a transient message in the browser's status line.

`top`
: A read-only reference to the top-level window that contains this window. If this window is a top-level window, `top` refers to the window itself.

`window`
: The `window` property is identical to the `self` property; it contains a reference to this window.

Netscape 4 Properties

`innerHeight, innerWidth`
: Read/write properties that specify the height and width, in pixels, of the document display area of this window. These dimensions do not include the height of the menubar, toolbars, scrollbars, and so on.

`outerHeight`, `outerWidth`
: Read/write integers that specify the total height and width, in pixels, of the window. These dimensions include the height and width of the menubar, toolbars, scrollbars, window borders, and so on.

`pageXOffset`, `pageYOffset`
: Read-only integers that specify the number of pixels that the current document has been scrolled to the right (`pageXOffset`) and down (`pageYOffset`).

`screenX`, `screenY`
: Read-only integers that specify the X and Y-coordinates of the upper-left corner of the window on the screen. If this window is a frame, these properties specify the X and Y-coordinates of the top-level window that contains the frame.

IE 4 Properties

`clientInformation`
: An IE-specific synonym for the `navigator` property. Refers to the Navigator object.

`event`
: The `event` property refers to an Event object that contains the details of the most recent event to occur within this window. In the IE event model, the Event object is not passed as an argument to the event handler, and is instead assigned to this property.

Methods

The Window object has the following portable methods. Since the Window object is the Global object in client-side JavaScript, it also defines the methods listed on the Global reference page.

`alert(`*`message`*`)`
: Displays *`message`* in a dialog box. Returns nothing. JS 1.0.

`blur()`
: Yields the keyboard focus and returns nothing. JS 1.1.

`clearInterval(`*`intervalId`*`)`
: Cancels the periodic execution of code specified by *`intervalId`*. See `setInterval()`. Returns nothing. JS 1.2.

`clearTimeout(`*`timeoutId`*`)`
: Cancels the pending timeout specified by *`timeoutId`*. See `setTimeout()`. Returns nothing. JS 1.0.

`close()`
: Closes a window and returns nothing. JS 1.0.

`confirm(`*`question`*`)`
: Displays *`question`* in a dialog box and waits for a yes-or-no response. Returns `true` if the user clicks the **OK** button, or `false` if the user clicks the **Cancel** button. JS 1.0.

`focus()`
: Requests keyboard focus; this also brings the window to the front on most platforms. Returns nothing. JS 1.1.

`getComputedStyle(`*`elt`*`)`
: Returns a read-only Style object that contains all CSS styles (not just inline styles) that apply to the specified document element *`elt`*. Positioning attributes such as

left, top, and width queried from this computed style object are always returned as pixel values. DOM Level 2.

moveBy(*dx, dy*)
: Moves the window the specified distances from its current position and returns nothing. JS 1.2.

moveTo(*x, y*)
: Moves the window to the specified position and returns nothing. JS 1.2

open(*url, name, features*)
: Displays the specified *url* in the named window. If the *name* argument is omitted or if there is no window by that name, a new window is created. The optional *features* argument is a string that specifies the size and decorations of the new window as a comma-separated list of features. Feature names commonly supported on all platforms are: width=*pixels*, height=*pixels*, location, menubar, resizable, status, and toolbar. In IE, set the position of the window with left=*x* and top=*y*. In Netscape, use screenX=*x* and screenY=*y*. Returns the existing or new Window object. JS 1.0.

print()
: Simulates a click on the browser's **Print** button and returns nothing. Netscape 4; IE 5.

prompt(*message, default*)
: Displays *message* in a dialog box and waits for the user to enter a text response. Displays the optional *default* as the default response. Returns the string entered by the user, or the empty string if the user did not enter a string, or null if the user clicked **Cancel**. JS 1.0.

resizeBy(*dw, dh*)
: Resizes the window by the specified amount and returns nothing. JS 1.2.

resizeTo(*width, height*)
: Resizes the window to the specified size and returns nothing. JS 1.2.

scroll(*x, y*)
: Scrolls the window to the specified coordinates and returns nothing. JS 1.1; deprecated in JS 1.2 in favor of scrollTo().

scrollBy(*dx, dy*)
: Scrolls the window by a specified amount and returns nothing. JS 1.2.

scrollTo(*x, y*)
: Scrolls the window to a specified position and returns nothing. JS 1.2.

setInterval(*code, interval, args...*)
: Evaluates the string of JavaScript *code* every *interval* milliseconds. In Netscape 4 and IE 5, *code* may be a reference to a function instead of a string. In that case, the function is invoked every *interval* milliseconds. In Netscape, any arguments after *interval* are passed to the function when it is invoked, but this feature is not supported by IE. Returns an interval ID value that can be passed to clearInterval() to cancel the periodic executions. JS 1.2.

setTimeout(*code, delay*)
: Evaluates the JavaScript code in the string *code* after *delay* milliseconds have elapsed. In Netscape 4 and IE5, *code* may be a function rather than a string; see the discussion under setInterval(). Returns a timeout ID value that can be passed to clearTimeout() to cancel the pending execution of *code*. Note that this

method returns immediately; it does not wait for *delay* milliseconds before returning. JS 1.0.

Event Handlers

Event handlers for a Window object are defined by attributes of the <body> tag of the document.

`onblur`
: Invoked when the window loses focus.

`onerror`
: Invoked when a JavaScript error occurs. This is a special event handler that is invoked with three arguments that specify the error message, the URL of the document that contained the error, and the line number of the error, if available.

`onfocus`
: Invoked when the window gains focus.

`onload`
: Invoked when the document (or frameset) is fully loaded.

`onresize`
: Invoked when the window is resized.

`onunload`
: Invoked when the browser leaves the current document.

See Also

Document

V

CGI and Perl

12
CGI Overview

The Common Gateway Interface (CGI) is an essential tool for creating and managing comprehensive web sites. With CGI, you can write scripts that create interactive, user-driven applications.

CGI allows the web server to communicate with other programs that are running on the server. For example, with CGI, the web server can invoke an external program, while passing user-specific data to the program (such as what host the user is connecting from, or input the user has supplied through an HTML form). The program then processes that data, and the server passes the program's response back to the web browser.

Rather than limiting the Web to documents written ahead of time, CGI enables web pages to be created on the fly, based upon the input of users. You can use CGI scripts to create a wide range of applications, from surveys to search tools, from Internet service gateways to quizzes and games. You can count the number of users who access a document or let them sign an electronic guestbook. You can provide users with all types of information, collect their comments, and respond.

This section provides a reference for the essential components of CGI. For a comprehensive treatment of CGI programming we recommend O'Reilly's *CGI Programming with Perl* by Scott Guelich, Shishir Gundavaram and Gunther Birznieks.

This chapter through Chapter 15 cover the following CGI topics:

- This chapter gives a quick introduction to the mechanism of CGI and lists the environment variables commonly defined by servers for CGI programs.
- Chapter 13 covers Server Side Includes, used with many CGI applications.
- Chapter 14 is a reference for the popular Perl module CGI.pm. CGI.pm defines one of the most widely used interfaces for creating CGI programs.
- Chapter 15 describes *mod_perl*, which embeds Perl into the Apache web server. *mod_perl* can greatly enhance the performance of CGI and also provides an interface to the Apache API for Perl programmers.

In addition, CGI programmers will probably also be interested in Chapter 6, and Chapter 17.

A Typical CGI Interaction

For an example of a CGI application, suppose you create a guestbook for your web site. The guestbook page asks users to submit their first name and last name using a fill-in form composed of two input text fields. Figure 12-1 shows the form you might see in your browser window.

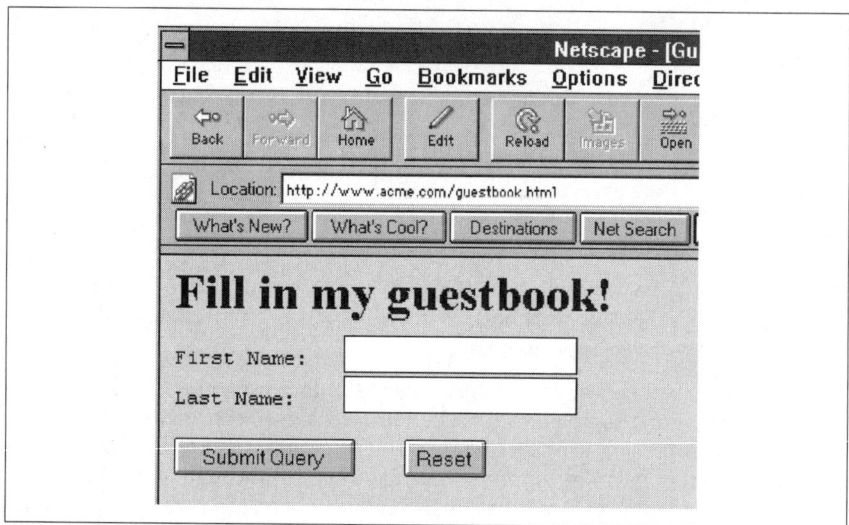

Figure 12-1. HTML form

The HTML that produces this form might read as follows:

```
<HTML><HEAD><TITLE>Guestbook</TITLE></HEAD>
<BODY>
<H1>Fill in my guestbook!</H1>
<FORM METHOD="GET" ACTION="/cgi-bin/guestbook.pl">
<PRE>
First Name:    <INPUT TYPE="TEXT" NAME="firstname">
Last Name:     <INPUT TYPE="TEXT" NAME="lastname">

<INPUT TYPE="SUBMIT">    <INPUT TYPE="RESET">
</FORM>
```

The form is written using special "form" tags (discussed in detail in Chapter 6):

- The `<form>` tag defines the *method* used for the form (either GET or POST) and the *action* to take when the form is submitted—that is, the URL of the CGI program to pass the parameters to.
- The `<input>` tag can be used in many different ways. In its first two invocations, it creates a text input field and defines the variable name to associate with the field's contents when the form is submitted. The first field is given the variable name "firstname," and the second field is given the name "lastname."

- In its last two invocations, the `<input>` tag creates a Submit button and a Reset button.
- The `</form>` tag indicates the end of the form.

When the user presses the Submit button, data entered into the `<input>` text fields is passed to the CGI program specified by the `action` attribute of the `<form>` tag (in this case, the */cgi-bin/guestbook.pl* program).

Transferring the Form Data

Parameters to a CGI program are transferred either in the URL or in the body text of the request. The method used to pass parameters is determined by the `method` attribute to the `<form>` tag. The GET method says to transfer the data within the URL itself; for example, under the GET method, the browser might initiate the HTTP transaction as follows:

```
GET /cgi-bin/guestbook.pl?firstname=Joe&lastname=Schmoe HTTP/1.1
```

See Chapter 17 for more information on HTTP transactions.

The POST method says to use the body portion of the HTTP request to pass parameters. The same transaction with the POST method would read as follows:

```
POST /cgi-bin/guestbook.pl HTTP/1.1
        ... [More headers here]

firstname=Joe&lastname=Schmoe
```

In both examples, you should recognize the `firstname` and `lastname` variable names that were defined in the HTML form, coupled with the values entered by the user. An ampersand (&) is used to separate the variable=value pairs.

The server now passes the variable=value pairs to the CGI program. It does this either through Unix environment variables or in standard input (STDIN). If the CGI program is called with the GET method, parameters are expected to be embedded in the URL of the request, and the server transfers them to the program by assigning them to the QUERY_STRING environment variable. The CGI program can then retrieve the parameters from QUERY_STRING as it would read any environment variable (for example, from the *%ENV* associative array in Perl). If the CGI program is called with the POST method, parameters are expected to be embedded into the body of the request, and the server passes the body text to the program as standard input.

(Other environment variables defined by the server for CGI programs are listed later in this chapter. These variables store such information as the format and length of the input, the remote host, the user, and various client information. They also store the server name, the communication protocol, and the name of the software running the server.)

The CGI program needs to retrieve the information as appropriate and then process it. The sky's the limit on what the CGI program actually does with the information it retrieves. It might return an anagram of the user's name, or tell them how many times their name uses the letter "t," or it might just compile the name into a list that the programmer regularly sells to telemarketers. Only the programmer knows for sure.

Creating Virtual Documents

Regardless of what the CGI program does with its input, it's responsible for giving the browser something to display when it's done. It must either create a new document to be served to the browser or point to an existing document. On Unix, programs send their output to standard output (STDOUT) as a data stream that consists of two parts. The first part is either a full or partial HTTP header that (at minimum) describes the format of the returned data (e.g., HTML, ASCII text, GIF, etc.). A blank line signifies the end of the header section. The second part is the body of the output, which contains the data conforming to the format type reflected in the header. For example:

```
Content-type: text/html

<HTML>
<HEAD><TITLE>Thanks!</TITLE></HEAD>
<BODY><H1>Thanks for signing my guest book!</H1>
      ...
</BODY></HTML>
```

In this case, the only header line generated is `Content-type`, which gives the media format of the output as HTML (`text/html`). This line is essential for every CGI program, since it tells the browser what kind of format to expect. The blank line separates the header from the body text (which, in this case, is in HTML format as advertised). See Chapter 17 for a listing of other media formats that are commonly recognized on the Web.

Notice that it does not matter to the web server what language the CGI program is written in. On Unix platforms, the most popular language for CGI programming is Perl. Other languages used on Unix are C, C++, Tcl, and Python. On Macintosh computers, programmers use Applescript and C/C++, and on Microsoft Windows, programmers use Visual Basic, Perl, and C/C++. As long as there's a way in a programming language to get data from the server and send data back, you can use it for CGI.

The server transfers the results of the CGI program back to the browser. The body text is not modified or interpreted by the server in any way, but the server generally supplies additional headers with information such as the date, the name and version of the server, etc. See Chapter 17 for a list of valid HTTP response headers.

CGI programs can also supply a complete HTTP header itself, in which case the server does not add any additional headers but instead transfers the response verbatim as returned by the CGI program. (The server may need to be configured to allow this behavior.)

Here is the sample output of a program generating an HTML virtual document, with a complete HTTP header:

```
HTTP/1.1 200 OK
Date:  Thursday, 28-June-96 11:12:21 GMT
Server: Apache/2.0.36
Content-type: text/html
Content-length: 2041
```

```
<HTML>
<HEAD><TITLE>Thanks!</TITLE></HEAD>
<BODY>
<H1>Thanks for signing my guestbook!</H1>
    ...
</BODY>
</HTML>
```

The header contains the communication protocol, the date and time of the response, and the server name and version. (The `200 OK` is a *status code* generated by the HTTP protocol to communicate the status of a request, in this case successful. See Chapter 17 for a list of valid HTTP status codes.) Most importantly, it also contains the content type and the number of characters (equivalent to the number of bytes) of the enclosed data.

As seen in Figure 12-2, the result is that after users click the Submit button, they see the message contained in the HTML section of the response thanking them for signing the guestbook.

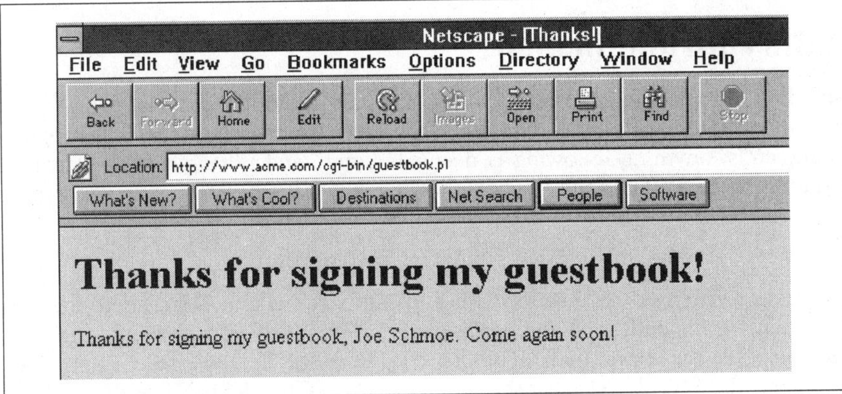

Figure 12-2. Guestbook acknowledgment

URL Encoding

Before data supplied on a form can be sent to a CGI program, each form element's name (specified by the `name` attribute) is equated with the value entered by the user to create a key-value pair. For example, if the user entered "30" when asked for his or her age, the key-value pair would be "age=30". In the transferred data, key-value pairs are separated by the ampersand (&) character.

Since under the GET method the form information is sent as part of the URL, form information can't include any spaces or other special characters that are not allowed in URLs, and also can't include characters that have other meanings in URLs, like slashes (/). (For the sake of consistency, this constraint also exists when the POST method is being used.) Therefore, the web browser performs some special encoding on user-supplied information.

Encoding involves replacing spaces and other special characters in the query strings with their hexadecimal equivalents. (Thus, URL encoding is also sometimes called *hexadecimal encoding*.) Suppose a user fills out and submits a form containing his or her birthday in the syntax mm/dd/yy (e.g., 11/05/73). The forward slashes in the birthday are among the special characters that can't appear in the client's request for the CGI program. Thus, when the browser issues the request, it encodes the data. The following sample request shows the resulting encoding:

```
POST /cgi-bin/birthday.pl HTTP/1.1
.
. [information]
.
Content-length: 21

birthday=11%2F05%2F73
```

The sequence `%2F` is actually the hexadecimal equivalent of the slash character.

CGI scripts have to provide some way to "decode" form data the client has encoded. The best way to do this is to use CGI.pm (covered in Chapter 14) and let it do the work for you.

Extra Path Information

In addition to passing query strings, you can pass additional data, known as *extra path information*, as part of the URL. The server gauges where the CGI program name ends; anything following is deemed "extra" and is stored in the environment variable PATH_INFO. The following line calls a script with extra path information:

```
http://some.machine/cgi-bin/display.pl/cgi/cgi_doc.txt
```

In this example, we use a script with a *.pl* suffix to make it clear where the CGI program's path ends and the extra path information begins. Everything after *display.pl* is the extra path. The PATH_TRANSLATED variable is also set, mapping the PATH_INFO to the document root (DOCUMENT_ROOT) directory (e.g., */usr/local/etc/httpd/public/cgi/cgi_doc.txt*).

CGI Environment Variables

Much of the information needed by CGI programs is made available via Unix environment variables. Programs can access this information as they would any environment variable (e.g., via the *%ENV* associative array in Perl). Table 12-1 lists the environment variables commonly available through CGI. However, since servers occasionally vary on the names of environment variables they assign, check with your own server documentation for more information.

Table 12-1. CGI environment variables

Environment variable	Content returned
AUTH_TYPE	The authentication method used to validate a user. See REMOTE_IDENT and REMOTE_USER.
CONTENT_LENGTH	The length of the query data (in bytes or the number of characters) passed to the CGI program through standard input.

Table 12-1. CGI environment variables (continued)

Environment variable	Content returned
CONTENT_TYPE	The media type of the query data, such as `text/html`. See Chapter 17 for a listing of commonly used content types.
DOCUMENT_ROOT	The directory from which web documents are served.
GATEWAY_INTERFACE	The revision of the Common Gateway Interface the server uses.
HTTP_ACCEPT	A list of the media types the client can accept.
HTTP_COOKIE	A list of cookies defined for that URL. (See Chapter 17 for more information.)
HTTP_FROM	The email address of the user making the query (many browsers do not support this variable).
HTTP_REFERER	The URL of the document the client points to before accessing the CGI program.
PATH_INFO	Extra path information passed to a CGI program.
PATH_TRANSLATED	The translated version of the path given by the variable PATH_INFO.
QUERY_STRING	The query information passed to the program. It is appended to the URL following a question mark (?).
REMOTE_ADDR	The IP address from which the user is making the request.
REMOTE_HOST	The hostname from which the user is making the request.
REMOTE_IDENT	The user making the request.
REMOTE_USER	The authenticated name of the user making the query.
REQUEST_METHOD	The method with which the information request was issued (e.g., GET, POST, HEAD). See Chapter 17 for more information on request methods.
SCRIPT_NAME	The virtual path (e.g., */cgi-bin/program.pl*) of the script being executed.
SERVER_NAME	The server's hostname or IP address.
SERVER_PORT	The port number of the host on which the server is running.
SERVER_PROTOCOL	The name and revision of the information protocol the request came in with.
SERVER_SOFTWARE	The name and version of the server software that is answering the client request.

Here's a simple Perl CGI script that uses environment variables to display various information about the server:

```
#!/usr/local/bin/perl

print "Content-type: text/html", "\n\n";

print "<HTML>", "\n";
print "<HEAD><TITLE>About this Server</TITLE></HEAD>", "\n";
print "<BODY><H1>About this Server</H1>", "\n";
print "<HR><PRE>";
print "Server Name:       ", $ENV{'SERVER_NAME'}, "<BR>", "\n";
print "Running on Port:   ", $ENV{'SERVER_PORT'}, "<BR>", "\n";
print "Server Software:   ", $ENV{'SERVER_SOFTWARE'}, "<BR>", "\n";
print "Server Protocol:   ", $ENV{'SERVER_PROTOCOL'}, "<BR>", "\n";
print "CGI Revision:      ", $ENV{'GATEWAY_INTERFACE'}, "<BR>", "\n";
print "<HR></PRE>", "\n";
print "</BODY></HTML>", "\n";

exit (0);
```

The preceding program outputs the contents of five environment variables into an HTML document. In Perl, you can access the environment variables using the *%ENV* associative array. Here's a typical output of the program:

```
<HTML>
<HEAD><TITLE>About this Server</TITLE></HEAD>
<BODY><H1>About this Server</H1>
<HR><PRE>
Server Name:          oreilly.com
Running on Port:      80
Server Software:      NCSA/1.4.2
Server Protocol:      HTTP/1.1
CGI Revision:         CGI/1.1
<HR></PRE>
</BODY></HTML>
```

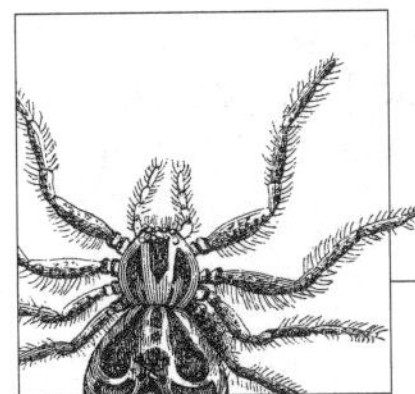

13

Server Side Includes

Server Side Includes (SSI) are directives you can place into an HTML document to execute other programs or to output data, such as file statistics or the contents of environment variables. SSI directives can save you the trouble of writing complete CGI programs to output documents containing a small amount of dynamic information. While Server Side Includes aren't technically CGI, they can be an important tool for incorporating CGI-like information as well as output from CGI programs.

In addition to output of specific directives, SSI can use conditional expressions to evaluate portions of documents. This extended SSI functionality is available in Apache 1.2 and later.

When a client requests a document from an SSI-enabled server and the document is coded appropriately, the server parses the specified document looking for SSI directives. We've already considered the advantages to this system; there are also a couple of liabilities. First, parsing documents before sending them to the client represents additional server overhead. Second, enabling SSI can create a security risk. For example, an unwise user might embed directives to execute system commands that output confidential information. In short, SSI can be very handy, but it must be used cautiously and efficiently.

This chapter summarizes the Server Side Includes directives and the extended expression syntax. There aren't many directives, but they perform some useful CGI-like operations and can spare you quite a bit of coding.

Configuring the Apache Server for SSI

To enable SSI, you must tell Apache what type of files to parse for includes, and enable them in any directory where they exist.

In the appropriate `<Directory>` sections of the server configuration file *httpd.conf* (or *.htaccess* files), include the following directive:

```
Options+ Includes
```

In the main configuration file, you must specify the parsed file type (*.shtml*) and associate it with the INCLUDES filter, which implements the SSI module *mod_include*. For example, the following two lines specify that the server should handle documents with the *.shtml* suffix as HTML documents, and parse them for SSI:

```
AddType text/html .shtml
AddOutputFilter INCLUDES .shtml
```

Prior to Apache 2.0, the server-parsed handler implemented the SSI module with:

```
AddHandler server-parsed .shtml
```

If you specify the suffix *.html* here, the server would parse all HTML documents. This would make it easier to modify files without having to worry about changing link and other issues, but it would cause a noticeable performance hit to the server. An alternate method to using the *.shtml* file extension is to use the XBitHack directive:

```
XBitHack on
```

This tells Apache to parse for SSI any file that has the executable permission set. You can do this for a file with the following command:

```
chmod +x filename.html
```

See Chapter 19 for more on configuring the Apache server.

Basic SSI Directives

All SSI directives have the format:

```
<!-#command parameter="value" ... ->
```

Each of the symbols is important; be careful not to forget the pound sign (#) or the dual dashes (--). Also, it is recommended that you place whitespace between the final arguments and the closing dashes to prevent it from being interpreted as part of an SSI argument.

Following is a list of the primary server-side directives, the parameters they take, and their function.

---

config

```
config errmsg|sizefmt|timefmt="string"
```

Modifies various aspects of SSI.

Arguments

errmsg

Default error message.

```
<!--#config errmsg="Error: File not found" ->
```

sizefmt

Format for the size of the file (returned by the fsize directive). Acceptable values are bytes, or abbrev, which rounds the file size to the nearest kilobyte. For example:

```
<!--#config sizefmt="abbrev" ->
```

timefmt
: Format for times and dates. SSI offers a wide range of formats. See the section "Configurable Time Formats for SSI Output" later in this chapter for more information.

echo

```
echo encoding="type" var="environment_variable"
```

Inserts value of special SSI variables, as well as other CGI environment variables. For example:

```
<H1>Welcome to my server at <!--#echo var="SERVER_NAME"
->...</H1>
```

Arguments

encoding
: Optional. This option is available in Apache 1.3.2 and later. It specifies how special characters contained in the variable are parsed before being output. none means no encoding is performed. url performs URL-style encoding. entity is the default value, which performs simple entity encoding. The encoding parameter must come before the var parameter, and is only in effect within the current echo directive.

Server Side Includes

exec

```
exec cmd|cgi="string"
```

Executes external programs and inserts output in the current document.

Arguments

cmd
: Any application on the host.

cgi
: A CGI program.

For example:

```
<!--#exec cmd="/bin/finger $REMOTE_USER@$REMOTE_HOST"-->
This page has been accessed
<!--#exec cgi="/cgi-bin/counter.pl"->
times.
```

flastmod

```
flastmod file="path"
```

Inserts the last modification date and time for a specified file.

```
The file was last modified on
<!--#flastmod file="/mybook.ps"->.
```

You can specify the format of the date and time returned using the config directive with the timefmt argument; timefmt takes a wide range of values described in the section "Configurable Time Formats for SSI Output" later in this chapter.

fsize

`fsize file|virtual="path"`

Inserts the size of a specified file.

Arguments

`file`
: Pathname relative to a document on the server.

`virtual`
: Virtual path to a document on the server.

For example:

```
The size of the file is
<!--#fsize file="/mybook.ps"--> bytes.
<!--#fsize virtual="/personal/mydata.txt"->
```

include

`include file|virtual="path"`

Inserts text of document into current file.

Arguments

`file`
: Pathname relative to a document on the server.

`virtual`
: Virtual path to a document on the server.

For example:

```
<!--#include file="stuff.html" -->
<!--#include virtual="/personal/stuff.html"->
```

printenv

`printenv`

Prints all environment variables on the server.

For example:

```
<!--#printenv->
```

set

`set var="name" value="value"`

Sets a server-side variable to a given value.

Arguments

`name`
: The name of the variable.

`value`
: The value to be assigned to the variable.

For example:

```
<!--#set name="myvar" value="activated"->
```

SSI Environment Variables

You can use SSI directives to output the values of environment variables in an otherwise static HTML document. These might be standard CGI variables (listed in Chapter 12); or they might be:

`DOCUMENT_NAME`
: The current file:

```
You are reading a document called:

<!--#echo var="DOCUMENT_NAME"->
```

`DOCUMENT_URI`
: Virtual path to the file:

```
You can access this document again by pointing to the URI:
<!--#echo var="DOCUMENT_URI"->
```

`DATE_LOCAL`
: Current date and time in the local time zone:

```
The time is now <!--#echo var="DATE_LOCAL" ->
```

`DATE_GMT`
: Current date and time in Greenwich Mean Time:

```
The Greenwich Mean Time is <!--#echo var="DATE_GMT"->
```

`LAST_MODIFIED`
: Last modification date and time for current file:

```
The current document was last modified on:
<!--#echo var="LAST_MODIFIED"->
```

Configurable Time Formats for SSI Output

Among its functions, the `config` SSI command allows you to specify the way the time and date are displayed with the `timefmt` argument. It takes a number of special values that are summarized in Table 13-1.

Table 13-1. SSI time formats

Status code	Meaning	Example
%a	Day of the week abbreviation	Sun
%A	Day of the week	Sunday
%b	Month name abbreviation (also %h)	Jan
%B	Month name	January
%d	Date	01
%D	Date as %m/%d/%y	06/23/95
%e	Date	1 (*not* 01)
%H	24-hour clock hour	13
%I	12-hour clock hour	01

Table 13-1. SSI time formats (continued)

Status code	Meaning	Example
%j	Decimal day of the year	360
%m	Month number	11
%M	Minutes	08
%p	AM | PM	AM
%r	Time as %I:%M:%S %p	09:21:13 PM
%S	Seconds	09
%T	24-hour time as %H:%M:%S	12:22:40
%U	Week of the year (also %W)	37
%w	Day of the week number (starting with Sunday=0)	2
%y	Year of the century	96
%Y	Year	1996
%Z	Time zone	EST

The config command in the following example makes use of two of those special time values:

```
<!--#config timefmt="%D %r" -->
The file address.html was last modified on:
        <!--#flastmod file="address.html"–>.
```

where %D specifies that the date appear in "mm/dd/yy" format, and %r specifies that the time appear as "hh/mm/ss AM|PM".

Thus the previous example produces output such as:

```
The file address.html was last modified on: 12/23/95 07:17:39 PM
```

Conditional Statements

Apache allows you to include only select portions of a server document using conditional statements. These conditional statements are based on the value of server-side variables initialized earlier using the SSI set command. The Apache flow-control statements allow you to effectively customize a document without adding more complex CGI programs to perform the same task.

There are four Apache flow-control statements:

```
<!–#if expr="expression" -->
<!–#elif expr="expression"-->
<!--#else-->
<!--#endif–>
```

Each works as you would expect from an ordinary scripting language. Note that each if must have a closing endif server-side statement. For example:

```
<!--#if expr="$myvar=activated" -->
<B>The variable appears to be activated</B>
<!--#elif expr="$myvar=inactive"-->
<B>The variable appears to be inactive</B>
```

```
<!--#else-->
<B>The variable has an unknown value</B>
<!--#endif->
```

Table 13-2 shows the allowed expressions, where the order of operations is as expected in a traditional programming language. Note that in some cases, *var2* is allowed to be an egrep-based regular expression if it is surrounded by slashes (/) on both sides.

Table 13-2. XSSI conditional expressions

Expression	Meaning
var	True if the variable is not empty
var1=var2	True if the variables match
var1!=var2	True if the variables do not match
var1<var2	True if the first variable is less than the second
var1<=var2	True if the first variable is less than or equal to the second
var1>var2	True if the first variable is greater than the second
var1>=var2	True if the first variable is greater than or equal to the second
(*expr*)	True if the enclosed condition is true
! *expr*	True if the condition is false
expr1&&expr2	True if both expressions evaluate to true
expr1||*expr2*	True if either expressions evaluates to true

Finally, you can place regular strings inside single quotes to preserve any whitespaces. If a string is not quoted, extra whitespaces are ignored. For example:

```
this    is    too  much    space
```

This string does not have quotes and will be collapsed to:

```
this is too much space
```

However, if you place the string in single quotes, the whitespace is preserved:

```
/'this    is    too  much    space/'
```

You can also place strings in double quotes, but you will have to escape each one while inside the expr="" expression, as shown here:

```
<!-#if expr="\" $HTTP_REFERER\" != " ->
```


Server Side Includes

14
The CGI.pm Module

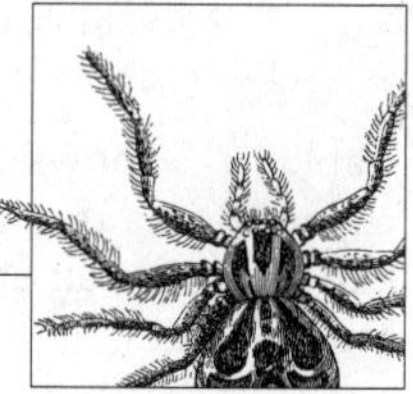

CGI.pm is a Perl module for creating and parsing CGI forms. It is distributed with core Perl as of Perl 5.004, but you can also retrieve CGI.pm from CPAN, and you can get the latest version at any time from *http://stein.cshl.org/WWW/software/CGI/*. This book doesn't include a complete reference for the Perl language, but if you already use Perl for CGI, you know how essential CGI.pm can be. So we include this chapter on CGI.pm as a convenience for Perl-savvy readers.

CGI.pm is an object-oriented module that is very easy to use, as evidenced by its overwhelming popularity among all levels of Perl programmers. To give you an idea of how easy it is to use CGI.pm, let's take a scenario in which a user fills out and submits a form containing her birthday. Without CGI.pm, the script would have to translate the URL-encoded input by hand (probably using a series of regular expressions) and assign it to a variable. For example, you might try something like this:

```
#!/usr/bin/perl
# cgi script without CGI.pm
$size_of_form_info = $ENV{'CONTENT_LENGTH'};
read ($STDIN, $form_info, $size_of_form_info);
# Split up each pair of key=value pairs
foreach $pair (split (/&/, $form_info)) {

    # For each pair, split into $key and $value variables
     ($key, $value) = split (/=/, $pair);
    # Get rid of the pesky %xx encodings
     $key =~ s/%([\dA-Fa-f][\dA-Fa-f])/pack ("C", hex ($1))/eg;
     $value =~ s/%([\dA-Fa-f][\dA-Fa-f])/pack ("C", hex ($1))/eg;
    # Use $key as index for $parameters hash, $value as value
     $parameters{$key} = $value;
}
# Print out the obligatory content-ytype line
print "Content-type: text/plain\n\n";
```

```
# Tell the user what they said
print "Your birthday is on " . $parameters{birthday} . ".\n";
```

Regardless of whether this code actually works, you must admit it's ugly. With CGI.pm, the script could be written:

```
#!/usr/bin/perl -w
# cgi script with CGI.pm

use CGI;

$query = CGI::new( );
$bday = $query->param("birthday");
print $query->header( );
print $query->p("Your birthday is $bday.");
```

Even for this tiny program, you can see that CGI.pm can alleviate many of the headaches associated with CGI programming.

As with any Perl module, the first thing you do is call the module with `use`. You then call the constructor `new( )`, creating a new CGI object called `$query`. Next, get the value of the `birthday` parameter from the CGI program using the `param` method. Note that CGI.pm does all the work of determining whether the CGI program is being called by the GET or POST methods, and it also does all the URL decoding for you. To generate output, use the `header` method to return the content type header, and the `p` method to generate a paragraph marker `<P>` tag.

However, this is only the tip of the iceberg as far as what CGI.pm can do for you. There are three basic areas covered by CGI.pm methods: handling CGI queries, retrieving environment variables, and creating HTML elements. Table 14-1 lists these methods. They are also covered in more detail later in this chapter.

Table 14-1. CGI.pm methods

CGI handling	
`append`	Append to a parameter
`cgi_error`	Get a CGI error
`cookie`	Get (or set) a cookie
`delete`	Delete a parameter
`delete_all`	Delete all parameters
`dump`	Print all name/value pairs
`header`	Create HTTP header
`import_names`	Import variables into a namespace
`keywords`	Get keywords from an `<ISINDEX>` search
`param`	Get (or set) the value of parameters
`param_fetch`	Get the value of parameters
`redirect`	Create redirection header
`save`	Save all parameters to a file
`self_url`	Create self-referencing URL
`url`	Get URL of current script without query information
`url_param`	Get submitted parameters appended to URLs as extra-path information

Table 14-1. CGI.pm methods (continued)

Handling environment variables	
accept	Get accept types from ACCEPT header
auth_type	Get value of AUTH_TYPE header
content_type	Get the value of the CONTENT_TYPE header
http	Get the values of specified header variables
path_info	Get value of PATH_INFO header
path_translated	Get value of PATH_TRANSLATED header
query_string	Get the query information appended to the URL following a question mark (?)
raw_cookie	Get value of HTTP_COOKIE header
referer	Get value of REFERER header
remote_addr	Get value of REMOTE_ADDR header
remote_host	Get value of REMOTE_HOST header
request_method	Get value of REQUEST_METHOD header
script_name	Get value of SCRIPT_NAME header
user_agent	Get value of USER_AGENT header
user_name	Get user name (not via headers)
HTML and form generation	
autoEscape	Set whether to use automatic escaping
button	Generate a JavaScript button
checkbox	Generate a single checkbox via a <INPUT TYPE=CHECKBOX> tag
checkbox_group	Generate a group of checkboxes via multiple <INPUT TYPE=CHECKBOX> tags
defaults	Generate a <DEFAULTS> tag
end_form	Generate a </FORM> end tag
end_html	Generate an </HTML> tag
end_multipart_form	Generate a </FORM> end tag for a multipart/form-data encoding
filefield	Generate an <INPUT TYPE=FILE> tag
hidden	Generate an <INPUT TYPE=HIDDEN> tag
image_button	Generate a clickable image button via a <SELECT> tag
password_field	Generate an <INPUT TYPE=PASSWORD> tag
popup_menu	Generate a pop-up menu via <SELECT SIZE=1> and <OPTION> tags
radio_group	Generate a group of radio buttons via <INPUT TYPE=RADIO> tags
reset	Generate a <RESET> tag.
scrolling_list	Generate a scrolling list via <SELECT> and <OPTION> tags
start_form	Generate a <FORM> tag
start_html	Generate an <HTML> tag
start_multipart_form	Generate a <FORM> tag for multipart/ form-data encoding
submit	Generate a <SUBMIT> tag
textarea	Generate an <TEXTAREA> tag
textfield	Generate an <INPUT TYPE=TEXT> tag

Each of these methods is covered later in this chapter.

HTML Tag Generation

In addition to the form-generation methods, CGI.pm also includes methods for generating HTML output. The names of the HTML output methods generally follow the HTML element names (e.g., `p` for `<P>`) and take named parameters that are assumed to be valid attributes for the tag (e.g., `img(src=>'camel.gif')` becomes `<IMG SRC="camel.gif">`). We do not list the HTML generating methods here, although the HTML element reference in Chapter 13 provides you with element names and attributes that are for the most part recognized by CGI.pm. See the CGI.pm manpage for complete information, or the book *Official Guide to Programming with CGI.pm* by Lincoln Stein (John Wiley & Sons, 1998).

Importing Method Groups

The syntax for calling CGI methods can be unwieldy. However, you can import individual methods and then call the methods without explicit object calls. The "birthday" example shown earlier could be written even more simply as follows:

```
#!/usr/bin/perl

use CGI param,header,p;

$bday = param("birthday");
print header( );
print p("Your birthday is $bday.");
```

By importing the `param`, `header`, and `p` methods into your namespace, you no longer have to use the `new` constructor (since it is called automatically now), and you don't need to specify a CGI object with every method call.

CGI.pm also lets you import groups of methods, which can make your programs much simpler and more elegant. For example, to import all form-creation methods and all CGI-handling methods:

```
use CGI qw/:form :cgi/;
```

The method groups supported by CGI.pm are:

`:cgi`
: All CGI-handling methods

`:cgi-lib`
: All methods supplied for backwards compatibility with *cgi-lib*

`:form`
: All form-generation methods

`:html`
: All HTML methods

`:html2`
: All HTML 2.0 methods

`:html3`
: All HTML 3.0 methods

CGI.pm

`:html4`
: All HTML 4.0 methods

`:netscape`
: All methods generating Netscape extensions

`:ssl`
: All SSL methods

`:standard`
: All HTML, form-generation, and CGI methods

`:all`
: All available methods

You can also define new methods for HTML tag generation by simply listing them on the import line and letting CGI.pm make some educated guesses. For example:

```
use CGI shortcuts,smell;

print smell {type=>'garlic',
           intensity=>'strong'}, "Scratch here!";
```

This causes the following tag to be generated:

```
<SMELL TYPE="garlic" INTENSITY="strong">Scratch here!</SMELL>
```

Maintaining State

One of the first complications for any nontrivial CGI script is how to "maintain state." Since HTTP is a stateless protocol, there's no built-in mechanism for keeping track of requests from the server end. A CGI transaction involving multiple forms, therefore, needs to find a way to remember information supplied on previous forms. One way to deal with this issue is to use *cookies*, which allow the CGI program to save information on the browser's end. HTTP Cookies are described in Chapter 17. CGI.pm uses the `cookie()` method to set and retrieve cookie information from a client.

CGI.pm implements other ways of maintaining state without cookies. To move around within a document containing form information, you can use the `self_url()` method to get a URL for the current document that saves the current form information. More generally, you can save query information from sessions in a variety of ways by saving to a filehandle with `$query->save()`. This method provides the pathway to connecting client sessions with outside data sources like databases and user directories.

Named Parameters

For most CGI.pm methods, there are two syntax styles. In the "standard" style, the position of the parameters determines how they will be interpreted; for example, parameter 1 is the name the script should assign, parameter 2 is the initial value, etc. For example:

```
print $query=textfield('username', 'anonymous');
```

In the "named parameters" style, the parameters can be assigned like a hash, and the order doesn't matter. For example:

```
print $query->textfield(-name=>'name', -default=>'value');
```

If you want to use named parameters, just call the use_named_parameters method early in the script.

Which syntax style should you use? It depends on how lazy you are and much control you need. Generally, "standard" syntax is faster to type. However, it is also harder to read, and there are many features that are simply not available using standard syntax (such as JavaScript support). In general, we recommend using the "named parameters" syntax for all but the most trivial scripts.

Using JavaScript Features

CGI.pm supports JavaScript scripting by allowing you to embed a JavaScript script in the HTML form within <SCRIPT> tags, and then calling the script using the -script parameter to the start_html method. You can then call the JavaScript functions as appropriate to the form elements.

Debugging

A complication of writing CGI scripts is that when debugging the script, you have to wrestle with the web server environment. CGI.pm provides support for debugging the script on the command line.

If you run the script on the command line without arguments, you will be placed into an "offline" mode, in which name-value pairs can be entered one-by-one. When you press CTRL-D, the script runs. For example:

```
% birthday
(offline mode: enter name=value pairs on standard input)
birthday=6/4/65
^D
Content-type: text/html

<P>Your birthday is 6/4/65.</P>
```

You can also supply the name/value parameters directly on the command line:

```
% test birthday=6/4/65
Content-type: text/html

<P>Your birthday is 6/4/65.</P>
```

Multiple values can be separated by spaces (as separate arguments on the command line) or by ampersands (as in URL-encoded syntax). In fact, you can use URL-encoded syntax on the command line. This makes it easy to supply raw CGI input to the script for testing purposes. Just remember to protect the ampersand from the shell. For example:

```
% test 'birthday=6%2f4%2f65&name=Fred%20Flintstone'
Content-type: text/html

<P>Fred Flintstone, your birthday is 6/4/65.</P>
```

CGI.pm Reference

The following methods are supported by CGI.pm.

Accept

```
$query->accept(['content_type'])
```

Returns a list of media types that the browser accepts.

content_type
: If specified, returns instead the browser's preference for the specified content type, between 0.0 and 1.0.

append

```
$query->append(-name=>'name',-values=>'value')
```

Appends a value or list of values to the named parameter.

`-name=>'name'`
: The parameter to be appended.

`-values=>'value'`
: The value to append. Multiple values can be specified as a reference to an anonymous array.

auth_type

```
auth_type()
```

Returns the authorization method.

autoEscape

```
$query->autoEscape(undef)
```

Turns off autoescaping of form elements.

button

```
print $query->button('name','function')
```

Generates a JavaScript button.

name
: The name of the button.

function
: The function to execute when the button is clicked.

Using named parameters, the syntax is:

```
print $query->button(-name=>'name',
                     -value=>'label',
                     -onClick=>"function");
```

`-value=>'label'`
: The label to display for the button.

checkbox

```
print $query->checkbox('name' [,'checked','value','label'])
```

Generates a single checkbox.

name
The name to assign the input to (required).

checked
Checkbox should be checked initially.

value
The value to return when checked (default is on).

label
The label to use for the checkbox (default is the name of the checkbox).

Using named parameters, the syntax is:

```
print $query->checkbox(-name=>'name',
                       -checked=>'checked',
                       -value=>'value',
                       -label=>'label',
                       -onClick=>function);
```

onClick=>*function*
Browser should execute *function* when the user clicks on any checkbox in the group.

---

checkbox_group

```
print $query->checkbox_group('name', \@list [,selected,
'true',\%labelhash ])
```

Generates a list of checkbox elements.

name
The name to assign the input to (required).

\@list
An array reference with the list items. You can also use an anonymous array reference.

selected
The menu item(s) to be initially selected (default is that nothing is selected). This can be a single value or a reference to an array of values.

true
Insert newlines between the checkboxes.

\%labelhash
A hash reference listing labels for each list item. Default is the list text itself. See popup_menu for an example.

Using named parameters, the syntax is:

```
print $query->checkbox_group(-name=>'name',
                             -values=>\@list,
                             -default=>selected,
                             -linebreak=>'true',
                             -labels=>\%labelhash,
                             -columns=>n,
                             -columnheader=>'string',
                             -rows=>m,
                             -rowheader=>'string',
                             -onClick=>function);
```

`-columns=>`*n*
: The number of columns to use.

`-columnheader=>'`*string*`'`
: A header for the column.

`-rows=`*m*
: The number of rows to use. If omitted and `-columns` is specified, the rows are calculated for you.

`-rowheader=>'`*string*`'`
: A header for the row.

`-onClick=>`*function*
: Browser should execute *function* when the user clicks on any checkbox in the group.

---

cookie

```
$cookie=$query->cookie('name')
```

Defines or retrieves a cookie. See also header .

name
: Name of the cookie (required).

Using named parameters, the syntax is:

```
$cookie = $query->cookie(-name=>'name',
                         -value=>'value',
                         -expires=>'expcode',
                         -path=>'partial_url',
                         -domain=>'domain_name',
                         -secure=>1);
print $query->header(-cookie=>$cookie);
```

`-value=>'`*value*`'`
: A value to assign to the cookie. You can supply a scalar value, or a reference to an array or hash. If omitted, a cookie is retrieved rather than defined.

`-expires=>`*expcode*
: Specify an expiration timestamp (such as `+3d` for 3 days). Values for *expcode* are:

n`s` *n* seconds

n`m` *n* minutes

n`h` *n* hours

n`d` *n* days

n`M` *n* months

n`Y` *n* years

day_of_week, dd-MMM-YY hh:mm:ss `GMT`
: At the specified time

`now` Expire immediately.

`-path=>'partial_url'`
The partial URL for which the cookie is valid. Default is the current URL.

`-domain=>'domain_name'`
The domain for which the cookie is valid.

`-secure=>1`
Only use this cookie for a secure session.

---

defaults

```
print $query->defaults('label')
```

Generates a button that resets the form to its defaults. See also `reset`.

label
The label to use for the button. If omitted, the label is "Defaults."

---

delete

```
$query->delete('parameter')
```

Deletes a parameter.

parameter
The parameter to delete.

---

delete_all

```
$query->delete_all()
```

Deletes the entire CGI object.

---

dump

```
print $query->dump([true])
```

Dumps all name/value pairs as an HTML list.

`true`
If specified, print as plain text.

---

end_html

```
print $query->end_html()
```

Ends an HTML document.

---

filefield

```
print $query->filefield('name' [,'default',size,maxlength])
```

Generates a file upload field for Netscape browsers.

name
The filename to assign the supplied file contents to (required).

default
The initial value (filename) to place in the text field.

size
The size of the text field (in characters).

maxlength
The maximum length of the text field (in characters).

Using named parameters, the syntax is:

```
print $query->textfield(-name=>'name',
                        -default=>'value',
                        -size=>size,
                        -maxlength=>maxlength,
                        -override=>1,
                        -onChange=>function,
                        -onFocus=>function,
                        -onBlur=>function,
                        -onSelect=>function);
```

`-override=>1`
Text field should not inherit its value from a previous invocation of the script.

`-onChange=>`*function*
Browser should execute *function* when the user changes the text field.

`-onFocus=>`*function*
Browser should execute *function* when the focus is on the text field.

`-onBlur=>`*function*
Browser should execute *function* when the focus leaves the text field.

`-onSelect=>`*function*
Browser should execute *function* when the user changes a selected portion of the text field.

header

```
print $query->header([content_type, status, headers])
```

Generates the HTTP header for the document.

content_type
The content type to return. Default is `text/html`.

status
The HTTP status code and description to return. Default is `200 OK`.

headers
Additional headers to include, such as `Content-Length: 123`.

Using named parameters, the syntax is:

```
print $query->header(-type=>'content_type',
                     -nph=>1,
                     -status=>'status_code',
                     -expires=>'expcode',
                     -cookie=>'cookie',
                     -target=>'frame',
                     -header=>'value');
```

`-type=>`*`content_type`*
: Specify the content type.

`-nph=>1`
: Use headers for a no-parse-header script.

`-status=>`*`status_code`*
: Specify the status code.

`-expires=>`*`expcode`*
: Specify an expiration timestamp (such as `+3d` for 3 days). Values for *expcode* are:

  n`s` *n* seconds

  n`m` *n* minutes

  n`h` *n* hours

  n`d` *n* days

  n`M` *n* months

  n`Y` *n* years

  day_of_week, dd-MMM-YY hh:mm:ss `GMT`
  At the specified time

  `now` Expire immediately.

`-cookie=>`*`cookie`*
: Specify a cookie. The cookie may be a scalar value or an array reference.

`-header=>`*`value`*
: Specify any HTTP header.

`-target=>`*`frame`*
: Write to specified frame.

CGI.pm

hidden

```
print $query->hidden('name', 'value' [,'value'... ])
```

Generates a hidden text field.

name
: The name to give the value (required).

value
: The value to assign to *name*. Multiple values can be specified.

Using named parameters, the syntax is:

```
print $query->hidden(-name=>'name',
                          -default=>'value');
```

With named parameters, the value can also be represented as a reference to an array, such as:

```
print $query->hidden(-name=>'name',
                        -default=>['value1', 'value2', ... ]);
```

image_button

```
print $query->image_button('name','url' [,'align'])
```

Generates a clickable image map.

name
: The name to use. When clicked, the *x,y* position is returned as *name.x* and *name.y*, respectively.

url
: The URL of the image for the image map.

align
: The alignment type. May be `TOP`, `BOTTOM`, or `MIDDLE`.

Using named parameters, the syntax is:

```
print $query->image_button(-name=>'name',
                           -src=>'url',
                           -align=>'align',
                           -onClick=>function);
```

`-onClick=>`*function*
: Browser should execute *function* when the user clicks on the image.

import_names

`$query->import_names('`*package*`')`

Creates variables in the specified package. Called `import` in older versions of CGI.pm.

package
: The package to import names into.

isindex

`print $query->isindex([`*action*`])`

Generates an `<ISINDEX>` tag.

action
: The URL of the index script. Default is the current URL.

Using named parameters, the syntax is:

```
print $query->isindex(-action=>$action);
```

keywords

`@keyarray = $query->keywords()`

Retrieves keywords from an `<ISINDEX>` search.

@keyarray
: The array to contain the retrieved keywords.

nph

`nph(1)`

Treats a CGI script as a no-parsed-header (NPH) script.

param

`@name = $query->param([`*parameter*`[`*newvalue1, newvalue2,...*`] ])`

Gets or sets parameter names.

@name
The array to contain the parameter names.

parameter
An optional single parameter to fetch. When used with no arguments, `param` returns a list of all known parameter names.

newvalue1, newvalue2, ...
The optional new values to assign to the parameter.

Using named parameters, the syntax is:

```
$query->param(-name=>'parameter',
                    -value=>'newvalue');
```

or:

```
$query->param(-name=>'parameter',
                    -values=>'newvalue1', 'newvalue2', ...);
```

password_field

```
print $query->password_field('name' [,'value',size,maxlength])
```

Generates a password input field.

name
The name to assign the input to (required).

value
The default password to place in the password field.

size
The size of the password field (in characters).

maxlength
The maximum length of the password field (in characters).

Using named parameters, the syntax is:

```
print $query->password_field(-name=>'name',
                             -default=>'value',
                             -size=>size,
                             -maxlength=>maxlength,
                             -override=>1,
                             -onChange=>function,
                             -onFocus=>function,
                             -onBlur=>function,
                             -onSelect=>function);
```

`-override=>1`
Text field should not inherit its value from a previous invocation of the script.

`-onChange=>`*function*
Browser should execute *function* when the user changes the text field.

`-onFocus=>`*function*
Browser should execute *function* when the focus is on the text field.

`-onBlur=>`*function*
Browser should execute *function* when the focus leaves the text field.

`-onSelect=>`*function*
Browser should execute *function* when the user changes a selected portion of the text field.

path_info

`path_info()`

Returns extra path information.

path_translated

`path_translated()`

Returns translated extra path information.

popup_menu

`print $query->popup_menu('`*name*`', \@`*array* `[,'`*selected*`', \%`*labelhash*`])`

Generates a pop-up menu.

name
The name to assign the input to (required).

\@array
An array reference listing the menu items. You can also use an anonymous array reference (see the second example).

selected
The menu item to be initially selected (default is first menu item or the item selected in previous queries).

\%labelhash
A hash reference listing labels for each menu item. Default is menu item text. For example:

```
%labels = ('UPS'=>'United Parcel Service (UPS)',
    'FedExO'=>'Federal Express Overnight - 10AM delivery',
    'FedExS'=>'Federal Express Standard - 2PM delivery',
    'FedEx2'=>'Federal Express 2nd Day Delivery');

print $query->popup_menu('delivery_method',
                    ['UPS', 'FedExO', 'FedExS', 'FedEx2'],
                        'FedExO',
                        \%labels);
```

Using named parameters, the syntax is:

```
print $query->popup_menu(-name=>'name',
                          -values=>\@array,
                          -default=>'selected',
                          -labels=>\%labelhash,
                          -onChange=>function,
                          -onFocus=>function,
                          -onBlur=>function);
```

`-onChange=>`*function*
: Browser should execute *function* when the user changes the text field.

`-onFocus=>`*function*
: Browser should execute *function* when the focus is on the text field.

`-onBlur=>`*function*
: Browser should execute *function* when the focus leaves the text field.

---

radio_group

`print $query->radio_group('`*name*`', \@`*list* `[, `*selected*`, 'true', \%`*label*`])`

Generates a set of radio buttons.

name
: The name to assign the input to (required).

\@list
: An array reference with the list items. You can also use an anonymous array reference.

selected
: The menu item to be initially selected.

true
: Insert newlines between radio buttons.

\%label
: A hash reference listing labels for each list item. Default is the list text itself. See popup_menu for an example.

Using named parameters, the syntax is:

```
print $query->radio_group(-name=>'name',
                          -values=>\@list,
                          -default=>'selected',
                          -linebreak=>'true',
                          -labels=>\%labelhash,
                          -columns=>n,
                          -columnheader=>'string',
                          -rows=>m,
                          -rowheader=>'string');
```

`-columns=>`*n*
: The number of columns to use.

`-columnheader=>`*'string'*
: A header for the column.

`-rows=`*m*
: The number of rows to use. If omitted and `-columns` is specified, the rows are calculated for you.

`-rowheader=>`*'string'*
: A header for the row.

raw_cookie

```
raw_cookie( )
```

Returns the value of the HTTP_COOKIE header.

ReadParse

```
ReadParse( )
```

Creates a hash named `%in` containing query information. Used for backward compatibility with the Perl4 *cgi-lib.pl*.

redirect

```
print $query->redirect('url')
```

Generates a header for redirecting the browser.

url The absolute URL to redirect to.

Using named parameters, the syntax is:

```
print $query->redirect(-uri=>'url',
                       -nph=>1);
```

referer

```
referer( )
```

Returns the referring URL.

remote_host

```
remote_host( )
```

Returns the remote hostname or IP address, depending on the configuration of the server.

remote_user

```
remote_user( )
```

Returns the username supplied for authorization.

request_method

```
request_method( )
```

Returns the request method.

reset

```
print $query->reset
```

Generates a button that resets the form to its initial values. See also `defaults`.

save

```
$query->save(filehandle)
```

Saves the form to the specified filehandle, to be read back with the `new` constructor.

filehandle
: The filehandle to save the file to.

script_name

```
script_name()
```

Returns the current partial URL.

scrolling_list

```
print $query->scrolling_list('name',\@list
[,selected,size,'true', \%labelhash])
```

Generates a scrolling list.

name
: The name to assign the input to (required).

\@list
: An array reference with the list items. You can also use an anonymous array reference.

selected
: The menu item(s) to be initially selected (default is that nothing is selected). This can be a single value or a reference to a list of values.

size
: The number of elements to display in the list box.

true
: Allow multiple selections.

\%labelhash
: A hash reference listing labels for each list item. Default is the list text itself. See popup_menu for an example.

Using named parameters, the syntax is:

```
print $query->scrolling_list(-name=>'name',
                             -values=>\@listarray,
                             -default=>selected,
                             -size=>size,
                             -multiple=>'true',
                             -labels=>\%labelhash,
                             -onChange=>function,
                             -onFocus=>function,
                             -onBlur=>function);
```

-onChange=>*function*
: Browser should execute *function* when the user changes the text field.

-onFocus=>*function*
: Browser should execute *function* when the focus is on the text field.

-onBlur=>*function*
: Browser should execute *function* when the focus leaves the text field.

self_url

```
$url = $query->self_url
```

Returns the URL of the current script with all its state information intact.

start_html

```
print $query->start_html(['title', 'email', 'base',
attribute='value'])
```

Generates <HTML> and <BODY> tags.

title
The title of the page.

email
The author's email address.

base
Whether to use a <BASE> tag in the header.

attribute=*'value'*
Specifies an attribute to the <BODY> tag.

Using named parameters, the syntax is:

```
print $query->start_html(-title=>'title',
                         -author=>'email_address',
                         -base=>'true',
                         -xbase=>'url',
                         -meta=>{'metatag1'=>'value1',
                                 'metatag2'=>'value2'},
                         -script=>'$script',
                         -onLoad=>'$function',
                         -onUnload=>'$function',
                          attribute=>'value');
```

-title=>*'title'*
Specifies the title of the page.

-author=>*'email_address'*
Specifies the author's email address.

-xbase=>*'url'*
Provides an HREF for the <BASE> tag. Default is the current location.

-meta=>*{'metatag1'=>'value1', ... }*
Adds arbitrary meta information to the header as a reference to a hash. Valid tags are:

keywords
Keywords for this document.

copyright
Description for this document.

attribute=>*'value'*
Specify an attribute to the <BODY> tag.

`-script=>'$script'`
: Specify a JavaScript script to be embedded within a `<SCRIPT>` block.

`-onLoad=>'$function'`
: Browser should execute the specified function upon entering the page.

`-onUnload=>'$function'`
: Browser should execute the specified function upon leaving the page.

---

startform

`print $query->startform([method, action, encoding])`

Generates a `<FORM>` tag.

method
: The request method for the form. Values are:

  `POST`
  : Use the POST method (default).

  `GET`
  : Use the GET method.

action
: The URL of the CGI script. Default is the current URL.

encoding
: The encoding scheme. Possible values are `application/x-www-form-urlencoded` and `multipart/form-data`.

Using named parameters, the syntax is:

```
print $query->startform(-method=>$method,
                        -action=>$action,
                        -encoding=>$encoding,
                        -name=>$name,
                        -target=>frame,
                        -onSubmit=>function);
```

`-name=>name`
: Names the form for identification by JavaScript functions.

`-target=>frame`
: Writes to the specified frame.

`-onSubmit=>function`
: A JavaScript function that the browser should execute upon submitting the form.

---

start_multipart_form

`print $query->start_multipart_form([method, action])`

Generates `<HTML>` and `<BODY>` tags. Same as `startform` but assumes `multipart/form-data` encoding as the default.

submit

```
print $query->submit([ 'label','value' ])
```

Generates a submit button.

label
: The label to use for the button.

value
: The value to return when the form is submitted.

Using named parameters, the syntax is:

```
print $query->submit(-name=>'name',
                     -value=>'value',
                     -onClick=>function);
```

`-onClick=>`*function*
: Browser should execute *function* when the user clicks the Submit button.

textarea

```
print $query->textarea('name' [,'value',rows,columns ])
```

Generates a large multiline text input box.

name
: The name to assign the input to (required).

value
: The initial value to place into the text input box.

rows
: The number of rows to display.

columns
: The number of columns to display.

Using named parameters, the syntax is:

```
print $query->textarea(-name=>'name',
                       -default=>'value',
                       -rows=>rows,
                       -columns=>columns,
                       -override=>1,
                       -onChange=>function,
                       -onFocus=>function,
                       -onBlur=>function,
                       -onSelect=>function);
```

`-override=>1`
: Text field should not inherit its value from a previous invocation of the script.

`-onChange=>`*function*
: Browser should execute *function* when the user changes the text field.

`-onFocus=>`*function*
: Browser should execute *function* when the focus is on on the text field.

-onBlur=>*function*
: Browser should execute *function* when the focus leaves the text field.

-onSelect=>*function*
: Browser should execute *function* when the user changes a selected portion of the text field.

---

textfield

```
print $query->textfield('name' [,'value', size, maxlength])
```

Generates a text input field.

name
: The name to assign the input to (required).

value
: The initial value to place in the text field.

size
: The size of the text field (in characters).

maxlength
: The maximum length of the text field (in characters).

Using named parameters, the syntax is:

```
print $query->textfield(-name=>'name',
                        -default=>'value',
                        -size=>size,
                        -maxlength=>maxlength,
                        -override=>1,
                        -onChange=>function,
                        -onFocus=>function,
                        -onBlur=>function,
                        -onSelect=>function);
```

-override=>1
: Text field should not inherit its value from a previous invocation of the script.

-onChange=>*function*
: Browser should execute *function* when the user changes the text field.

-onFocus=>*function*
: Browser should execute *function* when the focus is on the text field.

-onBlur=>*function*
: Browser should execute *function* when the focus leaves the text field.

-onSelect=>*function*
: Browser should execute *function* when the user changes a selected portion of the text field.

url

```
url = $query->url
```

Returns a URL of the current script without query information.

use_named_parameters

```
use_named_parameters( )
```

Specifies that functions should take named parameters.

user_agent

```
$query->user_agent( [string] )
```

Returns the value of the HTTP_USER_AGENT header.

string
: If specified, only returns headers matching the specified string.

user_name

```
user_name( )
```

Returns the remote user's login name; unreliable.

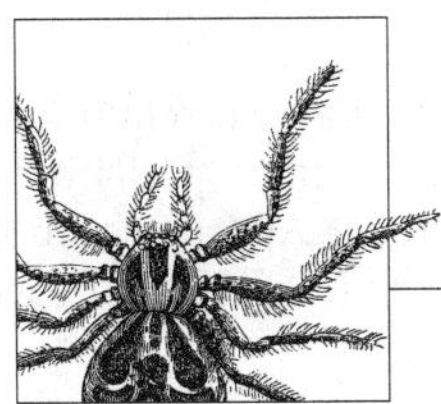

15
Web Server Programming with mod_perl

mod_perl is an Apache module that embeds the Perl interpreter directly into Apache. There are many advantages to mod_perl:

- Standard CGI programs can be converted to run significantly faster with little alteration under mod_perl.
- Databases can be accessed much more efficiently under mod_perl.
- You can write custom Apache modules and handlers easily, using Perl instead of C. mod_perl gives you access to all Apache request stages.
- Perl code can be embedded into Apache configuration files.
- Perl can be used for server-side includes.
- You have access to the many tools written for mod_perl servers, such as Mason and AxKit.

mod_perl isn't for everyone. By embedding Perl directly into the Apache `httpd` executable, mod_perl invokes significant overhead of its own. If you only have static documents, you certainly wouldn't use a mod_perl-enabled version of Apache to serve them. However, if you have a lot of dynamic content, you'll find mod_perl to be extremely powerful. You can also have the best of both worlds by designing your web site to serve static documents off a "normal" Apache server and dynamic documents off a mod_perl server.

At this writing, the release of mod_perl 2.0 is imminent, but mod_perl 1.3 is considered the stable version. mod_perl 2.0 is a near-complete rewrite that takes advantage of the threading features in Apache 2.0 and Perl 5.8. However, mod_perl 2.0 is still considered experimental. As the migration period to mod_perl 2.0 is expected to be long, this chapter covers mod_perl 1.3.

Installing mod_perl

If you already have Apache installed on your machine, you will have to rebuild it with mod_perl. You can get the source and documentation for mod_perl from *http://perl.apache.org/*. If there isn't already an Apache *httpd* in the Apache source tree, you must build one. Then build mod_perl as directed in the *INSTALL* file for the mod_perl distribution.

As we've mentioned, mod_perl allows you to hook in Perl modules as handlers for various stages of a request. By default, however, the only callback hook that is enabled is `PerlHandler`, which is the one that processes content (i.e., a CGI document). If you want to use other hooks—for example, to extend Apache's logging facilities via the `PerlLogHandler` directive; you need to specify it at build time as directed in the *INSTALL* file. For example:

```
% perl Makefile.PL PERL_LOG=1
```

The mod_perl Makefile replaces the *httpd* in the Apache source tree with a Perl-enabled one. When you install mod_perl, it installs not only the new *httpd* in your system area, but also several Perl modules, including Apache::Registry.

Design of mod_perl

mod_perl is not a Perl module. It is a module of the Apache server, which is currently the most commonly used web server. With mod_perl, you can use Apache configuration directives not only to process CGI scripts much more efficiently, but also to handle all stages in processing a server request.

mod_perl embeds a copy of the Perl interpreter into the Apache *httpd* executable, providing complete access to Perl functionality within Apache. This enables a set of mod_perl-specific configuration directives, all of which start with the string `Perl*`. Most of these directives are used to specify handlers for various stages of the request, but not all. In addition, mod_perl lets you embed Perl code into your Apache configuration files (within `<Perl> ... </Perl>` directives) and allows you to use Perl for server side includes.

mod_perl Handlers

To understand mod_perl, you should understand how the Apache server works. When Apache receives a request, it processes it in several stages. First, it translates the URL to the associated resource (i.e., filename, CGI script, etc.) on the server machine. Then it checks to see if the user is authorized to access that resource, perhaps by requesting and checking an ID and password. Once the user has passed inspection, the server figures out what kind of data it's sending back (e.g., it decides a file ending in *.html* is probably a `text/html` file), creates some headers, and sends those headers back to the client with the resource itself. When all is said and done, the server makes a log entry.

At each stage of this process, Apache looks for routines to "handle" the request. Apache supplies its own handlers; for example, one of the default handlers is `cgi-script`, often seen applied to */cgi-bin*:

```
<Location /cgi-bin>
  ...
SetHandler cgi-script
  ...
</Location>
```

mod_perl allows you to write your own handlers in Perl, by embedding the Perl runtime library directly into the Apache *httpd* server executable. To use mod_perl for CGI (which is all that most people want to do with it), assign the SetHandler directive to perl-script, and then assign the mod_perl-specific PerlHandler directive to a special Perl module called Apache::Registry:

```
SetHandler perl-script
PerlHandler Apache::Registry
```

PerlHandler is the mod_perl handler for the content retrieval stage of the transaction. To use other handlers, you don't need to reassign SetHandler. For example, to identify a handler for the logging stage of the request:

```
<Location /snoop/>
PerlLogHandler Apache::DumpHeaders
</Location>
```

In order for this to work, mod_perl must be built with logging hooks enabled and the Apache::DumpHeaders module must be installed. mod_perl looks in Apache::DumpHeaders for a routine called handler() and executes it as the logging handler for that resource.

The following is a list of each of the handler directives that can be enabled by mod_perl and the stages that each is used for. Only PerlHandler is enabled by default.

Handler	Purpose
PerlAccessHandler	Access stage
PerlAuthenHandler	Authentication stage
PerlAuthzHandler	Authorization stage
PerlChildInitHandler	Child initialization stage
PerlChildExitHandler	Child termination stage
PerlCleanupHandler	Cleanup stage
PerlFixupHandler	Fixup stage
PerlHandler	Response stage
PerlHeaderParserHandler	Header-parsing stage
PerlInitHandler	Initialization
PerlLogHandler	Logging stage
PerlPostReadRequestHandler	Post-request stage
PerlTransHandler	Translation stage
PerlTypeHandler	Type-handling stage

You can write your own handlers for each of these stages. But there are also dozens of modules you can download from CPAN, some of which are listed at the end of this chapter.

Running CGI Scripts with mod_perl

A common criticism of CGI is that it requires forking extra processes each time a script is executed. If you have only a few hits an hour, or even a few hits a minute, this isn't a big deal. But for a high-traffic site, lots of CGI scripts repeatedly spawning can have an unfortunate effect on the machine running the web server. The CGI scripts will be slow, the web server will be slow, and other processes on the machine will come to a crawl.

With mod_perl and Apache::Registry, however, your CGI scripts are precompiled by the server and executed without forking, thus running much more quickly and efficiently.

The mod_perl installation enables the `PerlHandler` callback hook by default and by installing the Apache::Registry module. `PerlHandler` is the handler used for the content retrieval stage of the server transaction. Apache::Registry is the Perl module that emulates the CGI environment so you can use "standard" Perl CGI scripts with mod_perl without having to rewrite them (much). This is by far the cheapest way to get improved CGI performance.

With Apache::Registry, each individual CGI program is compiled and cached the first time it is called (or whenever it is changed) and remains available for all subsequent instances of that CGI script. This process avoids the costs of startup time.

Whereas most CGI scripts are kept in */cgi-bin/*, scripts that use Apache::Registry are placed in a separate directory, e.g., */perl-bin/*. The *access.conf* Apache configuration file needs to point to this directory by setting an alias and defining a handler for this new location:

```
Alias /perl-bin/ /usr/local/apache/perl-bin/

<Location /perl-bin>
SetHandler perl-script
PerlHandler Apache::Registry
PerlSendHeader On
Options ExecCGI
</Location>
```

Instead of the `cgi-script` handler, use the `perl-script` handler to give control to mod_perl. Next, the `PerlHandler` directive tells mod_perl that the Apache::Registry module should be used for serving all files in that directory. `PerlSendHeader` is another mod_perl-specific directive; in this case, it tells mod_perl to send response lines and common headers; by default, none are sent. (For NPH scripts, you'll want to turn this feature off again.) `Options ExecCGI` is a standard Apache header needed to tell Apache to treat the script as a CGI script.

If you want to load Perl modules in addition to Apache::Registry, use the PerlModule directive:

```
PerlModule CGI
```

If you include this line, you shouldn't need to explicitly `use CGI` in each Perl CGI script anymore, as CGI.pm is loaded directly from the Apache server. Up to 10 modules can be listed with the `PerlModule` directive.

CGI scripts in the new directory should work now. However, if you have problems, the mod_perl manpage offers some words of wisdom:

Always `use strict`
: "Standard" CGI scripts start with a clean slate every time. When switching to mod_perl, CGI programmers are often surprised to learn how often they take advantage of this fact. `use strict` tells you when your variables haven't been properly declared and might inherit values from previous invocations of the script.

Don't call `exit()`
: Calling `exit()` at the end of every program is a habit of many programmers. While often totally unnecessary, it usually doesn't hurt... except with mod_perl. If you're using mod_perl without Apache::Registry, `exit()` kills the server process. If `exit()` is the last function call, just remove it. If the structure of your program is such that it is called from the middle of the script, you can put a label at the end of the script and use `goto()`. There's also an `Apache->exit()` call you can use if you're really attached to `exit()`. If you're using Apache::Registry, you don't have to worry about this problem. Apache::Registry is smart enough to override all `exit()` calls with `Apache->exit()`.

In addition, you should use recent versions of Perl and CGI.pm. You can scan the mod_perl documentation for the very latest compatibility news.

Server Side Includes with mod_perl

Server Side Includes (SSI) are tags embedded directly into an HTML file that perform special functions. They are most commonly used for running CGI scripts and displaying the result; most web page counters are performed using SSI.

If you use mod_perl with *mod_include* (another Apache server module), you can embed Perl subroutines into SSI directives. For example:

```
<!--#perl sub="sub {print ++Count}" -->
```

The Apache::Include module lets you include entire Apache::Registry scripts:

```
<!--#perl sub="Apache::Include" arg="/perl-bin/counter.pl" -->
```

You could have used standard SSI to include a CGI script for the same purpose, but this way is faster. To use *mod_include* with mod_perl, you need to configure mod_perl to do so at compile-time.

<Perl> Sections

With mod_perl, you can use Perl in Apache configuration files. This means you can make your Apache configuration much more flexible by using conditionals.

Any Perl code in Apache configuration files should be placed between `<Perl>` and `</Perl>` directives. This code can define variables and lists used by mod_perl to assign the associated Apache configuration directives; for example, assigning the `$ServerAdmin` variable redefines the `ServerAdmin` Apache configuration directive.

Suppose you share the same Apache configuration files across multiple servers, and you only want to allow personal directories on one of them. You can use Perl directives like this:

```
<Perl>
if (`hostname` =~ /public/) {
        $UserDir = "public.html";
} else {
        $UserDir = "DISABLED";
}
1;
</Perl>
```

Directive blocks (such as `<Location>...</Location>`) can be represented as a hash:

```
<Perl>
$Location{"/design_dept/"} = {
        DefaultType   => 'image/gif', FancyIndexing => 'On' }
</Perl>
```

Apache:: Modules

Apache::Registry is the most commonly used mod_perl module. But there are many more, all available on CPAN. Table 15-1 lists the Apache::* modules and which handler they're designed to be used with, but you should also check the *apache-modlist.html* file on CPAN for the very latest listing.

Table 15-1. Apache::Modules

PerlHandler	
Apache::CallHandler	Map filenames to subroutine calls
Apache::Dir	Control directory indexing
Apache::Embperl	Embed Perl code in HTML files
Apache::ePerl	Embedded Perl (ePerl) emulation
Apache::FTP	Emulate an FTP proxy
Apache::GzipChain	Compress output from another handler
Apache::JavaScript	Generate JavaScript code
Apache::OutputChain	Chain multiple handlers via "filter" modules
Apache::PassFile	Send files via OutputChain
Apache::Registry	Run unaltered CGI scripts
Apache::RobotRules	Enforce *robots.txt* rules
Apache::Sandwich	Add per-directory headers and footers
Apache::VhostSandwich	Add headers and footers for virtual hosts
Apache::SSI	Implement server side includes in Perl
Apache::Stage	Manage a document staging directory
Apache::WDB	Query databases via DBI
PerlHeaderParserHandler	
Apache::AgentDeny	Deny abusive clients
PerlAuthenHandler	
Apache::Authen	Authenticate users

Table 15-1. Apache::Modules (continued)

Apache::AuthCookie	Authenticate and authorize users via cookies
Apache::AuthenDBI	Authenticate via Perl's DBI
Apache::AuthExpire	Expire authentication credentials
Apache::AuthenGSS	Authenticate users with Generic Security Service
Apache::AuthenLDAP	Authenticate users with LDAP
Apache::AuthNIS	Authenticate users with NIS
Apache::BasicCookieAuth	Accept cookie or basic authentication credentials
Apache::DBILogin	Authenticate using a backend database
Apache::DCELogin	Authenticate within a DCE login context
Apache::AuthAny	Authenticate with any username/password
PerlAuthzHandler	
Apache::AuthCookie	Authenticate and authorize via cookies
Apache::AuthzAge	Authorize based on age
Apache::AuthzDCE	Authorize based on DFS/DCE ACL
Apache::AuthzDBI	Authorize groups via DBI
Apache::AuthNIS	Authenticate and authorize via NIS
Apache::RoleAuthz	Role-based authorization
PerlAccessHandler	
Apache::AccessLimitNum	Limit user access by the number of requests
Apache::DayLimit	Limit access based on the day of the week
Apache::RobotLimit	Limit access of robots
PerlTypeHandler	
Apache::AcceptLanguage	Send file types based on user's language preference
PerlTransHandler	
Apache::DynaRPC	Translate URIs into RPCs
Apache::Junction	Mount remote web-server namespace
Apache::LowerCaseGETs	Translate to lowercase URIs as needed
Apache::MsqlProxy	Translate URIs into mSQL queries
Apache::ProxyPassThru	Skeleton for vanilla proxy
Apache::ProxyCache	Caching proxy
PerlFixupHandler	
Apache::HttpEquiv	Convert HTML HTTP-EQUIV tags to HTTP headers
Apache::Timeit	Benchmark Perl handlers
PerlLogHandler	
Apache::DumpHeaders	Display HTTP transaction headers
Apache::Traffic	Log the number of bytes transferred on a per-user basis
Apache::WatchDog	Look for problematic URIs
PerlChildInitHandler	
Apache::Resource	Limit resources used by *httpd* children
Server configuration	
Apache::ConfigLDAP	Configure server via LDAP and `<Perl>` sections
Apache::ConfigDBI	Configure server via DBI and `<Perl>` sections

Table 15-1. Apache::Modules (continued)

Apache::ModuleConfig	Interface to configuration API
Apache::PerlSections	Utilities for `<Perl>` sections
Apache::httpd_conf	Methods to configure and run an *httpd*
Apache::src	Methods for finding and reading bits of source
Database	
Apache::DBI	Manage persistent DBI connections
Apache::Sybase	Manage persistent DBlib connections
Apache::Mysql	Manage persistent mysql connections
Interfaces and integration with various Apache C modules	
Apache::Constants	Constants defined in *httpd.h*
Apache::Include	Enable use of Apache::Registry scripts within SSI with *mod_include*
Apache::Global	Give access to server global variables
Apache::LogError	Give an interface to *aplog_error*
Apache::LogFile	Give an interface to Apache's piped logs, etc.
Apache::Mime	Give an interface to *mod_mime* functionality
Apache::Module	Give an interface to Apache C module structures
Apache::Options	Import Apache::Constants "options"
Apache::Scoreboard	Give an interface to scoreboard API
Apache::Servlet	Give an interface to the Java Servlet engine
Apache::Sfio	Give an interface to `r->connection->client->sf*`
Development and debug tools	
Apache::Debug	Provide debugging utilities to mod_perl
Apache::DProf	Hook Devel::DProf into mod_perl
Apache::FakeRequest	Implement Apache methods offline
Apache::Peek	Emulate Devel::Peek for mod_perl
Apache::SawAmpersand	Make sure no one is using $&, $', or $'
Apache::StatINC	Reloads `used` or `required` files when updated
Apache::Status	Get information about loaded modules
Apache::Symbol	Support symbols
Apache::test	Define handy routines for *make test* scripts
Miscellaneous	
Apache::Byterun	Run Perl bytecode modules
Apache::Mmap	Share data via Mmap module
Apache::Persistent	Store data via IPC::, DBI, or disk
Apache::PUT	Handler for the HTTP PUT method
Apache::RegistryLoader	Apache::Registry startup script loader
Apache::Safe	Adaptation of *safecgiperl*
Apache::Session	Maintain client <-> *httpd* session/state
Apache::SIG	Signal handlers for mod_perl
Apache::State	Powerful state engine

The Perl API

The Apache API is a set of routines that C programmers can use to write Apache modules. One of the most powerful features of mod_perl is its Perl API, which gives Perl programmers access to the Apache API. For information on how to program Apache modules in Perl, see *Writing Apache Modules in Perl and C* by Lincoln Stein and Doug MacEachern (O'Reilly).

The following methods are defined for the Perl API to Apache.

---

aborted `$c->aborted`

Returns true if the client aborted the transaction.

---

allow_options `$r->allow_options`

Checks the options allowed for this request.

---

allowed `$r->allowed($bitmask)`

Gets or sets the "allowed methods" bitmask.

---

args `$r->args( [$query_string] )`

Returns the query string portion of the URI either as a string (scalar context) or as a list of key/value pairs (list context).

---

as_string `$r->as_string`

Returns a string representation of the request object.

---

auth_name `$r->auth_name`

Returns a reference to the value of the AuthName directive.

---

auth_type `$c->auth_type`

Returns the authentication scheme.

---

auth_type `$r->auth_type`

Returns a reference to the value of the AuthType directive.

---

bytes_sent `$r->bytes_sent`

Returns the number of bytes sent to the client.

connection `$c = $r->connection`

Returns a reference to the request connection object.

content `$r->content`

If the request content type is `application/x-www-form-urlencoded`, returns the entity body either as a string (scalar context) or as a list of key/value pairs (list context).

content_encoding `$r->content_encoding( [$value] )`

Returns the content encoding of the entity.

content_languages `$r->content_languages( [$ref] )`

Returns the content language(s) of the entity as an array reference.

content_type `$r->content_type( [$value] )`

Returns the content type of the entity.

current_callback `$r->current_callback`

Returns the name of the current handler.

custom_response `$r->custom_response($code, $uri)`

Creates a custom response for the specified response code.

dir_config `$r->dir_config( $key )`

Returns the value associated with `$key` as specified by the PerlSetVar directive.

dir_config `$s->dir_config( $key )`

Same as Apache::dir_config.

document_root `$r->document_root ( [$docroot] )`

Returns a reference to the value of the DocumentRoot directive.

err_header_out

```
$r->err_header_out( $header, [$value] )
```

Retrieves a specific response header when an error is encountered.

err_headers_out

```
$r->err_headers_out
```

Returns a hash of server response headers when an error is encountered.

filename

```
$r->filename( [$filename] )
```

Returns the filename that the URI resolves to.

fileno

```
$c->fileno( [$n] )
```

Returns either the client output file descriptor, or the input file descriptor if an argument of 0 is given.

get

```
$r->dir_config->get( $key )
```

Returns the value associated with $key as specified by the PerlAddVar directive.

get_basic_auth_pw

```
$r->get_basic_auth_pw
```

Reports whether the request uses Basic authentication, or returns a value such as AUTH_REQUIRED that needs to be conveyed back to the client.

get_handlers

```
$r->get_handlers( $phase )
```

Returns a reference to a list of handlers enabled for the specified request phase.

get_remote_host

```
$r->get_remote_host
```

Returns the client's DNS hostname.

get_remote_logname

```
$r->get_remote_logname
```

Returns the client's login name.

get_server_port

```
$r->get_server_port
```

Returns server's port number.

gid `$s->gid`

Returns the group ID under the server uses.

handler `$r->handler( [$meth] )`

Specifies the handler for the request.

hard_timeout `$r->hard_timeout($string)`

Performs a hard timeout with the specified message.

header_only `$r->header_only`

Returns true if the request method is `HEAD`.

header_out `$r->header_out( $header, $value )`

Retrieves a specific response header.

headers_in `$r->headers_in`

Returns a hash of client request headers.

headers_out `$r->headers_out`

Returns a hash of server response headers.

hostname `$r->hostname`

Returns the server hostname.

internal_redirect `$r->internal_redirect( $location )`

Redirects transparently to a different location on the server.

internal_redirect_handler `$r->internal_redirect_handler( $location )`

Redirects transparently to a different location on the server, preserving the handler.

is_initial_req `$r->is_initial_req`

Returns true if the current request is the first request.

is_main

```
$r->is_main
```

Returns true if the main request is current.

is_virtual

```
$s->is_virtual
```

Returns true for virtual servers.

kill_timeout

```
$r->kill_timeout
```

Performs a kill timeout.

last

```
$r->last
```

Returns a reference to the last request structure.

local_addr

```
$c->local_addr
```

Returns the port and address on the local host.

location

```
$r->location
```

Returns the location that the current Perl handler is being called from.

log_error

```
$r->log_error($message)
```

Logs a message to the error log.

log_error

```
$s->log_error
```

Same as `Apache::log_error`.

log_reason

```
$r->log_reason($message, $logfile)
```

Logs a message to the specified error log.

loglevel

```
$s->loglevel
```

Returns the current LogLevel.

lookup_file

```
$r->lookup_file($filename)
```

Looks up the specified file.

lookup_uri

```
$r->lookup_uri($uri)
```

Looks up the specified URI.

main

```
$r->main
```

Returns a reference to the main request, or `undef` if the current request is the main request.

method

```
$r->method( [$meth] )
```

Returns the request method.

method_number

```
$r->method_number( [$num] )
```

Returns the request method number as defined by the M_GET and M_POST,... constants available from the Apache::Constants module.

names

```
$s->names
```

Returns aliases for the server.

next

```
$r->next
```

Returns a reference to the next request or `undef` if there is none.

no_cache

```
$r->no_cache( $boolean )
```

Specifies whether the returned data should be cached.

note_basic_auth_failure

```
$r->note_basic_auth_failure
```

Sets the HTTP headers requesting authentication for the realm.

notes

```
$r->notes( $key, [$value] )
```

Returns (or sets) a value from the Apache notes table. See also pnotes.

path_info

```
$r->path_info( [$path_info] )
```

Returns the path_info portion of the URI.

perl_hook

`Apache::perl_hook($hook)`

Reports whether the specified callback hook is in effect.

pnotes

`$r->pnotes( $key, [$value] )`

Returns (or sets) a value from the Apache notes table, taking any scalar as `$value`. The value is cleaned up after every request.

port

`$s->port`

Returns the server's port number.

post_ connection

`$r->post_connection($code_ref)`

Registers a cleanup function.

prev

`$r->prev`

Returns a reference to the previous request or undef if there is none.

print

`$r->print( @list )`

Sends the specified data to the client.

protocol

`$r->protocol`

Returns the HTTP protocol that the client uses.

proxyreq

`$r->proxyreq`

Returns true if the request is a proxy request.

push_handlers

`$r->push_handlers( $phase, \&handler )`

Specifies a new handler to be called for the specified request phase.

read

`$r->read($buf, $num_bytes, [$offset])`

Reads data from the client starting at the optional `$offset` until it reaches `$num_bytes` or reaches a timeout.

register_cleanup

`$r->register_cleanup($code_ref)`

Registers a cleanup function.

remote_addr

```
$c->remote_addr
```

Returns the port and address on the remote host.

remote_host

```
$c->remote_host
```

Returns the client's hostname.

remote_ip

```
$c->remote_ip
```

Returns the client's IP address.

remote_logname

```
$c->remote_logname
```

Returns the remote user's login name.

request

```
Apache->request([$r])
```

Returns a reference to the request object.

request_time

```
$r->request_time
```

Returns the timestamp of the request.

requires

```
$r->requires
```

Returns an array reference with information relating to the require directive.

reset_timeout

```
$r->reset_timeout
```

Resets the current timeout.

run

```
$subr->run
```

Executes the subroutine.

send_cgi_header

```
$r->send_cgi_header()
```

Specifies CGI headers and calls `send_http_header()`.

send_fd

```
$r->send_fd( $filehandle )
```

Sends the specified file to the client.

send_http_header

```
$r->send_http_header( [$content_type] )
```

Sends the http header to the client.

server

```
$s = $r->server
```

Return a reference to the server info object. Can also be used without a request object (i.e,, `Apache->server`) for startup files.

server_admin

```
$s->server_admin
```

Returns the webmaster's email address.

server_hostname

```
$s->server_hostname
```

Returns the server's hostname.

server_root_relative

```
$r->server_root_relative( [$path] )
```

Returns the value of the ServerRoot directory, or concatenates `$path` to that value. Can also be used without a request object (i.e., `Apache->server_root_relative`) for startup files.

set_handlers

```
$r->set_handlers( $phase, [\&handler, ... ] )
```

Specifies the handlers to be called for the specified request phase.

soft_timeout

```
$r->soft_timeout($string)
```

Performs a soft timeout with the specified message.

status

```
$r->status( $integer )
```

Returns the 3-digit response status code for the request.

status_line

```
$r->status_line( $string )
```

Returns the response status string for the request.

subprocess_env

```
$r->subprocess_env( $key, [$value] )
```

Returns (or sets) a value from the Apache `subprocess_env` table.

the_request

```
$r->the_request
```

Returns the request line sent by the client.

uid

```
$s->uid
```

Returns the user ID the server uses.

unescape_url

```
Apache::unescape_url($string)
```

Removes escapes for the specified URL.

unescape_url_info

```
Apache::unescape_url_info($string)
```

Removes escapes from the specified form data.

uri

```
$r->uri( [$uri] )
```

Returns the requested URI.

user

```
$c->user( [$user] )
```

Returns the authenticated user name.

warn

```
$r->warn($message)
```

Logs a message to the error log. Only works if the LogLevel is "warn" or higher under Apache 1.3 and later.

warn

```
$s->warn
```

Same as Apache::warn.

VI

PHP

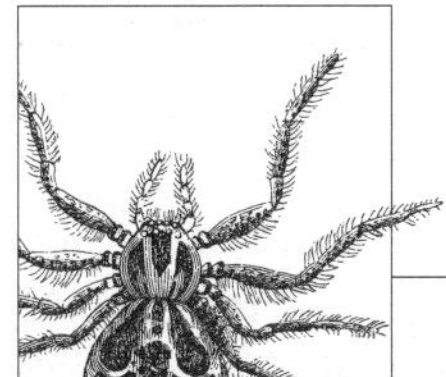

16
PHP

PHP (PHP Hypertext Preprocessor) is a web scripting language. PHP is easy to learn because it builds on the bits and pieces that most people already know. The pieces that you don't know are filled in by excellent online documentation and many high-quality books. This simple approach to solving the web problem has caught on with an amazing number of people.

This chapter provides an overview of the main concepts needed for most web applications, followed by quick reference material for most of the main PHP functions. For complete coverage of PHP, refer to *Programming PHP* by Rasmus Lerdorf and Keven Tatroe.

Installation and Configuration

PHP works with many different web servers in many different ways, but by far the most popular way to run PHP is as an Apache module with Apache 1.3.x. Full installation instructions for all the different ways to install PHP can be found in the PHP documentation. Here, I cover the Apache module installation.

If you are compiling from the PHP source tarball, follow the instructions in the *INSTALL* file found inside the PHP distribution file. A tarball is a compressed *tar* file. *tar* stands for tape archive, but these days it has little to do with tapes. It is simply a way to lump multiple files and directories into a single file for distribution. Normally tarballs have the *.tar.gz* extension to indicate a *tar* file compressed with *gzip*. To untar a tarball, use:

```
tar zxvf foo.tar.gz
```

On Windows, many utilities (including WinZip) understand tarballs.

If you are installing from a precompiled binary package such as an *rpm* file, most of the work should be done for you. But doublecheck that the Apache configuration described below is correct.

When you are using PHP as an Apache module, PHP processing is triggered by a special MIME type. This is defined in the Apache configuration file with a line similar to:

```
AddType application/x-httpd-php .php
```

This line tells Apache to treat all files that end with the *.php* extension as PHP files, which means that any file with that extension is parsed for PHP tags. The actual extension is completely arbitrary and you are free to change it to whatever you wish to use.

If you are running PHP as a dynamic shared object (DSO) module, you also need this line in your Apache configuration file:

```
LoadModule php4_module    modules/libphp4.so
```

Note that in many default *httpd.conf* files you will find AddModule lines. These really aren't necessary. They are only needed if you have a ClearModuleList directive somewhere in your *httpd.conf* file. I would suggest simply deleting the ClearModuleList directive and deleting all your AddModule lines. The idea behind ClearModuleList/AddModule is to make it possible to reorder already loaded modules in case module order is an issue. With most modules, the order that they are loaded—which governs the order they are called—is not important. And further, most binary distributions of Apache ship with most modules compiled as dynamically loadable modules, which means that if order is an issue for some reason, you can simply change the order of the LoadModule calls to fix it.

Don't forget to restart your server after making changes to your *httpd.conf* file. Once the server is restarted, you can check to see if PHP is working by creating a file in your document root named *info.php* containing the single line:

```
<?php phpinfo()?>
```

Load this up in your browser using *http://your.domain.com/info.php*. You should see all sorts of information about PHP. If you don't see anything, try selecting "View Source" in your browser. If you see the `phpinfo()` line, you probably forgot (or mistyped) the AddType line in your *httpd.conf* file. If the browser tries to download the file instead, it means that the AddType is there, but the PHP module is not being triggered—perhaps because you forgot the LoadModule line.

Once you have verified that PHP is working, have a look at the PHP initialization file called *php.ini*. The `phpinfo()` page will tell you where PHP is expecting to find it. PHP functions fine without this file, but with all the default settings. If you want to change the defaults, or perhaps more importantly, you want to be immune from any changes to the defaults when you upgrade, you should create a *php.ini* file. The source distribution of PHP comes with a *php.ini-dist* file that you can rename and copy into the location specified in the `phpinfo()` output. The *php.ini* file itself is well-commented and self-explanatory for the most part.

You can also put configuration directives inside the Apache *httpd.conf* file, and, in certain cases, in individual *.htaccess* files. This is very useful for setting things per-directory or per-virtual host. If you have this line in the *php.ini* file:

```
include_path = ".:/usr/local/lib/php:.."
```

you can set this in your *httpd.conf* file with:

```
php_value include_path .:/usr/local/lib/php:..
```

There are four *httpd.conf* directives used for setting PHP directives:

`php_value`
: For setting normal strings and values

`php_flag`
: For setting boolean values

`php_admin_value`
: For setting administrative values

`php_admin_flag`
: For setting boolean administrative values

The normal values and booleans can also be set in your *.htaccess* files, but only if the Apache AllowOverride setting (which sets what is allowed in a *.htaccess* file) includes `"Options"`.

More information can be found at *http://www.php.net/configuration*.

Embedding PHP in HTML

You embed PHP code into a standard HTML page. For example, here's how you can dynamically generate the title of an HTML document:

```
<html><head><title><?echo $title?></title>
</head>...
```

The `<?echo $title?>` portion of the document is replaced by the contents of the `$title` PHP variable. echo is a basic language statement that you can use to output data.

There are a few different ways that you can embed your PHP code. As you just saw, you can put PHP code between `<?` and `?>` tags:

```
<? echo "Hello World"; ?>
```

This style is the most common way to embed PHP, but it is a problem if your PHP code needs to co-exist with XML, as XML may use that tagging style itself. If this is the case, turn off this style in the *php.ini* file with the `short_open_tag` directive. Another way to embed PHP code is within `<?php` and `?>` tags:

```
<?php echo "Hello World"; ?>
```

This style is always available and is recommended when your PHP code needs to be portable to many different systems. Embedding PHP within `<script>` tags is another style that is always available:

```
<script language="php" > echo "Hello World";
</script>
```

One final style, in which the code is between `<%` and `%>` tags, is disabled by default:

```
<% echo "Hello World"; %>
```

PHP

You can turn on this style with the asp_tags directive in your *php.ini* file. The style is most useful when you are using Microsoft FrontPage or another HTML authoring tool that prefers that tag style for HTML-embedded scripts.

You can embed multiple statements by separating them with semicolons:

```
<?php
  echo "Hello World";
  echo "A second statement";
?>
```

It's legal to switch back and forth between HTML and PHP at any time. For example, if you want to output 100 <br /> tags for some reason, you can do it:

```
<?php for($i=0; $i<100; $i++) { ?>
  <br />
<?php } ?>
```

Of course, using the str_repeat() function here would make more sense.

When you embed PHP code in an HTML file, you need to use the *.php* file extension for that file, so that your web server knows to send the file to PHP for processing. Or, if you have configured your web server to use a different extension for PHP files, use that extension instead.

When you have PHP code embedded in an HTML page, you can think of that page as a PHP program. The bits and pieces of HTML and PHP combine to provide the functionality of the program. A collection of pages that contain programs can be thought of as a web application.

Including Files

An important feature of PHP is its ability to include files. These files may contain additional PHP tags. When you are designing a web application, you can break out common components and place them in a single file. This step makes it much easier to change certain aspects in one place later, and have the change take effect across the entire application. To include a file, use the include keyword:

```
<?php
    $title="My Cool Web Application";
    include "header.inc";
?>
```

The *header.inc* file might look as follows:

```
<html><head>
<title><?php echo $title?></title>
</head>
```

This example illustrates two important concepts of included files in PHP. First, variables set in the including file are automatically available in the included file. Second, each included file starts out in HTML mode. In other words, if you want to include a file that has PHP code in it, you have to embed that code just as you would any other PHP code.

Note also that I used the *.inc* extension here. This is not a special file type, just an arbitrary extension name I chose. Since your Apache server is not set up to treat *.inc* files as PHP files, if you put this file somewhere under your document_root, people can browse to it and see the PHP source in that file directly. This is usually not a good idea, so I add these lines to my *httpd.conf* file:

```
<Files ~ "\.inc$">
  Order allow,deny
  Deny from all
</Files>
```

This blocks any direct access to *.inc* files. The other option is to not put the files under document_root, or perhaps to name them *.php* instead. But be careful with that last approach. Keep in mind that people will then be able to execute these scripts, when they were probably not designed to be executed in a standalone fashion.

Other ways to include files are through include_once, require, and require_once. The difference between include and require is simply that with include, if the file to be included does not exist, you get a warning, whereas with require you get a fatal error and script execution stops. The include_once and require_once variations ensure that the file being included has not been included already. This helps avoid things like function redefinition errors.

Language Syntax

Variable names in PHP are case-sensitive. That means $A and $a are two distinct variables. However, function names in PHP are not case-sensitive. This rule applies to both built-in functions and user-defined functions.

PHP ignores whitespace between tokens. You can use spaces, tabs, and newlines to format and indent your code to make it more readable. PHP statements are terminated by semicolons.

There are three types of comments in PHP:

```
/* C style comments */
// C++ style comments
# Bourne shell style comments
```

The C++ and Bourne shell–style comments can be inserted anywhere in your code. Everything from the comment characters to the end of the line is ignored. The C-style comment tells PHP to ignore everything from the start of the comment until the end-comment characters. This means that this style of comment can span multiple lines.

Variables

In PHP, all variable names begin with a dollar sign ($). The $ is followed by an alphabetic character or an underscore, and optionally followed by a sequence of alphanumeric characters and underscores. There is no limit on the length of a variable name. Variable names in PHP are case-sensitive. Here are some examples:

```
$i
$counter
$first_name
$_TMP
```

In PHP, unlike in many other languages, you do not have to explicitly declare variables. PHP automatically declares a variable the first time a value is assigned to it. PHP variables are untyped; you can assign a value of any type to a variable.

PHP uses a symbol table to store the list of variable names and their values. There are two kinds of symbol tables in PHP: the global symbol table, which stores the list of global variables, and the function-local symbol table, which stores the set of variables available inside each function.

Dynamic Variables

Sometimes it is useful to set and use variables dynamically. Normally, you assign a variable like this:

```
$var = "hello";
```

Now let's say you want a variable whose name is the value of the `$var` variable. You can do that like this:

```
$$var = "World";
```

PHP parses `$$var` by first dereferencing the innermost variable, meaning that `$var` becomes `"hello"`. The expression that's left is `$"hello"`, which is just `$hello`. In other words, we have just created a new variable named `hello` and assigned it the value `"World"`. You can nest dynamic variables to an infinite level in PHP, although once you get beyond two levels, it can be very confusing for someone who is trying to read your code.

There is a special syntax for using dynamic variables, and any other complex variable, inside quoted strings in PHP:

```
echo "Hello ${$var}";
```

This syntax also helps resolve an ambiguity that occurs when variable arrays are used. Something like `$$var[1]` is ambiguous because it is impossible for PHP to know which level to apply the array index to. `${$var[1]}` tells PHP to dereference the inner level first and apply the array index to the result before dereferencing the outer level. `${$var}[1]`, on the other hand, tells PHP to apply the index to the outer level.

Initially, dynamic variables may not seem that useful, but there are times when they can shorten the amount of code you need to write to perform certain tasks. For example, say you have an associative array that looks like:

```
$array["abc"] = "Hello";
$array["def"] = "World";
```

Associative arrays like this are returned by various functions in the PHP modules. `mysql_fetch_array()` is one example. The indices in the array usually refer to fields or entity names within the context of the module you are working with. It's handy to turn these entity names into real PHP variables, so you can refer to them as simply `$abc` and `$def`. This is done as follows:

```
foreach($array as $index=>$value) {
  $$index = $value;
}
```

Data Types

PHP provides four primitive data types: integers, floating point numbers, strings, and booleans. In addition, there are two compound data types: arrays and objects.

Integers

Integers are whole numbers. The range of integers in PHP is equivalent to the range of the long data type in C. On 32-bit platforms, integer values range from –2,147,483,648 to +2,147,483,647. PHP automatically converts larger values to floating point numbers if you happen to overflow the range. An integer can be expressed in decimal (base-10), hexadecimal (base-16), or octal (base-8). For example:

```
$decimal=16;
$hex=0x10;
$octal=020;
```

Floating Point Numbers

Floating point numbers represent decimal values. The range of floating point numbers in PHP is equivalent to the range of the double type in C. On most platforms, a double can be between 1.7E – 308 to 1.7E + 308. A double may be expressed either as a regular number with a decimal point or in scientific notation. For example:

```
$var=0.017;
$var=17.0E-3
```

PHP also has two sets of functions that let you manipulate numbers with arbitrary precision. These two sets are known as the BC and the GMP functions. See *http://www.php.net/bc* and *http://www.php.net/gmp* for more information.

Strings

A string is a sequence of characters. A string can be delimited by single quotes or double quotes:

```
'PHP is cool'
"Hello, World!"
```

Double-quoted strings are subject to variable substitution and escape sequence handling, while single quotes are not. For example:

```
$a="World";
echo "Hello\t$a\n";
```

This displays "Hello: followed by a tab and then "World" followed by a newline. In other words, variable substitution is performed on the variable $a and the escape sequences are converted to their corresponding characters. Contrast that with:

```
echo 'Hello\t$a\n';
```

In this case, the output is exactly "Hello\t$a\n". There is no variable substitution or handling of escape sequences.

Another way to assign a string is to use what is known as the *heredoc* syntax. The advantage with this approach is that you do not need to escape quotes. It looks like this:

```
$foo = <<<EOD
  This is a "multiline" string
  assigned using the 'heredoc' syntax.
EOD;
```

The following table shows the escape sequences understood by PHP inside double-quoted strings.

Escape sequence	Meaning
\n	Linefeed (LF or 0x0A (10) in ASCII)
\r	Carriage return (CR or 0x0D (13) in ASCII)
\t	Horizontal tab (HT or 0x09 (9) in ASCII)
\\	Backslash
\$	Dollar sign
\"	Double quote
\123	Octal notation representation of a character
\x12	Hexadecimal notation representation of a character

Booleans

The boolean type only has two states: true and false. For example:

```
$flag = true;
```

Boolean values are most commonly used when the == or === operators perform a comparison and return the result.

Arrays

An array is a compound data type that can contain multiple data values, indexed either numerically or with strings. For example, an array of strings can be written like this:

```
$var[0]="Hello";
$var[1]="World";
```

Note that when you assign array elements like this, you do not have to use consecutive numbers to index the elements.

As a shortcut, PHP allows you to add an element onto the end of an array without specifying an index. For example:

```
$var[] ="Test";
```

PHP picks the next logical numerical index. In this case, the "Test" element is given the index 2 in our $var array: if the array has nonconsecutive elements, PHP selects the index value that is one greater than the current highest index value. This autoindexing feature is most useful when dealing with multiple-choice HTML <select> form elements, as we'll see in a later example.

Although we have called strings a primitive data type, it is actually possible to treat a string as a compound data type, where each character in the string can be accessed separately. In other words, you can think of a string as an array of characters, where the first character is at index 0. Thus, you can pick the third character out of a string with:

```
$string[2]
```

To solve an ambiguity problem between strings and arrays, a new syntax has been introduced to dereference individual characters from strings:

```
$string{2}
```

This syntax is equivalent to `$string[2]`, and is preferable.

Arrays can also be indexed using strings; these kinds of arrays are called *associative arrays*:

```
$var["January"]=1;
$var["February"]=2;
```

You can use a mix of numerical and string indices with a single array because PHP treats all arrays as hash tables internally, and the hash, or index, can be whatever you want.

All arrays in PHP can be traversed safely with the following mechanism:

```
foreach($array as $key=>$value) {
  echo "array[$key]=$value<br>\n";
}
```

This is the most common way to loop through each element of an array, whether it is a linear or an associative array. PHP provides a number of array manipulation functions; these are detailed later in the "Function Reference."

Objects

An object is a compound data type that can contain any number of variables and functions. PHP's support for objects is somewhat limited in Version 4. PHP Version 5 will improve the object-oriented capabilities of PHP. In PHP 4, the object-oriented support is designed to make it easy to encapsulate data structures and functions in order to package them into reusable classes. Here's a simple example:

```
class test {
  var $str = "Hello World";
  function init($str) {
    $this->str = $str;
  }
}

$class = new test;
echo $class->str;
$class->init("Hello");
echo $class->str;
```

This code creates a test object using the new operator. Then it sets a variable called str within the object. In object-speak, a variable in an object is known as a property of that object. The test object also defines a function, known as a method, called init(). This method uses the special-purpose $this variable to change the value of the str property within that object.

Inheritance is supported by using the extends keyword in the class definition. We can extend the previous test class like this:

```
class more extends test {
  function more() {
    echo "Constructor called";
  }
}
```

This means that the more class inherits from the test class and it also introduces the concept of a constructor. If a method inside a class has the same name as the class, it becomes the constructor function for that class. A constructor is called automatically when the class is instantiated.

Much more information is available at *http://www.php.net/oop*.

Type Casting

As I already mentioned, you do not need to specify a type when you create a variable, but that doesn't mean the variables do not have types associated with them. You can explicitly set the type, known as type casting, by using the C-style syntax in which you put the type you want in brackets before the variable or expression. For example:

```
$var = (int)"123abc";
```

Without the (int) in this example, PHP creates a string variable. With the explicit cast, however, we have created an integer variable with a value of 123. The following table shows the available cast operators in PHP.

Operators	Function
(int), (integer)	Cast to an integer
(real), (double), (float)	Cash to a floating point number
(string)	Cast to a string
(array)	Cast to an array
(object)	Cast to an object
(bool), (boolean)	Cast to a boolean
(unset)	Cast to NULL; the same as calling unset() on the value

Although they aren't usually needed, PHP provides the following built-in functions to check variable types in a program: gettype(), is_bool(), is_long(), is_float(), is_string(), is_array(), and is_object().

Expressions

An expression is the basic building block of the language. Anything with a value can be thought of as an expression. Examples include:

```
5
5+5
$a
$a==5
sqrt(9)
```

By combining many of these basic expressions, you can build larger, more complex expressions.

Note that the echo statement we've used in numerous examples cannot be part of a complex expression because it does not have a return value. The `print` statement, on the other hand, can be used as part of complex expression—it does have a return value. In all other respects, echo and `print` are identical: they output data.

Operators

Expressions are combined and manipulated using operators. The following table lists the operators from highest to lowest precedence; the second column (A) shows the operators' associativity. These operators should be familiar to you if you have any C, Java, or Perl experience.

Operators	Associativity
!, ~, ++, --, @, (the casting operators)	Right
*, /, %	Left
+, -, .	Left
<<, >>	Left
<, <=, >=, >	Nonassociative
==, !=, ===, !==	Nonassociative
&	Left
^	Left
|	Left
&&	Left
||	Left
? : (conditional operator)	Left
=, +=, -=, *=, /=, %=, ^=, .=, &=, |=, <<=, >>=	Left
AND	Left
XOR	Left
OR	Left

Control Structures

The control structures in PHP are very similar to those used by the C language. Control structures are used to control the logical flow through a PHP script.

PHP

PHP's control structures have two syntaxes that can be used interchangeably. The first form uses C-style curly braces to enclose statement blocks, while the second style uses a more verbose syntax that includes explicit ending statements. The first style is preferable when the control structure is completely within a PHP code block. The second style is useful when the construct spans a large section of intermixed code and HTML. The two styles are completely interchangeable, however, so it is really a matter of personal preference which one you use.

if

The `if` statement is a standard conditional found in most languages. Here are the two syntaxes for the `if` statement:

```
if(expr) {                 if(expr):
  statements                 statements
} elseif(expr) {           elseif(expr):
  statements                 statements
} else {                   else:
  statements               statements
}                            endif;
```

The `if` statement causes particular code to be executed if the expression it acts on is `true`. With the first form, you can omit the braces if you only need to execute a single statement.

switch

The `switch` statement can be used in place of a lengthy `if` statement. Here are the two syntaxes for `switch`:

```
switch(expr) {             switch(expr):
  case expr:                   case expr:
    statements                   statements
    break;                         break;
  default:                       default:
    statements                   statements
    break;                         break;
}                                 endswitch;
```

The expression for each `case` statement is compared against the `switch` expression and, if they match, the code following that particular case is executed. The `break` keyword signals the end of a particular case; it may be omitted, which causes control to flow into the next case. If none of the case expressions match the `switch` expression, the `default` case is executed.

while

The `while` statement is a looping construct that repeatedly executes some code while a particular expression is `true`:

```
while(expr) {              while(expr):
  statements                   statements
}                                endwhile;
```

The while expression is checked before the start of each iteration. If the expression evaluates to true, the code within the loop is executed. If the expression evaluates to false, however, execution skips to the code immediately following the while loop. Note that you can omit the curly braces with the first form of the while statement if you only need to execute a single statement.

It is possible to break out of a running loop at any time using the break keyword. This stops the current loop and, if control is within a nested set of loops, the next outer loop continues. It is also possible to break out of many levels of nested loops by passing a numerical argument to the break statement (break *n*) that specifies the number of nested loops it should break out of. You can skip the rest of a given loop and go onto the next iteration by using the continue keyword. With continue *n*, you can skip the current iterations of the *n* innermost loops.

do/while

The do/while statement is similar to the while statement, except that the conditional expression is checked at the end of each iteration instead of before:

```
do {
  statements
} while(expr);
```

Note that due to the order of the parts of this statement, there is only one valid syntax. If you only need to execute a single statement, you can omit the curly braces from the syntax. The break and continue statements work with this statement in the same way that they do with the while statement.

for

A for loop is a more complex looping construct than the simple while loop:

```
for(start_expr; cond_expr; iter_expr) {
  statements
}

for(start_expr; cond_expr; iter_expr):
  statements
endfor;
```

A for loop takes three expressions. The first is the start expression; it is evaluated once when the loop begins. This is generally used for initializing a loop counter. The second expression is a conditional expression that controls the iteration of the loop. This expression is checked prior to each iteration. The third expression, the iterative expression, is evaluated at the end of each iteration and is typically used to increment the loop counter. With the first form of the for statement, you can omit the braces if you only need to execute a single statement.

The break and continue statements work with a for loop like they do with a while loop, except that continue causes the iterative expression to be evaluated before the loop conditional expression is checked.

foreach

A foreach loop is used to loop through an array. Here are both forms of the syntax:

```
foreach(array_expression as $value) {
  statements
}

foreach(array_expression as $value):
  statements
endforeach;
```

This loops through the *array_expression* and assigns each value of the array to $value in turn. You can also get the key for each element with this syntax:

```
foreach(array_expression as $key=>$value) {
  statements
}
```

The break and continue statements work with a foreach loop like they do with a for loop.

Functions

A function is a named sequence of code statements that can optionally accept parameters and return a value. A function call is an expression that has a value; its value is the returned value from the function. PHP provides a large number of internal functions. The "Function Reference" section lists all of the commonly available functions. PHP also supports user-definable functions. To define a function, use the function keyword. For example:

```
function soundcheck($a, $b, $c) {
  return "Testing, $a, $b, $c";
}
```

When you define a function, be careful what name you give it. In particular, you need to make sure that the name does not conflict with any of the internal PHP functions. If you do use a function name that conflicts with an internal function, you get the following error:

```
Fatal error: Can't redeclare already declared function in
filename on line N
```

After you define a function, you call it by passing in the appropriate arguments. For example:

```
echo soundcheck(4, 5, 6);
```

You can also create functions with optional parameters. To do so, you set a default value for each optional parameter in the definition, using C++ style. For example, here's how to make all the parameters to the soundcheck() function optional:

```
function soundcheck($a=1, $b=2, $c=3) {
  return "Testing, $a, $b, $c";
}
```

Passing Arguments to Functions

There are two ways you can pass arguments to a function: by value and by reference. To pass an argument by value, you pass in any valid expression. That expression is evaluated and the value is assigned to the corresponding parameter defined within the function. Any changes you make to the parameter within the function have no effect on the argument passed to the function. For example:

```
function triple($x) {
  $x=$x*3;
  return $x;
}
$var=10;
$triplevar=triple($var);
```

In this case, `$var` evaluates to 10 when `triple()` is called, so `$x` is set to 10 inside the function. When `$x` is tripled, that change does not affect the value of `$var` outside the function.

In contrast, when you pass an argument by reference, changes to the parameter within the function do affect the value of the argument outside the scope of the function. That's because when you pass an argument by reference, you must pass a variable to the function. Now the parameter in the function refers directly to the value of the variable, meaning that any changes within the function are also visible outside the function. For example:

```
function triple(&$x) {
  $x=$x*3;
  return $x;
}
$var=10;
triple($var);
```

The `&` that precedes `$x` in the `triple()` function definition causes the argument to be passed by reference, so the end result is that `$var` ends up with a value of 30.

Variable Scope

The scope of a variable is the context within which a variable is available. There are two scopes for variables in PHP. Global variables are available directly from the mainline PHP execution. That is, if you are not inside a function, you can access global variables directly. Unlike most other languages, functions in PHP have their own, completely separate variable scope. Take this example:

```
<?php
  function test() {
    echo $a;
  }

  $a = "Hello World";
  test();
?>
```

If you run this script you will find that there is no output. This is because the `$a` you are trying to access inside the `test()` function is a completely different variable from the global $a you created in the global scope just before calling the function. In order to access a globally-scoped variable from inside a function, you need to tell the function to use the global scope for that particular variable. It can be done with the global keyword like this:

```
<?php
  function test() {
    global $a;
    echo $a;
  }

  $a = "Hello World";
  test();
?>
```

Alternatively, you can use the $GLOBALS array like this:

```
<?php
  function test() {
    echo $GLOBALS['a'];
  }

  $a = "Hello World";
  test();
?>
```

In this last example, the $GLOBALS array is known as a *superglobal*, which is a variable that is automatically available in all scopes without needing to be declared global in order to be accessed from within a function.

Static Variables

PHP supports declaring local function variables as static. A static variable retains its value between function calls, but is still accessible only from within the function it is declared in. Static variables can be initialized; this initialization only takes place the first time the static declaration is executed. Static variables are often used as counters, as in this example:

```
function hitcount( )
  static $count = 0;

  if ($count == 0) {
    echo "This is the first access to this page";
  } else {
    echo "This page has been accessed $count times";
  }
  $count++;
}
```

Web-Related Variables

PHP automatically creates variables for all the data it receives in an HTTP request. This can include GET data, POST data, cookie data, and environment variables.

The variables are either in PHP's global symbol table or in one of a number of superglobal arrays, depending on the value of the `register_globals` setting in your *php.ini* file.

Beginning with PHP 4.2.0, the default setting for `register_globals` is `off`. With `register_globals` off, all the various variables that are usually available directly in the global symbol table are now available via individual superglobal arrays. There is a limited set of superglobals and they cannot be created from a user-level script. The superglobal array to use depends on the source of the variable. Here is the list:

`$_GET`
: GET-method variables. These are the variables supplied directly in the URL. For example, with *http://www.example.com/script.php?a=1&b=2*, `$_GET['a']` and `$_GET['b']` are set to 1 and 2, respectively.

`$_POST`
: POST-method variables. Form field data from regular POST-method forms.

`$_COOKIE`
: Any cookies the browser sends end up in this array. The name of the cookie is the key and the cookie value becomes the array value.

`$_REQUEST`
: This array contains all of the above variables (i.e., GET, POST, and cookie). If a variable appears in multiple sources, the order in which they are imported into `$_REQUEST` is given by the setting of the `variables_order` *php.ini* directive. The default is `'GPC'`, which means GET-method variables are imported first, then POST-method variables (overriding any GET-method variables of the same name), and finally cookie variables (overriding the other two).

`$_SERVER`
: These are variables set by your web server. They are traditionally things like `DOCUMENT_ROOT`, `REMOTE_ADDR`, `REMOTE_PORT`, `SERVER_NAME`, `SERVER_PORT`, and many others. To get a full list, have a look at your `phpinfo()` output, or run a script like the following to have a look:

```
<?php
  foreach($_SERVER as $key=>$val) {
    echo '$_SERVER['.$key."] = $val<br>\n";
  }
?>
```

`$_ENV`
: Any environment variables that were set when you started your web server are available in this array.

`$_FILES`
: For RFC 1867–style file uploads the information for each uploaded file is available in this array. For example, for a file upload form containing:

```
<input name="userfile" type="file">
```

the `$_FILES` array will look something like this:

```
$_FILES['userfile']['name'] => photo.png
$_FILES['userfile']['type'] => image/png
```

```
$_FILES['userfile']['tmp_name'] => /tmp/phpo3kdGt
$_FILES['userfile']['error'] => 0
$_FILES['userfile']['size'] => 158918
```

Note that the `'error'` field is new for PHP 4.2.0 and the values are: `0` (no error, file was uploaded); `1` (the uploaded file exceeds the `upload_max_filesize` directive in *php.ini*); `2` (the uploaded file exceeds the `MAX_FILE_SIZE` directive that was specified in the HTML form); `3` (the actual number of bytes uploaded was less than the specified upload file size); and `4` (no file was uploaded).

Sessions

Sessions are used to help maintain the values of variables across multiple web pages. This is done by creating a unique session ID that is sent to the client browser. The browser then sends the unique ID back on each page request and PHP uses the ID to fetch the values of all the variables associated with this session.

The session ID is sent back and forth in a cookie or in the URL. By default, PHP tries to use cookies, but if the browser has disabled cookies, PHP falls back to putting the ID in the URL. The *php.ini* directives that affect this are:

`session.use_cookies`
: When on, PHP will try to use cookies

`session.use_trans_sid`
: When on, PHP will add the ID to URLs if cookies are not used

The `trans_sid` code in PHP is rather interesting. It actually parses the entire HTML file and modifies/mangles every link and form to add the session ID. The `url_rewriter.tags` *php.ini* directive can change how the various elements are mangled.

Writing an application that uses sessions is not hard. You start a session using `session_start()`, then register the variables you wish to associate with that session. For example:

```
<?php
  session_start();
  session_register('foo');
  session_register('bar');

  $foo = "Hello";
  $bar = "World";
?>
```

If you put the previous example in a file named *page1.php* and load it in your browser, it sends you a cookie and stores the values of `$foo` and `$bar` on the server. If you then load this *page2.php* page:

```
<?php
  session_start();
  echo "foo = $_SESSION[foo]<br />";
  echo "bar = $_SESSION[bar]<br />";
?>
```

You should see the values of $foo and $bar set in *page1.php*. Be sure to note the use of the $_SESSION superglobal. If you have register_globals on, you would be able to access these as $foo and $bar directly.

You can add complex variables such as arrays and objects to sessions as well. The one caveat with putting an object in a session is that you must load the class definition for that object before you call session_start().

A common error people make when using sessions is that they tend to use it as a replacement for authentication—or sometimes as an add-on to authentication. Authenticating a user once as he first enters your site and then using a session ID to identify that user throughout the rest of the site without further authentication can lead to a lot of problems if another person is somehow able to get the session ID. There are a number of ways to get the session ID:

- If you are not using SSL, session IDs may be sniffed.
- If you don't have proper entropy in your session IDs, they may be guessed.
- If you are using URL-based session IDs, they may end up in proxy logs.
- If you are using URL-based session IDs, they may end up bookmarked on publicly-accessible computers.

Forcing HTTP Authentication on each page over SSL is the most secure way to avoid this problem, but it tends to be a bit inconvenient. Just keep the above points in mind when building a web application that uses sessions to store users' personal details.

Examples

The best way to understand the power of PHP is to examine some real examples of PHP in action, so we'll look at some common uses of PHP in this section.

Showing the Browser and IP Address

Here is a simple page that prints out the browser string and the IP address of the HTTP request. Create a file with the following content in your web directory, name it something like *example.php3*, and load it in your browser:

```
<html><head><title>PHP Example</title></head>
<body>
   You are using
    <?php echo $_SERVER['HTTP_USER_AGENT'] ?>
   <br />
   and coming from
    <?php echo $_SERVER['REMOTE_ADDR'] ?>
</body></html>
```

You should see something like the following in your browser window:

```
You are using Mozilla/5.0 (X11; U; Linux i686; en-US;
rv:1.1b) Gecko/20020722
and coming from 127.0.0.1
```

PHP

Intelligent Form Handling

Here is a slightly more complex example. We are going to create an HTML form that asks the user to enter a name and select one or more interests from a selection box. We could do this in two files, where we separate the actual form from the data handling code, but instead, this example shows how it can be done in a single file:

```
<html><head><title>Form Example</title></head>
<body>
<h1>Form Example</h1>
<?
function show_form($first="", $last="", $interest="") {
 $options = array("Sports", "Business", "Travel", "Shopping", "Computers");
 if(!is_array($interest)) $interest = array();
 ?>
 <form action="form.php" method="POST">
 First Name:
 <input type="text" name="first"
        value="<?echo $first?>">
 <br />
 Last Name:
 <input type="text" name="last"
        value="<?echo $last?>">
 <br />
 Interests:
 <select multiple name="interest[ ]">
 <?php
  foreach($options as $option) {
   echo "<option";
   if(in_array($option, $interest)) {
    echo " selected ";
   }
   echo "> $option</option>\n";
  }
 ?>
 </select><br />
 <input type=submit>
 </form>
<?php } // end of show_form() function

if($_SERVER['REQUEST_METHOD']!='POST') {
 show_form();
} else {
 if(empty($_POST['first']) ||
    empty($_POST['last'])  ||
    empty($_POST['interest'])) {
  echo "<p>You did not fill in all the fields,";
  echo "please try again</p>\n";
  show_form($_POST['first'],$_POST['last'], $_POST['interest']);
 }
 else {
  echo "<p>Thank you, $_POST[first] $_POST[last], you ";
  echo 'selected '. join(' and ', $_POST['interest']);
```

```
    echo " as your interests.</p>\n";
  }
}
?>
</body></html>
```

There are a few things to study carefully in this example. First, we have isolated the display of the actual form to a PHP function called show_form(). This function is intelligent, in that it can take the default value for each of the form elements as an optional argument. If the user does not fill in all the form elements, we use this feature to redisplay the form with whatever values the user has already entered. This means the user only has to fill the fields he missed, which is much better than asking the user to hit the Back button or forcing him to reenter all the fields.

Notice how the file switches back and forth between PHP code and HTML. Right in the middle of defining our show_form() function, we switch back to HTML to avoid having numerous echo statements that just echo normal HTML. Then, when we need a PHP variable, we switch back to PHP code temporarily, just to print the variable.

We've given the multiple-choice <select> element the name interest[]. The [] on the name tells PHP that the data coming from this form element should be treated as an auto-indexed array. This means that PHP automatically gives each element the next sequential index, starting with 0 (assuming the array is empty to begin with).

The final thing to note is the way we determine what to display. We check if the SERVER variable REQUEST_METHOD is set to POST. If it isn't, we know that the user has not submitted the form yet, so we call show_form() without any arguments. This displays the empty form. If $first is set, however, we check to make sure that the $first and $last text fields are not empty and that the user has selected at least one interest.

Web Database Integration

To illustrate a complete database-driven application, we are going to build a little web application that lets people make suggestions and vote on what you should name your new baby. The example uses MySQL, a fast and easy to configure database (see *http://www.mysql.com*), but it can be changed to run on any of the databases that PHP supports.

PHP

The schema for our baby-name database looks like this:

```
CREATE TABLE baby_names (
  name varchar(30) NOT NULL,
  votes int(4),
  PRIMARY KEY (name)
);
```

This is in MySQL's query format and can be used directly to create the actual table. It simply defines a text field and an integer field. The text field is for the suggested baby name and the integer field is for the vote count associated with that name. We are making the name field a primary key, which means uniqueness is enforced, so that the same name cannot appear twice in the database.

We want this application to do a number of things. First, it should have a minimal check that prevents someone from voting many times in a row. We do this using a session cookie. Second, we want to show a fancy little barchart that depicts the relative share of the votes that each name has received. The barchart is created using a one pixel by one pixel blue dot GIF image and scaling the image using the height and width settings of the HTML `<img>` tag. We could also use PHP's built-in image functions to create a fancier-looking bar.

Everything else is relatively straightforward form and database work. We use a couple of shortcuts as well. For example, instead of reading all the entries from the database and adding up the votes in order to get a sum (which we need to calculate the percentages), we ask MySQL to do it for us with its built-in `sum()` function. The part of the code that displays all the names and their votes along with the percentage bar gets a little ugly, but you should be able to follow it. We are simply sending the correct HTML table tags before and after the various data we have fetched from the database.

Here's the full example:

```
<?
  if($vote && !$already_voted)
    SetCookie('already_voted',1);
?>
<html><head><title>Name the Baby</title>
</head><h3>Name the Baby</h3>
<form action="baby.php" method="POST">
<p>Suggestion:
<input type="text" name="new_name"></p>
<input type="submit"
       value="Submit idea and/or vote">
<?
 mysql_pconnect("localhost","","");
 $db = "test";
 $table = "baby_names";

 if($new_name) {
  if(!mysql_db_query($db, "insert into $table
      values ('$new_name',0)")) {
    echo mysql_errno().': '.
         mysql_error()."<br />\n";
  }
 }
 if($vote && $already_voted) {
  echo '<p><b>Hey, you voted already ';
  echo "Vote ignored.</b></p>\n";
 }
 else if($vote) {
  if(!mysql_db_query($db,
       "update $table set votes=votes+1
        where name='$vote'")) {
   echo mysql_errno().': '.
        mysql_error()."<br />\n";
  }
 }
```

```
$result=mysql_db_query($db,
    "select sum(votes) as sum from $table");
if($result) {
 $sum = (int) mysql_result($result,0,"sum");
 mysql_free_result($result);
}

$result=mysql_db_query($db,
   "select * from $table order by votes DESC");
echo <<<EOD
 <table border="0"><tr><th>Vote</th>
 <th>Idea</th><th colspan="2">Votes</th>
 </tr>
EOD;
while($row=mysql_fetch_row($result)) {
 echo <<<FOO
  <tr><td align="center">
  <input type="radio"
         name="vote" value="$row[0]"></td>
  <td>$row[0]</td>
  <td align="right">$row[1]</td>
  <td>
FOO;
 if($sum && (int)$row[1]) {
  $per = (int)(100 * $row[1]/$sum);
  echo '<img src="bline.gif" height=12 ';
  echo "width=$per> $per %</td>";
 }
 echo "</tr>\n";
}
echo "</table>\n";
mysql_free_result($result);
?>
<input type="submit"
       value="Submit idea and/or vote" />
<input type="reset" />
</form>
</body></html>
```

Function Reference

The rest of this chapter provides an alphabetical summary of the functions that are available in PHP. The synopsis for each function lists the expected argument types for the function, its return type, and the version of PHP in which the function was introduced. The possible types are `int`, `double`, `string`, `array`, `void`, and `mixed`. `mixed` means that the argument or return type can be of any type. Optional arguments are shown in square brackets. Note that PHP didn't start tracking version numbers for functions until PHP 3.0, so functions that are listed as 3.0 are likely to have existed in Version 2.x.

As of PHP 4.3, approximately 2,750 functions came bundled with PHP. The bulk of these are in optional extensions. Out of these functions, I selected 1,404 for this reference section. Even with close to half the functions cut, I'm still pushing the limits of what the average pocket can hold without busting a few seams. Here's a list of the function groups that survived the cut, followed by the ones that didn't:

In
: Apache, array, assert, aspell/pspell, base64, bcmath, bz2, calendar, crack, crc32, crypt, ctype, curl, date/time, dba, db, dbx, directory, DNS, exec, exif, file, ftp, gd, gettext, gmp, HTML, iconv, imap, iptc, java, lcg, ldap, link, mail, math, md5, mbstring, mcrypt, mhash, MySQL, Oracle 8, PDF, Perl regex, PostgreSQL, Posix, process control, recode, session, shmop, snmp, sockets, various standard built-in, syslog, SYSV shared mem/sem/msg, xml, xslt, zip, zlib.

Out
: COM, cpdf, Cybercash, Cybermut, Cyrus, dbase, direct io, DomXML, Frontbase, FDF, Filepro, Fribidi, Hyperwave, ICAP, Informix, Ingres, Interbase, ircg, mbregex, MCAL, MCVE, Ming, mnogosearch, msession, mSQL, mssql, ncurses, Lotus Notes, Birdstep, ODBC, OpenSSL, Oracle 7, Ovrimos, Payflow Pro, QTDom, readline, aggregation, browscap, cyrillic conversions, libswf, Sybase, Tokenizer, VPopMail, Win32 API, WDDX, XMLRPC, Yaz, YellowPages.

If your favorite functions were left out, please don't take it personally. I had a lot of tough choices to make. One of the hardest was DomXML. At 114 functions, the DomXML extension is huge and there just wasn't room. Leaving out the cool Ming functions was difficult as well. Please do check out the online manual at *http://www.php.net/manual* for more on both of these extensions and also all the others you see listed here.

int abs(int number) *3.0*
: Returns the absolute value of the number

float acos(float number) *3.0*
: Returns the arc cosine of the number in radians

float acosh(float number) *4.1.0*
: Returns the inverse hyperbolic cosine of the number (i.e., the value whose hyperbolic cosine is `number`)

string addcslashes(string str, string charlist) *4.0*
: Escapes all characters mentioned in `charlist` with backslashes, creating octal representations if asked to backslash characters with their 8th bit set or with an ASCII value greater than 32 (except `'\n'`, `'\r'`, `'\t'`, etc.)

string addslashes(string str) *3.0*
: Escapes single quotes, double quotes, and backslash characters in a string with backslashes

AND *4.0*
: Language keyword that is similar to the `&&` operator, except with lower precedence

bool apache_child_terminate(void) *4.0.5*
: Terminates Apache process after this request

object apache_lookup_uri(string URI) *3.0.4*
Performs a partial request of the given URI to obtain information about it

string apache_note(string note_name[, string note_value]) *3.0.2*
Gets and sets Apache request notes

array apache_request_headers(void) *4.3.0*
Fetches all HTTP request headers

array apache_response_headers(void) *4.3.0*
Fetches all HTTP response headers

bool apache_setenv(string variable, string value[, bool walk_to_top]) *4.1.0*
Sets an Apache `subprocess_env` variable

array array([mixed var[, ...]]) *3.0*
Creates an array

array array_change_key_case(array input[, int case=CASE_LOWER]) *4.1.0*
Returns an array with all string keys lowercased (or uppercased)

array array_chunk(array input, int size[, bool preserve_keys]) *4.1.0*
Splits array into chunks

array array_count_values(array input) *4.0*
Returns the value as key and the frequency of that value in `input` as value

array array_diff(array arr1, array arr2[, array ...]) *4.0.1*
Returns the entries of `arr1` that have values that are not present in any of the others arguments

array array_fill(int start_key, int num, mixed val) *4.1.0*
Creates an array containing `num` elements starting with index `start_key` each initialized to `val`

array array_filter(array input[, mixed callback]) *4.0.6*
Filters elements from the array via the callback

array array_flip(array input) *4.0*
Returns array with key/value pairs flipped

array array_intersect(array arr1, array arr2[, array ...]) *4.0.1*
Returns the entries of `arr1` that have values that are present in all the other arguments

bool array_key_exists(mixed key, array search) *4.1.0*
Checks if the given key or index exists in the array

array array_keys(array input[, mixed search_value]) *4.0*
Returns just the keys from the input array, optionally for only the specified `search_value`

array array_map(mixed callback, array input1[, array input2 ,...]) *4.0.6*
Applies the callback to the elements in the given arrays

array array_merge(array arr1, array arr2[, array ...]) *4.0*
Merges elements from passed arrays into one array

array array_merge_recursive(array arr1, array arr2[, array ...]) *4.0.1*
Recursively merges elements from passed arrays into one array

bool array_multisort(array ar1[, SORT_ASC|SORT_DESC[, SORT_REGULAR|SORT_NUMERIC|SORT_STRING]][, array ar2[, SORT_ASC|SORT_DESC[, SORT_REGULAR|SORT_NUMERIC|SORT_STRING]], ...]) *4.0*
Sorts multiple arrays at once similar to how `ORDER BY` clause works in SQL

array array_pad(array input, int pad_size, mixed pad_value) *4.0*
Returns a copy of input array padded with `pad_value` to size `pad_size`

mixed array_pop(array stack) *4.0*
Pops an element off the end of the array

int array_push(array stack, mixed var[, mixed ...]) *4.0*
Pushes elements onto the end of the array

mixed array_rand(array input[, int num_req]) *4.0*
Returns key/keys for random entry/entries in the array

mixed array_reduce(array input, mixed callback[, int initial]) *4.0.5*
Iteratively reduces the array to a single value via the callback

array array_reverse(array input[, bool preserve keys]) *4.0*
Returns `input` as a new array with the order of the entries reversed

mixed array_search(mixed needle, array haystack[, bool strict]) *4.0.5*
Searches the array for a given value and returns the corresponding key if successful

mixed array_shift(array stack) *4.0*
Pops an element off the beginning of the array

array array_slice(array input, int offset[, int length]) *4.0*
Returns elements specified by `offset` and `length`

array array_splice(array input, int offset[, int length[, array replacement]]) *4.0*
Removes the elements designated by `offset` and `length` and replaces them with supplied array

mixed array_sum(array input) *4.0.4*
Returns the sum of the array entries

array array_unique(array input) *4.0.1*
Removes duplicate values from array

int array_unshift(array stack, mixed var[, mixed ...]) *4.0*
Pushes elements onto the beginning of the array

array array_values(array input) *4.0*
Returns just the values from the input array

bool array_walk(array input, string funcname[, mixed userdata]) *3.0.3*
Applies a user function to every member of an array

bool arsort(array array_arg[, int sort_flags]) *3.0*
Sorts an array in reverse order and maintains index association

float asin(float number) *3.0*

Returns the arc sine of the number in radians

float asinh(float number) *4.1.0*

Returns the inverse hyperbolic sine of the number (i.e., the value whose hyperbolic sine is `number`)

bool asort(array array_arg[, int sort_flags]) *3.0*

Sorts an array and maintains index association

int aspell_check(aspell int, string word) *3.0.7*

Returns if `word` is valid

int aspell_check_raw(aspell int, string word) *3.0.7*

Returns if `word` is valid, ignoring case and without trying to trim it in any way

int aspell_new(string master[, string personal]) *3.0.7*

Loads a dictionary

array aspell_suggest(aspell int, string word) *3.0.7*

Returns an array of spelling suggestions

int assert(string|bool assertion) *4.0*

Checks if `assertion` is `false`

mixed assert_options(int what[, mixed value]) *4.0*

Sets or gets the various assert flags

float atan(float number) *3.0*

Returns the arc tangent of the number in radians

float atan2(float y, float x) *3.0.5*

Returns the arc tangent of y/x, with the resulting quadrant determined by the signs of y and x

float atanh(float number) *4.1.0*

Returns the inverse hyperbolic tangent of the number (i.e., the value whose hyperbolic tangent is `number`)

string base64_decode(string str) *3.0*

Decodes string using MIME base64 algorithm

string base64_encode(string str) *3.0*

Encodes string using MIME base64 algorithm

string base_convert(string number, int frombase, int tobase) *3.0.6*

Converts a number in a string from any base to any other base (where both bases are less than or equal to 36)

string basename(string path[, string suffix]) *3.0*

Returns the filename component of the path

string bcadd(string left_operand, string right_operand[, int scale]) *3.0*

Returns the sum of two arbitrary precision numbers

string bccomp(string left_operand, string right_operand[, int scale]) *3.0*

Compares two arbitrary precision numbers

string bcdiv(string left_operand, string right_operand[, int scale]) *3.0*
Returns the quotient of two arbitrary precision numbers (division)

string bcmod(string left_operand, string right_operand) *3.0*
Returns the modulus of the two arbitrary precision operands

string bcmul(string left_operand, string right_operand[, int scale]) *3.0*
Returns the product of two arbitrary precision numbers

string bcpow(string x, string y[, int scale]) *3.0*
Returns the value of an arbitrary precision number raised to the power of another arbitrary precision number

string bcscale(int scale) *3.0*
Sets default scale parameter for all BC math functions

string bcsqrt(string operand[, int scale]) *3.0*
Returns the square root of an arbitrary precision number

string bcsub(string left_operand, string right_operand[, int scale]) *3.0*
Returns the difference between two arbitrary precision numbers

string bin2hex(string data) *3.0.9*
Converts the binary representation of data to hexadecimal

string bind_textdomain_codeset (string domain, string codeset) *4.1.0*
Specifies the character encoding in which the messages from the `DOMAIN` message catalog will be returned

int bindec(string binary_number) *3.0*
Returns the decimal equivalent of a binary number

string bindtextdomain(string domain_name, string dir) *3.0.7*
Binds to the text domain `domain_name`, looking for translations in `dir`; returns the current domain

break *3.0*
Language keyword used inside `switch` statements and loops

string bzcompress(string source[, int blocksize100k[, int workfactor]]) *4.0.4*
Compresses a string into BZip2 encoded data

string bzdecompress(string source[, int small]) *4.0.4*
Decompresses BZip2 compressed data

int bzerrno(resource bz) *4.0.4*
Returns the error number

array bzerror(resource bz) *4.0.4*
Returns the error number and error string in an associative array

string bzerrstr(resource bz) *4.0.4*
Returns the error string

resource bzopen(string|int file|fp, string mode) *4.0.4*
Opens a new BZip2 stream

string bzread(int bz[, int length]) *4.0.4*
Reads up to `length` bytes from a BZip2 stream, or 1,024 bytes if `length` is not specified

int cal_days_in_month(int calendar, int month, int year) *4.1.0*
Returns the number of days in a month for a given year and calendar

array cal_from_jd(int jd, int calendar) *4.1.0*
Converts from Julian day count to a supported calendar and returns extended information

array cal_info(int calendar) *4.1.0*
Returns information about a particular calendar

int cal_to_jd(int calendar, int month, int day, int year) *4.1.0*
Converts from a supported calendar to Julian day count

mixed call_user_func(string function_name[, mixed parmeter][, mixed ...]) *3.0.3*
Calls a user function that is the first parameter

mixed call_user_func_array(string function_name, array parameters) *4.0.4*
Calls a user function that is the first parameter with the arguments contained in `array`

mixed call_user_method(string method_name, mixed object[, mixed parameter] [, mixed ...]) *3.0.3*
Calls a user method on a specific object or class

mixed call_user_method_array(string method_name, mixed object, array params) *4.0.5*
Calls a user method on a specific object or class using a parameter array

case arg: *3.0*
Language keyword used inside a `switch` statement

float ceil(float number) *3.0*
Returns the next highest integer value of the number

bool chdir(string directory) *3.0*
Changes the current directory

bool checkdate(int month, int day, int year) *3.0*
Returns `true` if passed a valid date in the Gregorian calendar

int checkdnsrr(string host[, string type]) *3.0*
Checks DNS records corresponding to a given Internet host name or IP address

bool chgrp(string filename, mixed group) *3.0*
Changes file group

bool chmod(string filename, int mode) *3.0*
Changes file mode

bool chown (string filename, mixed user) *3.0*
Changes file owner

PHP

string chr(int ascii) *3.0*

Converts ASCII code to a character

bool chroot(string directory) *4.0.5*

Changes root directory

string chunk_split(string str[, int chunklen[, string ending]]) *3.0.6*

Returns split line

class class_name *3.0*

Language keyword that defines a class

bool class_exists(string classname) *4.0*

Checks if the class exists

void clearstatcache(void) *3.0*

Clears file stat cache

void closedir([resource dir_handle]) *3.0*

Closes directory connection identified by `dir_handle`

bool closelog(void) *3.0*

Closes connection to system logger

array compact(mixed var_names[, mixed ...]) *4.0*

Creates a hash containing variables and their values

int connection_aborted(void) *3.0.7*

Returns `true` if client disconnected

int connection_status(void) *3.0.7*

Returns the connection status bitfield

mixed constant(string const_name) *4.0.4*

Returns the associated value, given the name of a constant

continue *3.0*

Language keyword used inside loops to skip to the next iteration

bool copy(string source_file, string destination_file) *3.0*

Copies a file

float cos(float number) *3.0*

Returns the cosine of the number in radians

float cosh(float number) *4.1.0*

Returns the hyperbolic cosine of the number

int count(mixed var[, int mode]) *3.0*

Counts the number of elements in a variable (usually an array)

mixed count_chars(string input[, int mode]) *4.0*

Returns information about what characters are used in `input`

string crack_check([int dictionary,] string password) *4.0.5*

Performs an obscure check with the given password

string crack_closedict([int link_identifier]) *4.0.5*

Closes an open *cracklib* dictionary

string crack_getlastmessage(void) *4.0.5*

Returns the message from the last obscure check

string crack_opendict(string dictionary) *4.0.5*

Opens a new *cracklib* dictionary

string crc32(string str) *4.0.1*

Calculates the crc32 polynomial of a string

string create_function(string args, string code) *4.0.1*

Creates an anonymous function and returns its name

string crypt(string str[, string salt]) *3.0*

Encrypts a string

bool ctype_alnum(mixed c) *4.0.4*

Checks for alphanumeric character(s)

bool ctype_alpha(mixed c) *4.0.4*

Checks for alphabetic character(s)

bool ctype_cntrl(mixed c) *4.0.4*

Checks for control character(s)

bool ctype_digit(mixed c) *4.0.4*

Checks for numeric character(s)

bool ctype_graph(mixed c) *4.0.4*

Checks for any printable character(s) except space

bool ctype_lower(mixed c) *4.0.4*

Checks for lowercase character(s)

bool ctype_print(mixed c) *4.0.4*

Checks for printable character(s)

bool ctype_punct(mixed c) *4.0.4*

Checks for any printable character that is not whitespace or an alphanumeric character

bool ctype_space(mixed c) *4.0.4*

Checks for whitespace character(s)

bool ctype_upper(mixed c) *4.0.4*

Checks for uppercase character(s)

bool ctype_xdigit(mixed c) *4.0.4*

Checks for character(s) representing a hexadecimal digit

void curl_close(resource ch) *4.0.2*

Closes a CURL session

int curl_errno(resource ch) *4.0.3*

Returns an integer containing the last error number

string curl_error(resource ch) *4.0.3*

Returns a string contain the last error for the current session

bool curl_exec(resource ch) *4.0.2*

Performs a CURL session

string curl_getinfo(resource ch, int opt) *4.0.4*

Gets information regarding a specific transfer

resource curl_init([string url]) *4.0.2*

Initializes a CURL session

bool curl_setopt(resource ch, string option, mixed value) *4.0.2*

Sets an option for a CURL transfer

string curl_version(void) *4.0.2*

Returns the CURL version string.

mixed current(array array_arg) *3.0*

Returns the element currently pointed to by the internal array pointer

string date(string format[, int timestamp]) *3.0*

Formats a local time/date

void dba_close(int handle) *3.0.8*

Closes the database

bool dba_delete(string key, int handle) *3.0.8*

Deletes the entry associated with key

bool dba_exists(string key, int handle) *3.0.8*

Checks if the specified key exists

string dba_fetch(string key, int handle) *3.0.8*

Fetches the data associated with key

string dba_firstkey(int handle) *3.0.8*

Resets the internal key pointer and returns the first key

bool dba_insert(string key, string value, int handle) *3.0.8*

Inserts value as key; returns `false` if key exists already

string dba_nextkey(int handle) *3.0.8*

Returns the next key

int dba_open(string path, string mode, string handlername[, string ...]) *3.0.8*

Opens path using the specified handler in specified mode

bool dba_optimize(int handle) *3.0.8*

Optimizes database

int dba_popen(string path, string mode, string handlername[, string ...]) *3.0.8*

Opens path persistently using the specified handler in specified mode

bool dba_replace(string key, string value, int handle) *3.0.8*

Inserts value as key; replaces key if key exists already

bool dba_sync(int handle) *3.0.8*

Synchronizes database

string dblist(void) *3.0*

Describes the DBM-compatible library being used

bool dbmclose(int dbm_identifier) *3.0*

Closes a DBM database

int dbmdelete(int dbm_identifier, string key) *3.0*

Deletes the value for a key from a DBM database

int dbmexists(int dbm_identifier, string key) *3.0*

Tells if a value exists for a key in a DBM database

string dbmfetch(int dbm_identifier, string key) *3.0*

Fetches a value for a key from a DBM database

string dbmfirstkey(int dbm_identifier) *3.0*

Retrieves the first key from a DBM database

int dbminsert(int dbm_identifier, string key, string value) *3.0*

Inserts a value for a key in a DBM database

string dbmnextkey(int dbm_identifier, string key) *3.0*

Retrieves the next key from a DBM database

int dbmopen(string filename, string mode) *3.0*

Opens a DBM database

int dbmreplace(int dbm_identifier, string key, string value) *3.0*

Replaces the value for a key in a DBM database

bool dbx_close(dbx_link_object dbx_link) *4.0.6*

Closes an open connection/database

int dbx_compare(array row_x, array row_y, string columnname[, int flags]) *4.1.0*

Compares two rows for sorting purposes

dbx_link_object dbx_connect(string module_name, string host, string db, string username, string password[, bool persistent]) *4.0.6*

Opens a connection/database; returns `dbx_link_object` on success or 0 on failure

void dbx_error(dbx_link_object dbx_link) *4.0.6*

Reports the error message of the latest function call in the module

dbx_result_object dbx_query(dbx_link_object dbx_link, string sql_statement[, long flags]) *4.0.6*

Sends a query and fetches all results; returns a `dbx_link_object` on success or 0 on failure

int dbx_sort(object dbx_result, string compare_function_name) *4.0.6*

Sorts a result from `dbx_query()` by a custom sort function

string dcgettext(string domain_name, string msgid, long category) *3.0.7*

Returns the translation of `msgid` for `domain_name` and `category` or `msgid` unaltered if a translation does not exist

string dcngettext (string domain, string msgid1, string msgid2, int n, int category) *4.1.0*

Plural version of `dcgettext()`

void debug_zval_dump(mixed var) *4.1.0*

Dumps a string representation of an internal Zend value to output

string decbin(int decimal_number) *3.0*

Returns a string containing a binary representation of the number

string dechex(int decimal_number) *3.0*
: Returns a string containing a hexadecimal representation of the number

declare(directive) *4.0.2*
: Language keyword used to mark a block of code; only used for ticks at this point

string decoct(int decimal_number) *3.0*
: Returns a string containing an octal representation of the number

default: *3.0*
: Language keyword used inside a `switch` statement

bool define(string constant_name, mixed value, case_sensitive=true) *3.0*
: Defines a new constant

void define_syslog_variables(void) *3.0*
: Initializes all syslog-related variables

bool defined(string constant_name) *3.0*
: Checks whether a constant exists

float deg2rad(float number) *3.0.4*
: Converts the number in degrees to the radian equivalent

string dgettext(string domain_name, string msgid) *3.0.7*
: Returns the translation of `msgid` for `domain_name` or `msgid` unaltered if a translation does not exist

object dir(string directory) *3.0*
: Directory class with properties for handle and class and methods to read, rewind, and close

string dirname(string path) *3.0*
: Returns the directory name component of the path

float disk_free_space(string path) *4.1.0*
: Gets free disk space for filesystem that path is on

float disk_total_space(string path) *4.1.0*
: Gets total disk space for filesystem that path is on

int dl(string extension_filename) *3.0*
: Loads a PHP extension at runtime

string dngettext (string domain, string msgid1, string msgid2, int count) *4.1.0*
: Plural version of `dgettext()`

do *3.0*
: Language keyword that forms the start of a `do`/`while` loop

array each(array arr) *3.0*
: Returns the current key/value pair in the passed array and advances the pointer to the next element

int easter_date([int year]) *3.0.9*
: Returns the timestamp of midnight on Easter of a given year (defaults to current year)

int easter_days([int year, [int method]]) *3.0.9*

Returns the number of days after March 21 that Easter falls on for a given year (defaults to current year)

echo string arg1[, string argn...] *3.0*

Outputs one or more strings

else *3.0*

Language keyword that reverses the current condition

elseif(cond) *3.0*

Language keyword that tests a condition only if current condition was not met

bool empty(mixed var) *3.0*

Determines whether a variable is empty

mixed end(array array_arg) *3.0*

Advances array argument's internal pointer to the last element and returns it

enddeclare *4.0.2*

Language keyword that ends a `declare:` block

endfor *3.0*

Language keyword that ends a `for:` block

endforeach *4.0*

Language keyword that ends a `foreach:` block

endif *3.0*

Language keyword that ends an `if:` block

endswitch *3.0*

Language keyword that ends a `switch:` block

endwhile *3.0*

Language keyword that ends a `while:` block

int ereg(string pattern, string string[, array registers]) *3.0*

Performs a regular expression match

string ereg_replace(string pattern, string replacement, string string) *3.0*

Performs a regular expression replacement

int eregi(string pattern, string string[, array registers]) *3.0*

Performs a case-insensitive regular expression match

string eregi_replace(string pattern, string replacement, string string) *3.0*

Performs a case-insensitive regular expression replacement

bool error_log(string message, int message_type[, string destination] [, string extra_headers]) *3.0*

Sends an error message somewhere

int error_reporting(int new_error_level=null) *3.0*

Returns the current `error_reporting` level, and, if an argument was passed, changes to the new level

string escapeshellarg(string arg) *4.0.3*

Quotes and escapes an argument for use in a shell command

string escapeshellcmd(string command) *3.0*

Escapes shell metacharacters

mixed eval(string code_str) *3.0*

Evaluates a string as PHP code

string exec(string command[, array output[, int return_value]]) *3.0*

Executes an external program

int exif_imagetype(string imagefile) *4.3.0*

Gets the type of an image

array|false exif_read_data(string filename[, sections_needed[, sub_arrays[, read_thumbnail]]]) *4.1.0*

Reads header data from the JPEG/TIFF image filename and optionally reads the internal thumbnails

string|false exif_tagname(index) *4.1.0*

Gets header name for `index` or `false` if not defined

string|false exif_thumbnail(string filename[, &width, &height[, &imagetype]]) *4.1.0*

Reads the embedded thumbnail

exit [([mixed status])] *3.0*

Language keyword that terminates execution of the script and prints status just before exiting

float exp(float number) *3.0*

Returns *e* raised to the power of the number

array explode(string separator, string str[, int limit]) *3.0*

Splits a string on string separator and returns an array of components

float expm1(float number) *4.1.0*

Returns `exp(number) - 1`, computed in a way that is accurate even when the value of `number` is close to zero

extends *3.0*

Language keyword used in a class definition to extend from a parent class

bool extension_loaded(string extension_name) *3.0.10*

Returns `true` if the named extension is loaded

int extract(array var_array[, int extract_type[, string prefix]]) *3.0.7*

Imports variables into symbol table from an array

int ezmlm_hash(string addr) *3.0.17*

Calculate EZMLM list hash value

bool fclose(resource fp) *3.0*

Closes an open file pointer

bool feof(resource fp) *3.0*

Tests for end-of-file on a file pointer

bool fflush(resource fp) *4.0.1*

Flushes output

string fgetc(resource fp) *3.0*
Gets a character from file pointer

array fgetcsv(resource fp, int length[, string delimiter[, string enclosure]]) *3.0.8*
Gets a line from file pointer and parses for CSV fields

string fgets(resource fp[, int length]) *3.0*
Gets a line from file pointer

string fgetss(resource fp, int length[, string allowable_tags]) *3.0*
Gets a line from file pointer and strips HTML tags

array file(string filename[, bool use_include_path]) *3.0*
Reads entire file into an array

bool file_exists(string filename) *3.0*
Returns `true` if filename exists

string file_get_contents(string filename[, bool use_include_path]) *4.3.0*
Reads the entire file into a string

resource file_get_wrapper_data(resource fp) *4.3.0*
Retrieves header/metadata from wrapped file pointer

bool file_register_wrapper(string protocol, string classname) *4.3.0*
Registers a custom URL protocol handler class

int fileatime(string filename) *3.0*
Gets last access time of file

int filectime(string filename) *3.0*
Gets inode modification time of file

int filegroup(string filename) *3.0*
Gets file group

int fileinode(string filename) *3.0*
Gets file inode

int filemtime(string filename) *3.0*
Gets last modification time of file

int fileowner(string filename) *3.0*
Gets file owner

int fileperms(string filename) *3.0*
Gets file permissions

int filesize(string filename) *3.0*
Gets file size

string filetype(string filename) *3.0*
Gets file type

float floatval(mixed var) *4.1.0*
Gets the `float` value of a variable

bool flock(resource fp, int operation[, int &wouldblock]) *3.0.7*
Provides portable file locking

float floor(float number) *3.0*
Returns the next lowest integer value from the number

void flush(void) *3.0*
Flushes the output buffer

float fmod(float x, float y) *4.1.0*
Returns the remainder of dividing `x` by `y` as a `float`

bool fnmatch(string pattern, string filename[, int flags]) *4.3.0*
Matches filename against pattern

resource fopen(string filename, string mode[, bool use_include_path [, resource context]]) *3.0*
Opens a file or a URL and returns a file pointer

for(init; cond; inc) *3.0*
Language keyword that implements a traditional `for` loop

foreach(array as key=>value) *4.0*
Language keyword that iterates through `array` and assigns each element to `key` and `value`

int fpassthru(resource fp) *3.0*
Outputs all remaining data from a file pointer

string fread(resource fp, int length) *3.0*
Provides a binary-safe file read

int frenchtojd(int month, int day, int year) *3.0*
Converts a French Republic calendar date to Julian day count

mixed fscanf(string str, string format[, string ...]) *4.0.1*
Implements a mostly ANSI-compatible `fscanf()`

int fseek(resource fp, int offset[, int whence]) *3.0*
Seeks on a file pointer

int fsockopen(string hostname, int port[, int errno[, string errstr[, float timeout]]]) *3.0*
Opens an Internet or Unix domain socket connection

int fstat(resource fp) *4.0*
Performs `stat()` on a filehandle

int ftell(resource fp) *3.0*
Gets file pointer's read/write position

int ftok(string pathname, string proj) *4.1.0*
Converts a pathname and a project identifier to a System V IPC key

int ftp_async_continue(resource stream) *4.3.0*
Continues retrieving/sending a file asynchronously

bool ftp_async_fget(resource stream, resource fp, string remote_file, int mode[, int resumepos]) *4.3.0*
Retrieves a file from the FTP server asynchronously and writes it to an open file

bool ftp_async_fput(resource stream, string remote_file, resource fp, int mode[, int startpos]) *4.3.0*

Stores a file from an open file to the FTP server asynchronously

int ftp_async_get(resource stream, string local_file, string remote_file, int mode[, int resume_pos]) *4.3.0*

Retrieves a file from the FTP server asynchronously and writes it to a local file

bool ftp_async_put(resource stream, string remote_file, string local_file, int mode[, int startpos]) *4.3.0*

Stores a file on the FTP server

bool ftp_cdup(resource stream) *3.0.13*

Changes to the parent directory

bool ftp_chdir(resource stream, string directory) *3.0.13*

Changes directories

void ftp_close(resource stream) *4.1.0*

Closes the FTP stream

resource ftp_connect(string host[, int port[, int timeout)]]) *3.0.13*

Opens an FTP stream

bool ftp_delete(resource stream, string file) *3.0.13*

Deletes a file

bool ftp_exec(resource stream, string command) *4.0.3*

Requests execution of a program on the FTP server

bool ftp_fget(resource stream, resource fp, string remote_file, int mode [, int resumepos]) *3.0.13*

Retrieves a file from the FTP server and writes it to an open file

bool ftp_fput(resource stream, string remote_file, resource fp, int mode[, int startpos]) *3.0.13*

Stores a file from an open file to the FTP server

bool ftp_get(resource stream, string local_file, string remote_file, int mode[, int resume_pos]) *3.0.13*

Retrieves a file from the FTP server and writes it to a local file

mixed ftp_get_option(resource stream, int option) *4.1.0*

Gets an FTP option

bool ftp_login(resource stream, string username, string password) *3.0.13*

Logs into the FTP server

int ftp_mdtm(resource stream, string filename) *3.0.13*

Returns the last modification time of the file or –1 on error

string ftp_mkdir(resource stream, string directory) *3.0.13*

Creates a directory and returns the absolute path for the new directory or `false` on error

array ftp_nlist(resource stream, string directory) *3.0.13*

Returns an array of filenames in the given directory

bool ftp_pasv(resource stream, bool pasv) *3.0.13*
Turns passive mode on or off

bool ftp_put(resource stream, string remote_file, string local_file, int mode[, int startpos]) *3.0.13*
Stores a file on the FTP server

string ftp_pwd(resource stream) *3.0.13*
Returns the present working directory

array ftp_rawlist(resource stream, string directory[, bool recursive]) *3.0.13*
Returns a detailed listing of a directory as an array of output lines

bool ftp_rename(resource stream, string src, string dest) *3.0.13*
Renames the given file to a new path

bool ftp_rmdir(resource stream, string directory) *3.0.13*
Removes a directory

bool ftp_set_option(resource stream, int option, mixed value) *4.1.0*
Sets an FTP option

bool ftp_site(resource stream, string cmd) *3.0.15*
Sends a `site` command to the server

int ftp_size(resource stream, string filename) *3.0.13*
Returns the size of the file or –1 on error

string ftp_systype(resource stream) *3.0.13*
Returns the system type identifier

int ftruncate(resource fp, int size) *4.0*
Truncates file to `size` length

mixed func_get_arg(int arg_num) *4.0*
Gets the specified argument that was passed to the function

array func_get_args() *4.0*
Gets an array of the arguments that were passed to the function

int func_num_args(void) *4.0*
Gets the number of arguments that were passed to the function

function func_name($arg1, $arg2, ...) *3.0*
Language keyword used to define a function

bool function_exists(string function_name) *3.0.7*
Checks if the function exists

int fwrite(resource fp, string str[, int length]) *3.0*
Provides a binary-safe file write

string get_cfg_var(string option_name) *3.0*
Gets the value of a PHP configuration option

string get_class(object object) *4.0*
Retrieves the class name

array get_class_methods(mixed class) *4.0*
Returns an array of method names for class or class instance

array get_class_vars(string class_name) *4.0*
Returns an array of default properties of the class

string get_current_user(void) *3.0*
Gets the name of the owner of the current PHP script

array get_declared_classes(void) *4.0*
Returns an array of all declared classes

array get_defined_constants(void) *4.1.0*
Returns an array containing the names and values of all defined constants

array get_defined_functions(void) *4.0.4*
Returns an array of all defined functions

array get_defined_vars(void) *4.0.4*
Returns an associative array of names and values of all currently defined variable names (variables in the current scope)

array get_extension_funcs(string extension_name) *4.0*
Returns an array with the names of functions belonging to the named extension

array get_html_translation_table([int table[, int quote_style]]) *4.0*
Returns the internal translation table used by `htmlspecialchars()` and `htmlentities()`

array get_included_files(void) *4.0*
Returns an array with the filenames that were included with `include_once`

array get_loaded_extensions(void) *4.0*
Returns an array containing names of loaded extensions

int get_magic_quotes_gpc(void) *3.0.6*
Gets the active configuration setting of `magic_quotes_gpc`

int get_magic_quotes_runtime(void) *3.0.6*
Gets the active configuration setting of `magic_quotes_runtime`

array get_meta_tags(string filename[, bool use_include_path]) *3.0.4*
Extracts all meta tag content attributes from a file and returns an array

array get_object_vars(object obj) *4.0*
Returns an array of object properties

string get_parent_class(mixed object) *4.0*
Retrieves the parent class name for object or class

string get_resource_type(resource res) *4.0.2*
Gets the resource type name for a given resource

array getallheaders(void) *3.0*
An alias for `apache_request_headers()`

mixed getcwd(void) *4.0*
Gets the current directory

PHP

array getdate([int timestamp]) *3.0*

Gets date/time information

string getenv(string varname) *3.0*

Gets the value of an environment variable

string gethostbyaddr(string ip_address) *3.0*

Gets the Internet hostname corresponding to a given IP address

string gethostbyname(string hostname) *3.0*

Gets the IP address corresponding to a given Internet hostname

array gethostbynamel(string hostname) *3.0*

Returns a list of IP addresses that a given hostname resolves to

array getimagesize(string imagefile[, array info]) *3.0*

Gets the size of an image as a four-element array

int getlastmod(void) *3.0*

Gets time of last page modification

int getmxrr(string hostname, array mxhosts[, array weight]) *3.0*

Gets MX records corresponding to a given Internet hostname

int getmygid(void) *4.1.0*

Gets PHP script owner's group ID

int getmyinode(void) *3.0*

Gets the inode of the current script being parsed

int getmypid(void) *3.0*

Gets current process ID

int getmyuid(void) *3.0*

Gets PHP script owner's user ID

int getprotobyname(string name) *4.0*

Returns protocol number associated with `name` as per */etc/protocols*

string getprotobynumber(int proto) *4.0*

Returns protocol name associated with protocol number `proto`

int getrandmax(void) *3.0*

Returns the maximum value a random number can have

array getrusage([int who]) *3.0.7*

Returns an array of usage statistics

int getservbyname(string service, string protocol) *4.0*

Returns port associated with service; protocol must be `"tcp"` or `"udp"`

string getservbyport(int port, string protocol) *4.0*

Returns service name associated with port; protocol must be `"tcp"` or `"udp"`

string gettext(string msgid) *3.0.7*

Returns the translation of `msgid` for the current domain or `msgid` unaltered if a translation does not exist

array gettimeofday(void) *3.0.7*

Returns the current time as array

string gettype(mixed var) *3.0*

Returns the type of the variable

array glob(string pattern[, int flags]) *4.3.0*

Finds pathnames matching a pattern

global var1[,var2[, ...]] *3.0*

Language keyword used inside functions to indicate all uses for specified variables will be global

string gmdate(string format[, int timestamp]) *3.0*

Formats a GMT/UTC date/time

int gmmktime(int hour, int min, int sec, int mon, int day, int year) *3.0*

Gets Unix timestamp for a GMT date

resource gmp_abs(resource a) *4.0.4*

Calculates absolute value

resource gmp_add(resource a, resource b) *4.0.4*

Adds a and b

resource gmp_and(resource a, resource b) *4.0.4*

Calculates logical AND of a and b

void gmp_clrbit(resource &a, int index) *4.0.4*

Clears bit in a

int gmp_cmp(resource a, resource b) *4.0.4*

Compares two numbers

resource gmp_com(resource a) *4.0.4*

Calculates one's complement of a

resource gmp_div_q(resource a, resource b[, int round]) *4.0.4*

Divides a by b, returns quotient only

array gmp_div_qr(resource a, resource b[, int round]) *4.0.4*

Divides a by b, returns quotient and reminder

resource gmp_div_r(resource a, resource b[, int round]) *4.0.4*

Divides a by b, returns reminder only

resource gmp_divexact(resource a, resource b) *4.0.4*

Divides a by b using exact division algorithm

resource gmp_fact(int a) *4.0.4*

Calculates factorial function

resource gmp_gcd(resource a, resource b) *4.0.4*

Computes greatest common denominator (GCD) of a and b

array gmp_gcdext(resource a, resource b) *4.0.4*

Computes G, S, and T, such that AS + BT = G, where G is the GCD of a and b

int gmp_hamdist(resource a, resource b) *4.0.4*
Calculates hamming distance between a and b

resource gmp_init(mixed number[, int base]) *4.0.4*
Initializes GMP number

int gmp_intval(resource gmpnumber) *4.0.4*
Gets signed long value of GMP number

resource gmp_invert(resource a, resource b) *4.0.4*
Computes the inverse of a modulo b

int gmp_jacobi(resource a, resource b) *4.0.4*
Computes Jacobi symbol

int gmp_legendre(resource a, resource b) *4.0.4*
Computes Legendre symbol

resource gmp_mod(resource a, resource b) *4.0.4*
Computes a modulo b

resource gmp_mul(resource a, resource b) *4.0.4*
Multiplies a and b

resource gmp_neg(resource a) *4.0.4*
Negates a number

resource gmp_or(resource a, resource b) *4.0.4*
Calculates logical OR of a and b

bool gmp_perfect_square(resource a) *4.0.4*
Checks if a is an exact square

int gmp_popcount(resource a) *4.0.4*
Calculates the population count of a

resource gmp_pow(resource base, int exp) *4.0.4*
Raises base to power exp

resource gmp_powm(resource base, resource exp, resource mod) *4.0.4*
Raises base to power exp and takes result modulo mod

int gmp_prob_prime(resource a[, int reps]) *4.0.4*
Checks if a is "probably prime"

resource gmp_random([int limiter]) *4.0.4*
Gets random number

int gmp_scan0(resource a, int start) *4.0.4*
Finds first zero bit

int gmp_scan1(resource a, int start) *4.0.4*
Finds first nonzero bit

void gmp_setbit(resource &a, int index[, bool set_clear]) *4.0.4*
Sets or clears bit in a

int gmp_sign(resource a) *4.0.4*
Gets the sign of the number

resource gmp_sqrt(resource a) *4.0.4*
Takes integer part of square root of a

array gmp_sqrtrem(resource a) *4.0.4*
Takes square root with remainder

string gmp_strval(resource gmpnumber[, int base]) *4.0.4*
Gets string representation of GMP number

resource gmp_sub(resource a, resource b) *4.0.4*
Subtracts b from a

resource gmp_xor(resource a, resource b) *4.0.4*
Calculates logical exclusive OR of a and b

string gmstrftime(string format[, int timestamp]) *3.0.12*
Formats a GMT/UCT time/date according to locale settings

int gregoriantojd(int month, int day, int year) *3.0*
Converts a Gregorian calendar date to Julian day count

string gzcompress(string data[, int level]) *4.0.1*
Gzip-compresses a string

string gzdeflate(string data[, int level]) *4.0.4*
Gzip-compresses a string

string gzencode(string data[, int level[, int encoding_mode]]) *4.0.4*
Gzip-encodes a string

array gzfile(string filename[, int use_include_path]) *3.0*
Reads and uncompresses an entire *.gz* file into an array

string gzinflate(string data[, int length]) *4.0.4*
Unzips a gzip-compressed string

int gzopen(string filename, string mode[, int use_include_path]) *3.0*
Opens a *.gz* file and returns a *.gz* file pointer

string gzuncompress(string data, int length) *4.0.1*
Unzips a gzip-compressed string

void header(string header[, bool replace, [int http_response_code]]) *3.0*
Sends a raw HTTP header

int headers_sent(void) *3.0.8*
Returns true if headers have already been sent, false otherwise

string hebrev(string str[, int max_chars_per_line]) *3.0*
Converts logical Hebrew text to visual text

string hebrevc(string str[, int max_chars_per_line]) *3.0*
Converts logical Hebrew text to visual text with newline conversion

int hexdec(string hexadecimal_number) *3.0*
Returns the decimal equivalent of the hexadecimal number

bool highlight_file(string file_name[, bool return]) *4.0*
Adds syntax highlighting to a source file

bool highlight_string(string string[, bool return]) *4.0*

Adds syntax highlighting to a string and optionally return it

string html_entity_decode(string string[, int quote_style][, string charset]) *4.3.0*

Converts all HTML entities to their applicable characters

string htmlentities(string string[, int quote_style][, string charset]) *3.0*

Converts all applicable characters to HTML entities

string htmlspecialchars(string string[, int quote_style][, string charset]) *3.0*

Converts special characters to HTML entities

string iconv(string in_charset, string out_charset, string str) *4.0.5*

Returns `str` converted to the `out_charset` character set

array iconv_get_encoding([string type]) *4.0.5*

Gets the internal and output encoding for `ob_iconv_handler()`

bool iconv_set_encoding(string type, string charset) *4.0.5*

Sets the internal and output encoding for `ob_iconv_handler()`

if(cond) *3.0*

Language keyword that tests a condition

int ignore_user_abort(bool value) *3.0.7*

Sets whether to ignore a user abort event or not

int image2wbmp(int im[, string filename[, int threshold]]) *4.0.5*

Outputs WBMP image to browser or file

array image_type_to_mime_type(int imagetype) *4.3.0*

Gets the MIME type for `imagetype` returned by `getimagesize()`, `exif_read_data()`, `exif_thumbnail()`, and `exif_imagetype()`

void imagealphablending(resource im, bool on) *4.0.6*

Turns alpha blending mode on or off for the given image

int imagearc(int im, int cx, int cy, int w, int h, int s, int e, int col) *3.0*

Draws a partial ellipse

int imagechar(int im, int font, int x, int y, string c, int col) *3.0*

Draws a character

int imagecharup(int im, int font, int x, int y, string c, int col) *3.0*

Draws a character rotated 90 degrees counterclockwise

int imagecolorallocate(int im, int red, int green, int blue) *3.0*

Allocates a color for an image

int imagecolorat(int im, int x, int y) *3.0*

Gets the index of the color of a pixel

int imagecolorclosest(int im, int red, int green, int blue) *3.0*

Gets the index of the closest color to the specified color

int imagecolorclosestalpha(resource im, int red, int green, int blue, int alpha) *4.0.6*

Finds the closest matching color with alpha transparency

int imagecolorclosesthwb(int im, int red, int green, int blue) *4.0.1*

Gets the index of the color that has the hue, white, and blackness nearest to the given color

int imagecolordeallocate(int im, int index) *3.0.6*

Deallocates a color for an image

int imagecolorexact(int im, int red, int green, int blue) *3.0*

Gets the index of the specified color

int imagecolorexactalpha(resource im, int red, int green, int blue, int alpha) *4.0.6*

Finds exact match for color with transparency

int imagecolorresolve(int im, int red, int green, int blue) *3.0.2*

Gets the index of the specified color or its closest possible alternative

int imagecolorresolvealpha(resource im, int red, int green, int blue, int alpha) *4.0.6*

Resolves/allocates a color with an alpha level; works for true color and palette based images

int imagecolorset(int im, int col, int red, int green, int blue) *3.0*

Sets the color for the specified palette index

array imagecolorsforindex(int im, int col) *3.0*

Gets the colors for an index

int imagecolorstotal(int im) *3.0*

Finds out the number of colors in an image's palette

int imagecolortransparent(int im[, int col]) *3.0*

Defines a color as transparent

int imagecopy(int dst_im, int src_im, int dst_x, int dst_y, int src_x, int src_y, int src_w, int src_h) *3.0.6*

Copies part of an image

int imagecopymerge(int src_im, int dst_im, int dst_x, int dst_y, int src_x, int src_y, int src_w, int src_h, int pct) *4.0.1*

Merges one part of an image with another

int imagecopymergegray(int src_im, int dst_im, int dst_x, int dst_y, int src_x, int src_y, int src_w, int src_h, int pct) *4.0.6*

Merges one part of an image with another

int imagecopyresampled(int dst_im, int src_im, int dst_x, int dst_y, int src_x, int src_y, int dst_w, int dst_h, int src_w, int src_h) *4.0.6*

Copies and resizes part of an image using resampling to help ensure clarity

int imagecopyresized(int dst_im, int src_im, int dst_x, int dst_y, int src_x, int src_y, int dst_w, int dst_h, int src_w, int src_h) *3.0*

Copies and resizes part of an image

int imagecreate(int x_size, int y_size) *3.0*

Creates a new image

int imagecreatefromgd(string filename) *4.1.0*

Creates a new image from GD file or URL

int imagecreatefromgd2(string filename) *4.1.0*
Creates a new image from GD2 file or URL

int imagecreatefromgd2part(string filename, int srcX, int srcY, int width, int height) *4.1.0*
Creates a new image from a given part of GD2 file or URL

int imagecreatefromgif(string filename) *3.0*
Creates a new image from GIF file or URL

int imagecreatefromjpeg(string filename) *3.0.16*
Creates a new image from JPEG file or URL

int imagecreatefrompng(string filename) *3.0.13*
Creates a new image from PNG file or URL

int imagecreatefromstring(string image) *4.0.4*
Creates a new image from the image stream in the string

int imagecreatefromwbmp(string filename) *4.0.1*
Creates a new image from WBMP file or URL

int imagecreatefromxbm(string filename) *4.0.1*
Creates a new image from XBM file or URL

int imagecreatefromxpm(string filename) *4.0.1*
Creates a new image from XPM file or URL

int imagecreatetruecolor(int x_size, int y_size) *4.0.6*
Creates a new true color image

int imagedashedline(int im, int x1, int y1, int x2, int y2, int col) *3.0*
Draws a dashed line

int imagedestroy(int im) *3.0*
Destroys an image

void imageellipse(resource im, int cx, int cy, int w, int h, int color) *4.0.6*
Draws an ellipse

int imagefill(int im, int x, int y, int col) *3.0*
Performs a flood fill

int imagefilledarc(int im, int cx, int cy, int w, int h, int s, int e, int col, int style) *4.0.6*
Draws a filled partial ellipse

void imagefilledellipse(resource im, int cx, int cy, int w, int h, int color) *4.0.6*
Draws an ellipse

int imagefilledpolygon(int im, array point, int num_points, int col) *3.0*
Draws a filled polygon

int imagefilledrectangle(int im, int x1, int y1, int x2, int y2, int col) *3.0*
Draws a filled rectangle

int imagefilltoborder(int im, int x, int y, int border, int col) *3.0*
Performs a flood fill to specific color

int imagefontheight(int font) *3.0*
Gets font height

int imagefontwidth(int font) *3.0*
: Gets font width

array imageftbbox(int size, int angle, string font_file, string text[, array extrainfo]) *4.1.0*
: Gives the bounding box of a text using fonts via freetype2

array imagefttext(int im, int size, int angle, int x, int y, int col, string font_file, string text, [array extrainfo]) *4.1.0*
: Writes text to the image using fonts via freetype2

int imagegammacorrect(int im, float inputgamma, float outputgamma) *3.0.13*
: Applies a gamma correction to a GD image

int imagegd(int im[, string filename]) *4.1.0*
: Outputs GD image to browser or file

int imagegd2(int im[, string filename]) *4.1.0*
: Outputs GD2 image to browser or file

int imagegif(int im[, string filename]) *3.0*
: Outputs GIF image to browser or file

int imageinterlace(int im[, int interlace]) *3.0*
: Enables or disables interlace

int imagejpeg(int im[, string filename[, int quality]]) *3.0.16*
: Outputs JPEG image to browser or file

int imageline(int im, int x1, int y1, int x2, int y2, int col) *3.0*
: Draws a line

int imageloadfont(string filename) *3.0*
: Loads a new font

int imagepalettecopy(int dst, int src) *4.0.1*
: Copies the palette from the `src` image onto the `dst` image

int imagepng(int im[, string filename]) *3.0.13*
: Outputs PNG image to browser or file

int imagepolygon(int im, array point, int num_points, int col) *3.0*
: Draws a polygon

array imagepsbbox(string text, int font, int size[, int space, int tightness, int angle]) *3.0.9*
: Returns the bounding box needed by a string if rasterized

int imagepscopyfont(int font_index) *3.0.9*
: Makes a copy of a font for purposes like extending or reencoding

bool imagepsencodefont(int font_index, string filename) *3.0.9*
: Changes a font's character encoding vector

bool imagepsextendfont(int font_index, float extend) *3.0.9*
: Extends or condenses (if `extend` is less than 1) a font

bool imagepsfreefont(int font_index) *3.0.9*
: Frees memory used by a font

int imagepsloadfont(string pathname) *3.0.9*
Loads a new font from specified file

bool imagepsslantfont(int font_index, float slant) *3.0.9*
Slants a font

array imagepstext(int image, string text, int font, int size, int xcoord, int ycoord[, int space, int tightness, float angle, int antialias]) *3.0.9*
Rasterizes a string over an image

int imagerectangle(int im, int x1, int y1, int x2, int y2, int col) *3.0*
Draws a rectangle

int imagesetbrush(resource image, resource brush) *4.0.6*
Sets the brush image for line drawing

int imagesetpixel(int im, int x, int y, int col) *3.0*
Sets a single pixel

void imagesetstyle(resource im, array styles) *4.0.6*
Sets the style for line drawing

void imagesetthickness(resource im, int thickness) *4.0.6*
Sets line thickness for line drawing

int imagesettile(resource image, resource tile) *4.0.6*
Sets the tile image for filling

int imagestring(int im, int font, int x, int y, string str, int col) *3.0*
Draws a string horizontally

int imagestringup(int im, int font, int x, int y, string str, int col) *3.0*
Draws a string vertically (rotated 90 degrees counterclockwise)

int imagesx(int im) *3.0*
Gets image width

int imagesy(int im) *3.0*
Gets image height

void imagetruecolortopalette(resource im, bool ditherFlag, int colorsWanted) *4.0.6*
Converts a true color image to a palette-based image with a number of colors, optionally using dithering.

array imagettfbbox(int size, int angle, string font_file, string text) *3.0.1*
Gives the bounding box of a text using TrueType fonts

array imagettftext(int im, int size, int angle, int x, int y, int col, string font_file, string text) *3.0*
Writes text to the image using a TrueType font

int imagetypes(void) *3 CVS Only*
Returns the types of images supported in a bitfield (1=GIF, 2=JPEG, 4=PNG, 8=WBMP, 16=XPM)

int imagewbmp(int im[, string filename,[, int foreground]]) *3.0.15*
Outputs WBMP image to browser or file

string imap_8bit(string text) *3.0*
Converts an 8-bit string to a quoted-printable string

array imap_alerts(void) *3.0.12*

Returns an array of all IMAP alerts generated since the last page load or the last `imap_alerts()` call, whichever came last, and clears the alert stack

int imap_append(int stream_id, string folder, string message[, string flags]) *3.0*

Appends a new message to a specified mailbox

string imap_base64(string text) *3.0*

Decodes base64 encoded text

string imap_binary(string text) *3.0.2*

Converts an 8-bit string to a base64 string

string imap_body(int stream_id, int msg_no[, int options]) *3.0*

Reads the message body

object imap_bodystruct(int stream_id, int msg_no, int section) *3.0.4*

Reads the structure of a specified body section of a specific message

object imap_check(int stream_id) *3.0*

Gets mailbox properties

int imap_clearflag_full(int stream_id, string sequence, string flag[, int options]) *3.0.3*

Clears flags on messages

int imap_close(int stream_id[, int options]) *3.0*

Closes an IMAP stream

int imap_createmailbox(int stream_id, string mailbox) *3.0*

Creates a new mailbox

int imap_delete(int stream_id, int msg_no[, int flags]) *3.0*

Marks a message for deletion

int imap_deletemailbox(int stream_id, string mailbox) *3.0*

Deletes a mailbox

array imap_errors(void) *3.0.12*

Returns an array of all IMAP errors generated since the last page load or the last `imap_errors()` call, whichever came last, and clears the error stack

int imap_expunge(int stream_id) *3.0*

Permanently deletes all messages marked for deletion

array imap_fetch_overview(int stream_id, int msg_no[, int flags]) *3.0.4*

Reads an overview of the information in the headers of the given message sequence

string imap_fetchbody(int stream_id, int msg_no, int section[, int options]) *3.0*

Gets a specific body section

string imap_fetchheader(int stream_id, int msg_no[, int options]) *3.0.3*

Gets the full unfiltered header for a message

object imap_fetchstructure(int stream_id, int msg_no[, int options]) *3.0*

Reads the full structure of a message

array imap_get_quota(int stream_id, string qroot) *4.0.5*

Returns the quota set to the mailbox account qroot

array imap_get_quotaroot(int stream_id, string mbox) *4.3.0*

Returns the quota set to the mailbox account `mbox`

array imap_getmailboxes(int stream_id, string ref, string pattern) *3.0.12*

Reads the list of mailboxes and returns a full array of objects containing names, attributes, and delimiters

array imap_getsubscribed(int stream_id, string ref, string pattern) *3.0.12*

Return a list of subscribed mailboxes in the same format as `imap_getmailboxes()`

object imap_headerinfo(int stream_id, int msg_no[, int from_length[, int subject_length[, string default_host]]]) *3.0*

Reads the headers of the message

array imap_headers(int stream_id) *3.0*

Returns headers for all messages in a mailbox

string imap_last_error(void) *3.0.12*

Returns the last error that was generated by an IMAP function; the error stack is not cleared after this call

array imap_list(int stream_id, string ref, string pattern) *3.0.4*

Reads the list of mailboxes

array imap_lsub(int stream_id, string ref, string pattern) *3.0.4*

Returns a list of subscribed mailboxes

int imap_mail(string to, string subject, string message[, string additional_headers[, string cc[, string bcc[, string rpath]]]]) *3.0.14*

Sends an email message

string imap_mail_compose(array envelope, array body) *3.0.5*

Creates a MIME message based on given envelope and body sections

int imap_mail_copy(int stream_id, int msg_no, string mailbox[, int options]) *3.0*

Copies specified message to a mailbox

int imap_mail_move(int stream_id, int msg_no, string mailbox[, int options]) *3.0*

Moves specified message to a mailbox

object imap_mailboxmsginfo(int stream_id) *3.0.2*

Returns information about the current mailbox

array imap_mime_header_decode(string str) *3.0.17*

Decodes MIME header element in accordance with RFC 2047 and returns an array of objects containing `charset` encoding and decoded `text`

int imap_msgno(int stream_id, int unique_msg_id) *3.0.3*

Gets the sequence number associated with a user ID

int imap_num_msg(int stream_id) *3.0*

Gives the number of messages in the current mailbox

int imap_num_recent(int stream_id) *3.0*

Gives the number of recent messages in current mailbox

int imap_open(string mailbox, string user, string password[, int options]) *3.0*
Opens an IMAP stream to a mailbox

int imap_ping(int stream_id) *3.0*
Checks if the IMAP stream is still active

string imap_qprint(string text) *3.0*
Converts a quoted-printable string to an 8-bit string

int imap_renamemailbox(int stream_id, string old_name, string new_name) *3.0*
Renames a mailbox

int imap_reopen(int stream_id, string mailbox[, int options]) *3.0*
Reopens an IMAP stream to a new mailbox

array imap_rfc822_parse_adrlist(string address_string, string default_host) *3.0.2*
Parses an address string

object imap_rfc822_parse_headers(string headers[, string default_host]) *4.0*
Parses a set of mail headers contained in a string and return an object similar to `imap_headerinfo()`

string imap_rfc822_write_address(string mailbox, string host, string personal) *3.0.2*
Returns a properly formatted email address given the mailbox, host, and personal information

array imap_scan(int stream_id, string ref, string pattern, string content) *3.0.4*
Reads list of mailboxes containing a certain string

array imap_search(int stream_id, string criteria[, long flags]) *3.0.12*
Returns a list of messages matching the given criteria

int imap_set_quota(int stream_id, string qroot, int mailbox_size) *4.0.5*
Sets the quota for `qroot` mailbox

int imap_setacl(int stream_id, string mailbox, string id, string rights) *4.1.0*
Sets the ACL for a given mailbox

int imap_setflag_full(int stream_id, string sequence, string flag[, int options]) *3.0.3*
Sets flags on messages

array imap_sort(int stream_id, int criteria, int reverse[, int options[, string search_criteria]]) *3.0.3*
Sorts an array of message headers, optionally including only messages that meet specified criteria

object imap_status(int stream_id, string mailbox, int options) *3.0.4*
Gets status information from a mailbox

int imap_subscribe(int stream_id, string mailbox) *3.0*
Subscribes to a mailbox

int imap_thread(int stream_id[, int flags]) *4.1.0*
Returns threaded by references tree

int imap_uid(int stream_id, int msg_no) *3.0.3*
Gets the unique message ID associated with a standard sequential message number

int imap_undelete(int stream_id, int msg_no) *3.0*
Removes the delete flag from a message

int imap_unsubscribe(int stream_id, string mailbox) *3.0*
Unsubscribes from a mailbox

string imap_utf7_decode(string buf) *3.0.15*
Decodes a modified UTF-7 string

string imap_utf7_encode(string buf) *3.0.15*
Encodes a string in modified UTF-7

string imap_utf8(string string) *3.0.13*
Converts a string to UTF-8

string implode(array src, string glue) *3.0*
Joins array elements placing `glue` string between items and returns one string

bool import_request_variables(string types[, string prefix]) *4.1.0*
Imports GET/POST/Cookie variables into the global scope

bool in_array(mixed needle, array haystack[, bool strict]) *4.0*
Checks if the given value exists in the array

bool include filename *3.0*
Includes and evaluates the given file, with a nonfatal warning on failure

bool include_once filename *4.0*
Includes and evaluates the given file if not already included, with a nonfatal warning on failure

string ini_get(string varname) *4.0*
Gets a configuration option

array ini_get_all([string extension]) *4.1.0*
Gets all configuration options

string ini_restore(string varname) *4.0*
Restores the value of a configuration option specified by `varname`

string ini_set(string varname, string newvalue) *4.0*
Sets a configuration option; returns `false` on error and the old value of the configuration option on success

int intval(mixed var[, int base]) *3.0*
Gets the integer value of a variable using the optional base for the conversion

int ip2long(string ip_address) *4.0*
Converts a string containing an (IPv4) Internet Protocol dotted address into a proper address

array iptcembed(string iptcdata, string jpeg_file_name[, int spool]) *3.0.7*
Embeds binary IPTC data into a JPEG image.

array iptcparse(string iptcdata) *3.0.6*
Parses binary IPTC data into associative array

bool is_a(object object, string class_name) *4.1.0*
Returns `true` if the object is of this class or has this class as one of its parents

bool is_array(mixed var) *3.0*
Returns true if variable is an array

bool is_bool(mixed var) *4.0*
Returns true if variable is a boolean

bool is_callable(mixed var[, bool syntax_only[, string callable_name]]) *4.0.6*
Returns true if variable is callable

bool is_dir(string filename) *3.0*
Returns true if file is directory

bool is_executable(string filename) *3.0*
Returns true if file is executable

bool is_file(string filename) *3.0*
Returns true if file is a regular file

bool is_finite(float val) *4.1.0*
Returns whether argument is finite

bool is_float(mixed var) *3.0*
Returns true if variable is float point

bool is_infinite(float val) *4.1.0*
Returns whether argument is infinite

bool is_link(string filename) *3.0*
Returns true if file is symbolic link

bool is_long(mixed var) *3.0*
Returns true if variable is a long (integer)

bool is_nan(float val) *4.1.0*
Returns whether argument is not a number

bool is_null(mixed var) *4.0.4*
Returns true if variable is NULL

bool is_numeric(mixed value) *4.0*
Returns true if value is a number or a numeric string

bool is_object(mixed var) *3.0*
Returns true if variable is an object

bool is_readable(string filename) *3.0*
Returns true if file can be read

bool is_resource(mixed var) *4.0*
Returns true if variable is a resource

bool is_scalar(mixed value) *4.0.5*
Returns true if value is a scalar

bool is_string(mixed var) *3.0*
Returns true if variable is a string

bool is_subclass_of(object object, string class_name) *4.0*
Returns true if the object has this class as one of its parents

bool is_uploaded_file(string path) *3.0.17*
: Checks if file was created by RFC 1867 upload

bool is_writable(string filename) *4.0*
: Returns `true` if file can be written

bool isset(mixed var[, mixed var[, ...]]) *3.0*
: Determines whether a variable is set

void java_last_exception_clear(void) *4.0.2*
: Clears last Java extension

object java_last_exception_get(void) *4.0.2*
: Gets last Java exception

mixed jddayofweek(int juliandaycount[, int mode]) *3.0*
: Returns name or number of day of week from Julian day count

string jdmonthname(int juliandaycount, int mode) *3.0*
: Returns name of month for Julian day count

string jdtofrench(int juliandaycount) *3.0*
: Converts a Julian day count to a French Republic calendar date

string jdtogregorian(int juliandaycount) *3.0*
: Converts a Julian day count to a Gregorian calendar date

string jdtojewish(int juliandaycount) *3.0*
: Converts a Julian day count to a Jewish calendar date

string jdtojulian(int juliandaycount) *3.0*
: Converts a Julian day count to a Julian calendar date

int jdtounix(int jday) *4.0*
: Convert Julian day count to a Unix timestamp

int jewishtojd(int month, int day, int year) *3.0*
: Converts a Jewish calendar date to a Julian day count

string join(array src, string glue) *3.0*
: An alias for `implode()`

void jpeg2wbmp (string f_org, string f_dest, int d_height, int d_width, int threshold) *4.0.5*
: Converts JPEG image to WBMP image

int juliantojd(int month, int day, int year) *3.0*
: Converts a Julian calendar date to a Julian day count

mixed key(array array_arg) *3.0*
: Returns the key of the element currently pointed to by the internal array pointer

bool krsort(array array_arg[, int sort_flags]) *3.0.13*
: Sorts an array by key value in reverse order

bool ksort(array array_arg[, int sort_flags]) *3.0*
: Sorts an array by key

float lcg_value() *4.0*
Returns a value from the combined linear congruential generator

string ldap_8859_to_t61(string value) *4.0.2*
Translates 8859 characters to t61 characters

bool ldap_add(resource link, string dn, array entry) *3.0*
Adds entries to an LDAP directory

bool ldap_bind(resource link[, string dn, string password]) *3.0*
Binds to an LDAP directory

bool ldap_compare(resource link, string dn, string attr, string value) *4.0.2*
Determines if an entry has a specific value for one of its attributes

resource ldap_connect([string host[, int port]]) *3.0*
Connects to an LDAP server

int ldap_count_entries(resource link, resource result) *3.0*
Counts the number of entries in a search result

bool ldap_delete(resource link, string dn) *3.0*
Deletes an entry from a directory

string ldap_dn2ufn(string dn) *3.0*
Converts DN to User Friendly Naming format

string ldap_err2str(int errno) *3.0.13*
Converts error number to error string

int ldap_errno(resource link) *3.0.12*
Gets the current LDAP error number

string ldap_error(resource link) *3.0.12*
Gets the current LDAP error string

array ldap_explode_dn(string dn, int with_attrib) *3.0*
Splits DN into its component parts

string ldap_first_attribute(resource link, resource result_entry, int ber) *3.0*
Returns first attribute

resource ldap_first_entry(resource link, resource result) *3.0*
Returns first result ID

resource ldap_first_reference(resource link, resource result) *4.0.5*
Returns first reference

bool ldap_free_result(resource result) *3.0*
Frees result memory

array ldap_get_attributes(resource link, resource result_entry) *3.0*
Gets attributes from a search result entry

string ldap_get_dn(resource link, resource result_entry) *3.0*
Gets the DN of a result entry

array ldap_get_entries(resource link, resource result) *3.0*
Gets all result entries

bool ldap_get_option(resource link, int option, mixed retval) *4.0.4*
Gets the current value of various session-wide parameters

array ldap_get_values(resource link, resource result_entry, string attribute) *3.0*
Gets all values from a result entry

array ldap_get_values_len(resource link, resource result_entry, string attribute) *3.0.13*
Gets all values with lengths from a result entry

resource ldap_list(resource link, string base_dn, string filter[, array attrs[, int attrsonly[, int sizelimit[, int timelimit[, int deref]]]]]) *3.0*
Performs a single-level search

bool ldap_mod_add(resource link, string dn, array entry) *3.0.8*
Adds attribute values to current

bool ldap_mod_del(resource link, string dn, array entry) *3.0.8*
Deletes attribute values

bool ldap_mod_replace(resource link, string dn, array entry) *3.0.8*
Replaces attribute values with new ones

string ldap_next_attribute(resource link, resource result_entry, resource ber) *3.0*
Gets the next attribute in result

resource ldap_next_entry(resource link, resource result_entry) *3.0*
Gets next result entry

resource ldap_next_reference(resource link, resource reference_entry) *4.0.5*
Gets next reference

bool ldap_parse_reference(resource link, resource reference_entry, array referrals) *4.0.5*
Extracts information from reference entry

bool ldap_parse_result(resource link, resource result, int errcode, string matcheddn, string errmsg, array referrals) *4.0.5*
Extracts information from result

resource ldap_read(resource link, string base_dn, string filter[, array attrs[, int attrsonly[, int sizelimit[, int timelimit[, int deref]]]]]) *3.0*
Reads an entry

bool ldap_rename(resource link, string dn, string newrdn, string newparent, bool deleteoldrdn); *4.0.5*
Modifies the name of an entry

resource ldap_search(resource link, string base_dn, string filter[, array attrs[, int attrsonly[, int sizelimit[, int timelimit[, int deref]]]]]) *3.0*
Searches LDAP tree under `base_dn`

bool ldap_set_option(resource link, int option, mixed newval) *4.0.4*
Set the value of various session-wide parameters

bool ldap_set_rebind_proc(resource link, string callback) *4.1.0*
Sets a callback function to do rebinds on referral chasing

bool ldap_sort(resource link, resource result, string sortfilter) *4.1.0*
Sorts LDAP result entries

bool ldap_start_tls(resource link) *4.1.0*

Starts TLS

string ldap_t61_to_8859(string value) *4.0.2*

Translates t61 characters to 8859 characters

bool ldap_unbind(resource link) *3.0*

Unbinds from LDAP directory

void leak(int num_bytes=3) *3.0*

Causes an intentional memory leak for testing/debugging purposes

int levenshtein(string str1, string str2) *3.0.17*

Calculates Levenshtein distance between two strings

int link(string target, string link) *3.0*

Creates a hard link

int linkinfo(string filename) *3.0*

Returns the `st_dev` field of the Unix C `stat` structure describing the link

void list(mixed var[, mixed var[, ...]]) *3.0*

Assigns variables as if they were an array

array localeconv(void) *4.0.5*

Returns numeric formatting information based on the current locale

array localtime([int timestamp[, bool associative_array]]) *4.0*

Returns the results of the C system call `localtime` as an associative array if the `associative_array` argument is set to 1 or as a regular array

float log(float number) *3.0*

Returns the natural logarithm of the number

float log10(float number) *3.0*

Returns the base-10 logarithm of the number

float log1p(float number) *4.1.0*

Returns `log(1 + number)`, computed in a way that is accurate even when the value of number is close to zero

string long2ip(int proper_address) *4.0*

Converts an (IPv4) Internet network address into a string in Internet standard dotted format

array lstat(string filename) *3.0.4*

Gives information about a file or symbolic link

string ltrim(string str[, string character_mask]) *3.0*

Strips whitespace from the beginning of a string

int mail(string to, string subject, string message[, string additional_headers[, string additional_parameters]]) *3.0*

Sends an email message

mixed max(mixed arg1[, mixed arg2[, mixed ...]]) *3.0*

Return the highest value in an array or a series of arguments

string mb_convert_encoding(string str, string to-encoding[, mixed from-encoding]) *4.0.6*
Returns converted string in desired encoding

string mb_convert_kana(string str[, string option][, string encoding]) *4.0.6*
Converts between full-width characters and half-width characters (Japanese)

string mb_convert_variables(string to-encoding, mixed from-encoding, mixed vars[, mixed ...]) *4.0.6*
Converts the string resource(s) in variable(s) to desired encoding

string mb_decode_mimeheader(string string) *4.0.6*
Decodes encoded-word string in MIME header field

string mb_decode_numericentity(string string, array convmap[, string encoding]) *4.0.6*
Converts HTML numeric entities to character codes

string mb_detect_encoding(string str[, mixed encoding_list]) *4.0.6*
Returns encoding of the given string

bool|array mb_detect_order([mixed encoding-list]) *4.0.6*
Sets the current `detect_order` or returns the current `detect_order` as a array

string mb_encode_mimeheader(string str[, string charset[, string transfer-encoding[, string linefeed]]]) *4.0.6*
Converts the string to a MIME encoded-word in the format of `=?charset?(B|Q)?encoded_string?=`

string mb_encode_numericentity(string string, array convmap[, string encoding]) *4.0.6*
Converts specified characters to HTML numeric entities

string mb_get_info([string type]) *4.1.0*
Returns the current settings of `mbstring`

false|string mb_http_input([string type]) *4.0.6*
Returns the input encoding

string mb_http_output([string encoding]) *4.0.6*
Sets the current `output_encoding` or returns the current `output_encoding` as a string

string mb_internal_encoding([string encoding]) *4.0.6*
Sets the current internal encoding or returns the current internal encoding as a string

string mb_language([string language]) *4.0.6*
Sets the current language or returns the current language as a string

string mb_output_handler(string contents, int status) *4.0.6*
Returns string in output buffer converted to the `http_output` encoding

bool mb_parse_str(string encoded_string[, array result]) *4.0.6*
Parses GET/POST/Cookie data and sets global variables

string mb_preferred_mime_name(string encoding) *4.0.6*
Returns the preferred MIME name (charset) as a string

int mb_send_mail(string to, string subject, string message[, string additional_headers[, string additional_parameters]]) *4.0.6*
Sends an email message with MIME scheme

string mb_strcut(string str, int start[, int length[, string encoding]]) *4.0.6*
Returns part of a string

string mb_strimwidth(string str, int start, int width[, string trimmarker[, string encoding]]) *4.0.6*
Trims the string in terminal width

int mb_strlen(string str[, string encoding]) *4.0.6*
Gets character numbers of a string

int mb_strpos(string haystack, string needle[, int offset[, string encoding]]) *4.0.6*
Finds position of first occurrence of a string within another

int mb_strrpos(string haystack, string needle[, string encoding]) *4.0.6*
Finds the last occurrence of a character in a string within another

int mb_strwidth(string str[, string encoding]) *4.0.6*
Gets terminal width of a string

mixed mb_substitute_character([mixed substchar]) *4.0.6*
Sets the current `substitute_character` or returns the current `substitute_character`

string mb_substr(string str, int start[, int length[, string encoding]]) *4.0.6*
Returns part of a string

string mcrypt_cbc(int cipher, string key, string data, int mode[, string iv]) *3.0.8*
CBC encrypts/decrypts data using key with `cipher` starting with optional `iv`

string mcrypt_cfb(int cipher, string key, string data, int mode[, string iv]) *3.0.8*
CFB encrypts/decrypts data using key with `cipher` starting with optional `iv`

string mcrypt_create_iv(int size, int source) *3.0.8*
Creates an initialization vector (IV)

string mcrypt_decrypt(string cipher, string key, string data, string mode[, string iv]) *4.0.2*
OFB encrypts/decrypts data using key with `cipher` starting with optional `iv`

string mcrypt_ecb(int cipher, string key, string data, int mode[, string iv]) *3.0.8*
ECB encrypts/decrypts data using key with `cipher` starting with optional `iv`

string mcrypt_enc_get_algorithms_name(resource td) *4.0.2*
Returns the name of the algorithm specified by the descriptor `td`

int mcrypt_enc_get_block_size(resource td) *4.0.2*
Returns the block size of the cipher specified by the descriptor `td`

int mcrypt_enc_get_iv_size(resource td) *4.0.2*
Returns the size of the IV in bytes of the algorithm specified by the descriptor `td`

int mcrypt_enc_get_key_size(resource td) *4.0.2*
Returns the maximum supported key size in bytes of the algorithm specified by the descriptor `td`

string mcrypt_enc_get_modes_name(resource td) *4.0.2*
Returns the name of the mode specified by the descriptor `td`

int mcrypt_enc_get_supported_key_sizes(resource td) *4.0.2*
Returns an array with the supported key sizes of the algorithm specified by the descriptor `td`

bool mcrypt_enc_is_block_algorithm(resource td) *4.0.2*
Returns `true` if the algorithm is a block algorithm

bool mcrypt_enc_is_block_algorithm_mode(resource td) *4.0.2*
Returns `true` if the mode is for use with block algorithms

bool mcrypt_enc_is_block_mode(resource td) *4.0.2*
Returns `true` if the mode outputs blocks of bytes

int mcrypt_enc_self_test(resource td) *4.0.2*
Runs the self test on the algorithm specified by the descriptor `td`

string mcrypt_encrypt(string cipher, string key, string data, string mode, string iv) *4.0.2*
OFB encrypts/decrypts data using key with `cipher` starting with `iv`

string mcrypt_generic(resource td, string data) *4.0.2*
Encrypts plain text with given parameters

bool mcrypt_generic_deinit(resource td) *4.1.0*
Initializes encryption specified by the descriptor `td`

bool mcrypt_generic_end(resource td) *4.0.2*
Terminates encryption specified by the descriptor `td`

int mcrypt_generic_init(resource td, string key, string iv) *4.0.2*
Initializes all buffers for the specific module

int mcrypt_get_block_size(int cipher) *3.0.8*
Gets the block size of `cipher`

int mcrypt_get_block_size(string cipher, string module) *3.0.8*
Gets the key size of `cipher`

string mcrypt_get_cipher_name(string cipher) *3.0.8*
Gets the key size of `cipher`

string mcrypt_get_cipher_name(int cipher) *3.0.8*
Gets the name of `cipher`

int mcrypt_get_iv_size(string cipher, string module) *4.0.2*
Get the IV size of `cipher` (usually the same as the block size)

int mcrypt_get_key_size(string cipher, string module) *3.0.8*
Gets the key size of `cipher`

int mcrypt_get_key_size(int cipher) *3.0.8*
Gets the key size of `cipher`

array mcrypt_list_algorithms([string lib_dir]) *4.0.2*
Lists all supported algorithms

array mcrypt_list_modes([string lib_dir]) *4.0.2*
Lists all supported modes

bool mcrypt_module_close(resource td) *4.0.2*
Frees the descriptor `td`

int mcrypt_module_get_algo_block_size(string algorithm[, string lib_dir]) *4.0.2*
Returns the block size of the algorithm

int mcrypt_module_get_algo_key_size(string algorithm[, string lib_dir]) *4.0.2*
Returns the maximum supported key size of the algorithm

int mcrypt_module_get_supported_key_sizes(string algorithm[, string lib_dir]) *4.0.2*
Returns an array with the supported key sizes of the algorithm

bool mcrypt_module_is_block_algorithm(string algorithm[, string lib_dir]) *4.0.2*
Returns `true` if the algorithm is a block algorithm

bool mcrypt_module_is_block_algorithm_mode(string mode[, string lib_dir]) *4.0.2*
Returns `true` if the mode is for use with block algorithms

bool mcrypt_module_is_block_mode(string mode[, string lib_dir]) *4.0.2*
Returns `true` if the mode outputs blocks of bytes

resource mcrypt_module_open(string cipher, string cipher_directory, string mode, string mode_directory) *4.0.2*
Opens the module of the algorithm and the mode to be used

bool mcrypt_module_self_test(string algorithm[, string lib_dir]) *4.0.2*
Does a self test of the specified module

string mcrypt_ofb(int cipher, string key, string data, int mode[, string iv]) *3.0.8*
OFB encrypts/decrypts data using key with `cipher` starting with optional `iv`

string md5(string str) *3.0*
Calculates the md5 hash of a string

string md5_file(string filename) *4.1.0*
Calculates the md5 hash of given filename

string mdecrypt_generic(resource td, string data) *4.0.2*
Decrypts plain text with given parameters

string metaphone(string text, int phones) *4.0*
Breaks English phrases down into their phonemes

bool method_exists(object object, string method) *4.0*
Checks if the class method exists

string mhash(int hash, string data[, string key]) *3.0.9*
Hashes data with `hash`

int mhash_count(void) *3.0.9*
Gets the number of available hashes

int mhash_get_block_size(int hash) *3.0.9*
Gets the block size of `hash`

string mhash_get_hash_name(int hash) *3.0.9*
Gets the name of `hash`

string mhash_keygen_s2k(int hash, string input_password, string salt, int bytes) *4.0.4*
Generates a key using hash functions

string microtime(void) *3.0*
Returns a string containing the current time in seconds and microseconds

PHP

string mime_content_type(string filename) *4.3.0*

Returns MIME Content-type for file

mixed min(mixed arg1[, mixed arg2[, mixed ...]]) *3.0*

Returns the lowest value in an array or a series of arguments

bool mkdir(string pathname[, int mode]) *3.0*

Creates a directory

int mktime(int hour, int min, int sec, int mon, int day, int year) *3.0*

Gets Unix timestamp for a date

string money_format(string format, float value) *4.3.0*

Converts monetary value(s) to string

bool move_uploaded_file(string path, string new_path) *4.0.3*

Moves a file if and only if it was created by an upload

resource msg_get_queue(long key[, long perms]) *4.3.0*

Attaches to a message queue

mixed msg_receive(resource queue, long desiredmsgtype, long &msgtype, long maxsize, mixed message [[, bool unserialize=true][, long flags=0[, long errorcode]]] *4.3.0*

Sends a message of type `msgtype` (must be greater than 0) to a message queue

bool msg_remove_queue(resource queue) *4.3.0*

Destroys the queue

bool msg_send(resource queue, long msgtype, mixed message [[, bool serialize=true][, bool blocking=true][, long errorcode]]) *4.3.0*

Sends a message of type `msgtype` (must be greater than 0) to a message queue

array msg_set_queue(resource queue, array data) *4.3.0*

Sets information for a message queue

array msg_stat_queue(resource queue) *4.3.0*

Returns information about a message queue

int mt_getrandmax(void) *3.0.6*

Returns the maximum value a random number from Mersenne Twister can have

int mt_rand([int min, int max]) *3.0.6*

Returns a random number from Mersenne Twister

void mt_srand([int seed]) *3.0.6*

Seeds Mersenne Twister random number generator

int mysql_affected_rows([int link_identifier]) *3.0*

Gets number of affected rows in previous MySQL operation

string mysql_character_set_name([int link_identifier]) *4.3.0*

Returns the default character set for the current connection

bool mysql_close([int link_identifier]) *3.0*

Closes a MySQL connection

resource mysql_connect([string hostname[:port][:/path/to/socket][, string username[, string password[, bool new[, int flags]]]]]) *3.0*
Opens a connection to a MySQL server

bool mysql_create_db(string database_name[, int link_identifier]) *3.0*
Creates a MySQL database

bool mysql_data_seek(int result, int row_number) *3.0*
Moves internal result pointer

resource mysql_db_query(string database_name, string query[, int link_identifier]) *3.0*
Sends an SQL query to a MySQL database

bool mysql_drop_db(string database_name[, int link_identifier]) *3.0*
Drops (deletes) a MySQL database

int mysql_errno([int link_identifier]) *3.0*
Returns the number of the error message from previous MySQL operation

string mysql_error([int link_identifier]) *3.0*
Returns the text of the error message from previous MySQL operation

string mysql_escape_string(string to_be_escaped) *4.0.3*
Escapes string for MySQL query

array mysql_fetch_array(int result[, int result_type]) *3.0*
Fetches a result row as an array (associative, numeric, or both)

array mysql_fetch_assoc(int result) *4.0.3*
Fetches a result row as an associative array

object mysql_fetch_field(int result[, int field_offset]) *3.0*
Gets column information from a result and returns it as an object

array mysql_fetch_lengths(int result) *3.0*
Gets maximum data size of each column in a result

object mysql_fetch_object(int result[, int result_type]) *3.0*
Fetches a result row as an object

array mysql_fetch_row(int result) *3.0*
Gets a result row as an enumerated array

string mysql_field_flags(int result, int field_offset) *3.0*
Gets the flags associated with the specified field in a result

int mysql_field_len(int result, int field_offset) *3.0*
Returns the length of the specified field

string mysql_field_name(int result, int field_index) *3.0*
Gets the name of the specified field in a result

bool mysql_field_seek(int result, int field_offset) *3.0*
Sets result pointer to a specific field offset

string mysql_field_table(int result, int field_offset) *3.0*
Gets name of the table the specified field is in

string mysql_field_type(int result, int field_offset) *3.0*
Gets the type of the specified field in a result

bool mysql_free_result(int result) *3.0*
Frees result memory

string mysql_get_client_info(void) *4.0.5*
Returns a string that represents the client library version

string mysql_get_host_info([int link_identifier]) *4.0.5*
Returns a string describing the type of connection in use, including the server host name

int mysql_get_proto_info([int link_identifier]) *4.0.5*
Returns the protocol version used by current connection

string mysql_get_server_info([int link_identifier]) *4.0.5*
Returns a string that represents the server version number

string mysql_info([int link_identifier]) *4.3.0*
Returns a string containing information about the most recent query

int mysql_insert_id([int link_identifier]) *3.0*
Gets the ID generated from the previous `INSERT` operation

resource mysql_list_dbs([int link_identifier]) *3.0*
Lists databases available on a MySQL server

resource mysql_list_fields(string database_name, string table_name[, int link_identifier]) *3.0*
Lists MySQL result fields

resource mysql_list_processes([int link_identifier]) *4.3.0*
Returns a result set describing the current server threads

resource mysql_list_tables(string database_name[, int link_identifier]) *3.0*
Lists tables in a MySQL database

int mysql_num_fields(int result) *3.0*
Gets number of fields in a result

int mysql_num_rows(int result) *3.0*
Gets number of rows in a result

resource mysql_pconnect([string hostname[:port][:/path/to/socket][, string username[, string password[, int flags]]]]) *3.0*
Opens a persistent connection to a MySQL server

bool mysql_ping([int link_identifier]) *4.3.0*
Pings a server connection or reconnects if there is no connection

resource mysql_query(string query[, int link_identifier][, int result_mode]) *3.0*
Sends an SQL query to a MySQL database

string mysql_real_escape_string(string to_be_escaped[, int link_identifier]) *4.3.0*
Escapes special characters in a string for use in a SQL statement, taking into account the current charset of the connection

mixed mysql_result(int result, int row[, mixed field]) *3.0*
Gets result data

bool mysql_select_db(string database_name[, int link_identifier]) *3.0*
Selects a MySQL database

string mysql_stat([int link_identifier]) *4.3.0*
Returns a string containing status information

int mysql_thread_id([int link_identifier]) *4.3.0*
Returns the thread ID of current connection

resource mysql_unbuffered_query(string query[, int link_identifier][, int result_mode]) *4.0.6*
Sends an SQL query to MySQL, without fetching and buffering the result rows

void natcasesort(array array_arg) *4.0*
Sorts an array using case-insensitive natural sort

void natsort(array array_arg) *4.0*
Sorts an array using natural sort

object new class_name() *3.0*
Language keyword that instantiates a class and returns the resulting object

mixed next(array array_arg) *3.0*
Moves array argument's internal pointer to the next element and returns it

string ngettext(string MSGID1, string MSGID2, int N) *4.1.0*
Plural version of `gettext()`

string nl2br(string str) *3.0*
Converts newlines to HTML line breaks

string nl_langinfo(int item) *4.1.0*
Queries language and locale information

string number_format(float number[, int num_decimal_places[, string dec_seperator, string thousands_seperator]]) *3.0*
Formats a number with grouped thousands

bool ob_clean(void) *4.1.0*
Cleans (deletes) the current output buffer

bool ob_end_clean(void) *4.0*
Cleans the output buffer and then deletes current output buffer

bool ob_end_flush(void) *4.0*
Flushes (sends) the output buffer and then deletes current output buffer

bool ob_flush(void) *4.1.0*
Flushes (sends) contents of the output buffer

string ob_get_contents(void) *4.0*
Returns the contents of the output buffer

string ob_get_length(void) *4.0.2*
Returns the length of the output buffer

int ob_get_level(void) *4.1.0*
Returns the nesting level of the output buffer

false|array ob_get_status([bool full_status]) *4.1.0*
Returns the status of the active or all output buffers

string ob_gzhandler(string str, int mode) *4.0.4*
Encodes `str` based on `accept-encoding` setting; designed to be called from `ob_start()`

string ob_iconv_handler(string contents, int status) *4.0.5*
Returns string in output buffer converted to the `iconv.output_encoding` character set

void ob_implicit_flush([int flag]) *4.0*
Turns implicit flush on/off; equivalent to calling `flush()` after every output call

false|array ob_list_handlers() *4.3.0*
Lists all output buffers in an array

bool ob_start([string|array user_function[, int chunk_size[, bool erase]]]) *4.0*
Turns on output buffering (specifying an optional output handler)

int ocibindbyname(int stmt, string name, mixed &var, int maxlength[, int type]) *3.0.4*
Binds a PHP variable to an Oracle placeholder by name

int ocicancel(int stmt) *3.0.8*
Prepares a new row of data for reading

string ocicloselob(object lob) *4.0.6*
Closes a large object descriptor

string ocicollappend(object collection, object object) *4.0.6*
Appends an object to the collection

string ocicollassign(object collection,object object) *4.0.6*
Assigns a collection from another existing collection

string ocicollassignelem(object collection, string ndx, string val) *4.0.6*
Assigns element `val` to collection at index `ndx`

string ocicollgetelem(object collection, string ndx) *4.0.6*
Retrieves the value at collection index `ndx`

string ocicollmax(object collection) *4.0.6*
Returns the maximum value of a collection; for a varray this is the maximum length of the array

string ocicollsize(object collection) *4.0.6*
Returns the size of a collection

string ocicolltrim(object collection, int num) *4.0.6*
Trims `num` elements from the end of a collection

int ocicolumnisnull(int stmt, int col) *3.0.4*
Tells whether a column is NULL

string ocicolumnname(int stmt, int col) *3.0.4*
Tells the name of a column

int ocicolumnprecision(int stmt, int col) *4.0*
Tells the precision of a column

int ocicolumnscale(int stmt, int col) *4.0*
Tells the scale of a column

int ocicolumnsize(int stmt, int col) *3.0.4*
Tells the maximum data size of a column

mixed ocicolumntype(int stmt, int col) *3.0.4*
Tells the data type of a column

mixed ocicolumntyperaw(int stmt, int col) *4.0*
Tells the raw Oracle data type of a column

string ocicommit(int conn) *3.0.7*
Commits the current context

int ocidefinebyname(int stmt, string name, mixed &var[, int type]) *3.0.7*
Defines a PHP variable to an Oracle column by name

array ocierror([int stmt|conn|global]) *3.0.7*
Returns the last error of `stmt|conn|global`; returns `false` if no error has occurred

int ociexecute(int stmt[, int mode]) *3.0.4*
Executes a parsed statement

int ocifetch(int stmt) *3.0.4*
Prepares a new row of data for reading

int ocifetchinto(int stmt, array &output[, int mode]) *3.0.4*
Fetches a row of result data into an array

int ocifetchstatement(int stmt, array &output[, int skip][, int maxrows][, int flags]) *3.0.8*
Fetches all rows of result data into an array

string ocifreecollection(object lob) *4.1.0*
Deletes collection object

string ocifreedesc(object lob) *4.0*
Deletes large object description

int ocifreestatement(int stmt) *3.0.5*
Frees all resources associated with a statement

void ociinternaldebug(int onoff) *3.0.4*
Toggles internal debugging output for the OCI extension

string ociloadlob(object lob) *4.0*
Loads a large object

int ocilogoff(int conn) *3.0.4*
Disconnects from database

int ocilogon(string user, string pass[, string db]) *3.0.4*
Connects to an Oracle database and logs on

string ocinewcollection(int connection, string tdo,[string schema]) *4.0.6*
Initializes a new collection

int ocinewcursor(int conn) *3.0.8*
Returns a new cursor (statement handle); use to bind ref cursors

string ocinewdescriptor(int connection[, int type]) *3.0.7*
Initializes a new empty LOB or FILE descriptor (LOB is default)

int ocinlogon(string user, string pass[, string db]) *3.0.8*
Creates a new connection to an Oracle database and logs on; returns a new session

int ocinumcols(int stmt) *3.0.4*
Returns the number of result columns in a statement

int ociparse(int conn, string query) *3.0.4*
Parses a query and returns a statement

int ociplogon(string user, string pass[, string db]) *3.0.8*
Connects to an Oracle database using a persistent connection and logs on

string ociresult(int stmt, mixed column) *3.0.4*
Returns a single column of result data

string ocirollback(int conn) *3.0.7*
Rolls back the current context

int ocirowcount(int stmt) *3.0.7*
Returns the row count of an OCI statement

string ocisavelob(object lob) *4.0*
Saves a large object

string ocisavelobfile(object lob) *4.0*
Saves a large object file

string ociserverversion(int conn) *3.0.4*
Returns a string containing server version information

int ocisetprefetch(int stmt, int prefetch_rows) *3.0.12*
Sets the number of rows to be prefetched for the statement

int ocistatementtype(int stmt) *3.0.5*
Returns the query type of an OCI statement

void ociwritelobtofile(object lob[, string filename][, int start][, int length]) *4.0*
Writes a large object into a file

int ociwritetemporarylob(int stmt, int loc, string var) *4.0.6*
Returns the row count of an OCI statement

int octdec(string octal_number) *3.0*
Returns the decimal equivalent of an octal string

mixed opendir(string path) *3.0*
Opens a directory and returns a `dir_handle`

bool openlog(string ident, int option, int facility) *3.0*
Opens connection to system logger

OR *4.0*

Language keyword that is similar to the || operator, except lower precedence

int ord(string character) *3.0*

Returns ASCII value of character

void overload(string class_entry) *4.1.0*

Enables property and method call overloading for a class

string pack(string format, mixed arg1[, mixed arg2[, mixed ...]]) *3.0*

Takes one or more arguments and packs them into a binary string according to the format argument

array parse_ini_file(string filename[, bool process_sections]) *4.0*

Parses configuration file

void parse_str(string encoded_string[, array result]) *3.0*

Parses GET/POST/Cookie data and sets global variables

array parse_url(string url) *3.0*

Parses a URL and returns its components

void passthru(string command[, int return_value]) *3.0*

Executes an external program and displays raw output

array pathinfo(string path) *4.0.3*

Returns information about a certain string

int pclose(resource fp) *3.0*

Closes a file pointer opened by `popen()`

int pcntl_alarm(int seconds) *4.3.0*

Sets an alarm clock for delivery of a signal

bool pcntl_exec(string path[, array args[, array envs]]) *4.1.0*

Executes specified program in current process space as defined by `exec()`

int pcntl_fork(void) *4.1.0*

Forks the currently running process following the same behavior as the Unix `fork()` system call

bool pcntl_signal(long signo, mixed handle) *4.1.0*

Assigns a system signal handler to a PHP function

int pcntl_waitpid(long pid, long status, long options) *4.1.0*

Waits on or returns the status of a forked child as defined by the `waitpid()` system call

int pcntl_wexitstatus(long status) *4.1.0*

Returns the status code of a child's exit

bool pcntl_wifexited(long status) *4.1.0*

Returns `true` if the child status code represents a successful exit

bool pcntl_wifsignaled(long status) *4.1.0*

Returns `true` if the child status code represents a process that was terminated due to a signal

bool pcntl_wifstopped(long status) *4.1.0*

Returns `true` if the child status code represents a stopped process (`WUNTRACED` must have been used with `waitpid()`)

int pcntl_wstopsig(long status) *4.1.0*

Returns the number of the signal that caused the specified process to stop

int pcntl_wtermsig(long status) *4.1.0*

Returns the number of the signal that terminated the specified process

void pdf_add_annotation(int pdfdoc, float xll, float yll, float xur, float xur, string title, string text) *3.0.12*

Sets annotation (deprecated; use `pdf_add_note()` instead)

int pdf_add_bookmark(int pdfdoc, string text[, int parent, int open]) *4.0.1*

Adds bookmark for current page

void pdf_add_launchlink(int pdfdoc, float llx, float lly, float urx, float ury, string filename) *4.0.5*

Adds link to web resource

void pdf_add_locallink(int pdfdoc, float llx, float lly, float urx, float ury, int page, string dest) *4.0.5*

Adds link to web resource

void pdf_add_note(int pdfdoc, float llx, float lly, float urx, float ury, string contents, string title, string icon, int open) *4.0.5*

Sets annotation

void pdf_add_pdflink(int pdfdoc, float llx, float lly, float urx, float ury, string filename, int page, string dest) *3.0.12*

Adds link to PDF document

void pdf_add_thumbnail(int pdf, int image); *4.0.5*

Adds an existing image as thumbnail for the current page.

void pdf_add_weblink(int pdfdoc, float llx, float lly, float urx, float ury, string url) *3.0.12*

Adds link to web resource

void pdf_arc(int pdfdoc, float x, float y, float radius, float start, float end) *3.0.6*

Draws an arc

void pdf_arcn(int pdf, float x, float y, float r, float alpha, float beta); *4.0.5*

Draws a clockwise circular arc from `alpha` to `beta` degrees

void pdf_attach_file(int pdf, float lly, float lly, float urx, float ury, string filename, string description, string author, string mimetype, string icon) *4.0.5*

Adds a file attachment annotation at the rectangle specified by the lower left and upper right corners

void pdf_begin_page(int pdfdoc, float width, float height) *3.0.6*

Starts page

int pdf_begin_pattern(int pdf, float width, float height, float xstep, float ystep, int painttype); *4.0.5*

Start a new pattern definition

int pdf_begin_template(int pdf, float width, float height); *4.0.5*

Start a new template definition

void pdf_circle(int pdfdoc, float x, float y, float radius) *3.0.6*
Draws a circle

void pdf_clip(int pdfdoc) *3.0.6*
Clips to current path

void pdf_close(int pdfdoc) *3.0.6*
Closes the PDF document

void pdf_close_image(int pdf, int pdfimage) *3.0.7*
Closes the PDF image

void pdf_close_pdi(int pdf, int doc); *4.0.5*
Closes all open page handles and closes the input PDF document

void pdf_close_pdi_page(int pdf, int page); *4.0.5*
Closes the page handle and frees all page-related resources

void pdf_closepath(int pdfdoc) *3.0.6*
Closes path

void pdf_closepath_fill_stroke(int pdfdoc) *3.0.6*
Closes, fills, and strokes current path

void pdf_closepath_stroke(int pdfdoc) *3.0.6*
Closes path and draws line along path

void pdf_concat(int pdf, float a, float b, float c, float d, float e, float f) *4.0.5*
Concatenates a matrix to the current transformation matrix for text and graphics

void pdf_continue_text(int pdfdoc, string text) *3.0.6*
Outputs text in next line

void pdf_curveto(int pdfdoc, float x1, float y1, float x2, float y2, float x3, float y3) *3.0.6*
Draws a curve

bool pdf_delete(int pdfdoc) *4.0.5*
Deletes the PDF object

void pdf_end_page(int pdfdoc) *3.0.6*
Ends page

void pdf_end_pattern(int pdf); *4.0.5*
Finishes the pattern definition

void pdf_end_template(int pdf); *4.0.5*
Finishes the template definition

void pdf_endpath(int pdfdoc) *3.0.6*
Ends current path

void pdf_fill(int pdfdoc) *3.0.6*
Fills current path

void pdf_fill_stroke(int pdfdoc) *3.0.6*
Fills and stroke current path

int pdf_findfont(int pdfdoc, string fontname, string encoding[, int embed]) *4.0.5*
Prepares the font `fontname` for later use with `pdf_setfont()`

int pdf_get_buffer(int pdfdoc) *4.0.5*
Fetches the full buffer containing the generated PDF data

int pdf_get_font(int pdfdoc) *4.0*
Gets the current font

string pdf_get_fontname(int pdfdoc) *4.0*
Gets the current font name

float pdf_get_fontsize(int pdfdoc) *4.0*
Gets the current font size

int pdf_get_image_height(int pdf, int pdfimage) *3.0.12*
Returns the height of an image

int pdf_get_image_width(int pdf, int pdfimage) *3.0.12*
Returns the width of an image

int pdf_get_majorversion() *4.1.0*
Returns the major version number of the PDFlib

int pdf_get_minorversion() *4.1.0*
Returns the minor version number of the PDFlib

string pdf_get_parameter(int pdfdoc, string key, mixed modifier) *4.0.1*
Gets arbitrary parameters

string pdf_get_pdi_parameter(int pdf, string key, int doc, int page, int index); *4.0.5*
Gets the contents of some PDI document parameter with string type

float pdf_get_pdi_value(int pdf, string key, int doc, int page, int index); *4.0.5*
Gets the contents of some PDI document parameter with numerical type

float pdf_get_value(int pdfdoc, string key, float modifier) *4.0.1*
Gets arbitrary value

void pdf_initgraphics(int pdf); *4.0.5*
Resets all implicit color and graphics state parameters to their defaults

void pdf_lineto(int pdfdoc, float x, float y) *3.0.6*
Draws a line

int pdf_makespotcolor(int pdf, string spotname); *4.0.5*
Makes a named spot color from the current color

void pdf_moveto(int pdfdoc, float x, float y) *3.0.6*
Sets current point

int pdf_new() *4.0.5*
Creates a new PDF object

int pdf_open([int filedesc]) *3.0.6*
Opens a new PDF document (deprecated; use `pdf_new()` and `pdf_open_file()` instead)

int pdf_open_ccitt(int pdf, string filename, int width, int height, int bitreverse, int k, int blackls1) *4.0.5*

Opens an image file with raw CCITT G3 or G4 compressed bitmap data

int pdf_open_file(int pdfdoc[, char filename]) *4.0.5*

Opens a new PDF document; if `filename` is NULL, document is created in memory

int pdf_open_gif(int pdf, string giffile) *3.0.7*

Opens a GIF file and returns an image for placement in a PDF document

int pdf_open_image(int pdf, string type, string source, string data, long length, int width, int height, int components, int bpc, string params) *4.0.5*

Opens an image of the given type and returns an image for placement in a PDF document

int pdf_open_image_file(int pdf, string type, string file, string stringparam, int intparam) *3 CVS Only*

Opens an image file of the given type and returns an image for placement in a PDF document

int pdf_open_jpeg(int pdf, string jpegfile) *3.0.7*

Opens a JPEG file and returns an image for placement in a PDF document

int pdf_open_memory_image(int pdf, int image) *3.0.10*

Takes an GD image and returns an image for placement in a PDF document

int pdf_open_pdi(int pdf, string filename, string stringparam, int intparam); *4.0.5*

Opens an existing PDF document and prepare it for later use

int pdf_open_pdi_page(int pdf, int doc, int page, string label); *4.0.5*

Prepares a page for later use with `pdf_place_image()`

int pdf_open_png(int pdf, string pngfile) *4.0*

Opens a PNG file and returns an image for placement in a PDF document

int pdf_open_tiff(int pdf, string tifffile) *4.0*

Opens a TIFF file and returns an image for placement in a PDF document

void pdf_place_image(int pdf, int pdfimage, float x, float y, float scale) *3.0.7*

Places image in the PDF document

void pdf_place_pdi_page(int pdf, int page, float x, float y, float sx, float sy) *4.0.6*

Places a PDF page with the lower left corner at `x`, `y` and scales it

void pdf_rect(int pdfdoc, float x, float y, float width, float height) *3.0.6*

Draws a rectangle

void pdf_restore(int pdfdoc) *3.0.6*

Restores formerly saved environment

void pdf_rotate(int pdfdoc, float angle) *3.0.6*

Sets rotation

void pdf_save(int pdfdoc) *3.0.6*

Saves current environment

void pdf_scale(int pdfdoc, float x_scale, float y_scale) *3.0.6*
Sets scaling

void pdf_set_border_color(int pdfdoc, float red, float green, float blue) *3.0.12*
Sets color of box surrounding annotations and links

void pdf_set_border_dash(int pdfdoc, float black, float white) *4.0.1*
Sets the border dash style of annotations and links

void pdf_set_border_style(int pdfdoc, string style, float width) *3.0.12*
Sets style of box surrounding annotations and links

void pdf_set_char_spacing(int pdfdoc, float space) *3.0.6*
Sets character spacing

void pdf_set_duration(int pdfdoc, float duration) *3.0.6*
Sets duration between pages

void pdf_set_font(int pdfdoc, string font, float size, string encoding[, int embed]) *3.0.6*
Selects the current font face, size, and encoding

void pdf_set_horiz_scaling(int pdfdoc, float scale) *3.0.6*
Sets horizontal scaling of text

bool pdf_set_info(int pdfdoc, string fieldname, string value) *4.0.1*
Fills an information field of the document

bool pdf_set_info_author(int pdfdoc, string author) *3.0.6*
Fills the author field of the document

bool pdf_set_info_creator(int pdfdoc, string creator) *3.0.6*
Fills the creator field of the document

bool pdf_set_info_keywords(int pdfdoc, string keywords) *3.0.6*
Fills the keywords field of the document

bool pdf_set_info_subject(int pdfdoc, string subject) *3.0.6*
Fills the subject field of the document

bool pdf_set_info_title(int pdfdoc, string title) *3.0.6*
Fills the title field of the document

void pdf_set_leading(int pdfdoc, float distance) *3.0.6*
Sets distance between text lines

void pdf_set_parameter(int pdfdoc, string key, string value) *4.0*
Sets arbitrary parameters

void pdf_set_text_pos(int pdfdoc, float x, float y) *3.0.6*
Sets the position of text for the next `pdf_show()` call

void pdf_set_text_rendering(int pdfdoc, int mode) *3.0.6*
Determines how text is rendered

void pdf_set_text_rise(int pdfdoc, float value) *3.0.6*
Sets the text rise

void pdf_set_transition(int pdfdoc, int transition) *3.0.6*
Sets transitions between pages

void pdf_set_value(int pdfdoc, string key, float value) *4.0.1*

Sets arbitrary value

void pdf_set_word_spacing(int pdfdoc, float space) *3.0.6*

Sets spacing between words

void pdf_setcolor(int pdf, string type, string colorspace, float c1[, float c2[, float c3[, float c4]]]); *4.0.5*

Sets the current color space and color.

void pdf_setdash(int pdfdoc, float black, float white) *3.0.6*

Sets dash pattern

void pdf_setflat(int pdfdoc, float value) *3.0.6*

Sets flatness

void pdf_setfont(int pdfdoc, int font, float fontsize) *4.0.5*

Sets the current font in the given `fontsize`

void pdf_setgray(int pdfdoc, float value) *3.0.6*

Sets drawing and filling color to gray value

void pdf_setgray_fill(int pdfdoc, float value) *3.0.6*

Sets filling color to gray value

void pdf_setgray_stroke(int pdfdoc, float value) *3.0.6*

Sets drawing color to gray value

void pdf_setlinecap(int pdfdoc, int value) *3.0.6*

Sets line cap parameter

void pdf_setlinejoin(int pdfdoc, int value) *3.0.6*

Sets line join parameter

void pdf_setlinewidth(int pdfdoc, float width) *3.0.6*

Sets line width

void pdf_setmatrix(int pdf, float a, float b, float c, float d, float e, float f) *4.0.5*

Sets the current transformation matrix

void pdf_setmiterlimit(int pdfdoc, float value) *3.0.6*

Sets miter limit

void pdf_setpolydash(int pdfdoc, float darray) *4.0.5*

Sets more complicated dash pattern

void pdf_setrgbcolor(int pdfdoc, float red, float green, float blue) *3.0.6*

Sets drawing and filling color to RGB color value

void pdf_setrgbcolor_fill(int pdfdoc, float red, float green, float blue) *3.0.6*

Sets filling color to RGB color value

void pdf_setrgbcolor_stroke(int pdfdoc, float red, float green, float blue) *3.0.6*

Sets drawing color to RGB color value

void pdf_show(int pdfdoc, string text) *3.0.6*

Outputs text at current position

int pdf_show_boxed(int pdfdoc, string text, float x_koor, float y_koor, float width, float height, string mode[, string feature]) *4.0*
Outputs text formatted in a boxed

void pdf_show_xy(int pdfdoc, string text, float x_koor, float y_koor) *3.0.6*
Outputs text at position

void pdf_skew(int pdfdoc, float xangle, float yangle) *4.0*
Skews the coordinate system

float pdf_stringwidth(int pdfdoc, string text[, int font, float size]) *3.0.6*
Returns width of text in current font

void pdf_stroke(int pdfdoc) *3.0.6*
Draws line along path

void pdf_translate(int pdfdoc, float x, float y) *3.0.6*
Sets origin of coordinate system

int pfsockopen(string hostname, int port[, int errno[, string errstr[, float timeout]]]) *3.0.7*
Opens persistent Internet or Unix domain socket connection

int pg_affected_rows(resource result) *4.1.0*
Returns the number of affected tuples

bool pg_cancel_query(resource connection) *4.1.0*
Cancels request

string pg_client_encoding([resource connection]) *3 CVS Only*
Gets the current client encoding

bool pg_close([resource connection]) *3.0*
Closes a PostgreSQL connection

resource pg_connect([string connection_string] | [string host, string port[, string options[, string tty,]] string database) *3.0*
Opens a PostgreSQL connection

bool pg_connection_busy(resource connection) *4.1.0*
Gets whether connection is busy or not

bool pg_connection_reset(resource connection) *4.1.0*
Resets connection (reconnects)

int pg_connection_status(resource connnection) *4.1.0*
Gets connection status

array pg_convert(resource db, string table, array values[, int options]) *4.3.0*
Checks and converts values for PostgreSQL SQL statement

bool pg_copy_from(int connection, string table_name, array rows[, string delimiter[, string null_as]]) *4.1.0*
Copies table from array

array pg_copy_to(int connection, string table_name[, string delimiter[, string null_as]]) *4.1.0*
Copies table to array

string pg_dbname([resource connection]) *3.0*
Gets the database name

bool pg_delete(resource db, string table, array ids[, int options]) *4.3.0*
Deletes records with values in `ids`

bool pg_end_copy([resource connection]) *4.0.3*
Completes the a copy command by syncing with the backend

string pg_escape_bytea(string data) *4.1.0*
Escapes a string for the bytea type

string pg_escape_string(string data) *4.1.0*
Escapes a string for text/char type

array pg_fetch_all(resource result) *4.3.0*
Fetches all rows into array

array pg_fetch_array(resource result[, int row[, int result_type]]) *3.0.1*
Fetches a row as an array

object pg_fetch_object(resource result[, int row[, int result_type]]) *3.0.1*
Fetches a row as an object

mixed pg_fetch_result(resource result, [int row_number,] mixed field_name) *4.1.0*
Returns values from a result identifier

array pg_fetch_row(resource result[, int row[, int result_type]]) *3.0.1*
Gets a row as an enumerated array

int pg_field_is_null(resource result, [int row,] mixed field_name_or_number) *4.1.0*
Tests if a field is NULL

string pg_field_name(resource result, int field_number) *4.1.0*
Returns the name of the field

int pg_field_num(resource result, string field_name) *4.1.0*
Returns the field number of the named field

int pg_field_prtlen(resource result, [int row,] mixed field_name_or_number) *4.1.0*
Returns the printed length

int pg_field_size(resource result, int field_number) *4.1.0*
Returns the internal size of the field

string pg_field_type(resource result, int field_number) *4.1.0*
Returns the type name for the given field

bool pg_free_result(resource result) *4.1.0*
Frees result memory

resource pg_get_result([resource connection]) *4.1.0*
Gets asynchronous query result

string pg_host([resource connection]) *3.0*
Returns the hostname associated with the connection

bool pg_insert(resource db, string table, array values[, int options]) *4.3.0*
Inserts an array of values into table

string pg_last_error([resource connection]) *4.1.0*
Gets the error message string

string pg_last_notice(resource connection) *4.0.6*
Returns the last notice set by the backend

string pg_last_oid(resource result) *4.1.0*
Returns the last object identifier

bool pg_lo_close(resource large_object) *4.1.0*
Closes a large object

int pg_lo_create([resource connection]) *4.1.0*
Creates a large object

bool pg_lo_export([resource connection,] int objoid, string filename) *4.1.0*
Exports a large object directly to filesystem

int pg_lo_import([resource connection,] string filename) *4.1.0*
Imports a large object directly from filesystem

resource pg_lo_open([resource connection,] int large_object_oid, string mode) *4.1.0*
Opens a large object and returns the file descriptor

string pg_lo_read(resource large_object[, int len]) *4.1.0*
Reads a large object

int pg_lo_read_all(resource large_object) *4.1.0*
Reads a large object and sends it straight to the browser

bool pg_lo_seek(resource large_object, int offset[, int whence]) *4.1.0*
Seeks position of large object

int pg_lo_tell(resource large_object) *4.1.0*
Returns current position of large object

bool pg_lo_unlink([resource connection,] string large_object_oid) *4.1.0*
Deletes a large object

int pg_lo_write(resource large_object, string buf[, int len]) *4.1.0*
Writes a large object

array pg_metadata(resource db, string table) *4.3.0*
Gets metadata

int pg_num_fields(resource result) *4.1.0*
Returns the number of fields in the result

int pg_num_rows(resource result) *4.1.0*
Returns the number of rows in the result

string pg_options([resource connection]) *3.0*
Gets the options associated with the connection

**resource pg_pconnect([string connection_string] | [string host,
string port[, string options[, string tty,]] string database)** *3.0*
Opens a persistent PostgreSQL connection

int pg_port([resource connection]) *3.0*
Returns the port number associated with the connection

bool pg_put_line([resource connection,] string query) *4.0.3*
Sends null-terminated string to backend server

resource pg_query([resource connection,] string query) *4.1.0*
Executes a query

string pg_result_error(resource result) *4.1.0*
Gets error message associated with result

int pg_result_status(resource result[, long result_type]) *4.1.0*
Gets status of query result

array pg_select(resource db, string table, array ids[, int options]) *4.3.0*
Selects records that have values in `ids`

bool pg_send_query(resource connection, string qeury) *4.1.0*
Sends asynchronous query

int pg_set_client_encoding([resource connection,] string encoding) *3 CVS Only*
Sets client encoding

bool pg_trace(string filename[, string mode[, resource connection]]) *4.0.1*
Enables tracing a PostgreSQL connection

string pg_tty([resource connection]) *3.0*
Returns the tty name associated with the connection

bool pg_untrace([resource connection]) *4.0.1*
Disables tracing of a PostgreSQL connection

bool pg_update(resource db, string table, array fields, array ids[, int options]) *4.3.0*
Updates table using values in `fields` and `ids`

string php_sapi_name(void) *4.0.1*
Returns the current SAPI module name

string php_uname(void) *4.0.2*
Returns information about the system PHP was built on

void phpcredits([int flag]) *4.0*
Prints the list of people who have contributed to the PHP project

void phpinfo([int what]) *3.0*
Outputs a page of useful information about PHP and the current request

string phpversion([string extension]) *3.0*
Returns the current PHP version

float pi(void) *3.0*
Returns an approximation of pi

void png2wbmp (string f_org, string f_dest, int d_height, int d_width, int threshold) *4.0.5*
Converts PNG image to WBMP image

resource popen(string command, string mode) *3.0*
Executes a command and opens either a read or a write pipe to it

string posix_ctermid(void) *3.0.13*
Generates terminal pathname (POSIX.1, 4.7.1)

int posix_get_last_error(void) *4.1.0*

Retrieves the error number set by the last Posix function that failed.

string posix_getcwd(void) *3.0.13*

Gets working directory pathname (POSIX.1, 5.2.2)

int posix_getegid(void) *3.0.10*

Gets the current effective group ID (POSIX.1, 4.2.1)

int posix_geteuid(void) *3.0.10*

Gets the current effective user ID (POSIX.1, 4.2.1)

int posix_getgid(void) *3.0.10*

Gets the current group ID (POSIX.1, 4.2.1)

array posix_getgrgid(long gid) *3.0.13*

Gets information about a group by group ID (POSIX.1, 9.2.1)

array posix_getgrnam(string groupname) *3.0.13*

Gets information about a group by group name (POSIX.1, 9.2.1)

array posix_getgroups(void) *3.0.10*

Gets supplementary group IDs (POSIX.1, 4.2.3)

string posix_getlogin(void) *3.0.13*

Gets user name (POSIX.1, 4.2.4)

int posix_getpgid(void) *3.0.10*

Gets the process group ID of the specified process (not a POSIX function, but a SVR4ism, so we compile conditionally)

int posix_getpgrp(void) *3.0.10*

Gets current process group ID (POSIX.1, 4.3.1)

int posix_getpid(void) *3.0.10*

Gets the current process ID (POSIX.1, 4.1.1)

int posix_getppid(void) *3.0.10*

Gets the parent process ID (POSIX.1, 4.1.1)

array posix_getpwnam(string groupname) *3.0.13*

Gets information about a user by username (POSIX.1, 9.2.2)

array posix_getpwuid(long uid) *3.0.13*

Gets information about a user by user ID (POSIX.1, 9.2.2)

int posix_getrlimit(void) *3.0.10*

Gets system resource consumption limits (not a POSIX function, but a BSDism and a SVR4ism, so we compile conditionally)

int posix_getsid(void) *3.0.10*

Gets process group ID of session leader (not a POSIX function, but a SVR4ism, so we compile conditionally)

int posix_getuid(void) *3.0.10*

Gets the current user ID (POSIX.1, 4.2.1)

bool posix_isatty(int fd) *3.0.13*

Determine if file descriptor is a tty (POSIX.1, 4.7.1)

bool posix_kill(int pid, int sig) *3.0.13*
Sends a signal to a process (POSIX.1, 3.3.2)

bool posix_mkfifo(string pathname, int mode) *3.0.13*
Makes a FIFO special file (POSIX.1, 5.4.2)

bool posix_setegid(long uid) *4.0.2*
Sets effective group ID

bool posix_seteuid(long uid) *4.0.2*
Sets effective user ID

bool posix_setgid(int uid) *3.0.13*
Sets group ID (POSIX.1, 4.2.2)

bool posix_setpgid(int pid, int pgid) *3.0.13*
Sets process group ID for job control (POSIX.1, 4.3.3)

int posix_setsid(void) *3.0.13*
Creates session and sets process group ID (POSIX.1, 4.3.2)

bool posix_setuid(long uid) *3.0.13*
Sets user ID (POSIX.1, 4.2.2)

string posix_strerror(int errno) *4.1.0*
Retrieves the system error message associated with the given `errno`

array posix_times(void) *3.0.13*
Gets process times (POSIX.1, 4.5.2)

string posix_ttyname(int fd) *3.0.13*
Determines terminal device name (POSIX.1, 4.7.2)

array posix_uname(void) *3.0.10*
Gets system name (POSIX.1, 4.4.1)

number pow(number base, number exponent) *3.0*
Returns base raised to the power of `exponent` (as an integer result when possible)

array preg_grep(string regex, array input) *4.0*
Searches array and returns entries that match regex

int preg_match(string pattern, string subject[, array subpatterns[, int flags]]) *3.0.9*
Performs a Perl-style regular expression match

int preg_match_all(string pattern, string subject, array subpatterns[, int flags]) *3.0.9*
Performs a Perl-style global regular expression match

string preg_quote(string str, string delim_char) *3.0.9*
Quotes regular expression characters plus an optional character

string preg_replace(mixed regex, mixed replace, mixed subject[, int limit]) *3.0.9*
Performs Perl-style regular expression replacement

string preg_replace_callback(mixed regex, mixed callback, mixed subject[, int limit]) *4.0.5*
Performs Perl-style regular expression replacement using replacement callback

array preg_split(string pattern, string subject[, int limit[, int flags]]) *3.0.9*
Splits string into an array using a Perl-style regular expression as a delimiter

mixed prev(array array_arg) *3.0*
Moves an array's internal pointer to the previous element and returns it

bool print(string arg) *3.0*
Outputs a string

bool print_r(mixed var[, bool return]) *4.0*
Prints out or returns information about the specified variable

int printf(string format[, mixed arg1[, mixed ...]]) *3.0*
Outputs a formatted string

int proc_close(resource process) *4.3.0*
Closes a process opened by `proc_open()`

resource proc_open(string command, array descriptorspec, array &pipes) *4.3.0*
Run a process with more control over its file descriptors

int pspell_add_to_personal(int pspell, string word) *4.0.2*
Adds a word to a personal list

int pspell_add_to_session(int pspell, string word) *4.0.2*
Adds a word to the current session

int pspell_check(int pspell, string word) *4.0.2*
Returns `true` if `word` is valid

int pspell_clear_session(int pspell) *4.0.2*
Clears the current session

int pspell_config_create(string language[, string spelling[, string jargon[, string encoding]]]) *4.0.2*
Creates a new configuration to be used later to create a manager

int pspell_config_ignore(int conf, int ignore) *4.0.2*
Ignore words with `ignore` characters or less

int pspell_config_mode(int conf, long mode) *4.0.2*
Selects mode for configuration (`PSPELL_FAST`, `PSPELL_NORMAL`, or `PSPELL_BAD_SPELLERS`)

int pspell_config_personal(int conf, string personal) *4.0.2*
Uses a personal dictionary for this configuration

int pspell_config_repl(int conf, string repl) *4.0.2*
Uses a personal dictionary with replacement pairs for this configuration

int pspell_config_runtogether(int conf, bool runtogether) *4.0.2*
Considers run-together words as valid components

int pspell_config_save_repl(int conf, bool save) *4.0.2*
Saves replacement pairs when a personal list is saved for this configuration

int pspell_new(string language[, string spelling[, string jargon[, string encoding[, int mode]]]]) *4.0.2*
Loads a dictionary

int pspell_new_config(int config) *4.0.2*
Loads a dictionary based on the given configuration

int pspell_new_personal(string personal, string language[, string spelling[, string jargon[, string encoding[, int mode]]]]) *4.0.2*
Loads a dictionary with a personal word list

int pspell_save_wordlist(int pspell) *4.0.2*
Saves the current (personal) wordiest

int pspell_store_replacement(int pspell, string misspell, string correct) *4.0.2*
Notifies the dictionary of a user-selected replacement

array pspell_suggest(int pspell, string word) *4.0.2*
Returns array of suggestions

bool putenv(string setting) *3.0*
Sets the value of an environment variable

string quoted_printable_decode(string str) *3.0.6*
Converts a quoted-printable string to an 8 bit string

string quotemeta(string str) *3.0*
Quotes meta characters

float rad2deg(float number) *3.0.4*
Converts the radian number to the equivalent number in degrees

int rand([int min, int max]) *3.0*
Returns a random number

array range(mixed low, mixed high) *3.0.8*
Creates an array containing the range of integers or characters from low to high (inclusive)

string rawurldecode(string str) *3.0*
Decodes a URL-encoded string

string rawurlencode(string str) *3.0*
URL-encodes a string

string readdir([resource dir_handle]) *3.0*
Reads directory entry from `dir_handle`

int readfile(string filename[, int use_include_path]) *3.0*
Outputs a file or a URL

int readgzfile(string filename[, int use_include_path]) *3.0*
Outputs a *.gz* file

string readlink(string filename) *3.0*
Returns the target of a symbolic link

string realpath(string path) *4.0*
Returns the resolved path

bool recode_file(string request, resource input, resource output) *3.0.13*
Recodes file input into file output according to `request`

PHP

string recode_string(string request, string str) *3.0.13*
Recodes string `str` according to `request` string

void register_shutdown_function(string function_name) *3.0.4*
Registers a user-level function to be called on request termination

bool register_tick_function(string function_name[, mixed arg[, mixed ...]]) *4.0.3*
Registers a tick callback function

bool rename(string old_name, string new_name) *3.0*
Renames a file

bool require filename *3.0*
Includes and evaluates the given file, with a fatal error on failure

bool require_once filename *4.0*
Includes and evaluates the given file if not already included, with a fatal error on failure

mixed reset(array array_arg) *3.0*
Sets an array's internal pointer to the first element and returns it

void restore_error_handler(void) *4.0.1*
Restores the previously defined error handler function

return(mixed result) *3.0*
Language keyword that returns its argument from a function or from current execution scope

bool rewind(resource fp) *3.0*
Rewinds the position of a file pointer

void rewinddir([resource dir_handle]) *3.0*
Rewinds `dir_handle` back to the start

bool rmdir(string dirname) *3.0*
Removes a directory

float round(float number[, int precision]) *3.0*
Returns the number rounded to specified precision

bool rsort(array array_arg[, int sort_flags]) *3.0*
Sorts an array in reverse order

string rtrim(string str[, string character_mask]) *3.0*
Removes trailing whitespace

int sem_acquire(int id) *3.0.6*
Acquires the semaphore with the given ID, blocking if necessary

int sem_get(int key[, int max_acquire[, int perm[, int auto_release]]) *3.0.6*
Returns an ID for the semaphore with the given key and allows `max_acquire` (default 1) processes to acquire it simultaneously

int sem_release(int id) *3.0.6*
Releases the semaphore with the given ID

int sem_remove(int id) *4.1.0*
Removes semaphore from Unix systems

string serialize(mixed variable) *3.0.5*

Returns a string representation of `variable` (that can later be unserialized)

int session_cache_expire([int new_cache_expire]) *4.1.0*

Returns the current `cache_expire`; if `new_cache_expire` is given, the current `cache_expire` is replaced with `new_cache_expire`

string session_cache_limiter([string new_cache_limiter]) *4.0.3*

Returns the current `cache_limiter`; if `new_cache_limiter` is given, the current `cache_limiter` is replaced with `new_cache_limiter`

bool session_decode(string data) *4.0*

Deserializes data and reinitializes the variables

bool session_destroy(void) *4.0*

Destroys the current session and all data associated with it

string session_encode(void) *4.0*

Serializes the current setup and returns the serialized representation

array session_get_cookie_params(void) *4.0*

Returns the session cookie parameters

string session_id([string newid]) *4.0*

Returns the current session ID; if `newid` is given, the session ID is replaced with `newid`

bool session_is_registered(string varname) *4.0*

Checks if a variable is registered in the session

string session_module_name([string newname]) *4.0*

Returns the current module name used for accessing session data; if `newname` is given, the module name is replaced with `newname`

string session_name([string newname]) *4.0*

Returns the current session name; if `newname` is given, the session name is replaced with `newname`

bool session_register(mixed var_names[, mixed ...]) *4.0*

Adds variable name(s) to the list of variables that are frozen at the session end

string session_save_path([string newname]) *4.0*

Returns the current save path; if `newname` is given, the save path is replaced with `newname`

void session_set_cookie_params(int lifetime[, string path[, string domain[, bool secure]]]) *4.0*

Sets session cookie parameters

void session_set_save_handler(string open, string close, string read, string write, string destroy, string gc) *4.0*

Sets user-level functions

bool session_start(void) *4.0*

Begins a session by reinitializing frozen variables, registers browsers, etc.

bool session_unregister(string varname) *4.0*

Removes `varname` from the list of variables that are frozen at the session end

void session_unset(void) *4.0*
Unsets all registered variables

void session_write_close(void) *4.0.4*
Writes session data and ends session

string set_error_handler(string error_handler) *4.0.1*
Sets a user-defined error handler function; returns the previously defined error handler, or `false` on error

int set_file_buffer(resource fp, int buffer) *3.0.8*
Sets file write buffer

bool set_magic_quotes_runtime(int new_setting) *3.0.6*
Sets the current active configuration setting of `magic_quotes_runtime` and return previous setting

bool set_socket_blocking(resource socket, int mode) *3.0*
Sets blocking/non-blocking mode on a socket

bool set_time_limit(int seconds) *3.0*
Sets the maximum time a script can run

bool setcookie(string name[, string value[, int expires[, string path[, string domain[, bool secure]]]]]) *3.0*
Sends a cookie

string setlocale(mixed category, string locale) *3.0*
Sets locale information

bool settype(mixed var, string type) *3.0*
Sets the type of the variable

string sha1(string str) *4.3.0*
Calculates the sha1 hash of a string

string sha1_file(string filename) *4.3.0*
Calculates the sha1 hash of given filename

string shell_exec(string cmd) *4.0*
Executes command via shell and returns complete output as string

int shm_attach(int key[, int memsize[, int perm]]) *3.0.6*
Creates or opens a shared memory segment

int shm_detach(int shm_identifier) *3.0.6*
Disconnects from shared memory segment

mixed shm_get_var(int id, int variable_key) *3.0.6*
Returns a variable from shared memory

int shm_put_var(int shm_identifier, int variable_key, mixed variable) *3.0.6*
Inserts or updates a variable in shared memory

int shm_remove(int shm_identifier) *3.0.6*
Removes shared memory from Unix systems

int shm_remove_var(int id, int variable_key) *3.0.6*
Removes variable from shared memory

void shmop_close (int shmid) *4.0.4*
Closes a shared memory segment

bool shmop_delete (int shmid) *4.0.4*
Marks segment for deletion

int shmop_open (int key, int flags, int mode, int size) *4.0.4*
Gets and attaches a shared memory segment

string shmop_read (int shmid, int start, int count) *4.0.4*
Reads from a shared memory segment

int shmop_size (int shmid) *4.0.4*
Returns the shared memory size

int shmop_write (int shmid, string data, int offset) *4.0.4*
Writes to a shared memory segment

bool shuffle(array array_arg) *3.0.8*
Randomly shuffles the contents of an array

int similar_text(string str1, string str2[, float percent]) *3.0.7*
Calculates the similarity between two strings

float sin(float number) *3.0*
Returns the sine of the number in radians

float sinh(float number) *4.1.0*
Returns the hyperbolic sine of the number

void sleep(int seconds) *3.0*
Delays for a given number of seconds

bool snmp_get_quick_print(void) *3.0.8*
Returns the current status of `quick_print`

void snmp_set_quick_print(int quick_print) *3.0.8*
Sets the value of `quick_print`

string snmpget(string host, string community, string object_id[, int timeout[, int retries]]) *3.0*
Fetches a SNMP object

array snmprealwalk(string host, string community, string object_id[, int timeout[, int retries]]) *3.0.8*
Returns all objects, including their respective object IDs, within the specified one

int snmpset(string host, string community, string object_id, string type, mixed value[, int timeout[, int retries]]) *3.0.12*
Sets the value of a SNMP object

array snmpwalk(string host, string community, string object_id[, int timeout[, int retries]]) *3.0*
Returns all objects under the specified object ID

resource socket_accept(resource socket) *4.1.0*
Accepts a connection on the listening socket

bool socket_bind(resource socket, string addr[, int port]) *4.1.0*
Binds an open socket to a listening port; `port` is only specified in AF_INET family

PHP

void socket_clear_error([resource socket]) *4.1.0*

Clears the error on the socket or the last error code

void socket_close(resource socket) *4.1.0*

Closes a file descriptor

bool socket_connect(resource socket, string addr[, int port]) *4.1.0*

Opens a connection to `addr:port` on the socket specified by `socket`

resource socket_create(int domain, int type, int protocol) *4.1.0*

Creates an endpoint for communication in the domain specified by `domain`, of type specified by `type`

resource socket_create_listen(int port[, int backlog]) *4.1.0*

Opens a socket on `port` to accept connections

bool socket_create_pair(int domain, int type, int protocol, array &fd) *4.1.0*

Creates a pair of indistinguishable sockets and stores them in `fd`

mixed socket_get_option(resource socket, int level, int optname) *4.3.0*

Gets socket options for the socket

array socket_get_status(resource socket_descriptor) *4.0*

Returns an array describing socket status

bool socket_getpeername(resource socket, string &addr[, int &port]) *4.1.0*

Queries the remote side of the given socket, which may result in either a host/port or a Unix filesystem path, depending on its type

bool socket_getsockname(resource socket, string &addr[, int &port]) *4.1.0*

Queries the remote side of the given socket, which may result in either a host/port or a Unix filesystem path, depending on its type

bool socket_iovec_add(resource iovec, int iov_len) *4.1.0*

Adds a new vector to the scatter/gather array

resource socket_iovec_alloc(int num_vectors[, int ...]) *4.1.0*

Builds a `struct iovec` for use with `sendmsg()`, `recvmsg()`, `writev()`, and `readv()`

bool socket_iovec_delete(resource iovec, int iov_pos) *4.1.0*

Deletes a vector from an array of vectors

string socket_iovec_fetch(resource iovec, int iovec_position) *4.1.0*

Returns the data that is stored in the iovec specified by `iovec_id[iovec_position]`

bool socket_iovec_free(resource iovec) *4.1.0*

Frees the iovec specified by `iovec_id`

bool socket_iovec_set(resource iovec, int iovec_position, string new_val) *4.1.0*

Sets the data held in `iovec_id[iovec_position]` to `new_val`

int socket_last_error([resource socket]) *4.1.0*

Returns the last socket error (either the last used or the provided socket resource)

bool socket_listen(resource socket[, int backlog]) *4.1.0*
Listens for a connection on a socket; `backlog` sets the maximum number of connections allowed to be waiting

string socket_read(resource socket, int length[, int type]) *4.1.0*
Reads a maximum of length bytes from socket

bool socket_readv(resource socket, resource iovec_id) *4.1.0*
Reads from an file descriptor, using the scatter-gather array defined by `iovec_id`

int socket_recv(resource socket, string &buf, int len, int flags) *4.1.0*
Receives data from a connected socket

int socket_recvfrom(resource socket, string &buf, int len, int flags, string &name[, int &port]) *4.1.0*
Receives data from a socket, connected or not

bool socket_recvmsg(resource socket, resource iovec, array &control, int &controllen, int &flags, string &addr[, int &port]) *4.1.0*
Receives messages on a socket, whether connection-oriented or not

int socket_select(array &read_fds, array &write_fds, &array except_fds, int tv_sec[, int tv_usec]) *4.1.0*
Runs the `select()` system call on the arrays of sockets with timeouts specified by `tv_sec` and `tv_usec`

int socket_send(resource socket, string buf, int len, int flags) *4.1.0*
Sends data to a connected socket

bool socket_sendmsg(resource socket, resource iovec, int flags, string addr[, int port]) *4.1.0*
Sends a message to a socket, regardless of whether it is connection-oriented or not

int socket_sendto(resource socket, string buf, int len, int flags, string addr[, int port]) *4.1.0*
Sends a message to a socket, whether it is connected or not

bool socket_set_block(resource socket) *4.1.0*
Sets blocking mode on a socket resource

bool socket_set_blocking(resource socket, int mode) *4.0*
Set blocking/non-blocking mode on a socket

bool socket_set_nonblock(resource socket) *4.1.0*
Sets non-blocking mode on a socket resource

bool socket_set_option(resource socket, int level, int optname, int|array optval) *4.3.0*
Sets socket options for the socket

bool socket_set_timeout(int socket_descriptor, int seconds, int microseconds) *4.0*
Sets timeout on a socket read to `seconds` plus `microseonds`

bool socket_shutdown(resource socket[, int how]) *4.1.0*
Shuts down a socket for receiving, sending, or both

string socket_strerror(int errno) *4.1.0*
Returns a string describing an error

int socket_write(resource socket, string buf[, int length]) *4.1.0*
Writes the buffer to the socket resource

bool socket_writev(resource socket, resource iovec_id) *4.1.0*
Writes to a file descriptor using the scatter-gather array defined by `iovec_id`

bool sort(array array_arg[, int sort_flags]) *3.0*
Sorts an array

string soundex(string str) *3.0*
Calculates the soundex key of a string

array split(string pattern, string string[, int limit]) *3.0*
Splits a string into an array with a regular expression

array spliti(string pattern, string string[, int limit]) *4.0.1*
Splits a string into an array with a case-insensitive regular expression

string sprintf(string format[, mixed arg1[, mixed ...]]) *3.0*
Returns a formatted string

string sql_regcase(string string) *3.0*
Makes a regular expression for a case-insensitive match

float sqrt(float number) *3.0*
Returns the square root of the number

void srand([int seed]) *3.0*
Seeds random number generator

mixed sscanf(string str, string format[, string ...]) *4.0.1*
Implements an ANSI C compatible `sscanf()`

array stat(string filename) *3.0*
Gives information about a file

static var1[,var2[, ...]] *3.0*
Language keyword used inside functions to mark a variable as static

string str_pad(string input, int pad_length[, string pad_string[, int pad_type]]) *4.0.1*
Returns input string padded on the left or right to specified length with `pad_string`

string str_repeat(string input, int mult) *4.0*
Returns the input string repeated `mult` times

mixed str_replace(mixed search, mixed replace, mixed subject[, bool boyer]) *3.0.6*
Replaces all occurrences of `search` in `subject` with `replace`

string str_rot13(string str) *4.1.0*
Performs the rot13 transform on a string

int strcasecmp(string str1, string str2) *3.0.2*
Performs a binary safe case-insensitive string comparison

string strchr(string haystack, string needle) *3.0*
An alias for `strstr()`

int strcmp(string str1, string str2) *3.0*
Performs a binary safe string comparison

int strcoll(string str1, string str2) *4.0.5*

Compares two strings using the current locale

int strcspn(string str, string mask) *3.0.3*

Finds length of initial segment consisting entirely of characters not found in `mask`

resource stream_context_create([array options]) *4.3.0*

Creates a file context and optionally sets parameters

array stream_context_get_options(resource context|resource stream) *4.3.0*

Retrieves options for a stream/wrapper/context

bool stream_context_set_option(resource context|resource stream, string wrappername, string optionname, mixed value) *4.3.0*

Sets an option for a wrapper

bool stream_context_set_params(resource context|resource stream, array options) *4.3.0*

Sets parameters for a file context

string strftime(string format[, int timestamp]) *3.0*

Formats a local time/date according to locale settings

string strip_tags(string str[, string allowable_tags]) *3.0.8*

Strips HTML and PHP tags from a string

string stripcslashes(string str) *4.0*

Strips backslashes from a string; uses C-style conventions

string stripslashes(string str) *3.0*

Strips backslashes from a string

string stristr(string haystack, string needle) *3.0.6*

Finds first occurrence of a string within another (case-insensitive)

int strlen(string str) *3.0*

Gets string length

int strnatcasecmp(string s1, string s2) *4.0*

Returns the result of case-insensitive string comparison using natural algorithm

int strnatcmp(string s1, string s2) *4.0*

Returns the result of string comparison using natural algorithm

int strncasecmp(string str1, string str2, int len) *4.0.2*

Performs a binary safe string comparison of `len` characters

int strncmp(string str1, string str2, int len) *4.0*

Performs a binary safe string comparison of `len` characters

int strpos(string haystack, string needle[, int offset]) *3.0*

Finds position of first occurrence of a string within another

string strrchr(string haystack, string needle) *3.0*

Finds the last occurrence of a character in a string within another

string strrev(string str) *3.0*

Reverses a string

int strrpos(string haystack, string needle) *3.0*
: Finds position of last occurrence of a character in a string within another

int strspn(string str, string mask) *3.0.3*
: Finds length of initial segment consisting entirely of characters found in `mask`

string strstr(string haystack, string needle) *3.0*
: Finds first occurrence of a string within another

string strtok([string str,] string token) *3.0*
: Tokenizes a string

string strtolower(string str) *3.0*
: Makes a string lowercase

int strtotime(string time, int now) *3.0.12*
: Converts string representation of date and time to a timestamp

string strtoupper(string str) *3.0*
: Makes a string uppercase

string strtr(string str, string from, string to) *3.0*
: Translates characters in `str` using given translation tables

string strval(mixed var) *3.0*
: Gets the string value of a variable

string substr(string str, int start[, int length]) *3.0*
: Returns part of a string

int substr_count(string haystack, string needle) *4.0*
: Returns the number of times a substring occurs in the string

string substr_replace(string str, string repl, int start[, int length]) *4.0*
: Replaces part of a string with another string

switch(expr) *3.0*
: Language keyword that implements the C-like `switch` construct

int symlink(string target, string link) *3.0*
: Creates a symbolic link

bool syslog(int priority, string message) *3.0*
: Generates a system log message

int system(string command[, int return_value]) *3.0*
: Executes an external program and displays output

float tan(float number) *3.0*
: Returns the tangent of the number in radians

float tanh(float number) *4.1.0*
: Returns the hyperbolic tangent of the number

string tempnam(string dir, string prefix) *3.0*
: Creates a unique filename in a directory

string textdomain(string domain) *3.0.7*
: Sets the textdomain to `domain`; returns the current domain

int time(void) *3.0*
Returns current Unix timestamp

resource tmpfile(void) *3.0.13*
Creates a temporary file that will be deleted automatically after use

bool touch(string filename[, int time[, int atime]]) *3.0*
Sets modification time of file

void trigger_error(string messsage[, int error_type]) *4.0.1*
Generates a user-level error/warning/notice message

string trim(string str[, string character_mask]) *3.0*
Strips whitespace from the beginning and end of a string

bool uasort(array array_arg, string cmp_function) *3.0.4*
Sorts an array with a user-defined comparison function and maintains index association

string ucfirst(string str) *3.0*
Makes a string's first character uppercase

string ucwords(string str) *3.0.3*
Uppercases the first character of every word in a string

bool uksort(array array_arg, string cmp_function) *3.0.4*
Sorts an array by keys using a user-defined comparison function

int umask([int mask]) *3.0*
Returns or changes the umask

string uniqid(string prefix[, bool more_entropy]) *3.0*
Generates a unique ID

int unixtojd([int timestamp]) *4.0*
Converts Unix timestamp to Julian day count

bool unlink(string filename) *3.0*
Deletes a file

array unpack(string format, string input) *3.0*
Unpacks binary string into named array elements according to `format` argument

void unregister_tick_function(string function_name) *4.0.3*
Unregisters a tick callback function

mixed unserialize(string variable_representation) *3.0.5*
Takes a string representation of variable and recreates it

void unset(mixed var[, mixed var[, ...]]) *3.0*
Unsets a given variable

string urldecode(string str) *3.0*
Decodes URL-encoded string

string urlencode(string str) *3.0*
URL-encodes a string

void usleep(int micro_seconds) *3.0*
Delays for a given number of microseconds

bool usort(array array_arg, string cmp_function) *3.0.3*
Sorts an array by values using a user-defined comparison function

string utf8_decode(string data) *3.0.6*
Converts a UTF-8 encoded string to ISO-8859-1

string utf8_encode(string data) *3.0.6*
Encodes an ISO-8859-1 string to UTF-8

var $prop *3.0*
Language keyword that defines a property in a class

void var_dump(mixed var) *3.0.5*
Dumps a string representation of a variable to output

mixed var_export(mixed var[, bool return]) *4.1.0*
Outputs or returns a string representation of a variable

int version_compare(string ver1, string ver2[, string oper]) *4.1.0*
Compares two PHP-standardized version number strings

bool virtual(string filename) *3.0*
Performs an Apache subrequest

int vprintf(string format, array args) *4.1.0*
Outputs a formatted string

string vsprintf(string format, array args) *4.1.0*
Returns a formatted string

while(cond) *3.0*
Language keyword that implements a loop that continues until cond is `false`

string wordwrap(string str[, int width[, string break[, int cut]]]) *4.0.2*
Wraps buffer to selected number of characters using string `break` character

string xml_error_string(int code) *3.0.6*
Gets XML parser error string

int xml_get_current_byte_index(resource parser) *3.0.6*
Gets current byte index for an XML parser

int xml_get_current_column_number(resource parser) *3.0.6*
Gets current column number for an XML parser

int xml_get_current_line_number(resource parser) *3.0.6*
Gets current line number for an XML parser

int xml_get_error_code(resource parser) *3.0.6*
Gets XML parser error code

int xml_parse(resource parser, string data[, int isFinal]) *3.0.6*
Starts parsing an XML document

int xml_parse_into_struct(resource parser, string data, array &struct, array &index) *3.0.8*
Parses a XML document

resource xml_parser_create([string encoding]) *3.0.6*
Creates an XML parser

resource xml_parser_create_ns([string encoding[, string sep]]) *4.0.5*
Creates an XML parser

int xml_parser_free(resource parser) *3.0.6*
Frees an XML parser

int xml_parser_get_option(resource parser, int option) *3.0.6*
Gets options from an XML parser

int xml_parser_set_option(resource parser, int option, mixed value) *3.0.6*
Sets options in an XML parser

int xml_set_character_data_handler(resource parser, string hdl) *3.0.6*
Sets up character data handler

int xml_set_default_handler(resource parser, string hdl) *3.0.6*
Sets up default handler

int xml_set_element_handler(resource parser, string shdl, string ehdl) *3.0.6*
Sets up start and end element handlers

int xml_set_end_namespace_decl_handler(resource parser, string hdl) *4.0.5*
Sets up character data handler

int xml_set_external_entity_ref_handler(resource parser, string hdl) *3.0.6*
Sets up external entity reference handler

int xml_set_notation_decl_handler(resource parser, string hdl) *3.0.6*
Sets up notation declaration handler

int xml_set_object(resource parser, object &obj) *4.0*
Sets up object that should be used for callbacks

int xml_set_processing_instruction_handler(resource parser, string hdl) *3.0.6*
Sets up processing instruction (PI) handler

int xml_set_start_namespace_decl_handler(resource parser, string hdl) *4.0.5*
Sets up character data handler

int xml_set_unparsed_entity_decl_handler(resource parser, string hdl) *3.0.6*
Sets up unparsed entity declaration handler

XOR *3.0*
Language keyword that is similar to the ^ operator, except lower precedence

resource xslt_create(void) *4.0.3*
Creates a new XSLT processor

int xslt_errno(resource processor) *4.0.3*
Returns an error number

string xslt_error(resource processor) *4.0.3*
Returns an error string

void xslt_free(resource processor) *4.0.3*
Frees the XSLT processor

string xslt_process(resource processor, string xml, string xslt[, mixed result[, array args[, array params]]]) *4.0.3*

Performs the XSLT transformation

void xslt_set_base(resource processor, string base) *4.0.5*

Sets the base URI for all XSLT transformations

void xslt_set_encoding(resource processor, string encoding) *4.0.5*

Sets the output encoding for the current stylesheet

void xslt_set_error_handler(resource processor, mixed error_func) *4.0.4*

Sets the error handler to be called when an XSLT error occurs

void xslt_set_log(resource processor, string logfile) *4.0.6*

Sets the log file to write the errors to (defaults to *stderr*)

void xslt_set_sax_handlers(resource processor, array handlers) *4.0.6*

Sets the SAX handlers to be called when the XML document gets processed

void xslt_set_scheme_handlers(resource processor, array handlers) *4.0.6*

Sets the scheme handlers for the XSLT processor

string zend_version(void) *4.0*

Get the version of the Zend Engine

void zip_close(resource zip) *4.1.0*

Closes a ZIP archive

void zip_entry_close(resource zip_ent) *4.1.0*

Closes a ZIP entry

int zip_entry_compressedsize(resource zip_entry) *4.1.0*

Returns the compressed size of a ZIP entry

string zip_entry_compressionmethod(resource zip_entry) *4.1.0*

Returns a string containing the compression method used on a particular entry

int zip_entry_filesize(resource zip_entry) *4.1.0*

Returns the actual file size of a ZIP entry

string zip_entry_name(resource zip_entry) *4.1.0*

Returns the name given a ZIP entry

bool zip_entry_open(resource zip_dp, resource zip_entry, string mode) *4.1.0*

Opens the ZIP file pointed to by the resource entry

string zip_entry_read(resource zip_ent[, int length]) *4.1.0*

Reads bytes from an opened ZIP entry

resource zip_open(string filename) *4.1.0*

Opens a new ZIP archive for reading

resource zip_read(resource zip) *4.1.0*

Returns the next file in the archive

VII

HTTP

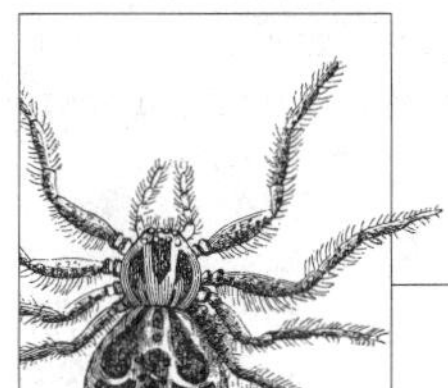

17
HTTP

The Hypertext Transfer Protocol (HTTP) is the language web clients and servers use to communicate with each other. It is essentially the backbone of the World Wide Web. While HTTP is largely the realm of server and client programming, a firm understanding of HTTP is also important for CGI programming. In addition, sometimes HTTP filters back to the users—for example, when server error codes are reported in a browser window.

This chapter covers all the basics of HTTP. For absolutely complete coverage of HTTP and all its surrounding technologies, see *HTTP: The Definitive Guide* by David Gourley and Brian Totty, with Marjorie Sayer, Sailu Reddy, and Anshu Aggarwal (O'Reilly).

All HTTP transactions follow the same general format. Each client request and server response has three parts: the request or response line, a header section, and the entity body. The client initiates a transaction as follows:

1. The client contacts the server at a designated port number (by default, 80). It sends a document request by specifying an HTTP command called a *method*, followed by a document address, and an HTTP version number. For example:

   ```
   GET /index.html HTTP/1.1
   ```

   This makes use of the GET method to request the document *index.html* using Version 1.1 of HTTP. HTTP methods are discussed in more detail later in this chapter.

2. Next, the client sends optional header information to inform the server of its configuration and the document formats it will accept. All header information is given line by line, each with a header name and value. For example, this header information sent by the client indicates its name and version number and specifies several document preferences:

   ```
   User-Agent: Mozilla/4.05(WinNT; I)
   Accept: image/gif, image/x-xbitmap, image/jpeg, image/pjpeg, */*
   ```

   The client sends a blank line to end the header.

3. After sending the request and headers, the client may send additional data. This data is mostly used by CGI programs that use the POST method. It may also be used by clients like Netscape Navigator Professional Edition to publish an edited page back onto the web server.

The server responds in the following way to the client's request:

1. The server replies with a status line containing three fields: HTTP version, status code, and description. The HTTP version indicates the version of HTTP the server is using to respond.The status code is a three-digit number that indicates the server's result of the client's request. The description following the status code is simply human-readable text that describes the status code. For example:

   ```
   HTTP/1.1 200 OK
   ```

   This status line indicates that the server uses Version 1.1 of HTTP in its response. A status code of 200 means that the client's request was successful, and the requested data will be supplied after the headers.

2. After the status line, the server sends header information to the client about itself and the requested document. For example:

   ```
   Date: Fri, 20 Sep 1998 08:17:58 GMT
   Server: NCSA/1.5.2
   Last-modified: Mon, 17 Jun 1998 21:53:08 GMT
   Content-type: text/html
   Content-length: 2482
   ```

   A blank line ends the header.

3. If the client's request is successful, the requested data is sent. This data may be a copy of a file or the response from a CGI program. If the client's request could not be fulfilled, the additional data may be a human-readable explanation of why the server could not fulfill the request.

In HTTP 1.0, after the server has finished sending the requested data, it disconnects from the client, and the transaction is over unless a `Connection: Keep Alive` header is sent. Beginning with HTTP 1.1, however, the default is for the server to maintain the connection and allow the client to make additional requests. Since many documents embed other documents (inline images, frames, applets, etc.), this saves the overhead of the client having to repeatedly connect to the same server just to draw a single page. Under HTTP 1.1, therefore, the transaction might cycle back to the beginning, until either the client or server explicitly closes the connection.

Being a stateless protocol, HTTP does not maintain any information from one transaction to the next, so the next transaction needs to start all over again. The advantage is that an HTTP server can serve a lot more clients in a given period of time, since there's no additional overhead for tracking sessions from one connection to the next. The disadvantage is that more elaborate CGI programs need to use hidden input fields (as described in Chapter 6), or external tools such as cookies (described later in this chapter) to maintain information from one transaction to the next.

Client Requests

Client requests are broken into three sections. The first line of a message always contains an HTTP command called a *method*, a URI that identifies the file or resource the client is querying, and the HTTP version number. The second section of a client request contains header information, which provides information about the client and the data entity it is sending the server. The third part of a client request is the *entity body*, the data being sent to the server.

A Uniform Resource Identifier (URI) is a general term for all valid formats of addressing schemes supported on the World Wide Web. The one in common use now is the Uniform Resource Locator (URL) addressing scheme. See Chapter 1 for more information on URLs.

Methods

A method is an HTTP command that begins the first line of a client request. The method tells the server the purpose of the client request. There are three methods defined for HTTP: GET, HEAD, and POST. Other methods are also defined but not as widely supported by servers (although the other methods will be used more often in the future, not less). Methods are case-sensitive, so a "GET" is different from a "get."

The GET method

The GET method is a request for information located at a specified URI on the server. It is the most commonly used method by browsers to retrieve information. The result of a GET request can be generated in many different ways; it can be a file accessible by the server, the output of a program or CGI script, the output from a hardware device, etc.

When a client uses the GET method in its request, the server responds with a status line, headers, and the requested data. If the server cannot process the request due to an error or lack of authorization, the server usually sends a textual explanation in the data portion of the response.

The entity-body portion of a GET request is always empty. GET is basically used to say "Give me this file." The file or program the client requests is usually identified by its full pathname on the server.

Here is an example of a successful GET request to retrieve a file. The client sends:

```
GET /index.html HTTP/1.0
Connection: Keep-Alive
User-Agent: Mozilla/2.02Gold (WinNT; I)
Host: www.oreilly.com
Accept: image/gif, image/x-xbitmap, image/jpeg, image/pjpeg, */*
```

The server responds with:

```
HTTP/1.0 200 Document follows
Date: Fri, 20 Sep 1998 08:17:58 GMT
Server: NCSA/1.5.2
Last-modified: Mon, 17 Jun 1998 21:53:08 GMT
```

```
Content-type: text/html
Content-length: 2482

(body of document here)
```

The GET method is also used to send input to programs like CGI through form tags. Since GET requests have empty entity-bodies, the input data is appended to the URL in the GET line of the request. When a `<form>` tag specifies the `method="GET"` attribute value, key-value pairs representing the input from the form are appended to the URL following a question mark (?). Pairs are separated by an ampersand (&). For example:

```
GET /cgi-bin/birthday.pl?month=august&date=24 HTTP/1.0
```

This causes the server to send the *birthday.pl* CGI program the `month` and `date` values specified in a form on the client. The input data at the end of the URL is encoded to CGI specifications. For literal use of special characters, the client uses hexadecimal notation. The character encoding is described in Chapter 12.

The GET method can also supply *extra-path information* in the same manner. This is achieved by adding the extra path after the URL, i.e., */cgi-bin/ display.pl/ cgi/cgi_doc.txt*. The server gauges where the program's name ends (`display.pl`); everything after that is read as the extra path.

The HEAD method

The HEAD method is functionally like GET except that the server will not send anything in the data portion of the reply. The HEAD method requests only the header information on a file or resource. The header information from a HEAD request should be the same as that from a GET request.

This method is used when the client wants to find out information about the document and not retrieve it. Many applications exist for the HEAD method. For example, the client may desire the following information:

- The modification time of a document, useful for cache-related queries
- The size of a document, useful for page layout, estimating arrival time, or determining whether to request a smaller version of the document
- The type of the document, to allow the client to examine only documents of a certain type
- The type of server, to allow customized server queries

It is important to note that most of the header information provided by a server is optional and may not be given by all servers. A good design for web clients is to allow flexibility in the server response and take default actions when desired header information is not given by the server.

The following is an example HTTP transaction using the HEAD request. The client sends:

```
HEAD /index.html HTTP/1.1
Connection: Keep-Alive
User-Agent: Mozilla/2.02Gold (WinNT; I)
Host: www.oreilly.com
Accept: image/gif, image/x-xbitmap, image/jpeg, image/pjpeg, */*
```

The server responds with:

```
HTTP/1.1 200 Document follows
Date: Fri, 20 Sep 1998 08:17:58 GMT
Server: NCSA/1.5.2
Last-modified: Mon, 17 Jun 1998 21:53:08 GMT
Content-type: text/html
Content-length: 2482
```

(No entity body is sent in response to a HEAD request.)

The POST method

The POST method allows data to be sent to the server in a client request. The data is directed to a data-handling program that the server has access to (e.g., a CGI script). The POST method can be used for many applications, such as:

- Network services, such as newsgroup postings
- Command-line interface programs
- Annotation of documents on the server
- Database operations

The data sent to the server is in the entity-body section of the client's request. After the server processes the POST request and headers, it passes the entity-body to the program specified by the URI. The encoding scheme most commonly used with POST is URL-encoding, which allows form data to be translated into a list of variables and values for CGI processing. Chapter 12 provides details on CGI and URL-encoded data.

Here is a quick example of a client request using the POST method to send birth-date data from a form:

```
POST /cgi-bin/birthday.pl HTTP/1.0
User-Agent: Mozilla/2.02Gold (WinNT; I)
Accept: image/gif, image/x-xbitmap, image/jpeg, image/pjpeg, */*
Host: www.oreilly.com
Content-type: application/x-www-form-urlencoded
Content-length: 20

month=august&date=24
```

Other methods

The following methods are also defined, although not as frequently used:

LINK
: Requests that header information is associated with a document on the server.

UNLINK
: Requests dissociation of header information from a document on the server.

PUT
: Requests that the entity-body of the request be stored at the specified URI.

HTTP

DELETE
Requests the removal of data at a URI on the server.

OPTIONS
Requests information about communications options available on the server. The request URI can be substituted with an asterisk (*) to indicate the server as a whole.

TRACE
Requests the request entity body be returned intact. Used for debugging.

CONNECT
A reserved method used specifically for Secure Sockets Layer (SSL) tunneling.

Server Responses and Status Codes

The server's response to a client request is grouped into three parts. The first line is the server response line, which contains the HTTP version number, a three-digit number indicating the status of the request (called a *server response code* or *status code*), and a short phrase describing the status. The response line is followed by the header information and an entity body if there is one.

Status codes are typically generated by web servers. However, they can also be generated by CGI scripts that bypass the server's precooked headers and supply their own. Status codes are grouped as follows.

Code range	Response meaning
100–199	Informational
200–299	Client request successful
300–399	Client request redirected, further action necessary
400–499	Client request incomplete
500–599	Server errors

HTTP defines only a few specific codes in each range, although servers may define their own as needed. If a client receives a code it does not recognize, it should understand its basic meaning from its numerical range. While most web browsers handle codes in the 100-, 200-, and 300-range silently, some error codes in the 400- and 500-range are commonly reported back to the user (e.g., "404 Not Found").

Informational

A response in the range of 100–199 is informational, indicating that the client's request was received and is being processed.

`100 Continue`
The initial part of the request has been received and the client may continue with its request.

`101 Switching Protocols`
The server is complying with a client request to switch protocols to the one specified in the `Upgrade` header field.

Client Request Successful

A response in the range of 200–299 means that the client's request was successful.

`200 OK`
: The client's request was successful, and the server's response contains the requested data.

`201 Created`
: This status code is used whenever a new URI is created. With this result code, the `Location` header is given by the server to specify where the new data was placed.

`202 Accepted`
: The request was accepted but not immediately acted upon. More information about the transaction may be given in the entity body of the server's response. Note that there is no guarantee that the server will actually honor the request, even though it may seem like a legitimate request at the time of acceptance.

`203 Non-Authoritative Information`
: The information in the entity header is from a local or third-party copy and not from the original server.

`204 No Content`
: A status code and header are given in the response, but there is no entity body in the reply. On receiving this response, browsers should not update their document view. This is a useful code for an imagemap handler to return when the user clicks on useless or blank areas of an image.

`205 Reset Content`
: The browser should clear the form used for this transaction for additional input. Appropriate for data-entry CGI applications.

`206 Partial Content`
: The server is returning partial data of the size requested. Used in response to a request specifying a `Range` header. The server must specify the range included in the response with the `Content-Range` header.

Redirection

A response code in the 300–399 range indicates that the request was not performed, and the client needs to take further action for a successful request.

`300 Multiple Choices`
: The requested URI refers to more than one resource. For example, the URI could refer to a document that has been translated into many languages. The entity body returned by the server could have a list of more specific data about how to choose the correct resource.

`301 Moved Permanently`
: The requested URI is no longer used by the server, and the operation specified in the request was not performed. The new location for the requested

document is specified in the `Location` header. All future requests for the document should use the new URI.

`302 Found`
: The requested URI temporarily has a new URI. The `Location` header points to the new location. If this is in response to a GET or a HEAD, the client should use the new URI to resolve the request immediately after receiving the response.

`303 See Other`
: The requested URI can be found at a different URI (specified in the `Location` header) and should be retrieved by a GET on that resource.

`304 Not Modified`
: This is the response code to an `If-Modified-Since` header, where the URI has not been modified since the specified date. The entity body is not sent, and the client should use its own local copy.

`305 Use Proxy`
: The requested URI must be accessed through the proxy in the `Location` header.

`307 Temporary Redirect`
: The requested URI has moved temporarily. The `Location` header points to the new location. Immediately after receiving this status code, the client should use the new URI to resolve the request, but the old URI should be used for all future requests.

Client Request Incomplete

A response code in the range of 400–499 means that the client's request was incomplete and may indicate further information is required from the client.

`400 Bad Request`
: This response code indicates that the server detected a syntax error in the client's request.

`401 Unauthorized`
: The result code is given along with the `WWW-Authenticate` header to indicate that the request lacked proper authorization, and the client should supply proper authorization when requesting this URI again.

`402 Payment Required`
: This code is not yet implemented in HTTP. However, it may, one day, indicate that a payment is required to receive the document on the server.

`403 Forbidden`
: The request was denied for a reason the server does not want to (or has no means to) indicate to the client.

`404 Not Found`
: The document at the specified URI does not exist.

405 `Method Not Allowed`
: This code is given with the `Allow` header and indicates that the method used by the client is not supported for this URI.

406 `Not Acceptable`
: The URI specified by the client exists, but not in a format preferred by the client. Along with this code, the server provides the `Content-Language`, `Content-Encoding`, and `Content-Type` headers.

407 `Proxy Authentication Required`
: The proxy server needs to authorize the request before forwarding it. Used with the `Proxy-Authenticate` header.

408 `Request Time-out`
: This response code means the client did not produce a full request within some predetermined time (usually specified in the server's configuration), and the server is disconnecting the network connection.

409 `Conflict`
: This code indicates that the request conflicts with another request or with the server's configuration. Information about the conflict should be returned in the data portion of the reply.

410 `Gone`
: This code indicates that the requested URI no longer exists and has been permanently removed from the server.

411 `Length Required`
: The server will not accept the request without a `Content-Length` header supplied in the request.

412 `Precondition Failed`
: The condition specified by one or more `If...` headers in the request evaluated to `false`.

413 `Request Entity Too Large`
: The server will not process the request because its entity body is too large.

414 `Request-URI Too Long`
: The server will not process the request because its requested URI is too large.

415 `Unsupported Media Type`
: The server will not process the request because its entity body is in an unsupported format.

416 `Requested Range Not Satisfiable`
: The server detected a `Range` header that contained no valid values for the target. In addition, an `If-Range` header was omitted.

417 `Expectation Failed`
: The condition specified in an `Expect` header could not be satisfied.

Server Errors

Response codes in the range of 500–599 indicate that the server encountered an error and may be unable to perform the client's request.

`500 Internal Server Error`
: This code indicates that a part of the server (for example, a CGI program) has crashed or encountered a configuration error.

`501 Not Implemented`
: This code indicates that the client requested an action that cannot be performed by the server.

`502 Bad Gateway`
: This code indicates that the server (or proxy) encountered invalid responses from another server (or proxy).

`503 Service Unavailable`
: This code means that the service is temporarily unavailable but should be restored in the future. If the server knows when it will be available again, a `Retry-After` header may also be supplied.

`504 Gateway Time-out`
: This response is like `408 (Request Time-out)` except that a gateway or proxy has timed out.

`505 HTTP Version not supported`
: The server will not support the HTTP protocol version used in the request.

HTTP Headers

HTTP headers are used to transfer all sorts of information between client and server. There are four categories of headers:

General
: Information not related to the client, server, or HTTP

Request
: Preferred document formats and server parameters

Response
: Information about the server sending the response

Entity
: Information on the data being sent between the client and server

General headers and entity headers are the same for both the server and client.

All headers in HTTP messages contain the header name followed by a colon (:), then a space, and the value of the header. Header names are case-insensitive (thus, `Content-Type` is the same as `Content-type`). The value of a header can extend over multiple lines by preceding each extra line with at least one space or tab character.

General Headers

General headers are used in both client requests and server responses. Some may be more specific to either a client or server message.

Cache-Control

`Cache-Control: directives`

Specifies caching directives in a comma-separated list.

Cache Request Directives

`no-cache` *2n*
: Do not cache.

`no-store`
: Remove information promptly after forwarding.

`max-age` = *seconds*
: Do not send responses older than *seconds*.

`max-stale [` = *seconds]*
: Send expired data. If *seconds* are specified, only send data expired by less than the specified number of seconds.

`min-fresh` = *seconds*
: Send data only if still fresh after the specified number of seconds.

`only-if-cached`
: Do not retrieve new data. Only return data already in the cache. Useful unless the network connection is down.

Cache Response Directives

`public`
: Cachable by any cache.

`private`
: Not cachable by a shared cache.

`no-cache`
: Do not cache.

`no-store`
: Remove information promptly after forwarding.

`no-transform`
: Do not convert data.

`must-revalidate`
: Client must revalidate the data.

`proxy-revalidate`
: Client must revalidate data except for private client caches.

`max-age=`*seconds*
: The document should be considered stale in the specified number of seconds.

Connection

`Connection: options`

Specifies options desired for this connection but not for further connections by proxies. The `close` connection option signifies that either the client or server wishes to end the connection (i.e., this is the last transaction).

Date

`Date: dateformat`

Indicates the current date and time. The preferred date format is described by RFC 1123. For example:

```
Mon, 06 May 1999 04:57:00 GMT
```

For backward compatibility, however, the RFC-850 and ANSI C *asctime()* formats are also acceptable:

```
Monday, 06-May-99 04:57:00 GMT
Mon May 6 04:57:00 1999
```

Use a two-digit year specification at your own risk.

MIME-Version

`MIME-Version:`*`version`*

Specifies the version of MIME (RFC-2045[7]) used in the HTTP transaction. If a message's entity-body does not conform to MIME, this header can be omitted. If the transaction involves MIME-encoded data, but this header is omitted, the default value is assumed to be 1.0.

Pragma

`Pragma: no-cache`

Specifies directives to a proxy system. This header is ignored by the target server. HTTP defines one directive for this header: `no-cache`. In HTTP 1.0, this tells the proxy to request the document from the server instead of the local cache. HTTP 1.1 prefers using `Cache Control: no-cache` instead.

Transfer-Encoding

`Transfer-Encoding:` *`encoding_type`*

Indicates what type of transformation has been applied to the message body for safe transfer. Currently only the `chunked` encoding type is defined by HTTP.

Upgrade

`Upgrade:` *`protocol/version`*

Specifies the preferred communication protocols. Used in conjunction with response code `101 Switching Protocols`. For example:

```
Upgrade: HTTP/1.2
```

Via

`Via: protocol` *`host [comment]`* `...`

Used by gateways and proxies to indicate the protocols and hosts that processed the transaction between client and server.

Client Request Headers

Client header data communicates the client's configuration and preferred document formats to the server. Request headers are used in a client message to provide information about the client.

Accept

`Accept: type/subtype [; q=qvalue]`

Specifies media types that the client prefers to accept. Multiple media types can be listed, separated by commas. The optional *qvalue* represents on a scale of 0 to 1 an acceptable quality level for accept types. Media types are listed at the end of this chapter.

Accept-Charset

`Accept-Charset: character_set  [; q=qvalue]`

Specifies the character sets the client prefers. Multiple character sets can be listed separated by commas. The optional *qvalue* represents on a scale of 0 to 1 an acceptable quality level for nonpreferred character sets.

Accept-Encoding

`Accept-Encoding: encoding_types`

Specifies the encoding schemes the client can accept, such as `compress` or `gzip`. Multiple encoding schemes can be listed, separated by commas. If no encoding types are listed, none are acceptable to the client.

Accept-Language

`Accept-Language: language [; q=qvalue]`

Specifies the languages the client prefers. Multiple languages can be listed, separated by commas. The optional *qvalue* represents on a scale of 0 to 1 an acceptable quality level for nonpreferred languages. Languages are written with their two-letter abbreviations (e.g., *en* for English, *de* for German, *fr* for French, etc.).

Authorization

`Authorization: scheme credentials`

Provides the client's authorization to access data at a URI. When a requested document requires authorization, the server returns a `WWW-Authenticate` header describing the type of authorization required. The client then repeats the request with the proper authorization information.

The authorization scheme generally used in HTTP is BASIC, and under the BASIC scheme the credentials follow the format *username:password* encoded in base64. For example, for the username "webmaster" and a password "zrma4v," the authorization header would look like this:

```
Authorization: BASIC d2VibWFzdGVyOnpycW1hNHY=
```

The value decodes into `webmaster:zrma4v`.

Cookie

`Cookie: name=value`

Contains a name/value pair of information stored for that URL. Multiple cookies can be specified, separated by semicolons. For browsers supporting Netscape persistent cookies; not included in the HTTP standard. See the discussion of cookies later in this chapter for more information.

From

`From: email_address`

Gives the email address of the user executing the client.

Host

`Host: hostname[:port]`

Specifies the host and port number of the URI. Clients must supply this information in HTTP 1.1, so servers with multiple hostnames can easily differentiate between ambiguous URLs.

If-Modified-Since

`If-Modified-Since: date`

Specifies that the URI data is to be sent only if it has been modified since the date given as the value of this header. This is useful for client-side caching. If the document has not been modified, the server returns a code of `304`, indicating that the client should use the local copy. The specified date should follow the format described under the `Date` header.

If-Match

`If-Match: entity_tag`

A conditional requesting the entity only if it matches the given entity tags (see the `ETag` entity header). An asterisk (*) matches any entity, and the transaction continues only if the entity exists.

If-None-Match

`If-None-Match: entity_tag`

A conditional requesting the entity only if it does not match any of the given entity tags (see the `ETag` entity header). An asterisk (*) matches any entity; if the entity doesn't exist, the transaction continues.

If-Range

`If-Range: entity_tag | date`

A conditional requesting only the portion of the entity that is missing if it has not been changed, and the entire entity if it has. Must be used in conjunction with a `Range` header. Either an entity tag or a date can identify the partial entity already received; see the `Date` header for information on the format for dates.

If-Unmodified-Since

`If-Unmodified-Since: date`

Specifies that the URI data is to be sent only if it has not been modified since the given date. The specified date should follow the format described under the `Date` header.

Max-Forwards

`Max-Forwards: n`

Limits the number of proxies or gateways that can forward the request. Useful for debugging with the `TRACE` method, avoiding infinite loops.

Proxy-Authorization

`Proxy-Authorization: credentials`

Used for a client to identify itself to a proxy requiring authorization.

Range

`Range: bytes=n-m`

Specifies the partial range(s) requested from the document. Multiple ranges can be listed, separated by commas. If the first digit in the comma-separated byte range(s) is missing, the range is assumed to count from the end of the document. If the second digit is missing, the range is byte *n* to the end of the document. The first byte is byte 0.

Referer

`Referer: url`

Gives the URI of the document that refers to the requested URI (i.e., the source document of the link).

User-Agent

`User-Agent: string`

Gives identifying information about the client program.

Server Response Headers

The response headers described here are used in server responses to communicate information about the server and how it may handle requests.

Accept-Ranges

`Accept-Ranges: bytes|none`

Indicates the acceptance of range requests for a URI, specifying either the range unit (e.g., `bytes`), or `none` if no range requests are accepted.

Age

`Age: seconds`

Indicates the age of the document in seconds.

Proxy-Authenticate

`Proxy-Authenticate: scheme realm`

Indicates the authentication scheme and parameters applicable to the proxy for this URI and the current connection. Used with response `407 (Proxy Authentication Required)`.

Retry-After

`Retry-After: date|seconds`

Used with response code `503 (Service Unavailable)`. It contains either an integer number of seconds or a GMT date and time (as described by the `Date` header formats). If the value is an integer, it is interpreted as the number of seconds to wait after the request was issued. For example:

```
Retry-After: 3600
Retry-After: Sat, 18 May 1996 06:59:37 GMT
```

Server

`Server: string`

Contains the name and version number of the server. For example:

```
Server: NCSA/1.3
```

Set-Cookie

`Set-Cookie: name=value [; options]`

Contains a name/value pair of information to retain for this URL. For browsers supporting Netscape persistent cookies; not included in the HTTP standard. See the discussion of cookies later in this chapter for more information. Options are:

`expires=`*`date`* *2n*
: The cookie becomes invalid after the specified date.

`path=`*`pathname`*
: The URL range for which the cookie is valid.

`domain=`*`domain_name`*
: The domain name range for which the cookie is valid.

`secure`
: Return the cookie only under a secure connection.

Vary

`Vary: *|` *`headers`*

Specifies that the entity has multiple sources and may therefore vary according to a specified list of request header(s). Multiple headers can be listed, separated by commas. An asterisk (*) means that another factor other than the request headers may affect the document that is returned.

Warning

`Warning:` *`code host`*`[:`*`port`*`]` *`string`*

Indicates additional information to that in the status code, for use by caching proxies. The *host* field contains the name or pseudonym of the server host, with an optional port number. The two-digit warning codes and their recommended descriptive strings are:

`10 Response is stale` *2n*
: The response data is known to be stale.

`11 Revalidation failed` *2n*
: The response data is known to be stale because the proxy failed to revalidate the data.

`12 Disconnected operation` *2n*
: The cache is disconnected from the network.

`13 Heuristic expiration` *2n*
: The data is older than 24 hours, and the cache heuristically chose a freshness lifetime greater than 24 hours.

`14 Transformation applied` *2n*
: The proxy has changed the encoding or media type of the document, as specified by the `Content-Encoding` or `Content-Type` headers.

`99 Miscellaneous warning` *2n*
: Arbitrary information to be logged or presented to the user.

WWW-Authenticate

`WWW-Authenticate:` *`scheme realm`*

Used with the `401 (Unauthorized)` response code. It specifies the authorization scheme and realm of authorization required from a client at the requested URI. Many different authorization realms can exist on a server. A common authorization scheme is BASIC, which requires a username and password. For example:

```
WWW-Authenticate: BASIC realm="Admin"
```

When returned to the client, this header indicates that the BASIC type of authorization data in the appropriate realm should be returned in the client's `Authorization` header.

Entity Headers

Entity headers are used in both client requests and server responses. They supply information about the entity body in an HTTP message.

Allow

`Allow:` *`methods`*

Contains a comma-separated list of methods that are allowed at a specified URI. In a server response, it is used with code `405` (`Method Not Allowed`) to inform the client of valid methods available for the requested information.

Content-Encoding

`Content-Encoding:` *`encoding_schemes`*

Specifies the encoding scheme(s) used for the transferred entity body. Values are `gzip` (or `x-gzip`) and `compress` (or `x-compress`). If multiple encoding schemes are specified (in a comma-separated list), they must be listed in the order in which they were applied to the source data.

Content-Language

`Content-Language:` *`languages`*

Specifies the language(s) the transferred entity body is intended for. Languages are represented by their two-digit code (e.g., *en* for English, *fr* for French).

Content-Length

`Content-Length:` *`n`*

This header specifies the length of the data (in bytes) of the transferred entity body. Due to the dynamic nature of some requests, the content length is sometimes unknown, and this header is omitted.

Content-Location

`Content-Location:` *`uri`*

Supplies the URI for the entity, in cases where a document has multiple entities with separately accessible locations. The URI can be either absolute or relative.

Content-MD5

`Content-MD5:` *`digest`*

Supplies a MD5 digest of the entity, for checking the integrity of the message upon receipt.

Content-Range

`Content-Range: bytes` *`n-m/length`*

Specifies where the accompanying partial entity body should be inserted and the total size of the full entity body. For example:

```
Content-Range: bytes 6143-7166/15339
```

Content-Transfer-Encoding

`Content-Transfer-Encoding:` *`scheme`*

Specifies any transformations that are applied to the entity body for transport over a network. Common values are: `7bit`, `8bit`, `binary`, `base64`, and `quoted-printable`.

Content-Type

`Content-Type:` *`type/subtype`*

Describes the media type and subtype of an entity body. It uses the same values as the client's `Accept` header, and the server should return media types that conform with the client's preferred formats.

ETag

`ETag: entity_tag`

Defines the entity tag for the `If-Match` and `If-None-Match` request headers.

Expires

`Expires:` *`date`*

Specifies the time when a document may change, or its information becomes invalid. After that time, the document may or may not change or be deleted. The value is a date and time in a valid format, as described for the `Date` header.

Last-Modified

`Last-Modified: date`

Specifies when the specified URI was last modified. The value is a date and time in a valid format, as described for the `Date` header.

Location

`Location: uri`

Specifies the new location of a document, usually with response codes `201` (`Created`), `301` (`Moved Permanently`), or `302` (`Moved Temporarily`). The URI given must be written as an absolute URI.

Cookies

Persistent-state, client-side cookies were introduced by Netscape Navigator to enable a server to store client-specific information on the client's machine and use that information when a server or a particular page is accessed again by the client. The cookie mechanism allows servers to personalize pages for each client, or remember selections the client has made when browsing through various pages of a site—all without having to use a complicated (or more time-consuming) CGI/database system on the server's side.

Cookies work in the following way: when a CGI program identifies a new user, it adds an extra header to its response containing an identifier for that user and other information the server may glean from the client's input. This header informs the cookie-enabled browser to add this information to the client's *cookies* file. After this, all requests to that URL from the browser will include the cookie information as an extra header in the request. The CGI program uses this information to return a document tailored to that specific client. The cookies are stored on the client user's hard drive, so the information remains even when the browser is closed and reopened.

The Set-Cookie Response Header

A cookie is created when a client visits a site or page for the first time. A CGI program looks for previous cookie information in the client request and, if it is not there, sends a response containing a `Set-Cookie` header. This header contains a name/value pair (the actual cookie) that comprises the special information you want the client to maintain. There are other optional fields you may include in the header.

The `Set-Cookie` header uses the following syntax:

```
Set-Cookie: name=value; expires=date;path=pathname; domain=domain-name; secure
```

Multiple `Set-Cookie` headers may be included in the server response. The *name=value* pair is the only required attribute for this header, and it should come first. The remaining attributes can be in any order and are defined as follows:

name=*value*

Both *name* and *value* can be any strings that do not contain either a semicolon, space, or tab. Encoding such as URL encoding may be used if these entities are required in the *name* or *value*, as long as your script is prepared to handle it.

expires=*date*

This attribute sets the date when a cookie becomes invalid. The date is formatted in a nonstandard way, like this:

```
Wednesday, 01-Sep-96 00:00:00 GMT
```

After this date, the cookie becomes invalid, and the browser no longer sends it. Only GMT (Greenwich Mean Time) is used. If no expires date is given, the cookie is used only for the current session.

path=*pathname*

The path attribute supplies a URL range for which the cookie is valid. If path is set to /pub, for example, the cookie is sent for URLs in /pub as well as lower levels such as/pub/docs and /pub/images. A *pathname* of "/" indicates that the cookie will be used for all URLs at the site from which the cookie originated. No path attribute means that the cookie is valid only for the originating URL.

domain=*domain-name*

This attribute specifies a domain name range for which the cookie is returned. The *domain-name* must contain at least two dots (.), e.g., .oreilly.com. This value covers both www.oreilly.com and software.oreilly.com, and any other server in the *oreilly.com* domain.

secure

The secure attribute tells the client to return the cookie only over a secure connection (via SHTTP and SSL). Leaving out this attribute means that the cookie is always returned, regardless of the connection.

The Cookie Request Header

Each time a browser goes to a web page, it checks its cookies file for any cookies stored for that URL. If there are any, the browser includes a Cookie header in the request containing the cookie's *name*=*value* pairs.

```
Cookie: name1=value1; name2
=value2; . . .
```

Returned cookies may come from multiple entries in the cookies files, depending on path ranges and domain ranges. For instance, if two cookies from the same site are set with the following headers:

```
Set-Cookie: Gemstone=Diamond; path=/
Set-Cookie: Gemstone=Emerald; path=/caves
```

when the browser requests a page at the site in the */caves* path, it returns:

```
Cookie: Gemstone=Emerald; Gemstone=Diamond
```

Both items share the same name, but since they are separate cookies, they both apply to the particular URL in */caves*. When returning cookies, the browser returns the most specific path or domain first, followed by less specific matches.

When the `Cookie` header is encountered, many servers pass the value of that header to CGI programs using the HTTP_COOKIE environment variable. See Chapter 12 for more information on CGI environment variables.

The preliminary cookies specification places some restrictions on the number and size of cookies:

- Clients should be able to support at least 300 total cookies. Servers should not expect a client to store more.

  The limit on the size of each cookie (name and value combined) should not exceed 4KB.
- A maximum of 20 cookies per server or domain is allowed. This limit applies to each specified server or domain, so *www.oreilly.com* is allowed 20, and *software.oreilly.com* is allowed 20, if they are each specified by their full names.

An issue arises with proxy servers in regard to the headers. Both the `Set-Cookie` and `Cookie` headers should be propagated through the proxy, even if a page is cached or has not been modified (according to the `If-Modified-Since` condition). The `Set-Cookie` header should also never be cached by the proxy.

Most web servers and clients still support the original cookie specification proposed by Netscape. Recently, the IETF has issued an Internet draft proposal for an updated cookie specification. This document describes new `Set-Cookie2` and `Cookie2` headers to eventually replace the original headers. They add additional attributes for comments and path specifiers.

Clients and servers that implement the new headers should be backwards-compatible with the original specification. The draft proposal can be found at the following URL:

```
http://www.ietf.org/internet-drafts/draft-ietf-http-state-man-mec-10.txt
```

Media Types and Subtypes

Media types are used to communicate the format of the content in HTTP transactions. Clients use media types in their `Accept` headers to indicate what formats they prefer to receive data in. Servers use media types in their `Content-Type` headers to tell the client what format the accompanying entity is in—i.e., whether the enclosed text is HTML that needs to be formatted, GIF or JPEG to be rendered, or PDF that requires opening an external viewer or using a plug-in.

Internet media types used by HTTP closely resemble MIME types. MIME (Multipurpose Internet Mail Extension) was designed as a method for sending attachments in email over the Internet. Like MIME, media types follow the format *type/subtype*. Asterisks (*) represent a wildcard. For example, the following client header means that documents of all formats are accepted:

```
Accept: */*
```

The following client header means that all `text` format types are accepted, regardless of the subtype:

```
Accept: text/*
```

Servers and CGI programs are expected to examine the format types reported by the `Accept` header and return data of an acceptable type when possible. Most servers determine the format of a document from its filename suffix—for example, a file ending with *.htm* or *.html* is assumed to be HTML format, so the server sends the document with a `Content-Type` of `text/html`. When calling a CGI program, servers cannot know the format of the data being returned, so the CGI program is responsible for reporting the content type itself. For that reason, every CGI program needs to include a `Content-Type` header such as:

```
Content-Type: text/html
```

Table 17-1 lists commonly used media types, along with the filename suffixes recognized by most servers. The current IANA-approved list can be found at *http://www.isi.edu/in-notes/iana/assignments/media-types/media-types*. Servers can be easily configured to recognize additional suffixes as well.

Table 17-1. Media types and subtypes

Type/subtype	Usual extension
application/activemessage	
application/andrew-inset	
application/applefile	
application/atomicmail	
application/cals-1840	
application/commonground	
application/cybercash	
application/dca-rft	
application/dec-dx	
application/EDI-Consent	
application/EDIFACT	
application/EDI-X12	
application/eshop	
application/hyperstudio	
application/iges	
application/mac-binhex40	
application/macwriteii	
application/marc	
application/mathematica	
application/msword	doc
application/news-message-id	
application/news-transmission	
application/octet-stream	bin
application/oda	oda
application/pdf	pdf
application/pgp-encrypted	
application/pgp-signature	
application/pgp-keys	

HTTP

Table 17-1. Media types and subtypes (continued)

Type/subtype	Usual extension
application/pkcs7-mime	
application/pkcs7-signature	
application/pkcs10	
application/postscript	ai, eps, ps
application/prs.alvestrand.titrax-sheet	
application/prs.cww	
application/prs.nprend	
application/remote-printing	
application/riscos	
application/rtf	rtf
application/set-payment-initiation	
application/set-payment	
application/set-registration-initiation	
application/set-registration	
application/sgml	sgm, sgml, gml, dtd
application/sgml-open-catalog	soc, cat
application/slate	
application/vemmi	
application/vnd.$commerce_battelle	
application/vnd.3M.Post-it-Notes	
application/vnd.acucobol	
application/vnd.anser-web-funds-transfer-initiation	
application/vnd.anser-web-certificate-issue-initiation	
application/vnd.audiograph	
application/vnd.businessobjects	
application/vnd.claymore	
application/vnd.comsocaller	
application/vnd.dna	
application/vnd.dxr	
application/vnd.ecdis-update	
application/vnd.ecowin.chart	
application/vnd.ecowin.filerequest	
application/vnd.ecowin.fileupdate	
application/vnd.ecowin.series	
application/vnd.ecowin.seriesrequest	
application/vnd.ecowin.seriesupdate	
application/vnd.enliven	
application/vnd.epson.salt	
application/vnd.fdf	
application/vnd.ffsns	
application/vnd.FloGraphIt	

Table 17-1. Media types and subtypes (continued)

Type/subtype	Usual extension
application/vnd.framemaker	
application/vnd.fujitsu.oasys	
application/vnd.fujitsu.oasys2	
application/vnd.fujitsu.oasys3	
application/vnd.fujitsu.oasysprs	
application/vnd.fujitsu.oasysgp	
application/vnd.fujixerox.docuworks	
application/vnd.hp-hps	
application/vnd.hp-HPGL	
application/vnd.hp-PCL	
application/vnd.hp-PCLXL	
application/vnd.ibm.MiniPay	
application/vnd.ibm.modcap	
application/vnd.intercon.formnet	
application/vnd.intertrust.digibox	
application/vnd.intertrust.nncp	
application/vnd.is-xpr	
application/vnd.japannet-directory-service	
application/vnd.japannet-jpnstore-wakeup	
application/vnd.japannet-payment-wakeup	
application/vnd.japannet-registration	
application/vnd.japannet-registration-wakeup	
application/vnd.japannet-setstore-wakeup	
application/vnd.japannet-verification	
application/vnd.japannet-verification-wakeup	
application/vnd.koan	
application/vnd.lotus-wordpro	
application/vnd.lotus-approach	
application/vnd.lotus-1-2-3	
application/vnd.lotus-organizer	
application/vnd.lotus-screencam	
application/vnd.lotus-freelance	
application/vnd.meridian-slingshot	
application/vnd.mif	
application/vnd.minisoft-hp3000-save	
application/vnd.mitsubishi.misty-guard.trustweb	
application/vnd.ms-artgalry	
application/vnd.ms-asf	
application/vnd.ms-excel	
application/vnd.ms-powerpoint	
application/vnd.ms-project	

Table 17-1. Media types and subtypes (continued)

Type/subtype	Usual extension
application/vnd.ms-tnef	
application/vnd.ms-works	
application/vnd.music-niff	
application/vnd.musician	
application/vnd.netfpx	
application/vnd.noblenet-web	
application/vnd.noblenet-sealer	
application/vnd.noblenet-directory	
application/vnd.novadigm.EDM	
application/vnd.novadigm.EDX	
application/vnd.novadigm.EXT	
application/vnd.osa.netdeploy	
application/vnd.powerbuilder6	
application/vnd.powerbuilder6-s	
application/vnd.rapid	
application/vnd.seemail	
application/vnd.shana.informed.formtemplate	
application/vnd.shana.informed.formdata	
application/vnd.shana.informed.package	
application/vnd.shana.informed.interchange	
application/vnd.street-stream	
application/vnd.svd	
application/vnd.swiftview-ics	
application/vnd.truedoc	
application/vnd.visio	
application/vnd.webturbo	
application/vnd.wrq-hp3000-labelled	
application/vnd.wt.stf	
application/vnd.xara	
application/vnd.yellowriver-custom-menu	
application/wita	
application/wordperfect5.1	
application/x-bcpio	bcpio
application/x-cpio	cpio
application/x-csh	csh
application/x-dvi	dvi
application/x-gtar	gtar
application/x-hdf	hdf
application/x-latex	latex
application/x-mif	mif
application/x-netcdf	nc, cdf

Table 17-1. Media types and subtypes (continued)

Type/subtype	Usual extension
application/x-sh	sh
application/x-shar	shar
application/x-sv4cpio	sv4cpio
application/x-sv4crc	sv4crc
application/x-tar	tar
application/x-tcl	tcl
application/x-tex	tex
application/x-texinfo	texinfo, texi
application/x-troff-man	man
application/x-troff-me	me
application/x-troff-ms	ms
application/x-troff	t, tr, roff
application/x-ustar	ustar
application/x-wais-source	src
application/xml	xml, dtd
application/x400-bp	
application/zip	zip
audio/32kadpcm	
audio/32kadpcm	
audio/basic	au, snd
audio/vnd.qcelp	wav
audio/x-aiff	aif, aiff, aifc
audio/x-wav	wav
image/cgm	cgm
image/g3fax	
image/gif	gif
image/ief	ief
image/jpeg	jpeg, jpg, jpe
image/naplps	
image/png	png
image/tiff	tiff, tif
image/vnd.dwg	
image/vnd.dxf	
image/vnd.fpx	
image/vnd.net-fpx	
image/vnd.svf	
image/vnd.xiff	
image/x-cmu-raster	ras
image/x-portable-anymap	rpnm
image/x-portable-bitmap	pbm
image/x-portable-graymap	pgm

Table 17-1. Media types and subtypes (continued)

Type/subtype	Usual extension
image/x-portable-pixmap	ppm
image/x-rgb	rgb
image/x-xbitmap	xbm
image/x-xpixmap	xpm
image/x-xwindowdump	xwd
message/external-body	
message/http	
message/news	
message/partial	
message/rfc822	
model/iges	
model/mesh	
model/vnd.dwf	
model/vrml	
multipart/alternative	
multipart/appledouble	
multipart/digest	
multipart/form-data	
multipart/header-set	
multipart/mixed	
multipart/parallel	
multipart/related	
multipart/report	
multipart/voice-message	
text/enriched	
text/html	html, htm
text/plain	txt
text/richtext	rtx
text/sgml	sgm, sgml, gml, dtd
text/tab-separated-values	tsv
text/xml	xml, dtd
text/x-setext	etx
video/mpeg	mpeg, mpg, mpe
video/quicktime	qt, mov
video/vnd.vivo	
video/vnd.motorola.video	
video/vnd.motorola.videop	
video/x-msvideo	qvi
video/x-sgi-movie	movie

VIII

Server Configuration

18
Apache Configuration

The Apache HTTP Server is the most widely used web server on the Internet. The Apache server was developed from an early version of the original NCSA server with the intent of providing further improvement while maintaining compatibility. Since then, all development efforts on the NCSA server have ceased. Apache has since earned the title of reigning king among web servers, and it isn't hard to see why: the base distribution is fast, free, and full-featured. It runs on many different platforms and has a multitude of third-party modules available to expand its functionality.

You can pick up a copy of the Apache server and its documentation from the Apache home page: *http://www.apache.org*. This chapter covers Version 2.0 of the Apache server. Most of the configuration and module functionality are similar to the last major release, 1.3, which is still in wide use. Major differences between the versions will be noted.

Understanding Apache

The Apache distribution consists of the source for the core binary, *httpd*, the standard set of modules, and numerous additional header and configuration files. You can compile the server for your particular architecture and preferences using the *config-make-make install* routing common to building open source software. The latest version of *gcc* or another up-to-date ANSI C compiler is required to compile and build Apache.

However, you may not have to compile Apache from source. Most Linux and Mac OS X distributions have Apache already built-in. Furthermore, binaries are available for most popular platforms. Refer to *www.apache.org* for details.

By itself, *httpd* doesn't do more than listen for requests and deliver files as is. Apache is designed to load special *modules* to implement additional functionality. These modules define much of the behavior of the Apache server. A set of standard modules is distributed with the server, including a set of core modules that is automatically compiled into the server binary. Apache will call on modules as needed to perform a dedicated task, such as user authentication or database queries.

Loading Modules

Modules must be compiled first to be used by the server, and can be loaded in two ways: statically or dynamically. Modules can be statically built directly into the server binary at compile time:

```
./configure --enable-module
./configure --disable-base_module
./configure --enable-modules=module_list
```

Alternatively, you can compile modules as DSO's (Dynamically Shared Objects) and load them as needed at run-time (when the server is started or restarted) by identifying them with the `LoadModule` directive in the configuration file.

To compile shared modules at compile time, use:

```
./configure --enable-MODULE=shared
```

DSO modules may also be compiled with *apxs* (Apache Extension Tool) at any time outside of the Apache source tree. See the Apache documentation for full details on *apxs*.

Server Configuration

At startup, Apache reads the main server configuration file *httpd.conf*. You can control the behavior of the server and its modules by inserting or modifying the directives within this file. Additional configuration can occur on a directory-specific level using *.htaccess* files. These are configuration files like *httpd.conf*, but the directives they contain apply only to the directory where they reside. This allows for delegation of control over separate content areas of a single server, and may simplify server management.

The Apache server uses one other configuration file, *mime.types*, to determine what MIME types should be associated with what file suffixes (see Chapter 17).

The configuration files contain directives, which are one-line commands that tell the server what to do. In addition to the directives themselves, the configuration files may contain any number of blank lines or comment lines beginning with a hash mark (#). Although directive names are not case-sensitive, we use the case conventions in the default files. Example copies of each of these files are included with the server software distribution, which you can refer to for more information.

The first things Apache needs from the configuration file are basics like the listening port, server name, the default locations for content, logs, and other important files, and what modules to load. After that, the wider server functionality is configured. This includes access control, virtual hosts, special resource handling, and module-specific directives.

Here are some basic directives you might find in the *httpd.conf* configuration file:

```
ServerType standalone
Port 80
ServerAdmin webmaster@oreilly.com
ServerName webnuts.oreilly.com
User nobody
Group nobody
```

Each directive here specifies a property of the server's configuration and binds it to a default setting or value. Since these directives exist on their own in the configuration file, their context is that of the whole server. Many directives will appear in special subsections that limit their scope. Directives that define subsections are bracketed, XML-like elements. For example:

```
<Directory /docs>
   Deny From All
</Directory>
```

This configuration section sets a directive for requests to a single directory */docs*. Many configuration sections apply to locations of file on the server, such as `<Files>`, `<Location>`, and `<Directory>`. Other configuration sections define virtual servers (`<VirtualHost>`) or contain directives specific to a module (`<IfModule>`)

All server configuration can occur in the *httpd.conf* file, but you may want to allow special configuration of only certain parts of your server—you could let a user configure some aspects of how documents in her directory are served. By default, Apache looks for *.htaccess* files in every directory it serves a file from. *.htaccess* may contain any configuration directives allowed by the server configuration file with the `AllowOverride` directive. For example, if *httpd.conf* contained the line:

```
AllowOverride AuthConfig
```

most of the directives from the user authorization modules (`Auth*`) could be used in an `.htaccess` file to limit access to the files in that directory. This is exactly equivalent to using the same directives within a specified `<Directory>` section in *httpd.conf*.

Since *.htaccess* files affect the directory they are in and any subdirectories, they have a cascading affect on configuration. A directive in a lower-level *.htaccess* requires an `AllowOverride` from a parent-level *.htaccess* to work. This places increased load on the server, which must search for *.htaccess* files and parse them for every request in the current *and* parent-level directories. If you want to completely ignore *.htaccess* files, use `AllowOverride None` in *httpd.conf*.

Handling Requests

On Unix systems, the Apache daemon *httpd* always starts itself as a system superuser (root). This is often done at startup through entries in the system initialization files. On Windows, the Apache service is called *apache* and runs with administrator privileges.

Once started, Apache's job is to listen for requests on any address and port to which it has been configured. When handling a request from a specific client, Apache spawns a separate process to handle the connection. This spawned process, however, doesn't run as the superuser; for security reasons, it instead runs as a restricted user that serves files to the client.

Apache normally has five such processes waiting for connections; hence, after startup, you will see one process (*httpd*) running as root and five processes owned by the Apache user ID, which stand to service requests. You can reconfigure that number, as well as the minimum and maximum number of service processes allowed with the `StartServers`, `MinSpareServers`, and `MaxSpareServers` directives. Each process handles specific HTTP requests for the client, such as GET or POST, which affect content on the server.

All resources available to visiting browsers (HTML documents, images, etc.) reside by default under a single root directory defined by the `DocumentRoot` directive. This defines the base directory that is prepended to a URL path to locate a file on the server. Most URL mapping is as simple as locating a file under the document root, but more complex mapping can be defined through aliasing, redirection, and URL rewriting using the *mod_alias* and *mod_rewrite* modules.

Access Control

Webmasters often find the need to restrict some or all of the data on their servers to authorized users. Access can be controlled by requiring username and password information or by restricting the originating IP address of the client request. The *mod_access* and *mod_auth* core modules provide basic access control for Apache.

Access control is usually confined to specific directories of the document tree. You can place authorization directives in *httpd.conf* within `<Directory>` sections, or within *.htaccess* files in the restricted directory itself (using `AllowOverride AuthConfig`).

This example shows the directives used to configure username and password access to a specific directory:

```
<Directory /projects>
 Options All
 AuthType Basic
 AuthName "Editorial Group"
 AuthUserFile /usr/local/etc/httpd.conf/.htpasswd
 AuthGroupFile /usr/local/etc/httpd.conf/.htgroup
 require group editors
</Directory>
```

The `AuthType` directive specifies the type of authentication used. "Basic" authentication describes the simple authorization scheme used by Apache where user password files are created with the *htpasswd* program. `AuthName` specifies the authorization "Realm". The realm can describe many different server locations so that an authorized user does not have to re-supply his password information as he navigates. AuthUserFile provides the user/password file location, and AuthGroupFile provides the group file location. require sets the restriction to only members of the group "editors".

The following configuration section limits access to a directory to requests from a specific domain:

```
<Directory /projects/golf>
   order deny,allow
   deny from all
   allow from .golf.org
</Directory>
```

Password and Group Files

A password file is needed for user and group-level authentication. The location and name of the password file are specified with the AuthUserName directive. The easiest and most common way to create a password file or add passwords is to use the *htpasswd* program that is distributed with the server. If a password file already exists for a location, you can type:

```
htpasswd pathname username
```

The program then asks you to type the password you wish for the given username twice, and the username and encrypted password are stored in the new file.

If a password file does not exist yet, you can create one by typing the same command with the -c option (e.g., htpasswd -c *pathname username*). But be careful, since the -c option will create a new file without checking if one already exists, thereby overwriting any existing passwords.

Password files created with *.htpasswd* are similar to Unix password files. Keep in mind, however, that there is no correspondence between valid users and passwords on a Unix server, and users and passwords on an Apache web server. You do not need an account on the Unix server to access the web server.

You can bundle several users into a single named group by creating a group file. The location and name of the group file are specified with the AuthGroupFile directive. Each line of a group file specifies the group name, followed by a colon, followed by a list of valid usernames that belong to the group:

```
groupname: username1 username2 username3 ...
```

Each user in a group needs to be entered into the Apache password file. When a group authentication is required, the server accepts any valid username/password from the group.

The *.htpasswd* user authentication scheme is known as the *basic* authentication method for HTTP servers. Apache allows other types of authentication methods, which are configured with a similar set of directives.

Virtual Hosting

Apache also has the ability to perform *virtual hosting*. This allows a single *httpd* process to serve multiple IP addresses or hostnames. Virtual hosting seems like a complicated procedure; however, it really isn't as bad as it seems. In each configuration file, you can structure directives that apply only to virtual hosts. For example, you can specify separate DocumentRoot directives for each virtual machine, such that someone connecting to *www.oreilly.com* is served one set of documents, while another client connecting to *www.onlamp.com* receives another, even though the content for each of these sites is served by the same server on the same machine.

To create a virtual server, simply enclose *httpd.conf* directives related to the server in a <VirtualHost> directive. Here is an example *httpd.conf* configuration that will set up two virtual servers:

```
ServerName www.oreilly.com
AccessConfig /dev/null
ResourceConfig /dev/null

<VirtualHost www.oreilly.com>
ServerAdmin webmaster@oreilly.com
DocumentRoot /usr/local/www/virtual/htdocs/oreilly
ServerName www.oreilly.com
ErrorLog /usr/local/www/virtual/htdocs/oreilly/error_log
TransferLog /usr/local/www/virtual/htdocs/oreilly/transfer_log
</VirtualHost>

<VirtualHost www.onlamp.com>
ServerAdmin webmaster@onlamp.com
DocumentRoot /usr/local/www/virtual/htdocs/onlamp
ServerName www.onlamp.com
ErrorLog /usr/local/www/virtual/htdocs/onlamp/error_log
TransferLog /usr/local/www/virtual/htdocs/onlamp/transfer_log
</VirtualHost>
```

Log Files

Apache creates two log files by default: the error log and the access log. The server's error log records any errors the server encounters during execution. The access log records all client requests made to the server. You can set the locations of these files with the ErrorLog and CustomLog directives.

Access logs are highly configurable. The LogFormat directive allows you to specify which data is recorded for each server transaction. For example, the following directive:

```
LogFormat "%h %l %u %t \"%r\" %>s %b" common
```

configures the access log to record information in the Common Log Format, which includes such data as the client IP, user ID, time of request, the request command, and the server's response.

Basic Server Configuration: Core Directives

The following section contains core directives that are independent of modules and can be used in the Apache server at all times. With each directive, we indicate any version constraints that are required, as well as the *context* the directive should appear in. Contexts include:

server config
: The directive is allowed in the *httpd.conf* or *srm.conf* configuration files.

`<VirtualHost>`
: The directive can appear inside a `<VirtualHost>` subsection, stating that the directive applies to a virtual server.

`<Directory>`
: The directive can appear inside a `<Directory>` subsection, stating that the directive applies to a specific directory tree on the server.

.htaccess
: The directive can appear inside the per-directory *.htaccess* access control files.

Directives pertaining to specific Apache modules are covered in Chapter 19.

AcceptPathInfo

`AcceptPathInfo on|off|default`

Determines if extra information following a valid URL pathname is accepted by the server or not. An `off` value means that a request is rejected if the pathname doesn't match exactly a server resource. `on` means that the server ignores the extra path information and returns the resource that will match a valid part of the path. The `default` setting allows the default handler to determine action. If the resource is a CGI script, extra path info may be allowed, but not if the request is for a file.

AccessConfig

`AccessConfig` *`filename`*

[*server config* or within `<VirtualHost>`]

Specifies the location of the access configuration file, either as an absolute path (with a beginning slash) or as a relative path from the `ServerRoot` directory. For example:

```
AccessConfig conf/access.conf
```

AccessFileName

`AccessFileName` *`filename filename ...`*

[*server config* or within `<VirtualHost>`]

Specifies the names of one or more per-directory access control files. The default is:

```
AccessFileName .htaccess
```

AddDefaultCharSet

```
AddDefaultCharSet on|off|charset
```

Specifies whether the server will add a default CharSet header to outgoing HTTP headers that do not have a Content Type set. If set to on the default Apache charset will be used. Otherwise, you can provide the character set string you wish.

AllowOverride

```
AllowOverride options ...
```

[Within `<Directory>`]

Controls the extent to which local per-directory *.htaccess* files can override the defaults defined by access control files in higher directories. The directive takes one or more options, which can be:

`None`
: Access control files are unrecognized in this directory.

`All`
: Access control files are unrestricted in this directory.

`Options`
: Allow use of the `Options` and `XBitHack` directives.

`Indexes`
: Allow use of directory indexing directives (`FancyIndexing`, `AddIcon`, and `AddDescription`, etc.).

`FileInfo`
: Allow use of the directive relating to document type: (`AddType`, `AddEncoding`, `AddLanguage`, etc.).

`AuthConfig`
: Allow use of these directives: `require`, `AuthName`, `AuthType`, `AuthUserFile`, `AuthGroupFile`, or any other `Auth*` directives.

`Limit`
: Allow use of the `allow`, `deny`, and `order` directives.

If omitted, the default is:

```
AllowOverride All
```

AuthName

```
AuthName name
```

[Within `<Directory>` or *.htaccess*]

Sets the name of the username/password authorization realm for this directory. The value is a short name describing this authorization realm; it can contain spaces.

AuthType

```
AuthType type
```

[Within `<Directory>` or *.htaccess*]

Sets the type of authorization used in this directory. `Basic` authorization is the most commonly used method. If used, this directive should be followed by `AuthName`, `require`, `AuthGroupFile`, and `AuthUserFile` directives, which better describe the authorization realm.

CGIMapExtension `CGIMapExtension` *`path extension`*

[Within `<Directory>` or *.htaccess*]

Provides an alternative method for assigning a script interpreter to a given file extension.

ContentDigest `ContentDigest on|off`

Computes an MD5 (Message Digest 5) hash of the body content of core data sent to the client. This value is stored in a header that looks like:

```
Content-MD5: AyTr28784eSp2k67d98n28a=
```

The receiver can use this hash value to determine whether the contents of the page have been altered in transit. The hash values are not cached for each page sent; hence, they must be recalculated each time data is requested.

DefaultType `DefaultType` *`mime_type`*

Establishes a default MIME type to be returned to a browser if mappings in the *mime.types* file fail to successfully identify a document or file type. The default is `text/html`.

<Directory> `<Directory>...</Directory>`

[*server config* or within `<VirtualHost>`]

`<Directory>` is a sectioning directive that identifies the directory (and its subdirectories) to which contained access-control directives apply. This directive cannot be used in a per-directory *.htaccess* file. The start tag has this format:

```
<Directory dir>
```

where *dir* is the absolute pathname of the directory. You can include wildcard characters (such as * and ?) to designate a set of directories or even use regular expressions if preceded by a tilde (~).

<DirectoryMatch> `<DirectoryMatch>...</DirectoryMatch>`

[*server config* or within `<VirtualHost>`]

`<DirectoryMatch>` is a sectioning directive that identifies the directory (and subdirectories) to which contained access-control directives apply. It cannot be used in a per-directory *.htaccess* file. The start tag has this format:

```
<DirectoryMatch regex>
```

where *regex* is a regular expression that designates one or more directories the enclosed directives apply to.

DocumentRoot `DocumentRoot directory_path`

[*server config* or within <VirtualHost>]

Specifies the root of the server document tree. For example:

```
DocumentRoot /usr/local/etc/httpd/htdocs/
```

This specifies that HTML documents for this server will reside in the given directory and its subdirectories. The default is:

```
DocumentRoot /usr/local/apache/htdocs/
```

ErrorDocument `ErrorDocument code filename|string|URL`

Allows you to customize the response sent by your server when an error is encountered. The error code is an HTTP status code as listed in Chapter 17. Possible values are:

filename .25i
: A local file to return upon encountering this error

string .25i
: A message to return upon encountering this error; the string must be surrounded by quotes

URL .25i
: A local or remote document to redirect the user to upon encountering this error

Example usage:

```
ErrorDocument 404 /errors/notfound.html
ErrorDocument 408 "Sorry, the server timed out
 - try again later"
ErrorDocument 402 http://www.oreilly.com/payment/
```

ErrorLog `ErrorLog filename`

[*server config* or within <VirtualHost>]

Specifies the location of the error log file, either an absolute path or relative path to the ServerRoot directory if an opening slash (/) is omitted. The default setting is:

```
ErrorLog logs/error_log
```

Beginning with Apache 1.3, you can specify syslog if the system supports logging via syslogd.

FileETag `FileETag flags`

Configures how the server forms the ETag response header used for network cache management. The header value is formed from a combination of certain file attributes. The flag keywords can be used in the directive with a plus or minus in front of them to indicate if they will be included or excluded from the determination with respect to a broader scope. The flags are:

INode
The file's inode number

MTime
The last-modified data and time of the file

Size
The size of the file

`All` indicates all three attributes should be used. `None` specifies that no ETag value should be added.

<Files>

`<Files>...</Files>`

The `<Files>` directive is a sectioning directive that identifies the file or files to which contained access-control directives apply. The start tag has this format:

```
<Files filename>
```

where *filename* is the name of any file that should have restrictions placed on it. Note that *filename* may include wildcard characters (such as * and ?) to designate a set of files. In addition, you may place it inside a `<Directory>` directive to further restrict which files are affected. You can also specify regular expressions by preceding them with a tilde (~).

<FilesMatch>

`<FilesMatch>...</FilesMatch>`

The `<FilesMatch>` directive is a sectioning directive that identifies the file or files to which contained access-control directives apply. The start tag has the following format:

```
<FilesMatch regex>
```

where *regex* is a regular expression that designates one or more files the enclosed directives apply to. Note that you may place this directive inside a `<Directory>` directive to further restrict which files are affected.

ForceType

`ForceType mime-type`

[Within `<Directory>` or *.htaccess*]

Forces all files in its scope to be served as the specified MIME type.

Group

`Group groupname`

[*server config* or within `<VirtualHost>`]

Specifies the group you want the server to process requests as. Either a group name or group ID can be specified; a group ID should be preceded by a hash mark (#). Setting this option to the same group as the superuser (i.e., `root`) is highly discouraged. Many administrators use the group `nobody` for the Apache server.

HostNameLookups `HostNameLookups on|off|double`

[*server config*, within `<VirtualHost>` or `<Directory>`]

Enables whether the server should perform hostname lookups on clients instead of simply recording the IP address in the connection logs. If the *double* option is specified, the server performs a forward and reverse DNS lookup; this ensures the client hostname maps to its IP, as well as the IP mapping to the DNS name. The default is `off`.

IdentityCheck `IdentityCheck on|off`

[*server config*, within `<VirtualHost>` or `<Directory>`]

Specifies whether the server should attempt to learn the user identity for each request by querying an *identd* process running on the user's machine. By default, identity checking is `off`.

<IfDefine> `<IfDefine>...</IfDefine>`

A sectioning directive for specifying directives that apply if a given define is entered on the command line. For example:

```
<IfDefine MD5Digest>
LoadModule mod_digest libexec/moddigest.so
</IfDefine>
```

This directive is executed if the Apache server is started using the following command line parameter:

```
httpd -DMD5Digest ...
```

Note that you can place an exclamation mark in front of the `<IfDefine>` parameter to include such directives if a definition is *not* made on the command line.

<IfModule> `<IfModule>...</IfModule>`

A sectioning directive for specifying directives that apply if a given module has been compiled into the Apache server. For example:

```
<IfModule mod_cgi>
LoadModule mod_speling libexec/modspelling.so
</IfModule>
```

This directive is executed if Apache is compiled with the `mod_cgi` module. Note that you can place an exclamation mark in front of the module name to include such directives if a module is not included in the Apache server build.

Include `Include` *`filename`*

[*server config*, within `<VirtualHost>`, or `<Directory>`]

Tells the server to include a specified file as part of its configuration.

KeepAlive

`KeepAlive on|off`

[*server config* or within `<VirtualHost>`]

Tells the server to allow persistent connections using the same TCP connection. The default is `on`. See also `KeepAliveTimeOut` and `MaxKeepAliveRequests`.

KeepAliveTimeOut

`KeepAliveTimeOut` *`seconds`*

[*server config* or within `<VirtualHost>`]

Specifies the number of seconds to wait for the next request before closing a persistent connection. Used only when persistent connections are enabled with the `KeepAlive On` setting. The default is 15.

<Limit>

`<Limit` *`methods`*`> ... </Limit>`

`<Limit>` is a sectioning directive that applies to the specified access methods (GET, POST, etc.). This directive restricts the boundaries of the access methods specified; if you wish to apply restrictions globally, omit the `Limit` directive completely. The start tag has the following syntax:

```
<Limit method1 method2 ...>
```

where a *method* is one of the following:

`GET`
: Allows clients to retrieve documents and execute scripts with the GET request method. The HEAD method is also restricted when you specify GET.

`POST`
: Allows clients to use scripts and resources using the POST request method (mostly CGI programs).

`PUT`
: Allows clients access to documents and resources using the PUT request method.

`DELETE`
: Allows clients access to documents and resources using the DELETE request method.

`CONNECT`
: Allows clients access to documents and resources using the CONNECT request method.

`OPTIONS`
: Allows clients access to documents and resources using the OPTIONS request method.

The `order`, `deny`, `allow`, and `require` directives are the usual inhabitants of the `Limit` sectioning directive.

<LimitExcept> `<LimitExcept methods> ... </LimitExcept>`

The reverse functionality of the `<Limit>` directive. `<LimitExcept>` restricts any methods that are not listed as parameters.

LimitRequestBody `LimitRequestBody size`

Limits the maximum size in bytes of the body of a client request. This setting can assist in addressing abnormal requests and some denial of service attacks. The default is 0.

LimitRequestFields `LimitRequestFields n`

[server config]

Limits the maximum number of HTTP headers accepted in a client request. This setting can assist in addressing abnormal requests and some denial of service attacks. The default is 100.

LimitRequest Fieldsize `LimitRequestFieldsize size`

[server config]

Limits the size in bytes of header fields accepted from a client request. The default is 8190.

LimitRequestLine `LimitRequestLine size`

[server config]

Limits the maximum size of the request line in a client request. The request line contains the HTTP method the URI of the requested resource and the protocol version number. This directive effectively limits the length of the URI. The request URI can vary widely in length, since it may contain extra-path info or CGI query strings. The default is 16380.

LimitXMLRequest Body `LimitXMLRequestBody size`

Limits the size in bytes of the body of an XML request that the server will accept. This setting would relate to SOAP requests and other XML-based services. The default is 0.

Listen `Listen [IP_address:]port`

[server config]

Tells the server to listen for requests on the specified port for the specified IP address (if supplied), instead of that specified by the `BindAddress` and `Port` directives. Multiple `Listen` directives can be used to bind the server to more than one port or address/port combination.

ListenBacklog `ListenBacklog` *`backlog`*

[*server config*]

Sets the length of the pending connection queue. Increasing this may be useful when the server is flooded with an unusually large number of pending connections. The default is 511.

<Location> `<Location` *`urlpath`*`>...</Location>`

[*server config* or within `<VirtualHost>`]

A sectioning directive for specifying directives that apply to a given URL. Basically just a more specific version of `<Directory>`. Wildcards and regular expressions are allowed.

<LocationMatch> `<LocationMatch` *`regexpr`*`>...</LocationMatch>`

[*server config* or within `<VirtualHost>`]

A sectioning directive for specifying directives that apply to a given URL. Basically, it's just a more specific version of `<DirectoryMatch>`.

LockFile `LockFile` *`filename`*

[*server config*]

Sets the path to the lockfile Apache uses while running. The lockfile must be on the local disk and cannot be NFS-mounted. This file should never be placed in a world-writable directory.

LogLevel `LogLevel` *`level`*

[*server config* or within `<VirtualHost>`]

This directive sets the verbosity of the Apache error logs. The level can be one of the following:

`emerg`
: Logs errors that cause the server to fail.

`alert`
: Reports alerts from program execution that had unexpected errors. The server may or may not perform correctly after such an error.

`crit`
: Reports critical conditions from server execution.

`error`
: Reports error conditions in Apache execution.

`warn`
: Reports warnings in Apache execution.

`notice`
: Reports common, noteworthy conditions.

`info`
: Reports informational items.

`debug`
: Reports simple debug-level items.

MaxClients

`MaxClients` *`number`*

[*server config*]

Specifies the maximum number of slave processes, and hence the number of client connections, the Apache server can support at a given time. The default is 256.

MaxKeepAliveRequests

`MaxKeepAliveRequests` *`number`*

[*server config*]

When persistent connections are enabled with `KeepAlive On`, the `MaxKeepAliveRequests` directive specifies the number of requests the server allows per persistent connection. If set to 0, the server allows unlimited connections. The default is 100.

MaxMemFree

`MaxMemFree` *`number`*

[*server config*]

Specifies the amount of memory (in KBytes) that can be held by the main allocator before calling *free()*. A zero value or no setting is equivalent to no limit at all.

MaxRequestsPerChild

`MaxRequestsPerChild` *`number`*

[*server config*]

Specifies how many requests a slave process may handle for a client during its life. If set to 0, the slave process may handle an unlimited number of connections; the default is 0. For example:

```
MaxRequestsPerChild 1000
```

This allows the slave process to handle up to 1000 requests per connection before the process dies, and the client is forced to reconnect to the server.

MaxSpareServers

`MaxSpareServers` *`number`*

[*server config*]

Specifies the upper range for how many idle slave processes the server should keep to handle requests. The default is 10.

MinSpareServers

`MinSpareServers number`

[*server config*]

Specifies the lower range for how many idle slave processes the server should keep around to handle requests. The default is 5.

NameVirtualHost

`NameVirtualHost [IP_address:]port`

[*server config*]

Specifies the name or address a virtual host on the server should resolve to. In addition to the address, you can also specify the port that should be used. For example, if you are accepting connections on the server under the IP 123.23.23.123, port 8001 (in addition to others), you would specify:

```
NameVirtualHost 123.23.23.123:8001
```

Options

`Options options ...`

[*server config*, or within `<VirtualHost>` or `<Directory>`, or *.htaccess*]

Controls the degree of advanced features that you wish to allow on your server. One or more options may be listed on the `Options` line, separated by spaces. Valid entries are:

`None`
: No features are enabled in this directory.

`Indexes`
: Allows clients to request a formatted index of this directory if no `DirectoryIndex` has been specified.

`Includes`
: Server-side includes are enabled in this directory.

`IncludesNoExec`
: Server-side includes (SSIs) are enabled in the directory, but the *exec* feature and the *include* of CGI scripts is disabled.

`ExecCGI`
: Execution of CGI scripts is allowed in this directory.

`MultiViews`
: Content-negotiated multiviews are allowed in this directory.

`FollowSymLinks`
: The server follows symbolic links in this directory. The pathname is not altered to reflect to the new location.

`SymLinksIfOwnerMatch`
: The server follows symbolic links only if the target file/directory is owned by the same user ID as the link.

`All`
: All features are enabled in this directory.

The Options directive can be used in both the global *access.conf* and in per-directory *.htaccess* files. There can be only one Options directive per Directory segment. If omitted, the default is:

```
Options All
```

PidFile

PidFile *filename*

[*server config*]

Specifies the location of the file into which the server should place its process ID when running in standalone mode, either as an absolute path or as a relative path from the ServerRoot directory if an opening slash (/) has been omitted. The default is:

```
PidFile logs/httpd.pid
```

---

require

require *entity* names ...

[Within <Directory>, or *.htaccess*]

Specifies which authenticated users or groups can access a given directory, typically in a <Limit> section of an access control file. A require line requires that all of the appropriate Auth* directives are specified for the directory. *entity* is one of the following:

user
: Only the named users can access this directory with the given methods. Each name is therefore a username that exists in the AuthUserFile (specified password file).

group
: Only users in the named groups can access this directory with the given methods. Each name is therefore a group name that is listed in the specified group file.

valid-user
: All users listed in the AuthUserFile (specified password file) are allowed access upon providing a valid password.

For example, the following restricts access to a directory to a few key users:

```
require user jdoe msmith
```

RLimitCPU

RLimitCPU *limit* [*limit*]

Specifies the soft resource limit and optionally the maximum resource limit of CPU time, in seconds per slave process.

```
RLimitCPU 5 5
```

In place of each parameter, you can also use the max keyword, which sets it to the maximum allowed by the host operating system.

RLimitMEM

```
RLimitMEM limit [limit]
```

Specifies the soft resource limit and optionally the maximum resource limit of memory usage, in bytes per process.

```
RLimitMEM 65535 65535
```

In place of each parameter, you can also use the max keyword, which sets it to the maximum allowed by the host operating system.

RLimitNPROC

```
RLimitNPROC limit [limit]
```

[*server config*, or within <VirtualHost>]

Specifies the soft resource limit and optionally the maximum resource limit of slave processes that the server can create.

```
RLimitNPROC 20 20
```

In place of each parameter, you can also use the max keyword, which sets it to the maximum allowed by the host operating system.

Satisfy

```
Satisfy any|all
```

[Within <Directory>, or *.htaccess*]

Specifies an access policy if access is restricted by both username-password and host address. The any parameter allows access if the client satisfies either the username-password or host address requirements. The all parameter requires that the client satisfy both.

ScoreBoardFile

```
ScoreBoardFile filename
```

[*server config*]

Specifies the location of the server status file, used by the server to communicate with slave processes. The location is specified as an absolute path, or as a relative path from the ServerRoot directory if the opening slash (/) is omitted. The default is:

```
ScoreBoardFile logs/apache_status
```

SendBufferSize

```
SendBufferSize bytes
```

[*server config*]

Resets the TCP buffer size, typically over the OS default.

ServerAdmin

```
ServerAdmin email_address
```

[*server config*, or within <VirtualHost>]

Specifies the email address to which complaints, suggestions, and questions regarding your server should be sent. Used when the server sends error messages in response to failed requests. This directive has no default. It may be specified as follows:

```
ServerAdmin webmaster@oreilly.com
```

ServerAlias

`ServerAlias` *`virtual_hostname`* `real_hostname`

[Within `<VirtualHost>`]

Specifies an alternate name for a server virtual host.

ServerName

`ServerName` *`hostname`*`[:`*`port`*`]`

[*server config*, or within `<VirtualHost>`]

Allows you to specify a preferred hostname for your server and its port address. (In 2.0, this directive replaces the functionality of the superseded `Port` directive.) This must be a valid, fully qualified DNS name for the server in question.

ServerPath

`ServerPath` *`pathname`*

[Within `<VirtualHost>`]

Specifies a pathname for a virtual host; that is, requests for this hostname are automatically routed to the specified pathname.

ServerRoot

`ServerRoot` *`directory_path`*

[*server config*]

Specifies the directory in which all the server's associated files reside. This path is used as the root directory when relative paths are specified with other directives. For example:

```
ServerRoot /etc/httpd/
```

ServerSignature

`ServerSignature on|off|EMail`

[*server config*, or within `<VirtualHost>` or `<Directory>`, or *.htaccess*]

Creates a footer line under all documents to identify the exact server this document originated from. This is useful in the event that there is a series of proxies, any one of which can return a specific document or error message. The default is `off`. If the `on` option is specified, the footer creates a line with the `ServerName` and version number. If the `EMail` option is used, the server creates a name and version number as well as a "mailto:" reference to the `ServerAdmin`.

ServerTokens

`ServerTokens Minimal|OS|Full`

[*server config*]

Specifies which type of header field is returned to clients when the information is requested. There are three options, listed with the appropriate formats:

`ProductOnly (Prod)`
    `Server: Apache`

`Major`
    `Server: Apache/2`

`Minor`
    `Server: Apache/2.0`

`Minimal (Min)`
    `Server: Apache/2.0.41`

`OS`
    `Server: Apache/2.0.41 (Unix)`

`Full`
    `Server: Apache/2.0.41 (Unix) PHP/4.2.2 MyMod/1.2`

ServerType

`ServerType standalone|inetd`

[*server config*]

Specifies whether your server is run standalone or from the *inetd* daemon. If the server is run from *inetd*, it's restarted each time a connection is made; hence, using this option is discouraged. The default is to run standalone.

SetHandler

`SetHandler` *`handler`*

Specifies a special handler for files requested from the location where this directive is used.

SetInputFilter

`SetInputFilter` *`filter[; filter2; filter3;...`*

Specifies a filter or filters to process client requests.

SetOutputFilter

`SetOutputFilter` *`filter[; filter2; filter3;...>`*

Specifes a filter or filters to process server responses before they are sent to the client.

StartServers

`StartServers` *`number`*

[*server config*]

Specifies the initial number of slave processes at server startup. The default is 5. This directive has no effect under the Windows platform.

TimeOut `TimeOut seconds`

[*server config*]

Specifies the number of seconds to wait before closing a presumably defunct connection. The default is 300 seconds.

UseCanonicalName `UseCanonicalName on|off|dns`

[*server config*, within `<Directory>`, or `<VirtualHost>`]

Used to build a self-referential URL. If `on`, Apache uses the `<ServerName>` directive to build a URL representing itself. If `off`, Apache attempts to construct its URL from the client parameters, which is typical when using the `VirtualHost` directive to represent different addresses. The `dns` value causes the server to use reverse DNS lookup to determine the self URL.

User `User username`

[*server config*, or within `<VirtualHost>`]

Specifies the user you want the Apache server to process requests as. Either a username or user ID can be specified; a user ID should be preceded by a hash mark (#). Setting this to `root` is highly discouraged. Many administrators create a user nobody for Apache.

<VirtualHost> `<VirtualHost>...</VirtualHost>`

[*server config*]

Used when the Apache server services multiple hostnames. Each hostname is given its own `<VirtualHost>` directive.

`<VirtualHost>` has a beginning and ending directive, with other configuration directives for the virtual host entered in between. Most directives are valid within `<VirtualHost>` except the following: `BindAddress`, `GroupId`, `MaxRequestsPerChild`, `MaxSpareServers`, `MinSpareServers`, `Listen`, `NameVirtualHost`, `PidFile`, `ServerType`, `ServerRoot`, `StartServers`, `TypesConfig`, and `UserId`. This is essentially a segmenting directive that applies directives solely to the virtual host specified. For example:

```
<VirtualHost sales.oreilly.com>
ServerAdmin webmaster@oreilly.com
DocumentRoot /ora/sales/www
ServerName sales.oreilly.com
ErrorLog /ora/sales/logs/error_log
TransferLog /ora/sales/logs/access_log
</VirtualHost>
```

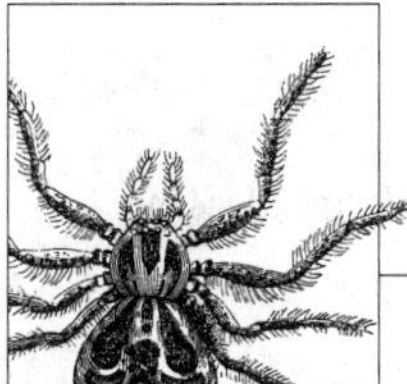

Apache Modules

Modules are a key part of Apache. They provide much of the functionality administrators expect in a modern web server, including user tracking, CGI scripting, authentication, SSL, etc. The set of modules distributed with Apache can be divided into a number of groups. Core modules provide the set of directives that are always available to Apache. The Base modules provide a common set of features for the server and are compiled in by default. You have to manually deselect them during compilation to not install them. The Extension modules comprise another set of common and useful server features, but are not required for every server setup. Therefore, they are not compiled by default. The remaining modules are classified as Experimental; they are either not completed to specification, or introduce instability to some environments.

This chapter contains information about the Base and Extension modules and their directives. The modules are present in versions 1.3 and 2.0, and differences in support are noted per version. Table 19-1 shows the Apache modules described in this chapter.

Table 19-1. Standard Apache modules

Module	Compiled	Description
mod_access	✓	Access control
mod_actions	✓	CGI scripting
mod_alias	✓	Aliasing and filesystem mapping
mod_asis	✓	Provides for *.asis* (as is) files
mod_auth	✓	User authentication
mod_auth_anon		Anonymous user authentication
mod_auth_db		User authentication with DB files. (Apache 1.1 to 1.3)
mod_auth_dbm		User authentication with DBM files
mod_autoindex	✓	Automatic directory listings
mod_cern_meta		Support for CERN metafiles

Table 19-1. Standard Apache modules (continued)

Module	Compiled	Description
mod_cgi	✓	Execution of CGI scripts
mod_cgid	✓	Execution of CGI scripts with external daemon (Apache 2.0 and up)
mod_dir	✓	Simple directory handling
mod_dav		Support for WevDAV (Apache 2.0 and up)
mod_deflate		Compress content sent to the client (Apache 2.0 and up)
mod_env	✓	Environment variable handling
mod_example		Example of Apache API usage
mod_expires		Automatic expire headers
mod_headers		Modification of HTTP response headers
mod_imap	✓	Image map handling
mod_include	✓	Server-side includes
mod_info		Server information
mod_isapi	✓	Support for ISAPI extensions in Windows
mod_log_config	✓	Configurable logging
mod_logio	✓	Logs input and output bytes (Apache 2.0 and up)
mod_mime	✓	MIME handling
mod_mime_magic		MIME handling via magic numbers
mod_negotiation	✓	Content negotiation
mod_proxy		Proxy capabilities
mod_rewrite		URL rewriting
mod_setenvif	✓	Conditional setting of environment variables
mod_so		Dynamic loading of modules and libraries
mod_speling		Spelling corrections
mod_ssl		Secure transaction over SSL (Apache 2.0 and up)
mod_status		Server status pages
mod_suexec		Select user and group for CGI (Apache 2.0 and up)
mod_userdir	✓	User HTML directories
mod_unique_id		Unique server request identifiers
mod_usertrack		User tracking (cookies)
mod_vhost_alias		Dynamic virtual host configuration (Apache 2.0 and up)

This chapter presents an overview of the runtime directives used with the Apache modules. Each of the directives listed in this chapter are grouped in association with the module they relate to.

mod_access

The `mod_access` module resolves which clients are allowed to access server directories based on their IP address or hostname.

allow

`allow from hostname hostname ...`

[Within <Directory> or *.htaccess*]

The `allow` directive specifies which hosts can access a given directory in the site. The *hostname* can be any of the following:

Domain name
: A domain name, like *.oreilly.com*. Only hosts from the domain are permitted access.

Hostname
: A full hostname.

Full IP address
: An IP address of a host.

Partial IP address
: The first 1 to 3 bytes of an IP address, for subnet restriction.

Network address/netmask
: A full network address, followed by a full netmask. (i.e., 192.168.220.110/255.255.255.0)

Network address/CIDR specification
: A full network address, followed by an abbreviated netmask. (i.e., 192.168.220.110/24 is equivalent to 192.168.220.110/255.255.255.0)

`all`
: Using this option means that all hosts are allowed.

There can be only one `allow` directive per section. If omitted, there is no default.

allow

`allow from env=variable`

[Within <Directory> or *.htaccess*]

The `allow from env` directive sets whether access to a directory should be granted if a specific environment variable exists. For example, the following grants access to the secret directory if the client is using Version 5.0 of the "InternetStar" browser, via a user-agent string:

```
BrowserMatch ^InternetStar/5.0 ACCESS_GRANTED
<Directory /secret>
order deny, allow
deny from all
allow from env=ACCESS_GRANTED
</Directory>
```

deny

`deny from hostname hostname ...`

[Within <Directory> or *.htaccess*]

The `deny` directive specifies which hosts are denied access to a directory. The *hostname* can be one of the following:

Domain name
: A domain name, like *.oreilly.com*. Hosts from that domain are denied access.

Hostname
: A full hostname.

Full IP address
: The IP address of a host.

Partial IP address
: The first 1 to 3 bytes of an IP address, for subnet restriction.

Network address with netmask
: A full network address, followed by a full netmask. (i.e., 192.168.220.110/255.255.255.0), or by an abbreviated netmask. (i.e., 192.168.220.110/24 is equivalent to 192.168.220.110/255.255.255.0)

`all`
: Using the word `all` means that all hosts are denied access.

---

deny

`deny from env=`*`variable`*

[Within `<Directory>` or *.htaccess*]

The `deny from env` directive sets whether access to a directory should be denied if a specific environment variable exists. Access to the `secret` directory is denied if the client is using Version 4.0 of the "InternetStar" browser, via a user-agent string:

```
BrowserMatch ^InternetStar/4.0 ACCESS_DENIED
<Directory /secret>
order deny, allow
deny from env=ACCESS_DENIED
allow from all
</Directory>
```

---

order

`order` *`order`*

[Within `<Directory>` or *.htaccess*]

The `order` directive specifies the order in which `deny` and `allow` directives are evaluated. The `order` directive can take one of the following forms:

`order deny,allow`
: `deny` directives are evaluated before `allow` directives (this is the default).

`order allow,deny`
: `allow` directives are evaluated before `deny` directives.

`order mutual-failure`
: This setting means that any host appearing on the `allow` list is allowed, and any host listed on the `deny` list is denied. Finally, any host not appearing on either list is denied.

mod_actions

The mod_actions module is responsible for handling the execution of CGI scripts based on content type.

Action

`Action mime_type cgi_script`

Directs the server to trigger the script *cgi_script* whenever a file of the specified MIME type is requested, sending the requested URL and file path as the PATH_INFO and PATH_TRANSLATED environment variables, respectively.

Script

`Script method cgi_script`

[*server config*, within <VirtualHost> or <Directory>]

Specifies a script *cgi_script* to be executed when a given HTTP request is used. The directive sends the requested URL and file path as the PATH_INFO and PATH_TRANSLATED environment variables, respectively, to the CGI script. The *method* can be GET, POST, PUT, or DELETE.

mod_alias

The mod_alias module assists filesystem mapping and URL redirection.

Alias

`Alias symbolic_path real_path`

[*server config*, within <VirtualHost>]

Creates a virtual name or directory by mapping a symbolic path that is used in a URL to a real path on the server. Aliasing is useful for organizing server documents, keeping URLs simpler for users, and hiding the structure of a filesystem. For example, the icon directory is aliased in the default configuration file:

```
Alias /icons /usr/local/etc/httpd/icons
```

With this setting, a request for */icons/image.gif* is handled by sending back the file */usr/local/etc/httpd/icons/image.gif*. If you specify a trailing slash on the *symbolic path*, the client must also enter that slash for the alias to take effect.

AliasMatch

`AliasMatch regex real_path`

[*server config*, within <VirtualHost>]

Similar to Alias but uses regular expressions. This option creates a virtual name or directory by mapping a symbolic pathname that matches the standard regular expression, *regex*, to a real path on the server. For example:

```
AliasMatch ^/images(.*) /etc/httpd/server/images$1
```

Redirect `Redirect [status] pathname url`

Tells the server to forward clients that request a given directory or document, *pathname*, to a new location, specified by *url*. This new location must be a complete path, unless the *status* given is gone, in which case the new location must be omitted. The Redirect directive supersedes any Alias or AliasMatch directives that are specified.

The *status* variable can be one of the following:

permanent
: This option uses an HTTP status 301 to indicate to the client that the redirect should be considered permanent.

temp
: This option uses an HTTP status 302 to indicate to the client that the redirect is only temporary. This is the default.

seeother
: This option uses an HTTP status 303 to indicate to the client that the resource requested has been superseded or replaced.

gone
: This option uses an HTTP status 410 to indicate to the client that the resource has been removed.

RedirectMatch `RedirectMatch [status] regex url`

Similar to Redirect but uses standard regular expressions. This option tells the server to forward clients that request a directory or document matching the regular expression *regex* to a new location, specified by *url*. For example:

```
RedirectMatch (.*).jpg http://imageserver.mycorp.com$1.jpg
```

RedirectPermanent `RedirectPermanent url-path url srm.conf`

Equivalent to Redirect with a status of permanent.

RedirectTemp `RedirectTemp url-path url`

Equivalent to Redirect with a status of temp.

ScriptAlias `ScriptAlias` *`symbolic_path`* `real_path`

[*server config*, within `<VirtualHost>`]

Creates a virtual directory of CGI programs by mapping a symbolic pathname that is used in a URL to a real directory of executable CGI programs on your server. Instead of returning a document in that directory, the server runs a requested file within a CGI environment and returns the output. For example:

```
ScriptAlias /cgi-bin/ /usr/local/frank/cgi-bin/
```

See Chapter 12, for more information on CGI.

ScriptAliasMatch `ScriptAliasMatch` *`regex`* `filename`

[*server config*, within `<VirtualHost>`]

Similar to `ScriptAlias`, but uses regular expressions. This option creates a virtual directory of CGI programs by mapping any symbolic pathnames that match the standard regular expression *regex* to a real directory of executable CGI programs on the server. For example:

```
ScriptAliasMatch ^/cgi-bin(.*) /usr/local/frank/cgi-bin$1
```

See Chapter 12 for more information on CGI.

mod_auth

The `mod_auth` module provides for user authentication using ordinary text files. Its directives override any core authentication directives given.

AuthAuthoritative `AuthAuthoritative on|off`

[Within `<Directory>`, or *.htaccess*]

Decides at which level authentication and authorization can be performed. If `off` is specified, and there is no user ID matching the requester, authentication and authorization are passed to lower-level modules, which allow access to their respective content based on individual settings. The default is `on`.

AuthGroupFile `AuthGroupFile` *`filename`*

[Within `<Directory>`, or *.htaccess*]

Specifies the user group filename, either as a fully qualified filename or relative to `ServerRoot`. For example:

```
AuthGroupFile /WWW/Admin/.htgroup
```

The format of the file should list on each line a group name, followed by a colon (:), followed by one or more users that belong to that group.

```
authors: robert stephen val
```

AuthUserFile

`AuthUserFile filename`

[Within `<Directory>`, or *.htaccess*]

Specifies a file that contains a list of users and passwords for user authentication, either as a fully qualified filename or relative to the `ServerRoot`. The password file is typically created with the *htpasswd* support program, which comes with the Apache distribution. It is best to place the password file outside the `DocumentRoot` for security purposes. For example:

```
AuthUserFile /etc/admin/.htpasswd
```

mod_auth_anon

The `mod_auth_anon` module determines which clients can access parts of the server anonymously. A standard anonymous connection uses the user `anonymous` with the client user's email address as password. Use of this module allows the server to track visitors and what pages they have requested.

Anonymous

`Anonymous user1 user2 ...`

[Within `<Directory>`, or *.htaccess*]

Specifies a list of users who do not require password authentication to access documents in this realm. The user IDs are case-insensitive. For example:

```
Anonymous anonymous guest "Some User"
```

Anonymous_Authoritative

`Anonymous_Authoritative on|off`

[Within `<Directory>`, or *.htaccess*]

Decides at which level authentication and authorization can be performed. If `off` is specified, and there is no user ID matching the requester, authentication and authorization are passed to lower-level modules, which allow anonymous access to their respective content based on individual settings.

Anonymous_ LogEmail

`Anonymous_LogEmail on|off`

[Within <Directory>, or *.htaccess*]

If set to on, logs the anonymous password entry (the requested email address) to the error log. The default is on.

Anonymous_ MustGiveEmail

`Anonymous_MustGiveEmail on|off`

[Within <Directory>, or *.htaccess*]

If set to on, prohibits blank passwords from being used. The default is on.

Anonymous_ NoUserID

`Anonymous_NoUserID on|off`

[Within <Directory>, or *.htaccess*]

If set to on, allows the user ID entry to be empty. The default is off, which specifies that the client must enter a user ID.

Anonymous_ VerifyEmail

`Anonymous_VerifyEmail on|off`

[Within <Directory>, or *.htaccess*]

If set to on, verifies that the password entered contains a @ and a . character. The default is off.

mod_auth_dbm

The mod_auth_dbm module allows user authentication using DBM files. Its directives overrides any core authentication directives specified.

AuthDBM Authoritative

`AuthDBMAuthoritative on|off`

[Within <Directory>, or *.htaccess*]

Decides at which level authentication and authorization can be performed. If off is specified, and there is no user ID matching the requester, authentication and authorization are passed to lower-level modules, which allow access to their respective contents based on individual settings. The default is on.

AuthDBMGroup File

`AuthDBMGroupFile filename`

[Within <Directory>, or *.htaccess*]

Specifies the group filename as a DBM file, using either a fully qualified filename or a path relative to ServerRoot. For example:

```
AuthDBMGroupFile /www/admin/.groupdbm
```

AuthDBMUserFile `AuthDBMUserFile` *`filename`*

[Within `<Directory>` or *.htaccess*]

Specifies the DBM file that contains a list of users and passwords for user authentication. For example:

```
AuthDBMUserFile /WWW/Admin/.passwddbm
```

mod_autoindex

The `mod_autoindex` module assists with automatic listings of server directory contents. This module can create icons and descriptions for each of the files in the directory, as well as display file content before and after the index itself.

AddAlt `AddAlt` *`string`* `filenames|suffixes ...`

[*server config*, within `<VirtualHost>` or `<Directory>`, or *.htaccess*]

Specifies alternative text for icons used with a given file listing in a directory index. The alternative text is used if the client is unable to load the image for any reason or has disabled the display of images. The text is used as the first argument to the directive, followed by one or more file extensions or names. For example:

```
AddAlt "Image" .gif .jpg .png
AddAlt "Logo" logo.gif
```

See also `FancyIndexing`.

AddAltByEncoding `AddAltByEncoding` *`string`* `mime-encoding ...`

[*server config*, within `<VirtualHost>` or `<Directory>`, or *.htaccess*]

Similar to `AddAlt`, except that it specifies alternative text based on the MIME content encoding of the file being listed. For example, to specify the string "gzip" for a file encoded using the *gzip* compression program, the directive would be:

```
AddAltByEncoding "gzip" x-gzip
```

See also `FancyIndexing`.

AddAltByType `AddAltByType` *`string`* `mime-type ...` *`access.conf/<Directory>`*

[*server config*, within `<VirtualHost>` or `<Directory>`, or *.htaccess*]

Similar to `AddAlt`, except that it specifies alternative text based on the media type of the file being listed. For example, to use the alt text "image" for all GIF files, the directive would be:

```
AddAltByType "image" image/gif
```

See also `FancyIndexing`.

AddDescription

`AddDescription string file ...`

[*server config*, within <VirtualHost> or <Directory>, or *.htaccess*]

Used to associate a descriptive text phrase with a particular type of file. The text appears to the right of the filename in a directory index. The descriptive text must be surrounded by quotes and should be fairly short. Files can be associated by extension or name. For example:

```
AddDescription "GIF image file" .gif
AddDescription "The bottom of Hoover Dam" /home/user/
vacation1.gif
```

See also FancyIndexing.

AddIcon

`AddIcon icon name ...`

[*server config*, within <VirtualHost> or <Directory>, or *.htaccess*]

Specifies an icon image to be displayed with a given type of file in a directory index. For example:

```
AddIcon /icons/image.gif .gif .jpg .png
```

An optional syntax lets you specify alternative text in this directive as well:

```
AddIcon (IMAGE,/icons/image.gif) .gif .jpg .png
```

Three values can be used for the file extensions in the AddIcon directive:

`^^DIRECTORY^^`
: The icon is used for subdirectory names.

`..`
: The icon is used for the parent directory.

`^^BLANKICON^^`
: The icon is used only for spacing in the header of the page.

See also FancyIndexing.

AddIconByEncoding

`AddIconByEncoding icon mime-encoding ...`

[*server config*, within <VirtualHost> or <Directory>, or *.htaccess*]

Specifies an icon to be displayed with a file in a directory index based on the file's encoding. For example:

```
AddIconByEncoding /icons/gzip.gif x-gzip
AddIconByEncoding (GZIP,/icons/gzip.gif) x-gzip
```

See also FancyIndexing.

AddIconByType

`AddIconByType icon mime-type`

[*server config*, within <VirtualHost> or <Directory>, or *.htaccess*]

Specifies an icon to be displayed with a file in a directory index based on the file's media type. For example:

```
AddIconByType /icons/image.gif image/*
AddIconByType (IMAGE,/icons/image.gif) image/*
```

See also `FancyIndexing`.

DefaultIcon

`DefaultIcon` *`url  access.conf/<Directory>`*

[*server config*, within `<VirtualHost>` or `<Directory>`, or *.htaccess*]

Specifies the default icon to use when no icon image has been assigned by one of the `AddIcon*` directives.

See also `FancyIndexing`.

FancyIndexing

`FancyIndexing on|off`

[*server config*, within `<VirtualHost>` or `<Directory>`, or *.htaccess*]

Specifies that the server should create a fancy index for a directory listing, including filenames and icons representing the files' types, sizes, and last-modified dates. By default, fancy indexing is `off`. If it's `on`, the module looks to other directives in this module to determine how to display the directory.

HeaderName

`HeaderName` *`filename`*

[*server config*, within `<VirtualHost>` or `<Directory>`, or *.htaccess*]

Specifies a file to be inserted at the top of the listing when generating a directory index. The example file uses the following setting:

```
HeaderName index.html
```

The server looks for this filename first with an *.html* extension and, failing that, without an extension to display at the top of the directory index.

IndexIgnore

`IndexIgnore` *`filename`* `...`

[*server config*, within `<VirtualHost>` or `<Directory>`, or *.htaccess*]

Tells the server to ignore (hide) certain files when automatically building a directory index on the fly. The files are specified as full server paths, and you can use the wildcards * and ? with their usual meanings. Thus, to ignore all hidden files (i.e., files whose names begin with a period) at every level, you could use the following setting:

```
IndexIgnore */.?*
```

Any number of `IndexIgnore` directives may be included.

IndexOptions `IndexOptions option ...   access.conf/<Directory>`

[*server config*, within `<VirtualHost>` or `<Directory>`, or *.htaccess*]

Specifies a number of options to use when creating a directory index on the fly. Possible options are:

`FancyIndexing`
: Equivalent to `FancyIndexing On`. Unless fancy indexing is turned on by either method, the other index options (except `None`) are ignored.

`IconsAreLinks`
: Make the icons link to the documents (in addition to making the names link).

`IconWidth[=Pixels]`
: Include a `WIDTH` attribute in the image tag for the file icon.

`IconHeight[=Pixels]`
: Include a `HEIGHT` attribute in the image tag for the file icon.

`ScanHTMLTitles`
: Scan any HTML files in the directory, extract their titles, and use them as descriptions for the files.

`SuppressLastModified`
: Omit the last-modified date from the fancy index.

`SuppressSize`
: Omit the size from the fancy index.

`SuppressDescription`
: Omit the description from the fancy index.

`SuppressHTMLPreamble`
: Deactivate the automatic generation of HTML preambles that accompany the `HeaderName`.

ReadmeName `ReadmeName filename`

[*server config*, within `<VirtualHost>` or `<Directory>`, or *.htaccess*]

Specifies a file to be appended to the end of a file listing when generating a directory index. The example file uses the following setting:

```
ReadmeName README
```

The server looks for this filename first with an *.html* extension and, failing that, without an extension. In this case, it will find the file *README* with such an extension.

mod_cern_meta

The `mod_cern_meta` module emulates the CERN web-server metafile semantics. The options listed here are correct as of Apache 1.3. This module is no longer in general use.

MetaDir

`MetaDir` *`directory`*

[*htaccess.conf*]

Indicates the directory in which metafiles can be found. For example:

```
MetaDir .hidden
```

MetaFiles

`MetaFiles on|off`

[*htaccess.conf*, *server config* before Apache 1.3]

Indicates whether metafiles should be used on a directory-by-directory basis.

MetaSuffix

`MetaSuffix` *`suffix`*

[*htaccess.conf*, *server config* before Apache 1.3]

Indicates the suffix of the file or files that contains the meta information.

mod_cgi

The `mod_cgi` module provides for execution of CGI scripts, including the handling of environment variables and logging. When a CGI script is started, this module creates an environment variable called `DOCUMENT_ROOT` that mimics the `DocumentRoot` directive. It also sets the `REMOTE_HOST`, `REMOTE_IDENT`, and `REMOTE_USER` environment variables if appropriate.

ScriptLog

`ScriptLog` *`filename`*

[*server config*]

Sets the name of the CGI-script error log, either as a fully qualified filename or relative to `ServerRoot`. All CGI errors are written out to this file. Note that there is no default log file; if this directive is omitted, the log file isn't created, and all errors are discarded.

ScriptLogLength `ScriptLogLength size`

[*server config*]

Specifies the maximum length of the CGI-script error log file. This is essentially a safety precaution. If the error log file exceeds this length, no more data will be written to it. The default is 10385760 bytes.

ScriptLogBuffer `ScriptLogBuffer size`

[*server config*]

Specifies how much data at a time can be logged to the CGI-script error log with an HTTP PUT or POST command. The default is 1024 bytes.

mod_cgid

On systems which use a multithreaded MPM module, *mod_cgid* automatically replaces *mod_cgi*, creating an external script processing daemon to execute CGI scripts. This saves the server system from spawning a new process to handle a CGI request, which greatly increases system load. The server communicates to the script daemon via Unix domain socket specified with the `ScriptSock` directive. Otherwise, this module is the same as mod_cgi. Apache 2.0 and up.

ScriptSock `ScriptSock socket`

[*server config*, or within `<VirtualHost>`]

Specifies the name of the socket that connects to the CGI daemon. The server's permissions are used to open the socket.

mod_dav

This module provides Apache functionality for WebDAV web-based Distributed Authoring and Versioning. This is an extension to the HTTP protocol that allows for authoring, editing and managing resources on a remote web server. Apache 2.0 and up.

Enable WebDAV for specific directories by placing `Dav on` in directory subsections of *httpd.conf*. In the main part of the server config file, you must specify a server-writable file to be used as the DAV lock database with `DavLockDB`.

Dav `Dav on|off`

[Within `<Directory>`]

Enables WebDAV methods to be used on files in the specified server location. You should also require user authentication to the affected files.

DavDepthInfinity `DavDepthInfinity on|off`

[Within `<Directory>`]

Allows PROPFIND requests containing the header "Depth: Infinity". The default is `off` because this type of request could be used as a denial of service attack.

DavLockDB `DavLockDB` *`path`*

[*server config*]

Specifies the name (full pathname, without extension) of the lock file database that manages user access to DAV-enabled files.

DavMinTimeout `DavMinTimeout` *`time`*

[Within `<Directory>`]

Sets the minimum amount of time, in seconds, that a lock on a DAV resource will be held by the server.

mod_deflate

This module implements an output filter (DEFLATE) that is used to compress content before it is sent to the client. This functionality can conserve network bandwidth and transfer time, but requires that the client be able to decompress the content it receives. Most browsers do not automatically handle compressed content. Apache 2.0 and up.

DeflateBufferSize `DeflateBufferSize` *`size`*

[*server config*, or within `<VirtualHost>`]

Specifies the fragment size in bytes that *zlib* should compress at one time.

DeflateFilterNote `DeflateFilterNote` *`name`*

[*server config*, or within `<VirtualHost>`]

Specifies the name of a note containing the compression ratio that is attached to the request for logging.

DeflateMemLevel `DeflateMemLevel` *`value`*

[*server config*, within `<VirtualHost>`]

Sets an amount of memory zlib may use for compression. *value* is a number from 1 to 9. The default is 9.

DeflateWindow Size `DeflateWindowSize` *`value`*

[*server config*, within `<VirtualHost>`]

Specifies the zlib compression window size. *value* is a number from 1 to 15. The default is 15.

mod_dir

The `mod_dir` module assists in locating various URL addresses that resolve to a directory or begin with a trailing slash.

DirectoryIndex `DirectoryIndex` *`url`* `...`

[*server config*, or within `<VirtualHost>` or `<Directory>` or *.htaccess*]

Specifies the files that should be searched for when the client requests a directory with a trailing slash. All *url* entries must be local to the server machine but do not have to be relative to `ServerRoot`. The server uses the first *url* entry that is found. If no entry is found, the server attempts to list the directory.

mod_env

The `mod_env` module manages how environment variables are passed to CGI/SSI scripts from the shell running the `httpd` server. It contains three straightforward directives.

PassEnv

`PassEnv` *`variable`* `...`

[*server config* or within `<VirtualHost>`]

Passes one or more environment variables to the server CGI scripts.

```
PassEnv HOME
```

SetEnv

`SetEnv` *`variable`* `value`

[*server config* or within `<VirtualHost>`]

Sets one or more environment variables in the context of a server CGI script.

```
SetEnv HOME /home/mike
```

UnsetEnv

`UnsetEnv` *`variable`* `...`

[*server config* or within `<VirtualHost>`]

Unsets (removes) one or more environment variables from the context of a server CGI script.

```
UnsetEnv HOME
```

mod_example

The `mod_example` module provides an example module from which Apache module developers can learn the Apache API.

Example

`Example`

[*server config*, or within `<VirtualHost>` or `<Directory>`, or *.htaccess*]

Used to activate the example module, which provides server calling information for Apache module developers.

mod_expires

The `mod_expires` module allows for the generation of HTTP `Expires` headers for server content. This prevents a document retrieved from the server from being cached and reused on the client machine for any duration past the stated expiration date.

ExpiresActive

```
ExpiresActive true|false
```

[*server config*, or within `<VirtualHost>` or `<Directory>`, or *.htaccess*]

Activates an expiration header for the documents in this realm. The default is `false`.

ExpiresByType

`ExpiresByType` *mime-type* `<A|M>`*seconds*

[*server config*, or within `<VirtualHost>` or `<Directory>`, or *.htaccess*]

Specifies the mime-type of a document and the number of seconds the document should expire in. For example:

```
ExpiresByType text/html A300000
ExpiresByType image/jpg M300000
```

The *seconds* field should be preceded by either the letter `A` or `M`. An `A` indicates that the resource should expire the specified number of seconds after the client's access. An `M` indicates that the resource should expire the specified number of seconds after the last modification date of the document as it resides on the server. The default is specified by the `ExpiresDefault` directive below; this directive overrides the default.

ExpiresDefault

`ExpiresDefault <A|M>`*seconds*

[*server config*, or within `<VirtualHost>` or `<Directory>`, or *.htaccess*]

Specifies the default type of expiry and the number of seconds that document in a specified realm should be cached before it expires. See `ExpiresByType` above.

mod_headers

The `mod_headers` module allows administrators to merge, remove, or replace customizable HTTP response headers to be distributed with documents from the server.

Header

`Header <set|append|add|unset>:`*header* `[`*value*`]`

[*server config*, or within `<VirtualHost>` or `<Directory>`, or *.htaccess*]

This directive allows administrators to merge, remove, or replace HTTP headers that are transmitted with server documents. The header action performed is specified after the `Header` directive; it can be one of four choices:

`set`
: The header specified is reset to the value specified.

`append`
: A header is appended to the specified response header, if it exists. The new value is listed after the old value and is separated by a comma.

`add`
: A new header is created and added to the response headers, even if one already exists.

`unset`
: This option deletes the first occurrence of the header in question.

Headers such as `Date` and `Server` cannot be overridden using this directive.

mod_imap

The `mod_imap` module provides support for *.map* files and imagemaps. Imagemaps allow a server to respond to clicks in various "hot zones" of an image, without creating an explicit link to redirect the client.

ImapBase

`ImapBase map|referer|url`

[*server config*, or within `<VirtualHost>` or `<Directory>`, or *.htaccess*]

Specifies the default base for imagemap files, if there is no `base` directive in the imagemap file itself. A URL can be specified, or one of the following options can be used:

`map`
: Uses the URL of the imagemap file.

`referer`
: Uses the referring document or the `ServerRoot` if a `Referer` header is not specified.

ImapDefault

`ImapDefault error|nocontent|map|referer|URL`

[*server config*, or within `<VirtualHost>` or `<Directory>`, or *.htaccess*]

Specifies the default action for imagemap files, if there is no `default` directive in the imagemap file itself. A URL can be specified, or one of the following options can be used:

`error`
: Fails with a server response code of 500 (see Chapter 17).

`nocontent`
: Sends a server response code of 204, telling the client to keep the same page displayed (see Chapter 17).

`map`
: Uses the URL of the imagemap file.

`referer`
: Uses the referring document, or the server root if a `Referer` header is not specified.

ImapMenu

`ImapMenu none|formatted|semiformatted|unformatted`

[*server config*, or within `<VirtualHost>` or `<Directory>`, or *.htaccess*]

Under Apache, if an imagemap is called without valid coordinates, the server can return a menu of the items in the imagemap file. The `ImapMenu` directive configures that menu. Options are:

`none`
: No menu is created. The action specified with `ImapDefault` is taken.

`formatted`
: A formatted menu is generated, with a listing of the possible links.

`semiformatted`
: A menu with comments from the imagemap file and simple breaks is generated, with a listing of the possible links.

`unformatted`
: A menu with the text of the imagemap file, unformatted. Useful if map files are written as HTML.

mod_include

The `mod_include` module provides support for server-side includes (SSIs). See Chapter 13 for further explanation.

XBitHack

`XBitHack` *`status`*

[*server config*, or within `<VirtualHost>` or `<Directory>`, or *.htaccess*]

Specifies the parsing of executable HTML documents. Options are:

`on`
: Files that are user-executable are treated as a server-parsed HTML document (SPML).

`off`
: Executable files are treated as regular files.

`full`
: Files that are both user- and group-executable have the last modified time altered to match that of the returned document.

mod_info

The mod_info module allows for addition information links to be placed in various documents sent by the server.

AddModuleInfo AddModuleInfo *module* string

[*server config*, or within <VirtualHost>]

Places the text specified by *string* as a link for additional information for the module specified. For example:

```
AddModuleInfo mod_include.c 'See <A HREF="/docs/mod/mod_
include.html" >
the following link </A> for more information.
```

mod_isapi

The mod_isapi module provides for ISAPI extensions when the server is running under Microsoft Windows. This module is compiled into the server by default if the target platform is Microsoft; otherwise, the module is left out. There are no directives in this module.

mod_log_config

The mod_log_config module provides logging of requests made to the server. See the Apache documentation for an explanation of the logging format.

CookieLog CookieLog *filename*

[*server config*, or within <VirtualHost>]

Specifies the location of the file where cookie requests can be logged, relative to the ServerRoot. This directive is deprecated.

CustomLog CustomLog *file* format

[*server config*, or within <VirtualHost>]

Specifies the location of the file where logs can be recorded, either as a fully qualified filename or relative to the ServerRoot. You can instruct the server to use a specific format to log the records using the *format* parameter. In addition, you can specify a formatting nickname as defined by the LogFormat directive.

LogFormat `LogFormat` *format* [*nickname*]

[*server config*, or within `<VirtualHost>`]

This sets the default format of the log file specified by the `TransferLog` directive. If you wish, you can also use the directive to declare a nickname for a format. If you specify a nickname, the command does not apply the format as the default. Log formats are defined using the "Common Log Format," which is explained in greater detail in the Apache documentation.

TransferLog `TransferLog` *file|pipe-command*

[*server config*, or within `<VirtualHost>`]

Specifies a default log file using a format dictated by the `LogFormat` command. If you wish, you can specify a pipe (|) followed by a shell command in place of the filename; this program runs as the user that started the *httpd* server and receives the log information as standard input. For example:

```
TransferLog |"grep PUT >>.putlog"
```

mod_logio

This module allows you to log the number of bytes that are sent and received during a server request. There are no directives for this module. It adds two new logging specifications that can be use for custom logfiles. Apache 2.0 and up.

%I Logs the number of bytes received in a request, including headers.

%O Logs the number of bytes returned by the server, including response headers.

mod_mime

The `mod_mime` module contains directives that help to organize various MIME types on the server.

AddCharset `AddCharset` *character_set extensions ...*

[*server config*, or within `<VirtualHost>` or `<Directory>`, or *.htaccess*]

Associates the specified filename extensions with the named MIME character set. If the extensions are already mapped to another characher set, they are remapped to this one.

AddEncoding

`AddEncoding` *`encoding`* `extension ...`

[*server config*, or within `<VirtualHost>` or `<Directory>`, or *.htaccess*]

Allows you to specify which MIME encodings should be associated with documents from your server. Encodings beginning with `x-` are used for unofficial encodings. For example:

```
AddEncoding x-gzip gz
```

AddHandler

`AddHandler` *`handler-name`* `extension ...`

[*server config*, or within `<VirtualHost>` or `<Directory>`, or *.htaccess*]

Maps one or more filename extensions to a specific handler for the server. For example, for CGI scripts, you might use the following:

```
AddHandler cgi-script cgi
```

AddLanguage

`AddLanguage` *`mime-lang`* `extension ...`

[*server config*, or within `<VirtualHost>` or `<Directory>`, or *.htaccess*]

Specifies that a certain extension should be associated with a specific language for purposes of content negotiation. For example, to associate the extension *.francais* with French documents, use the following setting:

```
AddLanguage fr .francais
```

AddType

`AddType` *`mime-type`* `extension ...`

[*server config*, or within `<VirtualHost>` or `<Directory>`, or *.htaccess*]

Specifies a MIME type and subtype to be associated with certain file extensions. For example, if you want to serve a Microsoft Word document:

```
AddType application/msword .doc
```

`AddType` directives overrides any extension-to-type mappings in your *mime.types* file.

DefaultLanguage

`DefaultLanguage` *`language`*

[*server config*, or within `<VirtualHost>` or `<Directory>`, or *.htaccess*]

Specifies the default language for any files that are not associated with a particular language via `AddLanguage`.

ForceType

`ForceType` *`mime_type`*

[Within `<Directory>`, or *.htaccess*]

Specifies that all files in this directory should be served with the specified type. Appropriate for inclusion in *.htaccess* files or within `<Directory>` section directives.

RemoveEncoding

`RemoveEncoding extensions ...`

[Within <Directory>, or *.htaccess*]

Removes any associated encodinges for files matching the specified extensions.

RemoveHandler

`RemoveHandler extensions ...`

[Within <Directory>, or *.htaccess*]

Removes any associated handlers for files matching the specified extensions.

RemoveType

`RemoveType extensions ...`

[Within <Directory>, or *.htaccess*]

Removes any associated MIME types for files matching the specified extensions.

SetHandler

`SetHandler handler`

[Within <Directory>, or *.htaccess*]

Specifies that all files in the directory should be passed through the specified handler. Values are:

`cgi-script`
: All files treated as CGI scripts (see Chapter 12)

`imap-file`
: All files treated as imagemap files

`send-as-is`
: All files sent as is without additional server-supplied HTTP headers

`server-info`
: All files sent with server configuration information

`server-parsed`
: All files parsed as server-side includes (see Chapter 12)

`type-map`
: All files parsed as type map files for content negotiation

TypesConfig

`TypesConfig filename`

[*server config*]

Specifies the location of the MIME types file. As with other configuration paths, the location may be given as either an absolute path or a relative path to the `ServerRoot` directory. The default is:

```
TypesConfig conf/mime.types
```

mod_mime_magic

The `mod_mime_magic` module enables looking up of specific MIME types by its initial contents, such as scanning for magic numbers.

MimeMagicFile `MimeMagicFile` *`file`*

[*server config* or `<VirtualHost>`]

Enables the `mod_mime_magic` module for this realm with the specified file. A default file is located at `conf/magic`.

mod_negotiation

The `mod_negotiation` module performs content negotiation between the server and the client.

CacheNegotiatedDocs `CacheNegotiatedDocs`

[*server config*]

Tells the server to allow remote proxy servers to cache negotiated documents. By default, Apache does not allow caching of negotiated documents.

LanguagePriority `LanguagePriority` *`language`* `...`

[*server config*, within `<VirtualHost>` or `<Directory>`, or *.htaccess*]

Allows you to specify a ranking of languages, which is used in the event that a user's preferences are equal among language choices. For example:

```
LanguagePriority de it
```

specifies German before Italian.

mod_proxy

The `mod_proxy` module handles a multitude of proxying and caching capabilities for the server. *Proxies* enforce security by screening and relaying requests made by a client; *caches* help to optimize transfer by storing recently requested information.

CacheDefault Expire

`CacheDefaultExpire` *`time`*

[*server config* or within `<VirtualHost>`]

This sets the default expiry time, in hours, of a document in the cache, assuming an expiry has not already been set. The default is one hour. After the document has been expired, the client must refetch it directly from the server.

CacheDirLength

`CacheDirLength` *`length`*

[*server config* or within `<VirtualHost>`]

This directive sets the number of characters a directory can contain in the proxy cache.

```
CacheDirLength 1024768
```

CacheDirLevels

`CacheDirLevels` *`level`*

[*server config* or within `<VirtualHost>`]

This directive sets the number of subdirectories in the cache.

```
CacheDirLevels 10
```

CacheForce Completion

`CacheForceCompletion` *`percentage`*

[*server config* or within `<VirtualHost>`]

This directive specifies the minimum percentage of a document required in order for it to be cached. This is useful in the event a document is canceled before completing a transfer. The default is 90 percent.

CacheGcInterval

`CacheGcInterval` *`time`*

[*server config* or within `<VirtualHost>`]

This directive instructs the server to garbage-collect the cache if the space usage is greater than the size specified by the `CacheSize` directive. The collection is performed every *time* hours. You can specify a noninteger for the *time* if you want to perform garbage collections between hours.

CacheLastModified Factor

`CacheLastModifiedFactor` *`factor`*

[*server config* or within `<VirtualHost>`]

This directive estimates an expiry date for a document by multiplying the *factor* specified by the time since the last modification. This is effective only if an expiry date for a document has not been set already. If the expiration date is greater than `CacheMaxExpire`, `CacheMaxExpire` is used instead.

CacheMaxExpire

`CacheMaxExpire` *`time`*

[*server config* or within `<VirtualHost>`]

This directive specifies the maximum amount of time a document should remain active. Once past this time, it is considered "expired" and should be reloaded directly from the server.

CacheRoot

`CacheRoot` *`directory`*

[*server config* or within `<VirtualHost>`]

This directive sets the name of the directory that will contain cache files.

CacheSize

`CacheSize` *`size`*

[*server config* or within `<VirtualHost>`]

This directive sets the maximum size, in kilobytes, of the cache. Once this size is exceeded, no more data is written to the cache.

NoCache

`NoCache` *`word|host|domain`* `list`

[*server config* or within `<VirtualHost>`]

This directive specifies a matching of documents that are not cached by the server. You can use one of three options:

`word`
: The server searches for any such word in the title of the document. If one is found, the document is not cached.

`host`
: A document that originates from the target host isn't cached.

`domain` *list*
: Documents originating from any domain in the list are not cached.

For example:

```
NoCache abc.com def.com ghi.com
NoCache somecompany
NoCache *
```

Note that you are allowed to use wildcards. The last example forces the server not to cache any documents at all.

NoProxy

`NoProxy` *`domain|subnet|ip|hostname`*

[*server config* or within `<VirtualHost>`]

Specifies a list of intranet addresses or domains the proxy should not attempt to intermediate between. The parameter can be one of the following:

domain
: A domain name, like *.oreilly.com*; hosts from the domain can bypass the proxy

hostname
: A full hostname that can bypass the proxy

IP
: An IP address of a host that can bypass the proxy

subnet
: A subnet of addresses that can bypass the proxy

For example, the following disables the proxy for all addresses in the subnet 192.168:

```
NoProxy 192.168.0.0
```

ProxyBlock

`ProxyBlock` *`word|host|domain`* `list`

[*server config* or within `<VirtualHost>`]

Specifies a list of intranet addresses or domains which the proxy should block access to any documents on the server. The parameter can be one of the following:

`word`
: The server searches for any such word in the title of the document. If one is found, the document is blocked.

`host`
: A document that originates from the target host will be blocked.

`domain` *list*
: Documents originating from any domain in the list are blocked.

For example, the following blocks all requests for documents from `dirtyrotten.com` and `hackers.com`:

```
ProxyBlock dirtyrotten.com hackers.com
```

ProxyDomain

`ProxyDomain` *`domain`*

[*server config* or within `<VirtualHost>`]

This directive specifies the default domain of the proxy. For example:

```
ProxyDomain .oreilly.com
```

ProxyPass

`ProxyPass` *`path`* `url`

[*server config* or within `<VirtualHost>`]

This directive translates requests for a specific *path* to be redirected to the corresponding *url*. This allows remote servers to act as if they existed in the local filesystem. Note that this directive takes place regardless of whether the ProxyRequests directive is activated. For example:

```
ProxyPass /mydir http://www.otherserver.com/mydir
```

ProxyPassReverse ProxyPassReverse *path* url

[*server config* or within <VirtualHost>]

Handles redirects made by a server pointed to by the ProxyPass directive by modifying the Location header in the HTTP redirect response. This directive alters redirect references to a specific *path* to the corresponding *url*.

ProxyReceive BufferSize ProxyReceiveBufferSize *bytes*

[*server config* or within <VirtualHost>]

Specifies the networking buffer size for outgoing connections through the proxy. The value must be greater than 512. However, you can use the value 0 to indicate that the system's default buffer size should be used. For example:

```
ProxyReceiveBufferSize 4096
```

ProxyRemote ProxyRemote *match* remote-server

[*server config* or within <VirtualHost>]

This directive specifies a remote proxy that should be used under user-definable conditions. The *match* parameter is either a URL scheme (http, ftp, etc.) that the server supports, or a partial URL which should be redirected to the remote proxy. The *remote-server* parameter should be organized as a fully qualified URL, as shown below:

```
ProxyRemote ftp http://ftpproxy.oreilly.com:8080
ProxyRemote * http://handle.everything.oreilly.com:9001
```

Currently, http is the only scheme supported for the *remote-server* parameter.

ProxyRequests ProxyRequests on|off

[*server config* or within <VirtualHost>]

This directive activates or deactivates proxy serving. The default is:

```
ProxyRequests Off
```

Note that even though proxy requests are deactivated, the ProxyPass directives are still valid.

mod_rewrite

The `mod_rewrite` module allows for rewriting URLs for clients based on specific rules. This is a powerful module with many rewriting features (too many to list here) that perform their functions on the fly.

RewriteBase

`RewriteBase` *`url`*

[Within `<Directory>` or *.htaccess*]

Sets the base directory for rewrites. This specifies a portion of the URI that will not be modified by any subsequent rewriting, even if the URI maps to a different filesystem. For example:

```
RewriteBase /files
```

This directive tells the rewriting engine to ignore the `files` directory in the URI when rewriting.

RewriteCond

`RewriteCond` *`string`* `condition`

Defines a rule condition for URI rewriting. See the Apache documentation for more information.

RewriteEngine

`RewriteEngine on|off`

[*server config*, within `<Directory>` or `<VirtualHost>`, or *.htaccess*]

This directive enables or disables the rewriting engine of this module. The default setting is:

```
RewriteEngine off
```

RewriteLock

`RewriteLock` *`filename`*

[*server config* or `<VirtualHost>`]

Sets a filename to serve as the lockfile used by the rewriting engine. It is recommended that this file reside on the local drive and not on an NFS-mounted drive.

RewriteLog

`RewriteLog` *`filename`*

[*server config* or `<VirtualHost>`]

This directive specifies the name of the log file to which it records any URL rewriting activities. *filename* can be a fully qualified filename or relative to the `ServerRoot` directive. For example:

```
RewriteLog "logs/rewrite.log"
```

RewriteLogLevel `RewriteLogLevel level`

[*server config* or <VirtualHost>]

Sets the amount of reporting that is done to the rewriting log file, a number between 0 and 9. The default is `RewriteLogLevel 0`. For example:

```
RewriteLogLevel 3
```

It is recommended that levels greater than 2 be used only for debugging purposes, as they can generate large amounts of data in a short period of time.

RewriteMap `RewriteMap name type:source`

[*server config* or <VirtualHost>]

Declares the rewriting map and its type. The map file performs substitutions for various URIs. The *name* parameter makes up the given name of the mapping. The *type* and *source* variables are determined by the *type*:

`txt` A plain-text file, with the *source* pointing to a regular file

`rnd` A plain-text file with a random mapping choice; the *source* variable points to a regular file

`dbm` The *source* variable points to a DBM-formatted file

`int` An internal Apache function; the *source* variable can be one of two functions: `toupper` or `tolower`

`prg` A program. The *source* variable points to a Unix executable

Here is an example that shows how to use a text-based rewriting file:

```
RewriteMap real-host txt:/usr/local/maps/mymap.txt
```

RewriteOptions `RewriteOptions option`

[*server config*, within <VirtualHost> or <Directory>, or *.htaccess*]

Sets options for the rewriting engine in this context. Currently, the only option available is:

`inherit`
: This option instructs the current rewriting configuration to inherit the values of its parent directory's access control file.

RewriteRule `RewriteRule pattern substitution`

[*server config*, within <VirtualHost> or <Directory>, or *.htaccess*]

Defines a single rewriting rule. See the Apache documentation for further information.

mod_setenvif

The mod_setenvif module sets environment variables based on the client's browser or other information.

BrowserMatch

```
BrowserMatch regex var[=value] var[=value] ...
```

[*server config*]

Sets environment variables based on the client's browser type. If the User-Agent HTTP header matches the regular expression specified by *regex*, set one or more environment variables as follows:

var
: The environment variable is defined and given the value of 1.

!var
: The environment variable is deleted.

var=value
: The environment variable is set to an initial value.

Here is an example of how to locate various browsers. The first sets compatible if the client is connecting with Versions 2 through 4 of Netscape. The second sets microsoft if Internet Explorer is detected:

```
BrowserMatch ^Mozilla/[2-4] compatible !microsoft
BrowserMatch MSIE microsoft
```

BrowserMatch NoCase

```
BrowserMatchNoCase regex var=value var=value ...
```

[*server config*]

Identical to BrowserMatch, except that matching is now case-insensitive. For example, the following would still work to detect Internet Explorer:

```
BrowserMatch msie microsoft
```

SetEnvIf

```
SetEnvIf attribute regex var[=value] var[=value]
```

[*server config*]

Sets environment variables based on the attributes of an HTTP request. Some of the more common attributes are:

Remote_Host
: The hostname of the client, if known

Remote_Addr
: The IP address of the client

Remote_User
: The user which is making the request, if known

`Request_Method`
: The name of the HTTP method being used to request information

`Request_URI`
: The latter portion of the URL, after the host information

`Referer`
: The URI of the referring page, if known

For example, the following sets the environment variable `SOMEONE_FROM_OREILLY` if the remote host resolves to the domain *oreilly.com*:

```
SetEnvIf Remote_Host oreilly.com SOMEONE_FROM_OREILLY
```

SetEnvIfNoCase

`SetEnvIfNoCase` *`attribute`* `regex var[=`*`value`*`] var[=`*`value`*`]`

[*server config*]

Identical to `SetEnvIf`, except that attribute matching is now case-insensitive.

mod_so

The `mod_so` module assists in loading shared object files into the server at startup. This includes modules and other shared libraries, including Dynamic Link Libraries (DLLs) and Unix `.so` shared libraries. See the Apache documentation for information on creating DLL modules for Windows.

LoadFile

`LoadFile` *`filename`* `...`

[*server config*]

This directive loads one or more specified object libraries when the server is started. The *filename* can be an absolute pathname or can be relative to `ServerRoot`.

LoadModule

`LoadModule` *`module`* `filename`

[*server config*]

This directive loads the given *filename* as a given module, adding it to the list of active modules. For example:

```
LoadModule status_module mod_stat.so
```

mod_speling

The `mod_speling` module (spelled with one "l") attempts to correct various spelling errors a user can make while requesting a document on the server.

CheckSpelling

`CheckSpelling on|off`

[*server config*, within `<VirtualHost>` or `<Directory>`, or *.htaccess*]

This directive enables or disables the spelling assistance.

mod_ssl

The `mod_ssl` enables encrypted, secure transactions between the server and client with SSL (Secure Sockets Layer) Versions 2 and 3, and TLS (Transport Layer Security) Version 1. Apache uses OpenSSL as its cryptography engine. Apache 2.0 and up.

The directives in this module set the locations of certificate and key files, specify options for the behavior of the encryption engine, and set up authorization requirements for access to protected parts of the server. The module also creates a number of new `SSL_*` environment variables, which will be available to SSI, CGI, and custom logging formats.

SSLCACertificateFile

`SSLCACertificateFile` *`filename`*

[*server config*, within `<VirtualHost>`]

Specifies the location of a single file that contains all of the certificates for the Certificate Authorities that you need for client verification. The file is a concatenation of the separate certificates, in order of preference. You can also use separate certificate files located in a single directory specified by `SSLCACertificatePath`.

SSLCACertificatePath

`SSLCACertificatePath` *`directory`*

[*server config*, within `<VirtualHost>`]

Specifies the directory containing the PEM-encoded certificate files for the Certificate Authorities that you need for client verification. Certificate files are accessed with hash filenames via symbolic links of the form *`hashname`*`.N`, This directory can be set up properly using the Makefile provided with `mod_ssl`.

SSLCARevocationFile

`SSLCARevocationFile` *`filename`*

[*server config*, within `<VirtualHost>`]

Specifies a file containing multiple, encoded Certificate Revocation Lists (CRLs) of the Certificate Authorities used by your clients. CRLs are used to revoke client certificates during authentication.

SSLCARevocationPath

`SSLCARevocationPath` *`directory`*

[*server config*, within `<VirtualHost>`]

Specifies the directory containing Certificate Revocation Lists (CRLs) for Certificate Authorities used by clients. Encoded CRL files are accessed with hash filenames via symbolic links of the form *`hashname`*`.rN`, This directory can be set up properly using the Makefile provided with `mod_ssl`.

SSLCertificateChainFile

`SSLCertificateChainFile` *`filename`*

[*server config*, within `<VirtualHost>`]

Specifies the single file containing all the server's certificates as a certificate chain establishing a path of trust. This will include the server's certificate and the certificate of the CA that issued it. It could possibly go to higher levels of CA certificates.

SSLCertificateFile

`SSLCertificateFile` *`filename`*

[*server config*, within `<VirtualHost>`]

Specifies the file containing the server's certificate and optionally, its RSA or DSA private key.

SSLCertificateKeyFile

`SSLCertificateKeyFile` *`filename`*

[*server config*, within `<VirtualHost>`]

Specifies the file containing the server's Private key. This directive must be used in conjunction with `SSLCertificateFile`, which specifies the certificate file (when the Private key is not included there).

SSLCipherSuite

`SSLCipherSuite` *`cipher_spec`*

[*server config*, within `<VirtualHost>` or `<Directory>`, or *.htaccess*]

This directive combines a number of cipher specifications to configure the Cipher Suite. The Cipher Suite is the set of methods or algorithms used by the server and client to establish secure communications. The cipher suite is negotiated during the handshake phase, just after a client sends an SSL request. The *cipher_spec* provided by this directive lists a set of methods that the server will support for a request. The client and server negotiate the most common and preferred methods in this list to use for transactions.

The *cipher_spec* is a rather complex string that requires at least one declaration for each of the following: a key exchange algorithm, an authentication algorithm, a cipher or encryption algorithm, and MAC digest algorithm. You can additionally declare an export cipher. There are many different tags for specific ciphers that can be combined for the cipher spec. Certain alias tags have been defined to group ciphers into specific sets that comprise certain protocols and levels of security. Table 19-2 lists the alias tags.

Table 19-2. Cipher tag aliases

Tag	Description
SSLv2	All SSL 2.0 ciphers
SSLv3	All SSL 3.0 ciphers
TLSv1	All TLS 1.0 ciphers
EXP	All export ciphers
EXPORT40	40-bit export ciphers only
EXPORT56	56-bit export ciphers only
LOW	All low strength ciphers (no export, single DES)
MEDIUM	All ciphers with 128-bit encryption
HIGH	All Triple-DES ciphers
RSA	All ciphers that use RSA key exchange
DH	All ciphers that use Diffie-Hellman key exchange
EDH	All ciphers that use Ephemeral Diffie-Hellman key exchange
ADH	All ciphers that use Anonymous Diffie-Hellman key exchange
DSS	All ciphers that use DSS authentication
NULL	All ciphers that don't use encryption

The *cipher_spec* string is composed of a list of cipher tags separated by colons. Each tag may also have a qualifier placed before it. No qualifier means that the cipher is added to the list. A + means that the cipher is added and is pulled to this location on the cipher order. A - means that the cipher is removed from the list, but can be added somewhere else. A ! means that the cipher cannot be used at all.

The default value for this directive demonstrates these features:

```
ALL:!ADH:RC4+RSA:+HIGH:+MEDIUM:+LOW:+SSLv2:+EXP
```

The *cipher_spec* first includes all ciphers, then removes the ones it doesn't want (!ADH) and adjusts the order of preference for the remaining ciphers. See the Apache and OpenSSL documentation for a complete list of cipher tags and complete information on using SSL for secure server communications.

SSLEngine

`SSLEngine off|on`

[*server config*, within `<VirtualHost>`]

Enables or disables the SSL/TLS protocol engine for the server or a virtual host.

SSLMutex

`SSLMutex` *`type`*

[*server config*]

Configures the SSL engines mutex (mutual exclusion) mechanism to synchronize multiple server processes' access to the SSL session cache. There are three types that can be used:

`file:`*`/path/name`*
: On Unix systems, you can specify a file that is used as the mutex lock. This option is not usable in the Win32 environment.

`sem`
: This options uses an IPC semaphore process flag for synchronization on Unix and a Windows Mutex flag on Win32.

`none`
: The default specifies that no exclusion mechanism is used. This may result in mangled information in the SSL session cache.

SSLOptions

`SSLOptions [+|-]`*`option...`*

[*server config*, within `<VirtualHost>` or `<Directory>`, or *.htaccess*]

Controls a number of SSL runtime options. Per-directory or location merging of options is controlled by the + or - prepended to an option. A + option adds to the set of options that are in place from an higher-level specification. A - options removes an localized option that was in place from a higher-level specification. The available options are:

`StdEnvVars`
: Creates the standard set of SSL-related environment variables. Since there are many of these and gathering this information can cause a performance hit, this configurable per directory, for example, is for CGI and SSL requests only.

`CompatEnvVars`
: Creates a set of environment variables that enable compatibility with previous Apache SSL programs.

`ExportCertData`
: Creates environment variables containing the encoded server and client certificate information for use with CGI.

`FakeBasicAuth`
: Allows basic authorization to be mocked using the Subject Distinguished Name (DN) of a client certificate as a valid username. No password is requested from the user, but the user file must have the appropriately encoded string for "password" for this scheme to work.

`StrictRequire`
: Forces strict SSL authorization (with `SSLRequire` or `SSLRequireSSL`) to be satisfied regardless of whether other authorization requirements are met when the `Satisfy` any directive is used. Without this option, `Satisfy` any overrides a forbidden access from SSL if other authorization requirements are met.

`OptRenegotiate`
: Allows for optimized renegotiation handling of SSL connections when directory-specific directives are specified. Normally, full renegotiation will be performed.

SSLPassPhrase Dialog

`SSLPassPhraseDialog` *`type`*

[*server config*]

Sets the type of dialog used to get the administrator's pass phrase for accessing encrypted private keys. The administrator needs to provide this information during server startup. The valid types are:

`builtin`
: This uses an interactive dialog at the terminal at startup. The administrator provides the pass phrase for each encrypted private key file. There is a reuse mechanism for multiple keys used on virtual hosts. Pass phrases will automatically be retried to see if it can be used for multiple key files, thus saving some input.

`exec:`*`/path/script`*
: This option calls a program at startup to produce the pass phrase however it sees fit, and send it to `stdout` for use with the terminal dialog described by the `builtin` option. The script is called with two arguments. The first argument is *`servername:portnumber`*, The second is either `RSA` or `DSA`, which is determined by the encryption used by the key file. This method is very flexible, and the administrator can provide any number of security checks to the process.

SSLProtocol

`SSLProtocol[+|-]`*`protocol`*

[*server config*, or within `<VirtualHost>`]

Specifies the SSL protocol(s) used by the server. The values can be: `SSLv2`, `SSLv3`, `TLSv1`, or `All`. The + or - flags are used to add or remove a protocol from a set.

SSLProxyCA CertificateFile

`SSLProxyCACertificateFile`

[*server config*, within `<VirtualHost>`]

Specifies the location of a single file that contains all of the certificates for the Certificate Authorities that you need for remote server verification. The file is a concatenation of the separate certificates, in order of preference. You can also use separate certificate files located in a single directory specified by `SSLProxyCACertificatePath`.

SSLProxyCA CertificatePath

`SSLProxyCACertificatePath`

[*server config*, within `<VirtualHost>`]

Specifies the directory containing the PEM-encoded certificate files for the Certificate Authorities that you need for remote server verification. Certificate files are accessed with hash filenames via symbolic links of the form *hashname*`.N`, This directory can be set up properly using the Makefile provided with `mod_ssl`.

SSLProxyCA RevocationFile

`SSLProxyCARevocationFile`

[*server config*, within `<VirtualHost>`]

Specifies a file containing multiple, encoded Certificate Revocation Lists (CRLs) of the Certificate Authorities used by remote servers. CRLs are used to revoke remote server certificates during authentication.

SSLProxyCA RevocationPath

`SSLProxyCARevocationPath`

[*server config*, within `<VirtualHost>`]

Specifies the directory containing Certificate Revocation Lists (CRLs) for Certificate Authorities used by remote servers. Encoded CRL files are accessed with hash filenames via symbolic links of the form *hashname*`.rN`. This directory can be set up properly using the Makefile provided with `mod_ssl`.

SSLProxyCipher Suite

`SSLProxyCipherSuite` *`cipher_spec`*

[*server config*, within `<VirtualHost>` or `<Directory>`, or *.htaccess*]

Specifies the cipher suite used for a proxy connection. The options are the same as `SSLCipherSuite`.

SSLProxyEngine

`SSLProxyEngine on|off`

[*server config*, within `<VirtualHost>`]

Enables or disables the SSL engine for proxy connections. The default is `off`.

SSLProxyMachine CertificateFile

`SSLProxyMachineCertificateFile`

[*server config*]

Specifies the location of a single file that contains all of the certificates for the Certificate Authorities that are needed to verify the proxy server to remote servers. The file is a concatenation of the separate certificates, in order of preference. You can also use separate certificate files located in a single directory specified by `SSLProxyMachineCertificatePath`.

SSLProxyMachine CertificatePath

`SSLProxyMachineCertificatePath`

[*server config*]

Specifies the directory containing the PEM-encoded certificate files for the Certificate Authorities that you need to verify the proxy server to remote servers. Certificate files are accessed with hash filenames via symbolic links of the form *hashname*`.N`, This directory can be set up properly using the Makefile provided with `mod_ssl`.

SSLProxyProtocol

`SSLProxyProtocol`

[*server config*, within `<VirtualHost>`]

Specifies the SSL protocols available for the proxy server. The options are the same as `SSLProtocol`.

SSLProxyVerify

`SSLProxyVerify` *`level`*

[*server config*, within `<VirtualHost>` or `<Directory>`, or *.htaccess*]

Specifies the verification level required for remote server verification. *value* can be one of the following:

none
: No remote server certificate is required.

require
: A valid certificate must be presented by the remote server.

optional
: A valid certificate may be required for the remote server. This option isn't very useful or supported.

optional_no_ca
: The remote server is verified with or without a valid certificate. This is useful for test purposes only.

SSLProxyVerify Depth

`SSLProxyVerifyDepth` *`number`*

[*server config*, within `<VirtualHost>` or `<Directory>`, or *.htaccess*]

Specifies the maximum verification depth that is allowed for determination of a valid certificate by a proxy server. The number is the number of unknown intermediate certificates allowed between the client and a certificate authority trusted by the client. For example, a depth of two would allow a client certificate that is certified by a CA unknown to the server. If that CA is certified by another CA known to the server, the verification is allowed. The default is 1.

SSLRandomSeed `SSLRandomSeed` *`context source`* `[`*`bytes`*`]`

[*server config*]

Specifies the source of seeding for the pseudorandom number generator used by OpenSSL. *context* determines the seeding source either at `startup` or when a new SSL connection is made (`connect`).

The *source* specifies the utility that provides the random seed. `builtin` indicates that mod_ssl's internal seeding utility is used. It is a simple utility, but doesn't provide a strong seeding source. Other seeding sources are: `file:`*`/path/file`*, which uses the contents of a file to determine the seeding. This usually points to a device file for a random generator like */dev/random*. exec:*/path/prog* points to an executable source for seeding. The source is the stream of bytes sent to `stdout`. For both file and executable sources, an optional argument specifying a number of bytes indicates that only the first *bytes* of the source (file or output) will be used. Without this argument, the complete source is used.

SSLRequire `SSLRequire` *`expression`*

[within `<Directory>` or *.htaccess*]

Specifies the requirements that must be met before access is allowed to a resource. The access requirement is an arbitrarily complex boolean expression, whose syntax is very similar to common programming language syntax like C or Java. Logical and comparison operators can be used in any combination with the values of environment variables to determine access. Environment variables are available with the following syntax: `%{`*`variable`*`}`.

SSLRequireSSL `SSLRequireSSL`

[within `<Directory>` or *.htaccess*]

When this directive is used (it has no arguments), it forbids access to a directory unless HTTP over SSL is used.

SSLSessionCache `SSLSessionCache` *`type`*

[*server config*]

Specifies the type of resource used for the SSL session cache. The session cache contains the SSL verification information for an open session, and allows access to this information to the multiple processes involved in a client request session. Clients will commonly use HTTP KeepAlive to retrieve numerous files associated with a resource like inline images, style sheets, etc., simultaneously to reduce loading time.

This directive specifies the type of resource used for the session cache with the following options:

`none`
: Disables the session cache. Functionality is not affected, but requests will take longer to complete.

`dbm:`*`/path/file`*
: Specifies the name of a DBM hash file to use as the session cache file.

`shm:`*`/path/file`*
: Specifies a hash table stored in shared memory for the session cache file. An optional *size* argument sets the size of the hashtable. This option is not available on all platforms.

SSLSessionCache Timeout

`SSLSessionCacheTimeout` *`time`*

[*server config*, within `<VirtualHost>` or `<Directory>`, or *.htaccess*]

Specifies the timeout in seconds for the information in the session cache to be valid between requests. The default is 300.

SSLVerifyClient

`SSLVerifyClient` *`level`*

[*server config*, within `<VirtualHost>` or `<Directory>`, or *.htaccess*]

Specifies the verification level required for client verification. *value* can be one of the following:

`none`
: No client certificate is required.

`require`
: A valid certificate must be presented by the client.

`optional`
: A valid certificate may be required for the client. This option isn't very useful or supported.

`optional_no_ca`
: The client is verified with or without a valid certificate. This is useful for test purposes only.

SSLVerifyDepth

`SSLVerifyDepth` *`number`*

[*server config*, within `<VirtualHost>` or `<Directory>`, or *.htaccess*]

Specifies the maximum verification depth is allowed for determination of a valid certificate by a client. The number is the number of unknown intermediate certificates are allowed between the client and a certificate authority trusted by the server. For example, a depth of 2 would allow a client certificate that is certified by a CA unknown to the server. If that CA is certified by another CA known to the server, the verification is allowed. The default is 1.

mod_status

The mod_status module enables server status pages to be generated, documenting the usage of the Apache server. If this module is compiled into the Apache server, you can enable server status reports with the following directives:

```
<Location /server-status>
SetHandler server-status

order deny,allow
deny from all
allow from .foo.com
</Location>
```

This automatically generates an HTML status page that is located in the server-status subdirectory of your document tree.

ExtendedStatus `ExtendedStatus on|off`

[*server config*]

This directive enables or disables the extended status information.

mod_suexec

This module allows Apache to switch the user and group permissions for CGI requests. Apache 2.0 and up.

SuexecUserGroup `SuexecUserGroup` *`user group`*

[*server config*, within `<VirtualHost>`]

Specifies the user and group under which CGI programs will be run. This only applies to CGI programs, and not other types of requested executables.

This directive replaces the use of `User` and `Group` within virtual host configuration, which was the behavior in Apache 1.3.

mod_unique_id

The mod_unique_id module generates an environment variable, UNIQUE_ID, which is guaranteed to be a unique number for each request given to the server. The variable consists of an encoding of the 32-bit IP address of the server, the httpd process ID, the current UTC timestamp, and an independent counter.

mod_userdir

The mod_userdir module provides automatic mapping to user directories for requested addresses.

UserDir

UserDir *directory|filename*

[*server config*, or within <VirtualHost>]

Translates a username to a specific directory and default filename. The default is the user's home directory in the subdirectory *public_html*, loading the file *index.html*. Alternatively, you can specify the enabled or disabled keyword followed by a series of usernames you wish to enable or disable access. For example:

```
UserDir enabled robert stephen
UserDir disabled john linda
```

mod_usertrack

The mod_usertrack module tracks various users who have accessed documents and other information from the server. Information is stored is a log file using the CustomLog directive.

CookieExpires

CookieExpires *period*

[*server config*, or within <VirtualHost>]

This specifies the number of seconds a cookie should exist before it is considered "expired." You can also specify the expiry period in a format such as:

```
5 weeks 4 days 12 hours
```

Otherwise, the cookies last only for the current browser session.

CookieTracking `XSCookieTracking on|off`

[*server config*, within `<VirtualHost>` or `<Directory>`, or *.htaccess*]

This directive enables or disables cookie tracking. If the directive is set to `on` for a directory, the Apache server sends cookies for all new HTTP requests. The default is `off`.

mod_vhost_alias

The mod_vhost_alias supports the dynamic configuration of document roots and script directories for virtual hosts. This functionality is useful when a server handles a large number of virtual hosts, usually by varying the subdomain sections of the hostname. Virtual hosts configured under the directives of this module are expected to share the same configuration since they won't have their own `<Virtual Directory>` sections.

The name of the virtual host is determined by the Host: header in the client request. (This requires `UseCanonicalName off`.) The IP address is the address assigned to the particular virtual host. The directives of this module use either the host name or IP address and interpolate it to locate unique document and script paths for each host.

The *interpolated path* parameter for each directive uses a *printf*-like format string to refashion parts of the virtual hostname or address into a directory. A %-sign followed by a short format specifier represent sections of the name in the interpolated directory. Each word between the dots in a name or address is a section numbered from left to right, starting with one. The whole name is represented by 0 (`%0`). For example:

`%0` The whole name

`%2` The second section

`%-1` The last section

`%-2` The next-to-last section

`%3+` The third section and all subsequent sections

Additionally, `%p` represents the port number.

The settings of this module will be overridden by any mod_alias and mod_userdir settings on the same host names.

VirtualDocumentRoot `VirtualDocumentRoot` *`interpolated_path`*

[*server config*, within `<VirtualHost>`]

Sets the root document directories for matching virtual hostnames.

VirtualDocumentRootIP

`VirtualDocumentRootIP` *`interpolated_path`*

[*server config*, within `<VirtualHost>`]

Sets the root document directories for virtual hosts with matching IP addresses.

VirtualScriptAlias

`VirtualScriptAlias` *`interpolated_path`*

[*server config*, within `<VirtualHost>`]

Sets the location of CGI directories for matching virtual hostnames.

VirtualScriptAliasIP

`VirtualScriptAliasIP` *`interpolated_path`*

[*server config*, within `<VirtualHost>`]

Sets the location of CGI directories for virtual hosts with matching IP addresses.

20

Web Performance

Sometimes it seems that no matter how fast your web site is, it's never fast enough. Pages don't load quickly enough, scripts always seem to take forever, and streaming video or audio brings everything to a standstill. The slower things are, the more likely it is that a user will become frustrated and give up. Improving web performance is a constant struggle for every webmaster.

In this chapter, we look at techniques to improve web performance from several different perspectives. Users can upgrade software or hardware, tweak some settings on their browser, or choose a faster modem or ISP. HTML authors can reduce the size of the content being transmitted. Programmers can do quite a bit to improve the execution of CGI programs or other scripts. Most importantly, administrators can reconfigure server software or their website design to greatly reduce the load. Most of this chapter concentrates on the administrator's role in improving performance.

This chapter gives only a brief discussion of web performance and how to improve it. See *Web Performance Tuning* by Patrick Killelea (O'Reilly) for a more thorough discussion.

Client-Side Performance

As a user, your ability to improve web performance is limited by the choices others have made about content, programming, and administration. A slow web site is not going to be fast no matter what client accesses it. Still, there are some things you can do to improve your overall experience.

Memory

If you have the money to improve your hardware, buy more memory rather than a machine with a faster CPU. Having the latest CPU will not make as much difference as having a lot of memory. These days, "a lot of memory" means 256 MB or 512 MB.

MTU Size

If you're more ambitious (or don't have a lot of money to throw away on hardware), another potential way to increase browser performance is to tune your MTU size. This can make a big difference if your current MTU is wrong for your connection to your ISP.

MTU stands for "Maximum Transmission Unit," which is the largest packet your PC will send out. You want it to be big enough to carry as much as the other end will accept, but not too big, or your performance will suffer when the other side keeps rejecting packets and telling your PC to send smaller ones. You can use one of the many MTU tuners on the market such as PPP Boost, MTU-speed pro, NetMedic, and Vital Signs.

You can manually figure out your optimum MTU from a Linux machine using the `ping` command:

```
% ping -M do -s 1500 www.myISP.com
```

From a Windows machine, use the following command from the DOS prompt:

```
C:\>ping -f -l 1500 www.myISP.com
```

(Use your own ISP's web site in place of *www.myISP.com*.)

A value of 1500 bytes may get you an error like "Packet needs to be fragmented, but DF set." Keep reducing the value until the `ping` works; this gives you the optimum value for your MTU.

How you set the MTU depends on the operating system. See *http://www.sysopt.com/maxmtu.html* for additional information on setting MTUs under Windows. On Linux, you can modify your MTU like this:

```
# /sbin/ifconfig eth0 mtu 1500
```

You can get the source code for a version of `traceroute` that finds MTUs along a route from the code published with Richard Stevens' book *TCP/IP Illustrated, Vol 1* (Addison-Wesley). The code is available at *ftp://ftp.uu.net/published/books/stevens/tcpipiv1.tar.Z*. Use the modified `traceroute` program to learn about the MTU between yourself and points you commonly visit. On an Ethernet LAN, the MTU is generally set to be 1500 bytes, and this is the way many clients such as Windows 95 are configured by default; but on the Internet you sometimes get better performance if you set the MTU to 576.

Switching Proxies

For those of you that use a proxy to get to the Internet, it pays to try out different proxies. Sometimes one proxy is much faster than others, and there is no automated way to get your browser to pick the fastest proxy.

You have to get a list of proxies to manually try them all out. Your system administrator should have the list of proxies, but if not, you may find their names yourself by examining the *proxy.pac* file that institutions often use to automatically configure browsers. If your browser was automatically configured via a URL such as *http://config.myinstitution.com/proxy.pac*, you will not be able to view that URL in the browser. Here is a simple way to retrieve the *proxy.pac* file via `telnet`:

```
% telnet config.myinstitution.com 80
Trying 192.1.14.53...
Connected to www.myinstitution.edu.
Escape character is '^]'
GET /proxy.pac HTTP/1.0

HTTP/1.1 200 OK
Date:
Sun, 08 Feb 1998 18:35:25 GMT
Server: Apache/1.2.5
...
(institution's proxy servers will be listed in body of response)
```

Rather than manually trying out each proxy, you may be able to figure out which one is least loaded by using the `rstat` program. `rstat` will report load statistics for any machine running the `rstatd` daemon, which Solaris, AIX, and Linux machines run by default. It doesn't hurt the proxy to try using `rstat` on it, and `rstat` is freely available from *http://patrick.net/software/rstat/rstat.html*.

Do You Have a Faulty DNS Library?

A last client side tip, for advanced Linux users: recent versions of the resolver DNS library that ships with RedHat Linux have a serious bug. The library will do DNS lookups for absolutely every machine name or address you surf, even names listed in */etc/hosts*, and even plain IP addresses. This happens regardless of how */etc/nsswitch.conf* is set. This will slow down your surfing of sites named by IP address, or machines you list in */etc/hosts* that do not have a DNS entry. As a fix, either downgrade your version of `libresolv`, or complain to RedHat.

HTML Authoring

Some HTML authors might think that the speed that their pages download is out of their control. That's not true at all: HTML authors are the ones who control what data, and how much of it, is actually sent.

Keep the Content Small

HTML authors sometimes put such heavy content on each page that performance suffers. You don't need style sheets, redirections, frames, Flash, JavaScript, or Java. Each one will hurt performance and portability, so keep it simple when you can. Most users are happy to load very simple pages as long as they can get them right this instant.

The basic performance principle is therefore to send fewer bits and make fewer requests. Try to think of size in terms of download time rather than absolute bits because the time a human being has to wait is the true measure of web page failure. If most of your users are on 56K modems, make a rule that no web page can be larger than 10 seconds. As a rule of thumb, remember that ten seconds on a 56K modem happens to correspond to about 56KB in size.

Short Pathnames

Short URL pathnames not only speed up downloads, but also save log file space on your servers. Using short pathnames may make it difficult to navigate your way around the directory tree, but that might be a reasonable trade-off for the improvement in speed.

Programming

Like HTML authors, some programmers do too much and want to use the latest thing. Distributed object schemes like CORBA and EJBs are complex and have poor performance, but are often preferred over CGI and servlets because they're more challenging. CGI and servlets may be boring, but they work quite well.

Unbuffered Reads and Writes

A very common performance problem is the use of unbuffered reads and writes. You can diagnose this problem by examining which system calls are being executed and what the parameters to those calls are, via a system call tracing utility such as `truss` on Solaris or `strace` on Linux. Other such utilities include `ktrace` and `par`. Shared library calls can be seen using `sotruss`.

These tools are especially useful for finding out that an application is doing single byte reads or writes, which is terribly inefficient. In Java, the single-byte read/write problem is easily fixed by using buffered readers and writers rather than single-byte I/O. If you run

```
% truss -t read,write -s\!all -p <process id>
```

You want to see fast buffered 8K reads, like this:

```
read(49, " B\r\n T R 0 8 0 6 5 9".., 8192) = 8192
read(49, " J".., 8192) = 8192
read(49, " 2 4 9 B D ".., 8192) = 8192
read(49, " 0 0 3 2 9 . 8 9 0 0 0 0".., 8192) = 8192
read(49, " . 0 0 R ".., 8192) = 8192
read(49, " B\r\n T R 0 8".., 8192) = 8192
read(49, " ".., 8192) = 8192
read(49, " 4 4 1 3 2 4 9 B ".., 8192) = 8192
read(49, " 0 0 0 2 4 5 6 1 5 . 0 3".., 8192) = 8192
```

You do not want to see one-byte unbuffered reads, like this:

```
read(49, " C", 1) = 1
read(49, " C", 1) = 1
read(49, " ", 1) = 1
read(49, " 0", 1) = 1
read(49, " 2", 1) = 1
read(49, " 3", 1) = 1
read(49, " 0", 1) = 1
read(49, " 0", 1) = 1
read(49, " 7", 1) = 1
read(49, " 5", 1) = 1
read(49, " 6", 1) = 1
```

```
read(49, " ", 1) = 1
read(49, " 0", 1) = 1
read(49, "\r", 1) = 1
```

Logging

Running a system call tracer may also show you that you are doing too much logging. You might be surprised to know how much debugging code gets left on by accident in a production environment. Logging from Java can be especially slow, because the VM may convert each byte from Unicode to ASCII before writing it to the log file.

Compressing Files

Consider using gzip compression on static files. If you compress your files on the server side with gzip and end them with the *.gz* suffix, most browsers will now automatically detect that and decompress the files. This can be a huge performance boost for users on slow connections like modems, because it can reduce by more than half the amount of data they need to download.

Administration

System administrators have the opportunity to improve performance in ways that users, HTML authors, and programmers do not, because administrators deal directly with web and application servers.

Apache, by far the most successful web server, is used on more than half of all web sites. Apache has real-time performance monitoring tools and an optional log format that tells you how long each transfer took (see *mod_log_config.html* in the server documentation). Try to ensure that the server has been compiled with the latest C compiler and libraries for your server platform, or compile the server yourself.

See Dean Gaudet's notes on tuning Apache servers at *http://www.apache.org/docs/misc/perf-tuning.html*.

AllowOverride

In the kind of full-path authentication used on Apache and some other servers, the current directory and each parent directory (up to the system root, not just up to the document root) are searched by default for a *.htaccess* authentication file to read and parse. You can speed up Apache by disabling this feature, turning off authentication for directories that don't need it (like the system root) by putting the following in the *access.conf* file:

```
<Directory />
     AllowOverride None
</Directory>

<Directory /usr/local/mydocroot>
     AllowOverride All (or any of the other AllowOverride options)
</Directory>
```

Even better, if you don't use *.htaccess* files at all, disable them completely:

```
<Directory /usr/local/mydocroot>
        AllowOverride None
</Directory>
```

The general web performance tip of keeping paths short takes on added importance for web servers that use directory-specific access control like Apache. Each directory traversal takes time not only because it follows the filesystem's linked list and checks Unix permissions, but also because of the *.htaccess* files, which are even less efficient.

Web Performance

Buffered Logs

For better performance, compile Apache with the `-DBUFFERED_LOGS` option so that log file writes are deferred until a certain number of bytes are accumulated. That number is the POSIX constant `PIPE_BUF`.

Max-Clients

You'll get much better performance by running only the number of server processes your RAM can hold. If you run too many, you'll start swapping and performance for each will drop. Knowing how many to run is tricky because some parts of each `httpd` process are shared with others, but a good rule of thumb for Apache is 1 MB per process. That is, if you have only 128 MB RAM, then don't try to run any more than 128 processes, even if you often have more than 128 concurrent users. Anyhow, you'll probably be limited by other factors at 128 processes.

You can configure the number of *httpd* processes in Apache with the `Max-Clients` directive. You don't want to run too few *httpd* processes either, because you need enough processes so that fast clients never have to wait for a slow client to finish and free up a process.

Persistent Connections

In older versions of Apache, the connection between client and server was closed after each transaction and needed to be reopened for every subsequent request. This made sense when you could assume that one page corresponded to one resource on the server, but became a huge performance liability as pages were increasingly crowded by images and multiple frames. The modern HTTP standard now supports persistent connections, also known as *keepalives*, whereby a client must explicitly close a connection.

To take full advantage of persistent connections, make sure the `KeepAlive` directive is set to `On` in *httpd.conf*. (`KeepAlive` is `On` by default with Apache 1.1 and higher.) Set the number of allowed requests per connection to a largish number (`MaxKeepAliveRequests 100`) to save the overhead of setting up new connections. Set the timeout fairly low, say 15 seconds (`KeepAliveTimeout 15`), so that clients that disconnect from the server without closing the connection properly will be timed out quickly. A keepalive timeout of 15 seconds should be a sufficient timeout parameter if your customers are generally coming from a LAN, or 30 seconds for modem customers.

Reverse DNS

The server is only given the IP address of the calling browser, but Apache and other servers can then translate the IP address to a fully-qualified hostname using DNS reverse lookup. This hostname is then available to CGI programs and is used in log files. Having a hostname instead of the IP address is convenient, but DNS reverse lookup takes up precious time in the transaction. Furthermore, you don't really need reverse DNS: log file analysis programs (such as the `logresolve` program that comes with Apache) can look up names offline, and CGI programs can do a reverse lookup themselves if they really need to.

As of Apache 1.3, reverse DNS is off by default. In older versions of Apache, edit the `HostnameLookups` directive in *httpd.conf*:

```
HostnameLookups off
```

The hazard to DNS is that it uses blocking system calls, which hang the entire server process until the call completes. DNS calls can take a noticeable amount of time for a single user, so a server servicing many users sees a large drag on performance from DNS lookups.

Do Not Restrict by Domain

You can allow and restrict requests from specific domains using the `allow from` and `deny from` directives in *httpd.conf*. However, using `allow` and `deny` from domains hurts performance twice. First, a reverse DNS lookup is done to check the domain of the client browser, and then a normal DNS lookup is done to be sure that reverse lookup is not a fake.

Instead of using domain names, use IP addresses with `allow` and `deny`, so DNS doesn't get involved.

Set FollowSymLinks

Set the `FollowSymLinks` option, because this will avoid the *lstat* system call that would otherwise have to be performed on every element of a path, including a symbolic link every single time you use that link. Here is an example of how to configure it.

```
DocumentRoot /www/htdocs
<Directory />
        Options FollowSymLinks
</Directory>
```

Beware, however, that this effectively turns off security for symbolic links. This means Unix-level users could then make a link point to any readable file on your server and actually serve that file.

FancyIndexing Off

One problem with Apache is fancy indexing. If `FancyIndexing` is set to `On`, then whenever you access a directory lacking an *index.html*, an HTML listing of the directory contents is generated on the fly and returned to the user. The fancy version of this directory listing uses different icons for different types of files, and assumes you have installed the icons that ship with the server in the */icons* directory. If you fail to install these icons, useless network traffic is generated looking for the icons, holding up the rendering of the page. This occurs every time you view the directory page, even if you set your browser to always use cached content and never check the network, because the missing images aren't in the cache. You could install the icons, but in the spirit of "doing less" (as we proclaimed towards the beginning of this chapter), we prefer just to turn `FancyIndexing Off`.

Use Specific Index Files

Instead of using a wildcard such as:

```
DirectoryIndex index
```

use a complete list of options:

```
DirectoryIndex index.cgi index.pl index.html
```

where you list the most common choice first.

MaxRequestsPerChild

`MaxRequestsPerChild` is the number of requests a child process will be allowed to serve before it is killed. The idea is to pre-empt memory leaks in the Apache code and in the system libraries. The default under Apache 1.3.9 seems to be 100, but this is far too low. Set it to 10,000 to avoid much of the overhead of spawning new child processes. Keep an eye on the size of your *httpd* processes and if they don't seem to grow, you can probably increase it to 100,000 or more safely.

Some Notes on Sizing Apache

For Apache, which handles load by dishing out requests to many child processes, you want to initially start as many processes as the number of simultaneous connections you expect. You specify the number of initial servers with the `StartServers` directive. A value of `10` is plenty for small sites, but would be inadequate for very busy sites.

Apache pre-spawns the number of processes specified and each process then waits for incoming connections. If you configure too many processes, then the `select()` call will have too much work to do. If you configure too few, you will find yourself forking at a time you can least afford to. However, as of Apache 1.3, forking rates double every second; that is, one child is forked the first second, then two the second second, then four the third second, and so on. This should be fast enough for most sites to cope with variations in load. The minimum (specified by the `MinSpareServers` directive) should be the average number of processes, plus a few for variation in load. The maximum should be the maximum the machine can handle, usually determined by memory size.

Using mod_status

If you include `mod_status` and set `Rule STATUS=yes` when building Apache, then on every request Apache will perform extra timing calls so that the status report generated will include timings. This slows down performance, but gives you performance data. Take your pick.

Using Analysis.cgi to Find A Bottleneck

A simple first step in diagnosing a performance problem is to break down performance into five categories:

- DNS lookup time
- Connection setup time
- Server silence
- Transmission time
- Connection close time.

These steps always happen in this order.

A tool that automatically times each of these 5 steps and generates a graph of the results (with advice) is *analysis.cgi*, which you can run from *http://patrick.net*. Simply enter a URL and it will try to graph the breakdown of these components for that URL. Figure 20-1 shows an example output graph.

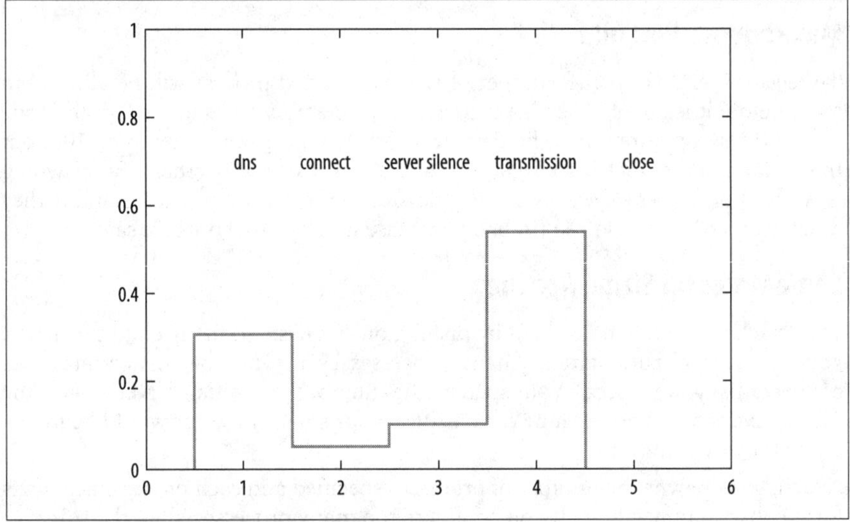

Figure 20-1. Sample output graph for analysis.cgi

The advice for *http://patrick.net* is as follows:

```
advice for http://patrick.net/

DNS

    I spent a cumulative 0.4052 seconds resolving hostnames. No problem with DNS.

network

    It took a cumulative total of 0.0650 seconds to set up the connections to
    download your content.  The average time to connect was 0.0325 seconds.  The
    latency to make a connection to your site was OK.  I spent 0.0012 seconds
    closing the socket.
```

```
server

There was a cumulative 0.1334 seconds of server silence.  The average period
of server silence was 0.0667 seconds.  Your server is using HTTP 1.1, which
has better performance than HTTP 1.0. Good.

content

Your content was a total of 4984 bytes, including headers.  It would take at
least 0.7120 seconds to download the content over a 56 Kbps modem.  It would
take at least 0.0791 seconds to download the content over a 500 Kbps DSL
line.

Your content size is well suited for surfing with a 56K modem: less than 3
seconds.  Here are URLs of the 2 elements on the page, with server response
headers:

    http://patrick.net:80/webpt_sm.gif
    HTTP/1.1 200 OK
    Date: Mon, 23 Apr 2001 19:14:29 GMT
    Server: Apache/1.3.9 (Unix)
    Last-Modified: Tue, 07 Nov 2000 05:56:29 GMT
    ETag: "11aaa93-865-3a07998d"
    Accept-Ranges: bytes
    Content-Length: 2149
    Connection: close
    Content-Type: image/gif

http://patrick.net/

HTTP/1.1 200 OK
Date: Mon, 23 Apr 2001 19:14:29 GMT
Server: Apache/1.3.9 (Unix)
Last-Modified: Sat, 03 Mar 2001 22:56:46 GMT
ETag: "11aaa81-929-3aa176ae"
Accept-Ranges: bytes
Content-Length: 2345
Connection: close
Content-Type: text/html

Multiple copies of the same element are counted only once, on the assumption
that the browser is smart enough to reuse them.

summary

The total is 1.3168 seconds.
The bottleneck was transmission.
```

We are told that the bottleneck was transmission time. The best way to make this page faster is to get it from a faster connection. A total content size of 4984 bytes is already small, so there's not much room for improvement there. There is little point in making the servers faster in this case because the potential gain from increased server speed is so small.

Here are some general guidelines for the five possible bottlenecks:

- If DNS is the bottleneck, then either the `analysis.cgi` client needs to point to a faster DNS server, or your web site's name needs to be more aggressively propagated to DNS servers around the Internet, where it will be cached. A more popular site will be a bit faster because the DNS-to-IP mapping will already be cached in many DNS servers.
- If connection time is the bottleneck, then there is a network problem. Maybe a packet was lost during connection setup because of an overloaded hub. Routers, interfaces, and cable should be examined for errors.
- If server silence is the bottleneck, then the server is overloaded in some way and could probably benefit from better hardware or a more optimized server application or database.
- If transmission time is the bottleneck, then client connection speed is too small or the content you are trying to push down it is too large.
- If connection close is the bottleneck, again we have a network problem.

Monitoring Web Performance Using Perl

You can set up an automated system to monitor web performance using Perl and *gnuplot*. It uses the LWP library to grab a web page and then deals with proxies, handling cookies, handling SSL, and handling login forms. Here's the basic code for getting the home page, logging in, logging out, and graphing all the times. Try to run monitoring and load testing from a machine that sits on the same LAN as the web server. This way, you know that network latency is not the bottleneck.

```
#!/usr/local/bin/perl -w

use LWP::UserAgent;
use Crypt::SSLeay;
use HTTP::Cookies;
use HTTP::Headers;
use HTTP::Request;
use HTTP::Response;
use Time::HiRes 'time','sleep';

# constants:

$DEBUG       = 0;
$browser     = 'Mozilla/4.04 [en] (X11; I; Patrix 0.0.0 i586)';
$rooturl     = 'https://patrick.net';
$user        = "pk";
$password    = "pw";
$gnuplot     = "/usr/local/bin/gnuplot";

# global objects:

$cookie_jar  = HTTP::Cookies->new;
$ua          = LWP::UserAgent->new;

MAIN: {
  $ua->agent($browser); # This sets browser for all uses of $ua.
```

```
    # home page
    $latency = &get("/home.html");
    # verify that we got the page
    $latency = -1 unless index "<title>login page</title>" > -1;
    &log("home.log", $latency);
    sleep 2;

    $content = "user=$user&passwd=$password";

    # log in
    $latency = &post("/login.cgi", $content);
    $latency = -1 unless m|<title>welcome</title>|;
    &log("login.log", $latency);
    sleep 2;

    # content page
    $latency = &get("/content.html");
    $latency = -1 unless m|<title>the goodies</title>|;
    &log("content.log", $latency);
    sleep 2;

    # logout
    $latency = &get("/logout.cgi");
    $latency = -1 unless m|<title>bye</title>|;
    &log("logout.log", $latency);

    # plot it all
    `$gnuplot /home/httpd/public_html/demo.gp`;
  }

  sub get {
    local ($path) = @_;

    $request = new HTTP::Request('GET', "$rooturl$path");

    # If we have a previous response, put its cookies in the new request.
    if ($response) {
        $cookie_jar->extract_cookies($response);
        $cookie_jar->add_cookie_header($request);
    }

    if ($DEBUG) {
        print $request->as_string();
    }

    # Do it.
    $start    = time();
    $response = $ua->request($request);
    $end      = time();
    $latency  = $end - $start;

    if (!$response->is_success) {
        print $request->as_string(), " failed: ",
        $response->error_as_HTML;
    }
```

```
    if ($DEBUG) {
        print "\n## Got $path and result was:\n";
        print $response->content;
        print   "## $path took $latency seconds.\n";
    }

    $latency;
  }

  sub post {

    local ($path, $content) = @_;

    $header  = new HTTP::Headers;
    $header->content_type('application/x-www-form-urlencoded');
    $header->content_length(length($content));

    $request = new HTTP::Request('POST',
                                 "$rooturl$path",
                                 $header,
                                 $content);

    # If we have a previous response, put its cookies in the new request.
    if ($response) {
        $cookie_jar->extract_cookies($response);
        $cookie_jar->add_cookie_header($request);
    }

    if ($DEBUG) {
        print $request->as_string();
    }

    # Do it.
    $start    = time();
    $response = $ua->request($request);
    $end      = time();
    $latency  = $end - $start;

    if (!$response->is_success) {
        print $request->as_string(), " failed: ", $response->error_as_HTML;
    }

    if ($DEBUG) {
        print "\n## Got $path and result was:\n";
        print $response->content;
        print   "## $path took $latency seconds.\n";
    }

    $latency;
  }

  # Write log entry in format that gnuplot can use to create an image.
  sub log {
```

```
    local ($file, $latency) = @_;
    $date = `date +'%Y %m %d %H %M %S'`;
    chop $date;
    # Corresponding to gnuplot command: set timefmt "%m %d %H %M %S %y"

    open(FH, ">>$file") || die "Could not open $file\n";

    # Format printing so that we get only 4 decimal places.
    printf FH "%s %2.4f\n", $date, $latency;

    close(FH);
}
```

This gives a set of log files with timestamps and latency readings. To generate a graph from that, you need a *gnuplot* configuration file. Here's the *gnuplot* configuration file for plotting the home page times.

```
set term png color
set output "/home/httpd/public_html/demo.png"
set xdata time
set ylabel "latency in seconds"
set bmargin 3
set logscale y
set timefmt "%Y %m %d %H %M %S"
plot "demo.log" using 1:7 title "time to retrieve home page"
```

Note that the output is set to write a PNG image directly into the web server's *public_html* directory. This way, you can merely click on a bookmark in your browser to see the output. Now just set up a *cron* job to run the monitor script every minute and you will have a log of the web page's performance and a constantly-updated graph. Use *crontab -e* to modify your *crontab* file. Here's an example entry in a *crontab* file.

```
# MIN   HOUR    DOM     MOY     DOW     Commands
#(0-59) (0-23)  (1-31)  (1-12)  (0-6)   (Note: 0=Sun)
*       *       *       *       *      cd /home/httpd/public_html; ./monitor
```

Figure 20-2 shows an example output image from a real site monitored for over a year.

Instead of running from *cron*, you could turn your monitoring script into a functional test by popping up each page in a Netscape browser as you get it, so you can see monitoring as it happens and also visually verify that pages are correct in addition to checking for a particular string on the page in Perl. For example, from within Perl, you can pop up the *http://www.oreilly.com* page in Netscape like this:

```
system "netscape -remote 'openURL(http://www.oreilly.com)'";
```

You can redirect the browser display to any Unix machine running X Windows, or any Microsoft Windows machine using an X Windows server emulator like Exceed. This capability of Netscape to be controlled from a script is described at *http://home.netscape.com/newsref/std/x-remote.html*.

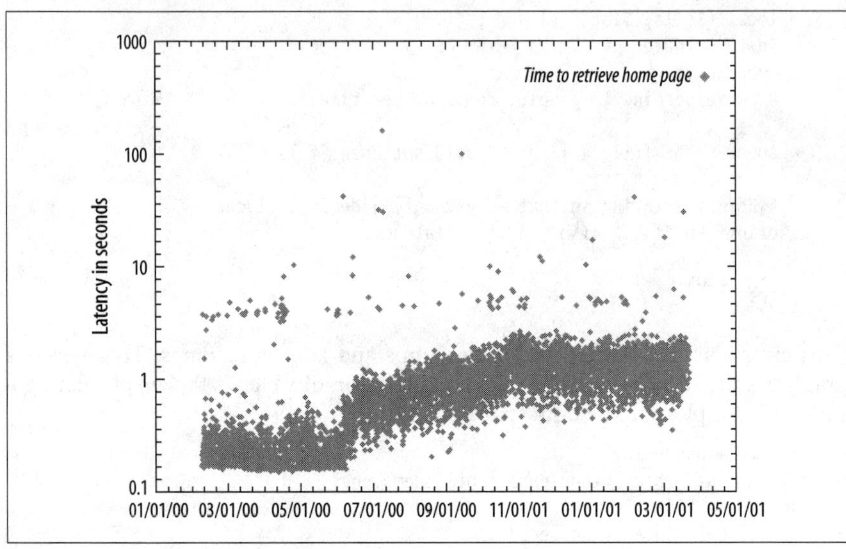

Figure 20-2. Graph of web site performance

There are many other things you can monitor besides raw performance. It is extremely useful to have an image of how much memory you are using. This allows you to visually see memory leaks, which can eventually crash your server. Memory leaks are memory allocations that get "lost," that is, lost track of by the application because of poor programming. There is no fix except stricter accounting of memory allocations and deallocations. Figure 20-3 shows an image of a memory leak in a web application, showing restarts on 11/3 and 11/7.

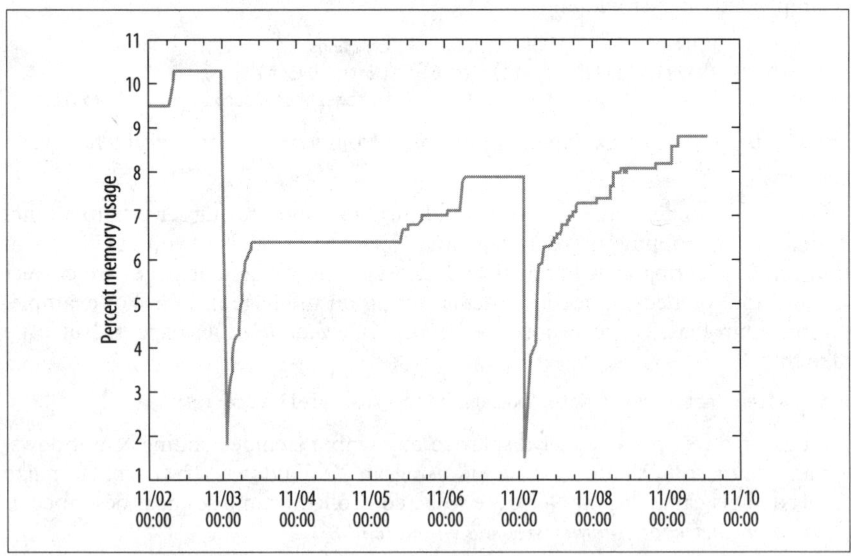

Figure 20-3. Memory leaks

Likewise, you can monitor database connections in use and create an image of a database connection leak, which is another common source of slowdowns and crashes. Database connection leaks have causes similar to memory leaks. Database connections are typically leaked in Java exceptions when the exception handling code does not release the connection. Figure 20-4 shows a graph showing how database connections build up between restarts of a Weblogic application server. The server was restarted 10/13, 10/25, 10/30, and 11/3.

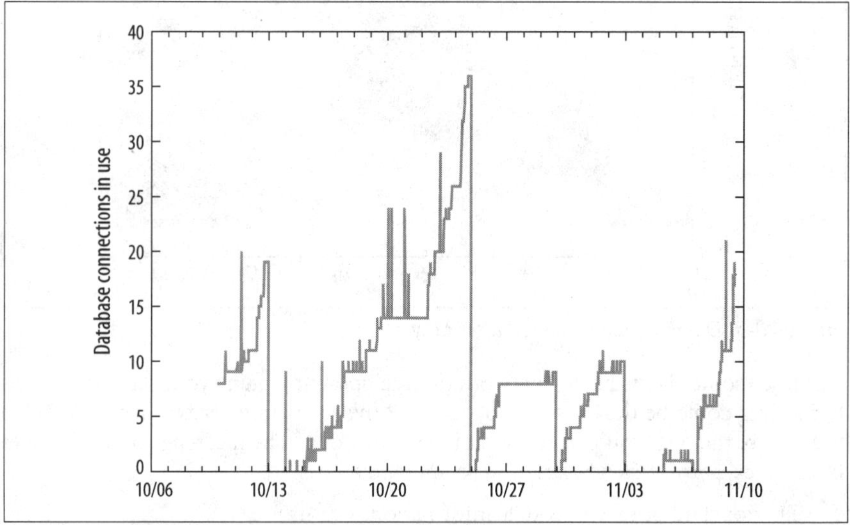

Figure 20-4. Database connection leaks

Monitoring web performance can help diagnose the common error of creating an unindexed database table growing without limit. A SQL `SELECT` statement using such a table will get slower and slower as the table grows. In Figure 20-5, you see the result of introducing a `select` from a large unindexed table in February, while the table continued to grow. When an index on that table was finally created in May, latency returned to normal.

Detailed instructions on how to set up your own monitoring and graphing system to make images like these can be found in *Web Performance Tuning*.

A final tip for system administrators: the recently introduced "selective acknowledgment" performance feature of TCP does not work with some old TCP stacks and older DSL hardware. Selective acknowledgment, or SACK, is defined in RFC 2018. The symptom is that browsers are occasionally sent blank pages and network error messages. Selective acknowledgment is supposed to work like this: say a server sends out four packets to a browser. Packet 2 gets lost while packets 1, 3, and 4 arrive just fine. Without selective acknowledgment, all a client can do is say that all packets arrived, or that they did not, and let the server time out and resend all 4 packets. But with selective acknowledgment, the client can tell the server exactly which packet was missing. This is a significant help to performance on lossy connections.

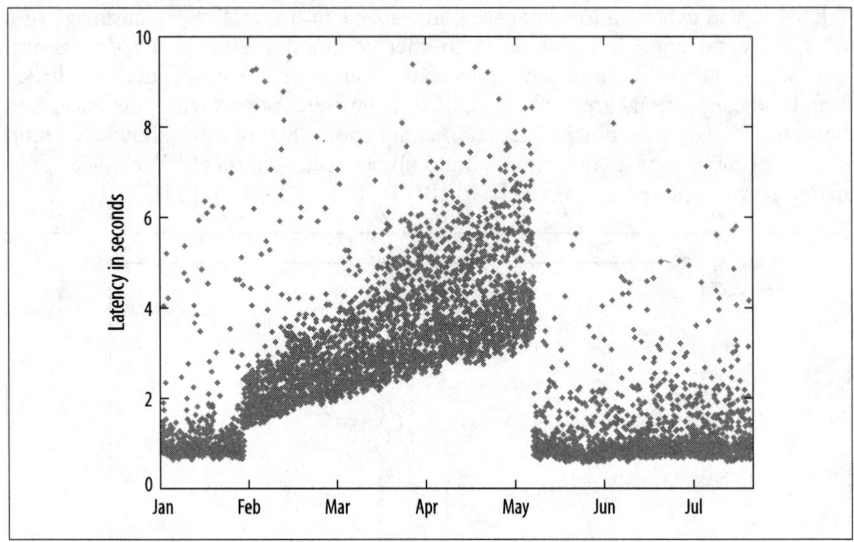

Figure 20-5. Database table indexed after May

If you see some clients having network trouble upon upgrading your server to Solaris 8, this bug could be the cause. As of Solaris 8 the `ndd` parameter `tcp_sack_permitted` is `2`. To fix the bug, you need only set it back to `1` or `0`. The meanings of the 3 values of `tcp_sack_permitted` in Solaris's `ndd` command are:

`0` Do not send or receive SACK information.

`1` Do not initiate with SACK, but respond with SACK if other side does.

`2` Initiate and accept connections with SACK.

Web performance is an ongoing challenge, but because of the widespread use of simple open standards like TCP/IP and HTTP, web performance problems are always understandable and solvable.

Index

Symbols

Numbers

A

We'd like to hear your suggestions for improving our indexes. Send email to *index@oreilly.com*.

B

C

D

E

F

G

I

J

K

L

M

N

O

Q

R

S

T

W

X

Z

About the Authors

Stephen Spainhour co-authored the first and second editions of *Webmaster in a Nutshell* and contributed to many other O'Reilly titles, including *Perl in a Nutshell* and *Linux in a Nutshell*. He is an avid fan of professional tennis, and when he's not checking for tennis scores on the Web, he enjoys cooking, electronic music, and watching too much television.

Robert Eckstein enjoys dabbling with just about anything related to computers. In fact, most of his friends agree that Robert spends far too much time in front of a computer screen. At O'Reilly, Robert mostly edits Java books, and in his spare time has been known to provide online coverage for popular conferences. Robert holds bachelor's degrees in computer science and communications from Trinity University in San Antonio, Texas. In the past, he has worked for the USAA insurance company and for Motorola's cellular software division. He now lives in Round Rock, Texas with his wife, Michelle, and their talking puppy, Ginger.

Colophon

Our look is the result of reader comments, our own experimentation, and feedback from distribution channels. Distinctive covers complement our distinctive approach to technical topics, breathing personality and life into potentially dry subjects.

The animal on the cover of *Webmaster in a Nutshell,* Third Edition, is a crab spider. Like the crustaceans after which they are named, crab spiders walk sideways or backwards. They feed on bees and other pollenizing insects, often lying in wait for their prey by hiding on flowers. Some species of crab spider can, over a period of several days, change color from white to yellow and back again to blend into the flower on which they are sitting. The spider grabs its prey quickly with its forward-facing legs. It then injects its victims with a fast-acting, highly poisonous venom, in order to protect itself from the bee's sting.

Spiders' insect-eating habits are extremely helpful to humans. Every year, billions of spiders do away with large numbers of disease-carrying and crop-destroying insects. Spiders are by far the most significant predator of insects in the world.

Colleen Gorman was the production editor and proofreader for *Webmaster in a Nutshell,* Third Edition. Emily Quill and Jane Ellin provided quality control. Nancy Crumpton wrote the index.

Edie Freedman designed the cover of this book. The cover image is a 19th-century engraving from the Dover Pictorial Archive. Emma Colby produced the cover layout with QuarkXPress 4.1 using Adobe's ITC Garamond font.

David Futato designed the interior layout. Linda Mui and Joe Wizda converted this book into FrameMaker 5.5.6 with a format conversion tool created by Erik Ray, Jason McIntosh, Neil Walls, and Mike Sierra that uses Perl and XML technologies. The text font is Linotype Birka; the heading font is Adobe Myriad Condensed; and the code font is LucasFont's TheSans Mono Condensed. The illustrations that appear in the book were produced by Robert Romano and Jessamyn Read using Macromedia FreeHand 9 and Adobe Photoshop 6. This colophon was written by Clairemarie Fisher O'Leary.